IN THE CROSSFIRE

IN THE CROSSFIRE

Marcus Foster and the Troubled History of American School Reform

JOHN P. SPENCER

PENN

UNIVERSITY OF PENNSYLVANIA PRESS

PHILADELPHIA

POLITICS AND CULTURE IN MODERN AMERICA

Series Editors: Margot Canaday, Glenda Gilmore,
Michael Kazin, and Thomas J. Sugrue

Volumes in the series narrate and analyze political and social change
in the broadest dimensions from 1865 to the present, including ideas
about the ways people have sought and wielded power in the public
sphere and the language and institutions of politics at all levels—local,
national, and transnational. The series is motivated by a desire to
reverse the fragmentation of modern U.S. history and to encourage
synthetic perspectives on social movements and the state, on gender,
race, and labor, and on intellectual history and popular culture.

Published by
University of Pennsylvania Press
Philadelphia, Pennsylvania 19104-4112
www.upenn.edu/pennpress

Printed in the United States of America on acid-free paper

10 9 8 7 6 5 4 3 2 1

Library of Congress Cataloging-in-Publication Data

Spencer, John P.
  In the crossfire : Marcus Foster and the troubled history of American school
reform / John P. Spencer. — 1st ed.
    p. cm. — (Politics and culture in modern America)
  Includes bibliographical references and index.
  ISBN 978-0-8122-4435-9 (hardcover : alk. paper)
  1. Foster, Marcus A., 1923–1973. 2. African Americans—Education. 3.
Educational change—United States. 4. African American school principals—
Pennsylvania—Philadelphia. 5. African American school superintendents—
California—Oakland. 6. Urban schools—Pennsylvania—Philadelphia. 7.
Urban schools—California—Oakland. I. Title. II. Series: Politics and culture in
modern America.
LA2317.F677S64 2012
370.92—dc23
[B]   2012002587

Frontispiece: Marcus A. Foster, 1969.
Urban Archives, Temple University Libraries.

For Eve,
and Ella and Owen

Contents

Introduction

O N November 6, 1973, Marcus Foster, the African American superintendent of the Oakland Public Schools, was assassinated by members
of the previously unknown Symbionese Liberation Army (SLA). This book
chronicles Foster's life and work, and it explores what his story can tell us
about the history and current circumstances of urban education and American school reform.

Who was Marcus Foster? Outside of Oakland and his native Philadelphia,
Foster tends to be remembered—if he is remembered at all—for the sensational nature of his death. When reminded, Americans of a certain age might
recall that the SLA killed him just before the group became famous for kidnapping publishing heiress Patty Hearst. And while I am younger and do not
remember Foster's assassination, it is certainly the detail that first caught my
eye as a historian. Why would the SLA (whose "brainwashing" of Hearst was
a source of great mystery to me as a nine-year-old just coming into awareness
of national events) kill a school superintendent—and a widely admired one
at that?

It was, in fact, Foster's position as the chief administrator in a troubled
school district that drew attention to him. After several years in Oakland,
Foster was caught in the middle of a heated controversy over a wave of school
violence and vandalism. On one side, a number of East Bay politicians, educators, and citizens were pressuring him to make a stronger showing of law
and order, including, perhaps, the placement of armed, uniformed police officers in some predominantly black schools. On the other side, the Black Panthers and other activists denounced the proposed security plan as a "fascist"
device for blaming school problems on students whom the system had failed.
Meanwhile, unbeknownst to the participants, a black escaped convict named

Donald DeFreeze latched onto the controversy in his own peculiarly chilling way. DeFreeze had been looking for a public figure to assassinate in order to launch the SLA and thereby ignite "the Revolution." In the end, he and a handful of white co-conspirators settled on Foster because they believed (incorrectly) that the superintendent was a driving force behind the police-in-schools proposal.[1]

Foster's bizarre and tragic death is an inescapable part of his story, especially for those who were closest to him. But as I quickly learned, Foster's life prior to 1973, and its enduring significance since then, are an even richer subject. In part, the richness is biographical. Born in 1923, Foster was the fifth and youngest child of a single mother who struggled to pass on a family legacy of African American achievement through education. As a dynamic teacher, principal, and administrator—first in his native Philadelphia and then in Oakland—he made success stories of urban schools and children whom others had dismissed as hopeless, only to be murdered by self-styled revolutionaries who denounced him as an Uncle Tom for trying to change the school system from within. At the same time, Foster's story offers a valuable lens on larger social and political changes in the decades following World War II: the great black migration from South to North, the civil rights movement, the violence and economic decline that rocked American cities, and the ever-increasing emphasis on educational achievement as a ticket to success in American life.

But why Foster? What can the experiences of a single educator teach us about the intersections of race, inequality, and education in the postwar era? Foster's story highlights how education, and especially the quintessentially American idea of schooling as the key to one's social and economic advancement, took on new importance in the context of postwar struggles over racial inequality and urban decline. In tracing Foster's life and work, we see, first of all, how the underachievement of black children became a contentious issue well before the 1960s and came to play a significant role in the crisis of postwar liberalism. This crisis played out in such divisive events as urban riots, fierce public debate over publication of the Moynihan Report (as *The Negro Family* came to be known), and African Americans' efforts to take direct control of the schools in their communities. By looking at these and other conflicts over education and inequality through the eyes of a black educator who wrestled with them on the ground in individual schools, we are able to see them in a new light.

From Foster's vantage point—in the classroom, from the principal's office, as superintendent—we see that the problems of access, of achievement, of resources, of responsibility, were more complicated than they appeared to be in polarized public debates over who was to blame. Moreover, in Foster's responses to these problems, we see more clearly the possibilities as well as the limitations of reform. In contrast to other stalemates that pitted communities against schools—the most infamous being the conflict over "community control" in the Ocean Hill–Brownsville section of New York City—Foster led school revitalization efforts that were notably successful because he was able to—indeed, had to—mobilize diverse constituencies. At the same time, his career dramatized the dangers of making too much out of such success—of assuming urban schools could bring equal opportunity and achievement to their students, if only educators (especially African American ones) would roll up their sleeves and insist on success. Ultimately, Foster's story shows us poignantly that schools and their students were shaped by larger social and economic forces that no educator, no matter how talented, hard working, and effective (as Foster surely was), could transcend on his or her own. To expect otherwise, as Foster increasingly emphasized when he rose to leadership at the district level, was to set the stage for disillusionment and retreat. In this sense, Foster's work—his achievements as well as his limitations—is not simply a matter of historical interest; it offers a cautionary lesson for current school reforms that aim to eliminate racial and socioeconomic achievement gaps, showing how those efforts build on, and at the same time ignore, important lessons from the 1960s.

*   *   *

The idea that education is the key to a person's social and economic advancement is an old and powerful one in the United States, going back to the founding of public school systems in the early nineteenth century. To be sure, the father of American public education, Horace Mann of Massachusetts, saw many purposes for state-supported school systems, including the Jeffersonian idea of educating citizens for democracy—and some critics continue to prefer civic and intellectual purposes of public schooling to a more instrumentalist economic agenda.[2] Still, one of Mann's most enduring ideas was that education would be "the great equalizer of the conditions of men." Perhaps no group of citizens has been as invested in this idea—or as frustrated by the gap between idea and reality—as African Americans. Blacks were initially barred altogether from access to public education, and in the process they were not only denied a possible avenue of social advancement; they were stigmatized as an intellectually inferior people. As a result, educational achievement has been a core value and goal for African Americans, especially since emancipation.[3] As we will see, there are serious problems with schooling as the "great equalizer." Yet it remains a powerful idea, and understandably so: in the wake of deindustrialization, civil rights progress, and an expansion of white-collar public sector jobs since the 1960s, education has come to play an increasingly important role in shaping social and economic opportunity in the United States.[4]

Given the importance of education to Americans in general and to black Americans in particular, it is not surprising that the persistent underachievement of African Americans has become an increasingly contentious issue over the past half century. The controversy in Oakland over placing police officers in schools is part of a much larger debate that has raged in educational and public policy circles ever since African American migration transformed the nation's cities during and after World War II: Why have urban blacks lagged so persistently behind other groups in school and in economic life generally? Who is responsible? What can and should be done about these inequalities? Argument over these questions has been fierce. Though Marcus Foster's murder in a crossfire of bullets was indeed extreme, it is, in some ways, symbolic of a larger political and ideological crossfire over how to effectively explain and respond to the "urban crisis" and, in particular, the persistent problems of urban schools that serve African American students.

For most of American history, until the years of Marcus Foster's childhood in the 1920s, the predominant answer to the question of why blacks lagged behind in educational attainment was racist: blacks were supposedly unequal to whites because they were biologically different and inferior. As Foster came of age in the 1930s and 1940s, however, racist ideologies were giving way to a new "racial liberalism" associated most famously with the sociologist Gunnar Myrdal and his landmark book, *An American Dilemma* (1944). According to postwar liberals, racial inequality was not a product of inborn racial differences, nor did it result, as more left-leaning critics contended, from white privilege and power in an exploitative system. Rather, it was a matter of attitudes that could be adjusted—a correctable flaw in an otherwise free and fair society. Blacks were not inherently different or inferior; they had been blocked from participating and succeeding in American society by irrational white "prejudice." Compounding the problem, according to Myrdal and many other liberals, blacks had responded to their exclusion by developing dysfunctional attitudes and behaviors that reinforced existing white prejudices and kept them at the bottom of the social system—in all, a vicious cycle of discrimination and "cultural pathology."[5]

The story of how postwar liberals optimistically looked to the nation's schools to break this alleged cycle of white prejudice and black failure is at the center of this book. To an extent that has not been widely emphasized among historians, urban schools were a focal point in the development of racial liberalism after World War II.[6] It is important to note that liberals were not a monolithic group in this or any other period. Some were rooted primarily in civil rights activism and tended to prioritize the fight against various forms of prejudice and discrimination, including segregated schools and low academic expectations. In education, the most familiar outgrowth of these efforts was the 1954 Supreme Court decision in *Brown v. Board of Education* (though much research remains to be done on the implementation and meaning of *Brown* in urban settings outside of the South).[7] Others, including social scientists, government officials, and foundation officers, tended to emphasize the "cultural pathology" part of the vicious circle, emphasizing the need for blacks to assimilate white, middle-class cultural norms. An important expression of this view was the Johnson administration's War on Poverty, which included a heavy focus on "compensatory" education programs for "deprived" inner-city children. In spite of these differences in focus, however, racial liberals shared an overarching belief that some combination of these impediments (prejudice, discrimination, and cultural pathology, as opposed to black inferiority or a fundamentally exploitative system) was responsible for black inequality, and that the time had come to eliminate these obstacles to racial integration. Unlike their predecessors in the New Deal era, postwar liberals put racial inequality on the nation's political agenda—and by the 1960s they came to emphasize education and training (as opposed to 1930s-style jobs programs and other elements of an economic safety net for vulnerable citizens) as a centerpiece of federal law and antipoverty policies.[8]

If this book traces the rise of the education-oriented racial liberalism that shaped Foster's development, it also examines the splintering of that liberal vision into a more polarized debate, stretching from the later years of his career into our own time. Conflicts over busing are already an iconic example of how K–12 education figured into the crisis of liberalism and the social and political turmoil of the 1960s and 1970s.[9] But just as *Brown* was part of a larger story of educational ferment in the 1940s and 1950s, so, too, was busing part of a wider struggle over the status of African American youth in the nation's big cities and schools—a struggle that played a role in splitting the liberal political coalition that built the New Deal and the Great Society. No sooner had President Johnson launched the War on Poverty in 1964 (based partly on a pilot project that involved Foster in the Philadelphia public schools) than the ghettos of North Philadelphia, Harlem, and several other cities erupted in violence and looting, much of it involving teenagers.[10] A few years later, in one of the most traumatic racial incidents of the 1960s in Philadelphia, police brutally assaulted a multitude of black high school students who had gathered at the school administration building to protest racial discrimination and a Eurocentric curriculum.[11]

Americans came into sharp disagreement as they attempted to explain these and other urban problems—including what came to be called the "achievement gap" between students of different racial and socioeconomic backgrounds. Some zeroed in on the strand of liberalism that emphasized cultural deprivation among low-income African Americans—though often with a more somber emphasis on the schools' relative inability to overcome these deficits. The massive federal study *Equality of Educational Opportunity,* better known as the Coleman Report, was especially influential in this vein.[12] Others, especially civil rights activists, sharpened their critique of discrimination and racism: black children were failing not because of deficiencies in their own culture and home environments but because white-run schools were not educating them. To these critics, liberals such as James Coleman and Daniel Patrick Moynihan (author of the controversial report, *The Negro Family: The Case for National Action,* better known as the Moynihan Report) were guilty of "blaming the victim" for institutional and societal failures.[13] Still others—especially sociologists and historians—began to pursue more radical critiques, challenging the very notion that schools could foster equal opportunity in a fundamentally unequal capitalist society.[14]

These arguments were not mutually exclusive. The problems of educational and social inequality were more complex than liberals had realized, and the various critiques of liberalism held the possibility of a more sophisticated approach to urban schooling, one that would emphasize the need for reforms (especially in terms of academic expectations, teacher quality, and funding) *and* the importance of addressing social, cultural, and economic conditions beyond school walls. Often, though, debates over the problems of cities and their schools became polarized in a more simplistic way, between those who blamed the schools for achievement gaps and demanded that those gaps be eliminated and those who insisted that urban schools were victims of social and cultural forces beyond their control.

A striking example of such polarization was the notorious 1968 battle between white teachers and black activists over community control of public schools in the Ocean Hill–Brownsville section of New York City. In one sense, Ocean Hill–Brownsville was a power struggle: black parents and community activists gained a measure of local control over their neighborhood schools and used it to fire white teachers who were members of the United Federation of Teachers. (After a series of strikes that divided white and black New Yorkers as bitterly as any event of the 1960s, the UFT prevailed in reinstating the teachers.) But community control was not just about power; it was also a clash between warring interpretations of who was responsible for low achievement: culturally deprived black students or racist white teachers?[15]

By focusing on a school-based educator who had a reputation for bridging the divide, *In the Crossfire* offers a different perspective on this ideological crossfire over race and achievement. Of course, teachers and principals do not have all the answers simply because they are "in the trenches"; being in schools may, in fact, lead to a myopic view. But in Foster's case, long experience with the daily life of schools and children was one reason he tended to take a more eclectic and less ideologically pure approach to urban educational problems than did many of the policymakers, commentators, and activists who weighed in on those problems from the outside.

Foster's friend and colleague Bob Blackburn was especially well positioned to grasp the significance of what he calls Foster's "long apprenticeship as an educator." Blackburn worked with Foster in Philadelphia and went with him to Oakland to serve as his deputy superintendent—in which capacity he was nearly killed in the assassination—but by comparison with his boss, he was an outsider in the world of school reform, having come to it as a civil rights activist with no classroom experience. "We were kids on the bus coming down to meet [Mississippi civil rights activist] Fannie Lou Hamer—and Marcus *was* Fannie Lou Hamer," Blackburn says of himself and others of his generation who gravitated to urban school reform as a way to work for social justice. "Almost all the people that you think of being superintendents or educational hell-raisers or foundation officials or national organizations . . . they simply weren't as steeped in their craft as [Marcus] was . . . I mean, it's the difference between those who have the political zeal to see injustice ended, and those whose personal history is drenched in that injustice. And in Marcus's case, it was drenched in struggling to get kids to be effective readers and to see what social studies really meant to children in primary grades."[16]

As a result of this long immersion in school improvement from the ground up, Foster was able to combine an activist's sense of urgency with a practitioner's sense of the complexity of the job. As a principal of three all-black schools and later as a superintendent, he insisted that educators raise academic expectations of low-income and minority children and be held more accountable for their achievement or failure; in that sense, he helped pioneer a critique of racial and class bias in American public education. But Foster was a critic of the system from within. In contrast to some outside the profession, he did not single out educators for blame; he recognized a range of factors, both inside and beyond the schools, that affect student achievement. Moreover, he translated this critique into actual change, energizing a wide range of people, including teachers, students, parents, politicians, and taxpayers, to work together and help turn around troubled schools.

Foster's ability to engage a wide spectrum of people emerged as a major theme of the oral history interviews I conducted for this project; interviewees invariably praised his ability to communicate with and mobilize diverse constituencies in the name of reform. Partly this was due to his varied life experiences and his legendary charisma and communication skills. School reformer Theodore Sizer, who was a thirty-something dean of the Harvard Graduate School of Education when he encountered Foster in the 1960s, was struck by his infectious optimism and his ability to relate to all kinds of students: "He was a roaming-the-halls principal. He had a remarkable ability to sense the wavelength, even among kids who had good reason to be distressed."[17] Foster could relate to even his toughest students because he, too, was a product of gritty urban neighborhoods in South Philadelphia. For this reason, for example, student militants at Gratz High School not only were willing to let him know they wanted to use violent tactics during a conflict between the school and the school board; they were willing to obey him when he responded, "Fellas, that's not the way. Violence is not the way."[18]

But Foster's effectiveness with diverse people and groups was not just a matter of personal charm and shared life experiences; it also came from his willingness to take competing viewpoints seriously and synthesize them into a more complete and inclusive response to urban school problems. This sounded like a very different story than Ocean Hill–Brownsville, and I was motivated to write this book partly to explore the apparent contrast. In this sense, *In the Crossfire* is first and foremost a work of history that culminates in the early 1970s and provides a kind of alternative to the New York story.

At the same time, I have been struck by the continuing relevance of Foster's story in our own time, and as a result, the book is not only about the past: it draws on history to make an argument about school reform debates in the present. Foster lamented the powerful correlation between social background and academic achievement; before the term was in common usage, he was dedicated, above all, to eliminating achievement gaps. Since his time, and in particular since the passage of the No Child Left Behind Act of 2002 (NCLB), relationships between race, inequality, and schooling have continued to fuel intense controversy. NCLB made racial and socioeconomic achievement gaps a central focus of national policy. In particular, the law calls on the states to regularly test all students in math and reading, to break down the achievement data by race and socioeconomic status in order to shine a light on achievement gaps, and, ultimately, to penalize or close those schools that fail to make inroads on the problem.[19]

The specific provisions and implementation of NCLB have been widely criticized, but the basic idea of holding schools accountable has been overwhelmingly popular, at least outside the schools themselves.[20] The law was a centerpiece of the domestic policy agenda of Republican president George W. Bush, yet it passed Congress with overwhelming bipartisan support. The election of a Democrat to the White House in 2008 did little to change the basic thrust of federal education policy. Under President Barack Obama, the U.S. Department of Education has continued to emphasize the use of standardized test scores to hold schools accountable for student achievement—especially the roughly five thousand lowest-performing schools in the nation. Indeed, Obama has pushed accountability even further than did his predecessor, using his $4 billion grant program, Race to the Top (RTT), to pressure Democratic-leaning teachers' unions to accept student test scores as a basis for teacher evaluation. On education, in contrast to other key issues such as health care and financial reform, the president has enjoyed support from politicians across the spectrum—not to mention media and business figures, such as Bill Gates and Oprah Winfrey, and major media such as *Time, Newsweek,* and the *New York Times.*[21]

Everyone seems to support the idea of holding schools accountable—everyone, that is, except educators. Echoing the debates of the 1960s, teachers and other educators have tended to argue that accountability singles them out for blame—that it scapegoats them for social problems beyond their control.

Is it fair for NCLB to hold schools accountable for reducing the achievement gap between students of different backgrounds? Is it reasonable for Obama's Secretary of Education, Arne Duncan, to insist that state and local school leaders find a way to "turn around" the five thousand worst-performing schools in the nation? Or, on the contrary, are schools and educators at the mercy of larger social and economic forces—inadequate resources, for instance, or economic hardship among students and parents? By 2011, Americans were being inundated by media coverage that broke down along these lines, with educators often being portrayed as excuse makers and villains in the story of educational inequality in America.[22]

Marcus Foster's story provides a valuable perspective on these debates. Broadly speaking, Foster charted a course between the extremes of demanding too little and expecting too much of the schools as agents of equal opportunity in America, and it is this approach, I think, that has fruitful lessons for our own time. On the one hand, Foster insisted that educators take responsibility for raising achievement at failing urban schools, and in this sense, I argue, he was an early advocate of the "accountability" argument. Commentators tend to say that movements for educational "excellence" and accountability have arisen since the 1980s, in opposition to the "equity" agenda of the 1960s, with its emphasis on such issues as desegregation and the equalization of access and resources.[23] This is certainly true in significant ways, but Foster's story reminds us that in other respects, the excellence and accountability agendas are also *legacies* of the black freedom movement of the 1960s and, prior to that, a longstanding tradition of African American educational achievement and activism. To be clear: I am not suggesting a straight line of continuity from the activism of the 1960s to the accountability movement of the NCLB era. But I do mean to say that we cannot fully understand the latter without reference to the former. The concerns of educators and activists from Marcus Foster's time—in particular, the notion of taking responsibility for student learning and making no excuses—have informed the current movement for accountability and helped to imbue it with a sense of moral urgency. When presidents and legislators promote education as the "new civil right" and insist that schools eradicate the achievement gap—as they did during the Bush administration and have continued to do since the election of Barack Obama—they are tapping into powerful hopes and expectations that rose to prominence in the 1960s.[24]

On the other hand, this book reconstructs a vision of what I call *shared* accountability, which stands in contrast to the recent school reform agendas spearheaded by No Child Left Behind and Race to the Top. Foster insisted on accountability not only from educators but from families, taxpayers, and political and economic institutions as well. This effort to mobilize multiple constituencies was essential to the urban educational success stories that dotted his career—and a lesson for current policymakers who would take aim at the achievement gap without addressing the full range of school *and* non-school factors that have created it.

*   *   *

In the Crossfire develops and embeds these arguments in a narrative of Marcus Foster's career as a student, teacher, school principal, and superintendent. As I trace his efforts in local schools and communities, I emphasize how this work interacted with the larger urban context in Philadelphia and Oakland and with national developments. In the process, biography, urban study, and policy history emerge as interconnected and indispensable lenses for analyzing urban education.

The book begins in the time of Marcus Foster's own schooling, in the 1930s and 1940s—a time when achievement gaps between black and white students were not only accepted but expected in the urban North as well as the Jim Crow South. In such a climate, it was not necessarily school so much as a mixture of outside influences that pushed Foster on his path toward successful leadership. One such influence, ironically, was the education he received in the streets, dancehalls, and youth gangs of South Philadelphia; for the rest of his life, it seems, these experiences gave him a visceral understanding of the challenges and circumstances faced by black teenagers in the inner city. At the same time, the gritty side of urban life did not fully define or consume Foster, partly due to a second major influence: his family, which exemplified a history of African American striving to excel in education. Foster's mother, Alice, immersed her five children in this legacy and, in spite of humble finances, she managed to impart to them a good deal of "cultural capital"—the knowledge, skills, resources, and attitudes that some parents (most often affluent ones) pass on to their children to help ensure their academic success.[25] Blessed by this foundation of literacy and learning—and a scholarship—young Marcus ended up at historically black Cheyney State Teachers College, under the tutelage of a strict headmaster, Leslie Pinckney Hill, who preached the power of education as a lever of progress for the Negro race.

Foster was able to synthesize these various influences and rise to positions of educational leadership partly because of his personal attributes; by all accounts he was exceedingly bright, ambitious, and charismatic. But Foster's rise to leadership was also shaped by timing and history. Beginning especially in the 1940s, events in the wider world converged to elevate Foster and his educational aspirations to a larger stage. In public life (though not necessarily in most schools and classrooms), racism increasingly gave way to racial liberalism, and liberals looked to education for solutions to racial inequality and the unfolding urban crisis. As he embarked on a career in the Philadelphia public schools in the 1950s, Marcus Foster was positioned to test the idea that, for African Americans, urban schools could be an advantage, as opposed to an obstacle, in the quest for educational and life success.

Foster took up that challenge of African American achievement in the 1960s, as the principal of three troubled, all-black schools in Philadelphia. The middle chapters of the book examine his efforts to transform those schools, as conflicts over race and inequality increasingly tore the country apart. In all three examples, we can see how urban school policies and reforms played out at the school and classroom level.[26] In the first, from 1958 to 1963, Foster served as principal of the Dunbar Elementary School in North Philadelphia, where he participated in a Ford Foundation pilot project in compensatory education, which in turn helped shape national education and antipoverty policies during the Great Society. Proponents of the compensatory approach, or "deficit model," expressed key tenets of postwar liberalism: low-achieving urban students were not unintelligent, as racist ideology had long asserted; they and their families were declared to be educationally and culturally deprived. Schools, in turn, were said to have both the ability and obligation to compensate for such deprivation by instilling the attitudes and skills needed in a modern, technological society.[27] Even as the Johnson administration adopted it as a cornerstone of federal education policy in the mid-1960s, however, compensatory education was on its way to being widely discredited. African American leaders increasingly denounced the cultural deprivation thesis as a new and more subtle form of racism—a liberal way for white educators to avoid desegregation and blame underachievement on black students and families.[28]

Foster offers a different perspective on compensatory education, however, by showing how it was developed and implemented by innovative educators at particular urban schools. In the late 1950s and 1960s, at schools like Dunbar, Foster and other educators developed pilot projects that began to reverse a legacy of racial discrimination and pave the way for the current policy era of high academic expectations of all students. Drawing on African American traditions of educational activism and achievement as well as the liberal creed of equal opportunity, the Dunbar program raised academic expectations, motivated students, reached out to parents, and not least, provided much-needed infusions of financial and human resources. This brand of compensatory education anticipated subsequent research on how student achievement is shaped both by the social and cultural capital that parents pass on to their children *and* by the attitudes, instructional approaches, and resources the children encounter in school.[29] Foster and other black educators addressed school as well as non-school factors in their pilot programs. As they did so, they began to confront the intertwined problems of racism, poverty, and underachievement that continue to haunt urban schools.

As compensatory education rapidly expanded into a nationwide federal program, liberals not only spent too little and promised too much for it as a social policy (in hindsight, the most serious problems with the approach); even more damaging at the time, they continued to alienate previous allies in the black freedom movement with pejorative-sounding language that ignored the persistence of racism in schools and society. The escalating critique of liberal condescension—including the critics' insistence that schools be more responsive to, perhaps even governed by, their communities—forms a context for Foster's work in the later 1960s at the Catto Disciplinary School and Simon Gratz High School. In that era of heated challenges to authority in education, Foster was among those who called for urban schools to be more responsive and accountable to their communities. He did so, however, from within the system, as an African American principal who helped bridge divisions between families, teachers, and administrators who increasingly blamed each other for urban school problems. Foster revamped Catto, turning it from the "cesspool of the system" into a school that some parents requested for their children (to no avail, unless the child was "lucky" enough to have a record of delinquent behavior). Foster declared that Catto students were not "hoodlums," as many believed (especially after the riot of 1964); they were victims of racial injustice, and the schools had an obligation to educate them. But the teachers and administration could not do it alone. At Catto, as at Dunbar, Foster not only raised staff members' expectations of the students; he also motivated parents, students, and even neighborhood merchants to help meet those expectations. Under his leadership from 1963 to 1966, Catto students were less likely to engage in delinquent behavior and more likely to attend and succeed in their classes.

Similarly, Foster's emphasis on "total school community" was key to his effort to transform perhaps the most troubled school in the system, Gratz High School in North Philadelphia. At Gratz, Foster forcefully expressed a sense of urban school accountability that echoes today: "Inner city folks . . . want people in there who get the job done, who get youngsters learning *no matter what it takes.* They won't be interested in beautiful theories that explain why the task is impossible. The people believe that the job can be done. And they want it done now."[30] As at his previous schools, however, Foster attempted to "get the job done" in a variety of ways, with change coming not only from educators but from students, parents, and others in the community. A black history program and a school-led confrontation with the city to expand Gratz's facilities showed how educators like Foster responded to the increasingly insistent demands of their school communities. In this sense, schools were important sites in an antiracist struggle for Black Power, defined broadly as poor and working-class citizens organizing to challenge power structures in the city and improve the quality of their immediate lives.[31] At the same time, a compensatory education program, outreach to parents, and efforts to generate college scholarships and internships in local businesses were the work of a liberal who continued to believe schools should fill gaps in the background of urban students, providing them with the skills, confidence, and connections—again, the cultural capital—that more affluent students typically got from their parents. As measured by improved attendance, higher college admission rates, and a dramatically energized mood in the Gratz community overall, Foster's mix of approaches offered a ray of hope for urban school reform.

Foster's work at Gratz brought him public acclaim and propelled him to administrative leadership, first as an associate superintendent in Philadelphia and shortly thereafter as superintendent in Oakland. The end of the book analyzes his Oakland years as a culmination of the conflicts of the 1960s and, at the same time, as a prelude to more recent attempts to hold schools accountable for eliminating achievement gaps. In Oakland, in contrast to the Ocean Hill–Brownsville crisis, the Foster administration created a vibrant citizen participation process that resolved the city's crisis over school governance. Foster continued to insist that the schools produce results for the parents and communities they served, and he increasingly expressed this goal in terms of accountability and grade-level achievement. However, in Oakland, as in Philadelphia, Foster's approach was neither punitive nor focused on schools and educators alone. He called on taxpayers, politicians, businesspeople, and parents to join educators in taking responsibility for the performance of all students in Oakland. He insisted on *shared* accountability.

*   *   *

As this overview suggests, *In the Crossfire* is partly a story of how leadership and activism changed the conversation about race and education in America. When the SLA took Marcus Foster's life, they cut short one of America's most promising efforts to sever the links between race, socioeconomic status, and achievement. And even so, Foster's work had already helped ensure that the racism of the society in which he had been raised, while not eliminated in all quarters (especially individual classrooms), was for the most part gone from public and scholarly debates over education and inequality.[32]

But Foster's story is also a cautionary tale. Even as he made notable progress in Oakland, Foster confronted the difficulties of achieving equal educational opportunity in an unequal society—difficulties that haunt educators and reformers to this day. As a superintendent, he grew increasingly bitter over what he saw as a narrow approach to accountability that singled out educators and set up a self-fulfilling prophecy of failure: political institutions and the public did not provide urban school systems with the "massive doses" of support they needed, and then blamed either the schools or their largely poor and minority students for the resulting failure to produce dramatic progress. By the time of his assassination, Foster had come to see inadequate resources and a lack of *public* accountability as the biggest obstacles to his effort to eliminate the achievement gap. Speaking in 1973 at a conference of school administrators, Foster surprised his audience with an uncharacteristically caustic commentary on the plight of urban schools and educators: "We go through a coronary alley at all those tough high schools," he said, alluding to the heart attack he had suffered while working fourteen-hour days as a high school principal—"and they tell us, 'Here it is, baby; make it fly.' Then, when you can't make it, they say, 'I told you those niggers can't do it.'"[33]

Foster's searing statements pointed to the limits of isolated efforts at school reform in the nation's big cities. Writers and filmmakers have inspired audiences with the exploits of dynamic educators like Foster who pushed their students to unexpected heights of accomplishment. (The charter schools in the widely discussed 2010 documentary film, *Waiting for "Superman,"* are a recent example.)[34] Yet, as Foster's experience showed, and as sociologists and historians have emphasized since, urban school reform must be part of a larger social and economic policy response to the urban crisis—a response that also addresses the problems of inadequate housing, health care, and unemployment.[35] To ignore this insight—and to expect educators like Foster to defy the odds with all-consuming, after-hours dedication, at the expense of their families and personal health—is to turn them into martyrs and scapegoats.

Americans of the 1960s often made that mistake. From compensatory education, which policymakers expected to cancel out the effects of poverty with a few modestly funded programs, to the black freedom movement, which exposed institutional racism but said little about the impact of social and cultural capital on achievement, to advocates of fiscal retrenchment in the early 1970s, Foster's contemporaries tended to expect too much of school reforms and provide too little support for them.

Instead of learning from these mistakes, however, Americans in recent years have compounded them. Since the 1970s, the tendency to hold urban schools solely responsible for the low achievement of their students—and, in a larger sense, the tendency to look to schools for solutions to the problems of urban poverty—has only intensified. Proponents of No Child Left Behind and Race to the Top have espoused the accountability and antiracist themes of the 1960s and 1970s—noble sentiments, for sure—while too often ignoring the larger structural dimensions of urban school problems and social inequality. The period of rising expectations in school reform has coincided with economic trends that undermine the idea of education as the key to social mobility. Disparities in wealth and income have steadily increased since the Reagan era, as have the barriers blocking access to higher education for poor and working-class citizens. In their focus on school-based solutions, federal policies have ignored—indeed, diverted attention away from—a variety of other factors that prevent urban children from reaching their full potential in school and in life. It is hard enough to fix urban schools so that low-achieving students get the knowledge and skills they need for college—but even that is not enough, if the students cannot pay for it.[36]

In pointing out that schools are not in fact the great equalizer that Horace Mann said they were, I do not mean to suggest that they cannot be reformed or that they do not matter as a mechanism of opportunity. I do not mean to make "excuses" for their failings.[37] Rather, I seek to emphasize complexity—even paradox—in the relationship between schooling and opportunity in America. Like the Sixties-era debates that this book reconstructs, recent debates over race, urban schooling, and achievement gaps have tended to emphasize either the power and responsibility of schools to reduce the achievement gap, or the larger social and economic forces that impede such efforts.[38] Both are important arguments, and this book will develop them still further. At its core, however, this book is about the tension *between* stories of educational uplift and analyses of entrenched inequality.[39] It has been difficult for Americans to espouse the dream of educational empowerment and uplift without turning schools into what one historian called the "imperfect panacea."[40] At the same time, it has been hard to emphasize the social and economic forces that limit what the schools can accomplish without diminishing the importance of school reform. With the pendulum swinging from one of these positions to the other, the result has been a recurring cycle of overheated expectation and disillusioned retrenchment in American school reform.

This account of the remarkable but tragic career of Marcus Foster tries to synthesize these conflicting arguments and impulses into a more complete analysis of race, poverty, and educational inequality—one that captures the importance of schools as agents of opportunity in an unequal society, as well as their inability to transcend that unequal society on their own.

Schools are not the answer to problems of social inequality—but we cannot solve those problems without them.

CHAPTER 1

Schooling as Social Reform: Racial Uplift, Liberalism, and the Making of a Black Educator

PUBLIC education has been intimately tied to American dreams of social mobility since Horace Mann helped found the first school system in the early nineteenth century, and it has held an especially potent meaning for African Americans. Initially barred from public schools, blacks not only were denied an avenue of opportunity (and an increasingly important one as the twentieth century unfolded); they were stigmatized as intellectually inferior. As a result, access to education has been at the core of African Americans' identities as free people, and academic achievement—especially the acquisition of literacy—has been a way for African Americans to transcend racist assumptions and assert themselves as equal citizens.[1]

Marcus Foster's upbringing vividly illustrates the obstacles that African Americans faced in pursuing educational achievement as well as the importance they attached to doing so. Foster's family moved from Georgia to Philadelphia in the 1920s, when he was two or three years old—part of the "Great Migration" of African Americans who left the South with the hope of making a better life in the cities of the North. The migration changed the cities and their schools—and, for blacks hoping to escape racism and Jim Crow, the changes were not always promising. Foster went to public schools during the 1930s. When he graduated from high school in 1941, the system was more segregated than it had been when he started. This was no accident. The de facto segregation of the North may not have been imposed by law (de jure), as it was in the South, but it was a product of intentional actions, nonetheless. As African Americans became a larger presence in Philadelphia and other cities, whites worked to contain them in separate neighborhoods, workplaces, and schools. In those cases in which black children did end up in the same schools as whites—especially at the high school level—they faced discrimination in the form of separate curricula, lower expectations, and sometimes overt hostility from white teachers. And if, after all that, black students managed to make it to graduation, they were likely to face job discrimination that prevented them from applying their schooling. For many African American youths who faced such dismal educational and employment prospects, the streets, the poolrooms, and the underground economy became alternative arenas for achieving an identity.[2]

Marcus Foster was a product of this gritty South Philadelphia subculture. As a teenager, he wore a zoot suit and was a leading member of a social club, or gang, called the Trojans. He could "hold his hands up" as a street fighter, according to his lifelong best friend, Leon Frisby. Frisby was a member of Club Zigar—"you had to smoke a 'stogie' and drink a lot of wine to get in"—and he remembers meeting Foster at a club dance in a gymnasium that doubled, at night, as "Club Benezet." The two boys went to the same junior and senior high schools, but most of Frisby's memories of Foster from this period revolve around parties, "rumbles," and life in the streets. "We were worldly," Frisby laughs.[3]

At the same time, though, Marcus Foster was an excellent student whose achievements were part of a larger dream of racial progress and self-improvement through education—a dream held dear by African Americans since the days when slaveowners had made it a crime for them to be literate. Foster was immersed in that educational legacy by a mother who named him after the Roman emperor Marcus Aurelius and nurtured a family culture of striving and learning. And as she imparted the legacy of African American achievement, Alice Foster also endowed her children with forms of cultural capital—especially literacy in Standard English—that would help them succeed in a school system run by white educators.[4] Young Marcus was as ambitious, competitive, and as proud in school as he was in the activities of the Trojans. He graduated with honors from South Philadelphia High, won a scholarship to all-black Cheyney State Teachers College outside of Philadelphia, and made one of the few legitimate, upwardly mobile career moves available to a young black man: he became a teacher. And he did so not because of, but in spite of, a public school system that expected little of him and other black students.

Foster's mixed identity—his immersion in street life and his drive for mainstream success—had at least two implications for his future as an educator. First, he was a living example of how education could be a ticket to social mobility for an African American boy of limited means. In spite of the obstacles and distractions that he faced—including some within the schools themselves—Foster and his family prioritized education both as a path to college and a career choice, and this would prove to be the key to a life of financial security. At the same time, though, Foster's "worldly" background gave him a basis for understanding just what a challenge it was for many urban students to achieve success in education and life. Foster was not the straitlaced young man that his mother or the Cheyney president Leslie Pinckney Hill wanted him to be, and this, as much as his more respectable accomplishments, was part of why he held such promise as a mentor and educator of urban youth.

Another factor that shaped Foster's rise to educational leadership was timing. During the World War II era when Foster was at Cheyney, social changes in the larger society, including a "Second Great Migration" of southern blacks to cities like Philadelphia, gave wider urgency to black education, making it a more mainstream cause. The 1940s gave rise in the northern cities to a new racial liberalism that predated the southern civil rights struggles of the 1950s. As historians have begun to show, white and black liberals joined forces during and after the war to fight discrimination in the workplace and in private housing markets.[5] Yet racial liberals did not focus solely on jobs and housing; in the 1940s and especially in the 1950s, they also began to move urban schools and educators toward the center of the struggle against racial inequality.[6] Educators, reformers, and other city leaders began to address racial inequality in urban schools as a result of "intergroup tensions" that escalated during World War II; as blacks entered the city in larger numbers and whites resisted their integration into urban life, some liberals looked to the schools for solutions. Education took on new importance for Americans who increasingly conceived of racial inequality as a vicious circle of white prejudice and black social pathology. Hoping to break this cycle and extend equal opportunity to African Americans, racial liberals created school-based "intergroup education" programs aimed at eradicating "prejudice."[7]

Foster's African American upbringing had a different educational focus than did the racial liberalism of the 1940s and 1950s: academic achievement and literacy as opposed to the eradication of prejudice. Moreover, as a young educator, Foster was not driven first and foremost by idealistic intentions to uplift his people or fight racial prejudice and inequality; he seems to have been motivated more by a personal ambition to work within the system toward his own professional accomplishments and advancement. As Frisby says, he had to "come out on top" in everything he did.

Still, Foster's personal path would be shaped and altered by the movement of history. Due to the rise of racial liberalism, his potential to achieve a position of leadership was greater than that of many black men in earlier generations. And due to the rising importance of education within the struggle for racial equality, an up-and-coming black educator like him was on a path to becoming a leader in the larger struggle of his people, whether he intended to be one or not. Foster would have the chance—and the burden—of showing that his personal story of educational achievement and social mobility could be the rule, rather than the exception.

"You Can't Teach Them Anything": Separate and Unequal Schooling in Philadelphia

Marcus Foster was born March 31, 1923, in Athens, Georgia, about seventy miles from Atlanta. He was the youngest of five children born to William Henry Foster, a mailman, and Alice Johnson Foster, a schoolteacher. (A sixth child, who died of diphtheria during infancy, would have been the oldest.) The parents separated when Marcus was two or three, and Alice took the children to Philadelphia, where they moved in with her younger sister, Susan, and Susan's husband John Jordan. "All six of us descended upon them," laughs Alfred Foster, who was two years older than Marcus, "so growing up in Philadelphia, it was a family of eight." The Jordans and Fosters initially lived in a small row house at 20th and Gerritt Streets in South Philadelphia; a short time later, they bought a three-story row house at 18th and Latona.[8]

Foster's family had its own distinctive reasons for moving north, but the six of them were also part of the Great Migration of African Americans out of the South. Philadelphia had always been an important center of African American settlement, but World War I marked a turning point for the city's black community. Southern migrants, lured initially by recruiters from the city's railroad corporations, kept coming of their own volition into the late 1920s, causing the city's black population to more than double between 1910 and 1930, from 85,000 (5.5 percent of the city's total) to 220,000 (11.3 percent). The migrants established a more visible presence for African Americans in Philadelphia; while roughly a third of them moved into Center City's seventh and thirtieth wards, the somewhat isolated black ghetto that W. E. B. DuBois spotlighted in his 1899 study *The Philadelphia Negro,* most, including the Fosters, branched out into neighborhoods where blacks were still significantly outnumbered by Jewish, Italian, and Irish immigrants.[9]

Foster's brother, Alfred, remembers the South Philadelphia neighborhood of his and Marcus's youth as "very integrated," full of Italian and Jewish immigrant families with whom the Fosters got along. "Our childhood days were full of activities and pleasant memories. Lots of children and lots of fun playing games—street games like rugby, stickball, and jump rope." Alfred had heard about, but never experienced, turf battles involving the Italians and the Irish; in his small world, at least in memory, the ethnic and racial groups lived in peace.[10]

Alfred Foster's memories suggest a degree of social fluidity in the northern cities that absorbed the Great Migration of southern blacks. Indeed, prior to 1930 the northern cities were actually less segregated than they would become in the four decades thereafter. Still, for migrants who had envisioned the North as the promised land, segregation and second-class citizenship remained a bitter fact of life. Philadelphia was a border city, just north of the Mason-Dixon line, and many of its public and commercial facilities were segregated. Its manufacturing sector went into long-term decline in the late 1920s, depriving the migrants of manufacturing jobs the war only recently had made available to blacks for the first time.

To make matters worse, the newcomers became scapegoats for social and economic problems that coincided with their arrival. Native-born Philadelphians, fixating on a derelict element in the early wave of railroad recruits, blamed the migrants en masse for rising crime rates, a booming underground economy, public disorder, and deteriorating neighborhoods—despite evidence that most of them came from stable families and that many of those who engaged in underground activity did so because the world of legitimate enterprise had shut them out. Some of the southerners' toughest critics included the so-called Old Philadelphians, or O.P.s—native-born blacks who were eager to maintain the modicum of status and security they had achieved as butlers, caterers, postal workers, ministers, teachers, and, in some cases, professionals. The O.P.s resented the newcomers for stirring up anti-black attitudes.[11]

Better schooling for their children was a top priority among African Americans who fled the segregated South during the Great Migration. Instead, the migrants faced new variations on an old problem of separate and inferior schooling in a system that stigmatized their children as intellectually inferior. Black children were not a major presence in the Philadelphia schools in the first two decades of the twentieth century; in 1920 they made up only 8.1 percent of the total school population. Black students who did attend school were usually mixed with whites in integrated facilities.[12] During the Great Migration, however, the school district began to steer white children away from schools with black children and, in some cases, to build new schools to accommodate the rising black enrollments. Gerrymandering and informal pressure were less overt than Jim Crow, but they produced similar results: roughly a dozen all-black, often under-equipped, elementary schools. Even within junior and senior high schools, which drew from a wider geographic area and therefore remained somewhat integrated, tracking and separate curricula channeled white children into academic subjects and limited black children to the vocational courses that allegedly suited their abilities.[13]

One of the most potent mechanisms for segregating and stigmatizing black children, whether in separate schools or within the same building, was the battery of new intelligence tests that came into vogue after World War I. Testing put a pseudo-scientific gloss on the idea of racial differences, explaining them as products of natural intelligence rather than discrimination and oppression. Researchers, for instance, drew unflattering conclusions from the presence of "large numbers of big, unschooled, overage southern children in the lower grades," as one black teacher described the effect of the Great Migration, without considering that the roots of this phenomenon lay partly in the dreadful lack of educational opportunities and expectations for black children in the Jim Crow South. What is more, IQ testing did not always work to a black child's advantage even when he or she got a high score; in 1924, for example, the Philadelphia High School for Girls segregated all of its black students into the same class, citing IQ scores as the reason, when in fact the girls' scores ranged from low to high.[14] Such practices were all the more likely because the teachers and administrators in Philadelphia's junior and senior high schools were segregated, too. Using separate eligibility lists, the school district placed black teachers only in predominantly black schools, thus limiting them to the elementary grades. As a result, they were stigmatized as unfit to teach white children and prevented from working with and supporting older black students.

In the face of such obstacles, black educators, parents, and activists did their best to secure a quality education for their children. One strategy was to resist the ghettoization of black teachers and students in separate schools. That approach especially gained momentum after 1932, when African American activist Floyd Logan founded the Educational Equality League (EEL), an organization through which he would lead black Philadelphia's fight against educational segregation and discrimination for more than thirty years. Logan was a product of segregated southern schools, and he hoped to eradicate what he saw as the destructive psychological effects of separate education. In 1937, he successfully pressured the district to abolish dual eligibility lists for teaching assignments.

The results of the fight for integration were meager, however, and racism remained a potent force even as some barriers began to fall. By 1942, only two African Americans were teaching in integrated schools above the elementary level, and both were at Sulzberger Junior High School, where the student body was increasingly black. The elementary schools remained as segregated as ever, and the practices of the junior and senior high schools showed that integration was no panacea. One of Sulzberger's two black teachers, Ruth Wright Hayre, recalled that white colleagues openly disparaged black children in her presence, complaining that "It's not anything like it used to be" (when the school was predominantly white); "You can't teach them anything"; and, "I'm going to transfer where I can teach children, instead of animals." Hayre, who went on to become a pillar of black educational leadership in Philadelphia, nurturing the careers of Marcus Foster and the future superintendent Constance Clayton, among many others, announced at a Sulzberger faculty meeting that in seven years of teaching throughout the country, she had never seen such "insulting condescension toward young people that I've seen here . . . You should be ashamed." And students were not the only targets of insult. When Dr. James Duckrey came to Sulzberger as Philadelphia's first black principal at the post-elementary level, the social studies chair asked for a transfer, telling Hayre that "I just can't let my friends know that I'm working under a colored principal."[15]

Hayre was no stranger to "insulting condescension"; she had faced it as a student whose high school counselor tried to steer her away from a college-prep program and into home economics because, according to the counselor, there were "just not any opportunities for colored girls for scholarships or professional jobs." Hayre's mother intervened, scolding the counselor for her "ignorance, prejudice, and low expectations" and lamenting that "many of our children are lost because no parent or knowledgeable person is there to go to bat for them" in such situations.[16]

Ruth Hayre's experiences as both teacher and student convinced her that integration, while a worthy ideal, often meant discrimination, exclusion, and "overall dullness." Her assessment echoed the 1935 article in which W. E. B. Du-Bois famously abandoned the cause of integrated education. DuBois had come to believe, in a foreshadowing of the Black Power sentiment of the 1960s, that African American children were better off learning in black-run classrooms and schools. He wrote that, "other things being equal," mixed schools were a "more natural basis" for the education of all youth. But things were nowhere near equal, as far as DuBois was concerned. As the NAACP and Floyd Logan's EEL stepped up the attack on segregation, DuBois argued that white institutions were so racially biased that blacks had to embrace their own schools or not be educated at all. "A separate black school, where children are treated like human beings, trained by teachers of their own race, who know what it means to be black in the year of salvation 1935," was, he wrote, "infinitely better than making our boys and girls doormats to be spit and trampled upon and lied to by ignorant social climbers, whose sole claim to superiority is the ability to kick 'niggers' when they are down." Moreover, black schools and educators could provide black history instruction that was impossible to find in white schools. DuBois's position ran afoul of the NAACP, which expelled its co-founder for rejecting the integrationist creed, and of some African Americans who, he wrote, "disparage their own schools" and "treat the Negro teachers in them with contempt." Still, he spoke for at least some urban blacks who perceived that, in the early twentieth century, schooling by and for one's own people was the most realistic path to academic achievement.[17]

DuBois made a powerful case for the potential of black schools, especially in the field of black history, but his article underscored the dismal educational choices that African Americans faced in the days of Marcus Foster's youth. The mixed schools were bad—but so were separate schools when plagued, as he admitted they often still were, by "ignorant placeholders, inadequate equipment, poor salaries, and wretched housing."[18] Neither integration nor self-help could fully offset the inferior status that white educators imposed on African American children in Philadelphia and other cities. And even those persistent black students who went on to graduate from high school got little economic reward for their efforts, meeting instead with discrimination from employers who feared racist reactions from white employees and customers.[19] Far from being the "great equalizer" Horace Mann had described when he helped create public education in the nineteenth century, the schools in the Fosters' adopted city of Philadelphia were, if anything, an obstacle to African American achievement.

"You Had to Be Twice as Good": An African American Culture of Achievement

In the schools, Foster and other black students faced what education scholar Theresa Perry describes as the "dilemma of achievement" for African Americans: Why should one work hard to excel in school if one has little expectation of being recognized or rewarded? Since the 1980s, some scholars have made the controversial claim that African American students respond to this dilemma by developing an "oppositional culture" that rejects academic achievement as "acting white."[20] But historical perspective and context are crucially important to this debate. For much of American history, and certainly during Marcus Foster's youth in the early twentieth century, many African Americans responded to educational discrimination not by rejecting the ideal of academic achievement, but by dedicating themselves even more tenaciously to it, in spite of its apparent limitations as an avenue of social mobility. For African Americans who were excluded from labor unions and denigrated as an intellectually inferior people, academic achievement was not only one of the few *possible* paths to social mobility (however flawed); it was also a way to assert one's basic dignity and worth as a free person.[21]

Marcus Foster was among those African Americans who transcended the school system's and the larger society's low expectations of him, excelling in academic subjects as he made his way toward a high school diploma. He made a strong start in the segregated environment of Smith Elementary School, thriving in academics and dramatics. According to his brother, he was the only student to be accelerated a grade ahead of his age group.[22] Foster was talented, and at Smith, he may also have benefited from the new facilities and the supportive environment that some commentators attributed to all-black schools. There is no question, however, that one key ingredient to his high achievement was the set of knowledge, skills, and attitudes he developed outside of school, under the tutelage of his mother and extended family.

Alfred Foster's memories of his family stand in contrast to those critics, black as well as white, who blamed the southern migrants for ruining the fabric of social life and race relations in Philadelphia. Indeed, the Fosters exemplified the resilience and resourcefulness with which many African American families responded to the challenges of urban life. Not having a father in the house was, of course, a setback. Alfred recalls that his father, William, had been a "good disciplinarian"—"he would have us select the switches off the peach tree if we were naughty"—and a good provider. There was talk of his rejoining the household in Philadelphia before he died in the late 1920s.[23] But William's absence did not doom the Fosters. Later in life, Marcus Foster cited his own story to show, against what some observers believed, that children raised by single mothers could succeed. In his case, this was especially true because of two factors: the strength of his mother's family and the material assistance of government in hard times.

Alice Foster had been a teacher before her marriage ended, and she retrained herself to do clerical work, but in Philadelphia the key to her survival was her extended family. Sue and John Jordan not only provided shelter; they played a major role in raising and supporting Marcus and his siblings. John was a father figure and partial provider, initially with paychecks from Baldwin Locomotive and later, after he was laid off when the company stopped making steam engines during the Depression, with odd jobs. Sue helped support the family with a hairdressing shop on the first floor of their house on Latona Street. One of Alice and Sue's brothers, William Decker Johnson, worked in the postal service in New York City and sent the Philadelphians some money every two weeks. Another brother, Hall Johnson, who gained fame as the head of a choir that sang Negro spirituals, helped them financially as well.

Even with this variety of family sources, Alfred notes the family's reliance on federal relief programs during the Great Depression, when his uncle John had difficulty finding work: "With the help of FDR's programs"—surplus food distribution is the one he recalls best—"we were able to live a comfortable life . . . We never lacked for food, clothing, or shelter." When it came to bread lines, young Marcus did his part, sometimes changing his jacket to go through the line for seconds.[24]

The Johnsons shared material resources to help each other survive; less tangibly, but no less important to the development of Marcus and his siblings, they also shared a proud legacy of striving and accomplishment. Alice's father, William Johnson, had been a bishop in the African Methodist Episcopal (AME) Church and a speaker of Greek and Latin; the latter fact perhaps helped to explain the name Marcus Aurelius Foster. (Curiously, Marcus believed his middle initial stood for "Albert" until just a few years before his death, when, to his amazement, he discovered the truth on a birth certificate he obtained from the state of Georgia.)[25] William Johnson's eminence as a black cultural figure was most closely matched in Alice's generation by her brother Hall, the choir leader. But Alice, too, was "very intellectual," as Alfred Foster recalls.

Alice Foster's intellectual streak may have played a role in her leaving her father's Methodist church to become a devout Christian Scientist; as Alfred says, she loved reading and may have been influenced by some of the group's literature. Whatever the reason, the decision helps paint a picture of a strong-willed woman, especially when it came to her children's growth and success.

Alice nurtured a family culture of excellence and achievement. It was important, Alfred says, "not to fail, to achieve something. To impress people, to avoid being on the short end of something. It wasn't enough to be good; you had to be better, twice as good."

For Alice Foster's children, being "good" was partly a matter of morals and manners. She was not harsh; Alfred describes her as "a very loving person, a very gentle disciplinarian" who guided her children "more through precepts and examples than lecturing." But she was strict. "She was of the idea that the world was in trouble when parents stopped requiring their children to say, 'Yes sir, no ma'am, thank you, you're welcome,'" Alfred says. "We learned respect for all people, especially our elders."[26]

As for many African Americans, however, the most important element in the Foster family culture of excellence was education. As Alfred says, the family "came up in an aura of learning" that was passed down from William to Alice Johnson and from Alice to her children. "She saw that we valued education."[27] In sociological terms, she saw that the children inherited the kind of cultural capital that would help them succeed in school and in society.

The concept of cultural capital does not involve a value judgment about the relative merits of particular cultural forms or behaviors; it does not suggest, for instance, that Standard English is better than Black English. It does remind us, however, that because schools and other institutions of the larger society *do* place a higher valuation on Standard English and other privileged forms of knowledge and skill (without explicitly teaching these in schools), the children who possess these forms of knowledge and skill will be at an advantage.[28] Children of privilege tend to inherit the largest supplies of cultural capital, from parents who are knowledgeable about the ways of the dominant culture and financially capable of cultivating such competence in their children (for instance, by providing such amenities as summer camps and private lessons, or by going to bat for the child, as Ruth Hayre's mother did when the guidance counselor tried to steer Ruth away from an academic curriculum). Nonetheless, Marcus Foster and his siblings—African American kids from a single-parent, working-class family—inherited a good deal of cultural capital in their home as well.

Alice Foster not only taught her children to "value education" (as many poor and working-class parents do); she was able to provide them with some of the knowledge, skills and self-confidence they needed to succeed in a system that held low expectations of children from their racial and social class background. As Standard English was (and is) the linguistic form that dominated the world of formal schooling, perhaps the most important element in the Fosters' supply of cultural capital was the ability to read, write, and speak that version of the language. A lifelong reader and learner herself, Alice Foster doggedly developed the linguistic skills of her children.

"She didn't want Marcus playing sports," Bob Blackburn recalls Foster telling him in later years, "and she didn't want him hanging on the corner and so forth." Instead, she made him take "elocution" lessons.[29] Alfred Foster says that his mother supervised the children's homework and "saw that we had adequate books of all kinds, and library cards." She also "gave us every opportunity to develop interest in music or whatever." She gave the children a religious upbringing that made an educational impact. Religion not only shaped the Fosters' "approach to life and the love for humanity and people," as Alfred says; it shaped their minds and reading skills. As young children, the Fosters dressed up every week and went to Sunday school at the Fifth Church of Christ, Scientist, in South Philadelphia—a predominantly white church. As teenagers they went less regularly, but Marcus and Alfred continued to read and distribute the *Christian Science Monitor*. At home, Alice led the children in readings from the bible and a Christian Science textbook.[30]

Alice Foster also fueled her children's aspirations by involving them in cultural and social activities beyond their immediate neighborhood. The family went on picnics and visited museums, the zoo, and other local attractions. They went to Robin Hood Dell, an outdoor amphitheater, to hear Uncle Hall's choir perform under starry skies with the Philadelphia Orchestra. Alfred and Marcus went to Boy Scout meetings at the famous Mother Bethel A.M.E. Church, and the troop's camping trips expanded their horizons: "For any city kid to get out into the countryside was a big deal," says Alfred.[31]

The Foster family culture of achievement helped propel young Marcus from Smith Elementary to Barrett Junior High and eventually to South Philadelphia High School for Boys. At the latter two schools he was now in the minority, but this fact apparently did not affect his performance. He was an honor student, ranked near the top of his class, and he competed on the speech and debate team.[32]

Foster fulfilled his mother's expectations of academic achievement partly because she prepared him to be comfortable and competent in the cultural milieu of the public schools. But Foster was not always the straitlaced son his mother groomed him to be. He was apparently as comfortable and content in the streets of South Philadelphia as he was in its public school classrooms. "Marcus had his set of friends he went with, and he was into dancing and that kind of thing, and the girls," says Alfred Foster, who grew less close to his brother as their interests diverged. "I wasn't involved in those kind[s] of activities with him . . . I couldn't verify the friends he had."[33] One of those friends was Leon Frisby, who went to the same junior and senior high schools as Foster and who knew a side of the educator's life that has received no mention in written sources about him.

Frisby does not remember Foster from school so much as from their participation in teenage male social clubs—Club Zigar and the Trojans, respectively. The clubs' main social activity was to sponsor dances, for which they hired a "radio boy" to play the latest big band records, and it was at one such event that Frisby recalls meeting Foster. Peers from different clubs had much in common and generally socialized without incident. They all took pride in cultivating the hipster fashions that were emerging as the signature of an urban black subculture: wide-lapel zoot suits with custom-tapered "peg" pants, "conked" (straightened) hair, suede shoes, dangling pocket watch chains. They used the same jazzy slang—"the narrower the peg in your pants, the more 'hep' or 'on time' you looked," says Frisby. And they all loved to do the jitterbug, either at one of their own dances or in nightclubs like The Strand, on Broad and Bainbridge, that featured the big band sounds of Billy Eckstine and Jimmy Gorham.[34]

At any moment, though, social encounters within this subculture might end in a fight over girls or some other territorial matter. "Sometimes we'd try to get their girls and they'd try to get our girls," Frisby says. Problems especially arose when gangs were involved. Frisby recalls gangs as being less organized and respectable than clubs; their members were "street people" whose main concern was battling over turf. Clubs fought less often, he says, but "we defended ourselves when put upon" by a gang. Frisby remembers the violence being black-on-black rather than interracial. In a typical rumble, the club chose a representative for a fistfight that would settle the matter. Foster's club often selected him for this role, Frisby says, "and he won, I can tell you that. He could hold his hands up."[35]

Historians have analyzed the black hipster culture of the 1940s, and especially the wearing of the zoot suit, as an act of subversion—a rejection of the work ethic and other aspects of bourgeois respectability.[36] Foster's life as model student and zoot-suit-wearing jitterbug blurred the lines between conformity and rebellion; he apparently devoted himself equally to the norms of the classroom and the dance hall. Both aspects of his identity are perhaps best understood as products of an intensely ambitious and competitive nature. "Anything he was in, he had to come to the top, he had to be first," says Frisby. "Whatever it was—playing cards, shooting pool, teaching . . . And girls, too."[37] Alfred Foster prefers to say his brother possessed an intense pride in excellence: "He didn't want to ever appear to be lacking in some way. He wanted to put his best foot forward. I don't think it was thought of in terms of being competitive or better than someone else. It was something that he had to do, it was his nature to do it."[38] However one describes it, Foster expressed a will to excel and to lead in every area of his life, both socially respectable and otherwise.

By 1941, Foster's ambition and effort had helped propel him to a high school diploma and a college scholarship—notable accomplishments among his peers. Later in his career, a reporter would write that Foster had always wanted to be a teacher.[39] Frisby says that his friend simply wanted to go to college, and as a financially strapped black applicant, his only option was a small, all-black teacher training institution—the Cheyney State Teachers College, outside of Philadelphia. "We couldn't think about the University of Pennsylvania or Temple or any of those schools, or Penn State; that was just out," he says. "So he went, as I went, because it was a college, and he wanted to get a college education."[40]

Cheyney actively recruited black students from Philadelphia who showed signs of promise, offering them partial scholarships through its Student Loan Fund. Alice Foster also had a hand in the process. "My mother had arranged for us to be considered by Cheyney," Alfred says, because their scholarship program made it the only affordable option.[41] Alice Foster no doubt liked Cheyney for another reason; its president, the poet and educator Leslie Pinckney Hill, was as stern an advocate of excellence and right conduct as she was.

Foster's exact motives and feelings concerning college are unknown. Once he went to Cheyney, though, it is clear he encountered a new kind of environment and set of influences. The faculty and president of the college not only would emphasize the high personal and academic standards his mother had tried to instill in him; they would push him toward leadership and the lofty goal of "uplifting" his race.

Cheyney College and Racial Uplift

Cheyney had been founded in 1852 by Quakers, in Philadelphia, as a small secondary school called the Institute for Colored Youth. The Quakers let African Americans run the school, though in 1903 the governing board disappointed blacks by moving the institution twenty-five miles southwest of the city in the hope of insulating students from the vices of city life. In 1913, the board hired Leslie Pinckney Hill as headmaster, a position he would hold until 1951. By the time Foster arrived in 1941, Hill had first transformed Cheyney from a tiny secondary school to a two-year state Normal school, and then to a nationally accredited, four-year black teachers college.[42] For Hill, Cheyney was more than just a place where African American men and women were credentialed to earn a livelihood as teachers; it was a "fulcrum" for the grand enterprise that many black leaders since Reconstruction had called "uplifting the race."

Uplift has had conflicting meanings in African American history, with the most familiar of these divisions involving the contrasting ideas of Booker T. Washington and W. E. B. DuBois. Where Washington preached manual education and economic self-help, DuBois called on blacks to agitate in the political arena for civil and social equality. Leslie P. Hill was an associate of both men, and at Cheyney he forged a vision of black educational uplift that does not fit neatly into the Washington-versus-DuBois framework. Born in 1880 as the second son of former slaves, Hill attended Harvard. After his graduation in 1903, Washington hired him to head the Tuskegee Institute's education department, which was part of the small academic division of the school. After several years at the flagship of the industrial education movement, Hill moved on to run a similar institution, the Manassas Industrial School. But Hill's heart lay in books and culture; he was a poet, and he had soured somewhat on Washington's anti-intellectualism even before he left Tuskegee. He was not against manual instruction. However, like DuBois, who was a fellow Harvard alum and eventually a good friend, he believed African American students should receive the same classical academic education as whites. Washington's alma mater and educational model had been a vocationally oriented freedmen's school, the Hampton Institute in Virginia; Hill's was the Ivy League, which he invoked with his slogan, "Harvard, Yale, and Cheyney."[43]

Hill's slogan was belied by Cheyney's curriculum, which was limited to preparation for elementary, industrial arts, or home economics teachers. Still, among students and alumni, President Hill was famous for the "Cheyney legacy," an inspirational blend of moral and academic preparation for life as a positive black role model. Like Washington, Hill largely put the onus for racial progress on blacks and black institutions—especially educational ones—rather than on whites. The Cheyney legacy included an emphasis on conduct and etiquette that Hill believed would earn respect for African Americans within the larger society. At regular assemblies and in conversations around campus, Hill dwelled on the virtues of personal initiative and reprimanded students for deficiencies in their manners, posture, grooming, and eating habits. He required them to go to chapel on Sundays and to teach Sunday school to neighboring children. He demanded that the "gentlemen" tip their hats and give up seats for women.[44] In these respects Harriet Braxton Logan, a classmate of Marcus Foster and a longtime admirer of Hill, compared the college to a finishing school.[45] For Hill, the key to racial progress lay largely with blacks themselves, including the efforts of enlightened black educators to promote self-help and cultural uplift in black communities. The main goal was not to change the existing society so much as to prepare oneself for acceptance within it.

If Hill accepted existing institutions and emphasized self-help, however, he was also a passionate advocate of full equality for his people; like DuBois, he rejected Washington's acceptance of a segregated sphere of ambition for blacks. In the spirit of the New Negro movement of the 1920s, Hill wrote, "We must have a new type of Negro teacher for Negro youth," one who could "inspire them that there is no attainment, no character, no service that black boys and girls may not reach."[46] Cheyney's curriculum may have been limited, but as in some of Philadelphia's all-black elementary schools, segregation (combined with Hill's academic connections and interests) steered a number of highly capable African American educators toward the college, giving it an atmosphere of high standards.[47] Hill expected these men and women to put Cheyney on a "plane of uncompromising equality" with white higher education. At the same time, like DuBois, he believed that black colleges had special contributions to make in the teaching of black history, black music, and other areas that inculcated "wholesome race pride."[48] Cheyney taught that African Americans were a proud people, capable of intellectual achievement and worthy of participating equally in all aspects of American society.[49]

In the broadest sense, Hill, like both Washington and DuBois, was committed to education as a tool to advance not just individual opportunity, but the progress of all African Americans. Over time, Marcus Foster's goals and ideas would come to resemble those of the Cheyney president. During his time at the college, however, Foster's social vision was still in an early stage of development.

To be sure, Foster quickly gained notice for his academic excellence and his potential as a leader. The first issue of the student newspaper—edited by his brother Alfred, also a high achiever—reported that the freshmen had chosen

"Marcus Foster, a brilliant student from South Philadelphia High School," as their class president. "Young Foster," the article said, "seems a good bet to duplicate his brother's distinguished scholastic record." And he was. A few months later Foster was the highest-ranking freshman, by grade point average, among twenty-two students honored at "Scholar's Night." He also found time to appear in a school play and to serve as assistant manager of the football team.[50]

Still, Foster's path through Cheyney included struggle and a degree of rebellion against the moralistic leadership of President Hill. In the fall of his junior year, by which time Foster was one of only a few male students who had not been drafted, a campus newspaper cartoon poked fun at his habit of arriving late in the morning and sleeping through class. The accompanying article noted how a defense job at the Sun Shipyard in nearby Chester had reduced the time Foster could devote to campus activities.[51] As Ruth Hayre, whose husband Talmadge Hayre was one of Foster's professors, later noted, the evening shift at Sun also helped explain Foster's inability to stay awake in class.[52]

Hard work was not the only reason Foster was tired, though; with the companionship of Leon Frisby, who accompanied him to Cheyney and to Sun Shipyard, Foster maintained aspects of his South Philadelphia lifestyle that would have chagrined Hill and his faculty had they been aware of them. Formerly acquaintances in the city, Foster and Frisby became best friends at Cheyney. Foster began to call Frisby his "home boy." When Frisby accidentally set his dorm room on fire with an illicit cigarette, Foster, who had the better reputation, took the blame to prevent his friend from getting suspended. On weekends, when their shift at the shipyard ended around midnight, Foster and Frisby headed to all-night clubs to carouse with fellow workers. On Sunday morning, they went straight from the bars to their respective churches. "We felt we were superior because we went to church," says Frisby.[53] A more conservative classmate, J. David Bowick, who followed in Foster's footsteps to become superintendent of schools in Oakland in the early 1980s, alluded to such behavior when, in later years, he expressed amazement at how Frisby had "mellowed"; "after all," he wrote to Frisby in 1982, "you and Marcus were crazy when we were at Cheyney."[54] Granted, Foster and Frisby toned down their urban styles of dress and slang and generally conformed to Cheyney's conservative climate. "We weren't strong enough to *rebel* against it, because everybody else was doing it," Frisby says of Hill's dress codes and his Sunday night sermons on philosophy, history and religion. "But we just thought it was an imposition—you know, that it was being forced on us . . . Anything to get out and to graduate, we did."[55]

Foster did not yet share Leslie P. Hill's zealous commitment to promoting racial uplift and equality through education. What he did share with Hill, though, was a powerful orientation toward excellence and achievement, and over time, this trait carried him ever further on a path to success and leadership in the larger society. Too proud to keep dozing through class, he left school for a few years until he could afford to quit the shipyard and spend more time pursuing the straight A's he demanded of himself. After leaving the job and being drafted and nearly inducted into military service—a last-minute test of his terrible eyesight made him 4F—Foster devoted himself to Cheyney's elementary education curriculum.[56] He was not overly excited about elementary education, according to Frisby, but he chose it over the two alternatives, industrial arts and home economics—and when he did, his pride in achievement kicked in. "He wanted to excel in whatever he did. If it was just recreation, playing cards . . . whatever it was, he wanted to be the best. When he got into elementary education, then he wanted to be first in that."[57] And he was: in addition to earning excellent grades, Foster was honored as the best student teacher in his program.

Outside the classroom, Foster exemplified the leadership qualities Leslie Pinckney Hill hoped to instill in his students, though, as Foster's story shows, those qualities were inborn as much as they were instilled. Alfred Foster, who got somewhat reacquainted with his younger brother while they both attended Cheyney and worked at Sun Ships, recalls his natural charisma: "Everybody liked him, because Marcus had a great sense of humor . . . We had to put on skits; he was the emcee, because he was recognized as the one with a good social presence, able to relate with the audience. He loved the stage."[58] In these and other settings, Foster always emerged as a leader. At the shipyard, he was a foreman. In the Omega Psi Phi fraternity, he was president. The latter accomplishment was all the more notable because Cheyney did not have a chapter of Omega Psi Phi, so Foster and Frisby traveled into West Philadelphia to join the University of Pennsylvania chapter. At Penn they were outsiders among students from what Frisby calls a more "professional" background. Even so, Foster rose to be president of his pledge class and eventually the president, or "basileus," of the chapter—a leadership position that for the first time made him an official representative of a larger social agenda. (The fraternity's Cardinal Principles were scholarship, manhood, perseverance, and uplift, and it had a history of advocating for racial equality.)[59]

Estella Johnson, a sociologist who taught in Cheyney's elementary education program and who in 1961 became the first African American to teach in a predominantly white college or university in Pennsylvania, says Foster had a self-confidence that did not come easily to blacks in a segregated society. "When you come from a closed society that is antithetical, you've got to have something extra," she says. Among a student body in which "all seemed to have extraordinary characteristics," Johnson remembers that Foster in particular "wasn't fearful. You see, a lot of people grow up in a closed society, and they're fearful. But he wasn't. His whole persona was different. . . You have to have a sense of self-identity, to make it." Johnson's husband, Rufus, who was a professor in the Industrial Arts department, adds, "He was more than a student; he was like a faculty person." As a senior after the war, Foster helped Johnson re-establish the school's athletic program, serving as manager of the football team, and he assisted the administration and faculty with other postwar expansion projects. When his professors had to be absent, he sometimes taught class.[60]

Foster met his future wife at Cheyney, and this relationship, too, was indicative of his ambition to rise in the world. Albertine Ramseur ("Abbe") came from a different social world than the one Foster and Frisby were accustomed to inhabiting. "We were used to drinking people and carousing folks and going out overnight and staying out and sex," says Frisby. "That was our lifestyle." By contrast, Ramseur came from "a stable home" in the Philadelphia suburb of Darby. Her father was a church deacon, and her mother did social work. She was of a "higher caliber than the people we had been associating with in South Philadelphia," Frisby says. She was "very stern."[61] Estella Johnson was Ramseur's freshman adviser, and she echoes Frisby's characterization. Above all, Johnson remembers Ramseur's independence and her "high personal standards." "Abbe always had as a basic cultural value for herself, excellence. She always wanted to be right—right and proper."[62] Foster had made a mark for himself at Cheyney, and according to Frisby, he, too, was "a good catch"—but still, his courtship of Ramseur was "like the tramp and the lady." Ramseur was the kind of woman an ambitious young man like Foster was interested in marrying. "She was opinionated, and strong in her thinking, and strong in her commitments," Frisby explains. "And he liked that." Foster was "popular with the ladies" and accustomed to "get[ting] away with almost anything," but Ramseur was a different story. She was "a standard for him to achieve"—"a *challenge*."[63] In this challenge, as in most others, Foster's efforts ended in success: on graduation day in the spring of 1947, he and Albertine got engaged under the flagpole at Cheyney, and later that year they were married.[64]

Apart from whatever personal feelings he may have had for her (which are not well documented), Foster's courtship of Albertine Ramseur was part of a larger process of social mobility in his life—a process that may be helpful to understanding his life as an educator. As a black man coming of age in the 1940s, Foster had limited opportunities, and elementary education may not have been his dream. But it turned out he was well suited to a career in education, perhaps in part because of the complicated mix of identities and experiences he had embraced in his own life. Foster applied himself to education, and in doing so, he put himself on a long-term path to a stable and secure livelihood. He also took an interest in "marrying up." His scholastic efforts as well as his choice of a partner marked a move away from the streets and clubs in which he had spent a good portion of his youth. And yet, that lifestyle was part of who he was, too. Foster would never fully give it up; in particular, he struggled over time with a drinking problem.[65] His personal weaknesses seem to have caused him some pain—but they also may have played a role in his effectiveness as an educator. In particular, the gritty underside of Foster's young life seems to have been a foundation for his legendary ability to relate to all kinds of people, undergoing all kinds of struggle—especially young people for whom the challenges and lifestyle of the inner city represented obstacles to educational achievement.

Little is known about Foster's early years of teaching, but the few fragments of evidence that do exist point to this very quality of relating to all kinds of students, families, and environments. Like many of his classmates who faced discrimination and job shortages in Philadelphia and other northern cities, Foster went south for his first teaching job, to rural Princess Anne, Maryland. In Princess Anne, he taught science in a four-room, wood-frame school. He began his day by gathering wood to build a fire in the stove that stood in the middle of the classroom. Foster's remembrances suggest a respect for his students' humble social and cultural backgrounds and at the same time a desire to expand their horizons. "I was forced to do creative teaching," he later said, "because there weren't many materials available."[66] Some of those materials included the hog farms and oyster houses in which the students and their parents worked; the class made field trips to those locations for teaching units like "Finding Myself in Respect to the Land and Water Resources of Maryland." Foster's goal, in this instance as in the rest of his career, was to build academic skills as well as aspirations in disadvantaged children. "Those kids were ten feet tall when they walked around," he recalled; "'these water resources depend on me!'"[67]

Foster spent a year in Maryland, and while it seems to have been a productive time educationally, it was problematic for other reasons. Ramseur had taken a teaching job in Florida, and though the couple got married over Christmas vacation, she returned to her job. After three days of marriage, "he put me on a train and I cried all the way to Florida," she said later. "We took separate honeymoons," Foster recalled.[68] After a year of separation in the South, however, the Fosters were able to move to Philadelphia, where they soon had their daughter Marsha, and where Marcus landed a position at the E. M. Stanton Elementary School.

Stanton was in South Philadelphia, not far from where Foster had grown up. Like his own elementary school, it was a product of the segregationist policies of the Great Migration era, a formerly mixed school that became a black school in 1920 and moved into a new building shortly thereafter. Foster stayed at Stanton for at least several years, though the record of his experience there, as in Maryland, is limited to fragments. Still, one anecdote hints at the responsive kind of educator he was to become. Foster was the only man on the staff, and for that reason his principal, a tough, diminutive Irish American woman, looked to him as the resident disciplinarian. Once she delivered a boy to Foster with instructions to "fix him so he can't walk." Foster laughed about the incident with Frisby, though he no doubt saw it as an example of how *not* to respond to discipline problems. We do not know how he handled the boy at Stanton, but he did go on to make a name for himself precisely because of his ability to defuse conflicts with dialogue and mutual understanding rather than harsh punishments.[69]

Identification with diverse students came naturally to Foster, and this, together with his ambitious nature, may have done more than the teachings of Leslie P. Hill to put him on his path to educational leadership. In the end, in fact, what role did Hill and his "Cheyney legacy" play in Foster's development? Hill had tried to mold Foster and his classmates into African American role models who would further the social advancement of their people. At the time, Frisby says, he and Foster perceived this agenda as an imposition; they simply wanted to graduate and "get out." Moreover, when Foster did move on from Cheyney, the day-to-day realities of his early career stood in striking contrast to Hill's lofty notions about uplifting the race. By day, Foster labored in obscurity as an elementary school teacher. Most evenings, he focused on providing additional support for his wife and daughter by teaching night school and driving a cab (which, of course, came at the cost of spending less time at home with them). He was a far cry from being any kind of public figure or leader of his people.

Indeed, what impact could any educator have in the grand struggle for black progress and racial equality? Hill focused on what black people could do as individuals, especially through education, to uplift themselves and fellow members of their race. By the time Foster graduated in the late 1940s, other black thinkers and leaders increasingly were pointing to a need for changes in the larger society. In 1944, Howard University professor Rayford Logan edited an anthology entitled *What the Negro Wants,* and as he noted in his foreword, the contributors included five liberals, five radicals, and four who "might be called conservatives." Leslie Pinckney Hill was presumably one of the conservatives; his essay emphasized the virtues of endurance, forgiveness, and family that he was preaching to Marcus Foster and the rest of the Cheyney student body on a weekly basis. In contrast, labor leader A. Philip Randolph's essay called for "the people" to turn a war between fascism and monopoly capitalism into a "Peoples' Revolution." The poet Sterling Brown stressed the problem of racial discrimination and demanded that white society "count us in."[70] Around the same time, the novelist Ralph Ellison began work on *Invisible Man,* his prizewinning portrait of a young black man who strives to succeed by virtue of diligent study and meritorious behavior, only to grow disillusioned by white society's repeated refusal even to see him.

The "Cheyney legacy" was not a complete and satisfactory answer to the ravages of racism and poverty—but it was not irrelevant, either. In the decades after his graduation, the ideals of African American achievement and uplift that Foster was exposed to at Cheyney would play an increasingly important role in his career and in nationwide struggles for racial equality. Hill may have been more conservative than leaders and critics like Randolph, Ellison, and DuBois, but his basic goal was the same: for African Americans to be granted the "rights, opportunities, and privileges that were vouchsafed to all other Americans and to fulfill all the obligations that are required of all other Americans," as Rayford Logan summarized the central agreement at the heart of *What the Negro Wants.*[71] In a society that disparaged African Americans and held them to lower standards, Cheyney emphasized the intellectual capacity of black children and looked to education as a tool of racial advancement. These ideas would become hallmarks of Marcus Foster's career, and they would resonate in the larger society as well, not least because, in the 1940s, the blatantly racist society of his childhood years was changing.

Pushed by the turbulent events of World War II and its aftermath, at least some white people began to listen more intently to "what the Negro wanted."

Schooling as Social Reform

For decades, a standard view of the civil rights movement was that it began in the South in the 1950s as a campaign against Jim Crow segregation in buses and other public facilities and culminated in the mid-1960s with passage of the Civil Rights Act (1964) and Voting Rights Act (1965). In recent years, historians have presented a strikingly different view, situating this "classical" phase of the movement within a "long civil rights movement" that began earlier (in the 1930s), lasted longer (into our own time), and took place over a wider geographic setting (nationally, as opposed to just the South).[72] A look at the time and context in which Marcus Foster began his career reinforces this more recent view. As Foster left Cheyney in 1947, American race relations were in flux. The Great Depression, World War II, and the Cold War unleashed major social, political, and cultural changes in Philadelphia and other cities across the nation. The war and its aftermath further eroded a post-Reconstruction racial order that had begun to unravel during the interwar years. Foster's early career unfolded against an urban backdrop of black migration, white-black conflict, and civil rights activism. Together, these forces would push racial inequality to the top of local and national agendas—and place powerful new pressures on educators like Foster.

Foster's family had been part of the Great Migration of African Americans out of the South. In the 1930s, a new wave of black migration, even larger than the first one, began to transform the cities and give new prominence to the plight of black Americans. Driven off the land by an agricultural depression, African Americans migrated from farms to the cities of the South and North. During the 1930s, some 400,000 of these migrants expanded the black population of the urban North by 25 percent. In the 1940s, as the rise of mechanical cotton-picking machines pushed unprecedented numbers of blacks out of the South and war-related employers pulled them north, the steady flow of the previous decade turned into a second great migration. Philadelphia was a dramatic case in point. In 1940, the city already had a large black population of about 250,000. In the next few decades that number would more than double, rising above 650,000 in 1970. Starting in the 1930s and accelerating thereafter, blacks went from being a rural to an urban people—and as they did, race went from being a southern to a national issue.[73]

Black migration went hand in hand with white resistance and new levels of interracial conflict. Like Alice Johnson Foster and others who had come a generation before, the new migrants expected to make a better life in a less hostile environment. And once again, whites fought to ghettoize them in separate and inferior workplaces, neighborhoods, and schools. Depression-era Philadelphia, far from being a "city of brotherly love," was rife with racial and religious tensions, including the activities of Nazi sympathizers, the Ku Klux Klan (which had almost nine thousand members in the city), and followers of Father Coughlin.[74] During the war, when white transit workers rampaged through black neighborhoods in protest against the hiring of black workers, the city appeared to teeter on the brink of a race riot such as the ones that erupted in 1943 in Harlem and Detroit.[75]

Out of the ferment of the war years came new ideas and policies with regard to the "race problem" in America—ideas and policies that would set a context for much of Marcus Foster's work as an educator. In particular, the 1940s marked a key turning point in a shift from racism to racial liberalism in public life. Racial liberalism was partly an intellectual and ideological development with roots in the interwar years. During the 1920s and 1930s, social scientists had begun to discredit racist ideology: that is, the biological explanations of racial inequality that had dominated American society, in various incarnations, since slavery and Reconstruction. In the 1940s, the war against Hitler and his race-based genocide did even more to discredit explicitly racist ideologies in America. Together, social science and the war against fascism bolstered the liberal idea that blacks deserved an equal opportunity to participate in American society.[76]

At the same time, and closely related to these intellectual and ideological changes, racial liberals promoted government action, especially in the form of new antidiscrimination laws and agencies, to turn the idea of equal opportunity for blacks into a reality. As historians have shown, New Deal liberalism redefined the meaning of American citizenship, expanding it to include government protection for the individual's right to own a home and get a college education, among other benefits, but it did so unevenly, largely leaving African Americans out of the bargain.[77] During and after World War II, however, as African Americans streamed into northern cities and developed a larger presence within the Democratic Party, they and their white liberal allies worked to ensure equal opportunity under the law for all citizens. In 1941, pressure from A. Philip Randolph and the Brotherhood of Sleeping Car Porters led President Roosevelt to establish a Fair Employment Practices Committee (FEPC), thus putting racially discriminatory hiring practices on the national agenda. After 1945, the liberal civil rights agenda gained even more steam as the war against fascism shifted to a Cold War against Communism, and American leaders faced a new imperative to eradicate racial hatred and live up to democratic ideals: it was difficult to win allies in the newly independent nations of Africa and Asia while the Soviet Union went about publicizing the injustices of Jim Crow. Following this logic of "Cold War civil rights," and in response to anti-lynching appeals from the NAACP and other allied groups, President Truman created a blue ribbon Committee on Civil Rights, whose report, *To Secure These Rights* (1947), called for an end not only to Ku Klux Klan terrorism but to discriminatory housing and labor markets, as well as segregated schools.[78]

Northern cities like Philadelphia were key sites in the unfolding of this liberal agenda. After 1947, the Cold War stalled the momentum toward civil rights at the national level, as southern Democrats and others fiercely resisted social change in the name of anti-Communism; it would remain for the mass movement in the South, arising after 1955, to force national leaders of the Democratic Party to choose civil rights over the racial status quo.[79] But in northern cities, local activist groups and new municipal agencies had better success at promoting the kind of antidiscriminatory, "color-blind" agenda that the Truman Administration had laid out in *To Secure These Rights*. In Philadelphia, the key players were the Philadelphia Fellowship Commission (FC), an "intergroup relations" agency that activists launched during the war to coordinate various crusades against racial and religious bigotry; a group of liberal business leaders known as the Greater Philadelphia Movement (GPM); and the GPM-sponsored reform mayors, Joe Clark and Richardson Dilworth.[80] In 1951, these leaders and groups helped persuade Philadelphia voters to approve a new city charter that created a municipal agency, the Commission on Human Relations (CHR), which was charged with promoting racial harmony and opposing housing and job discrimination.[81]

Racial liberalism was not embraced by all Americans, nor did all liberals see America's racial problems in exactly the same way. Even the most famous statement and synthesis of racial liberalism—Gunnar Myrdal's *An American Dilemma* (1944)—was partly a testament to the variety of views on racial inequality in mid-century America. Sponsored by the Carnegie Corporation, the Myrdal study was a massive research project involving collaboration among dozens of social scientists. As director of the study, Myrdal shaped the argument to emphasize the key liberal themes of racial tolerance and equal

opportunity: blacks were unequal to whites because whites harbored irratio-
nally "prejudiced" attitudes toward them and had shut them out of full participation in American life. This was a violation of the "American creed" of
equal opportunity under the law, and Myrdal called on white Americans to
shed their prejudices and put an end to racial discrimination.[82] Racial liberals
differed, however, in the extent to which they emphasized changing either
attitudes of white prejudice or laws and institutions.[83] (And over time, they
would place different degrees of emphasis on another aspect of the study,
namely, an alleged vicious cycle in which prejudice and discrimination led
to damaged black psyches and cultural pathology.) Meanwhile, some of the
scholars involved in *An American Dilemma* had pushed for a more radical
interpretation of the race problem. Especially forceful were the contributions
of the black political scientist Ralph Bunche, who pushed Myrdal to go beyond individualistic, psychological notions of social mobility and emphasize
the economic underpinnings of racial inequality. As Bunche and other left-
leaning analysts argued, racial inequality was not merely a byproduct of bad
laws or irrational white prejudices; it was the inevitable result of a capitalist
economy based on exploited black (and white) labor, and it could only be
eliminated through a mass mobilization of black and white workers such as
was being undertaken by the Congress of Industrial Organizations (CIO),
formed after passage of the Wagner Act in 1935.[84]

These differences of interpretation were consequential, and as we will see
in later chapters, they came to the fore in the 1960s. Still, in the 1940s and
1950s, racial liberalism gained momentum and became a major touchstone
for a wide variety of intellectuals, policymakers, and educators, including
the young Marcus Foster. In contrast to racial conservatism, with its focus
on black inferiority and the need for separation, racial liberalism said that
African Americans were unequal only because whites had deprived them of
an equal opportunity to succeed. Moreover, whites now had an obligation,
individually and through government, to remove those barriers and facilitate
the full inclusion of blacks in American life. Most importantly, in terms of our
focus on Marcus Foster, the liberal understanding of racial inequality led to a
new level of importance for education, especially in the nation's cities.

It is important to note that expectations of public education were on the
rise in postwar America even apart from concerns over racial inequality. As
high school and college diplomas became a key requirement for jobs in a
deindustrializing economy, families approached education as consumers of a
private good, scrambling for access to the best schools and, most important,

the credentials they conferred.[85] At the same time, reformers continued to place schooling at the heart of broader social and political agendas. Perhaps the most influential of these men was James B. Conant, the president of Harvard and an architect of the Manhattan Project and the Marshall Plan. During the war Conant came to worry that the nation's social structure had grown dangerously rigid and stratified and that tensions between labor and capital carried the explosiveness of "social dynamite." Fortunately, he argued (like others before him), public education held the potential to save American democracy. In particular, Conant believed schools could sort Americans fairly and rationally into the courses of study and careers that best suited them—but after the war they faced major challenges in doing so.[86] In response to rising enrollments, inadequate budgets and buildings, and a shortage of trained teachers, Conant persuaded his friend Roy Larsen, president of Time, Inc., to launch the National Citizens Commission for the Public Schools, a body that, in turn, would foster local citizens committees to support the public schools.[87] In Philadelphia, Larsen's organization helped stir the activist energies of citizens like Annette Temin, a mother of three who, in 1952, followed Larsen's lead and founded the Citizen's Committee on Public Education (CCPE). By 1957, as the Soviet launch of Sputnik fueled growing national concerns over the state of American education, the CCPE was stirring citizen interest in public schooling with town hall meetings, school visitations, and a study of the effects of low teacher pay on the quality of instruction.[88]

If racial inequality was not the only prominent educational issue in postwar America, however, it was an increasingly important one. Of course, for many Americans the first thing that will come to mind in this connection is the U.S. Supreme Court decision in *Brown v. Board of Education* (1954). But while accounts of *Brown* have established the importance of schooling to the struggle for racial equality, those accounts have important limits.[89] For one thing, their focus has been mainly on events in the South, which tends to obscure the fact that, prior to the late 1960s, other parts of the nation were also struggling over relationships between race, education, and opportunity. Second, if we expand our focus to take in events outside the South, we are reminded that *Brown* was not the beginning of the modern struggle over race and education so much as a milestone in a set of longer stories that date back at least to the World War II era. Racial problems in northern schools prior to the 1960s have been overshadowed by stories such as the Little Rock Nine and the struggles over busing in the 1970s (in educational history), or by civil rights struggles over jobs and housing (in urban history). However, a look at

Philadelphia during and after World War II reveals the rising prominence of urban schooling within struggles against racial inequality.[90]

The interracial tension and violence of the World War II era laid a foundation for urban school reform just as it did for the attempt to change employment and housing practices. In 1943, against the backdrop of race riots in Detroit and Harlem, Philadelphia schools chief Alexander Stoddard revealed his concern with racial tensions by naming Dr. Tanner Duckrey, a black educator, as the first assistant superintendent in charge of intergroup relations. (Prior to that appointment, Duckrey had been principal of the Dunbar Elementary School in North Philadelphia, leaving a legacy that Marcus Foster would inherit when he assumed leadership of that school in the late 1950s.) In 1944, Duckrey's office launched the Committee on School and Community Tensions (CSCT). Each month, district leaders and representatives from civic and governmental agencies, including Maurice Fagan of the Fellowship Commission and Marjorie Penney of Fellowship House, gathered to analyze and respond to "intergroup incidents" in schools and communities.[91] In 1944, Superintendent Stoddard also formed the Committee on Living Together, a group of teachers, counselors, and administrators who regularly swapped information on successful human relations practices.[92]

The district's early initiatives in intergroup education were intended more to maintain social order in a time of crisis than to extend high standards and quality education to blacks. Administrators hoped to contain disruptive, interracial violence in Philadelphia schools. But as they pursued that goal, they also began to forge a deeper link between schooling and the problem of racial inequality. Schools continued to be an important site of urban change and racial conflict in the 1940s and 1950s. Between 1945 and 1960, African Americans went from composing 25 to 47 percent of the student population in the Philadelphia schools.[93] Southern blacks kept migrating to the inner city, and violent interracial incidents continued to erupt on the borders of the expanding black sections in South, North, and West Philadelphia.[94] Whites increasingly moved to segregated outer neighborhoods and suburbs—partly because the federal government offered them discriminatory incentives to do so, but also because they tended to believe that an influx of blacks would lead to lower educational standards.[95] In this context, school programs played an increasingly important role for racial liberals who believed that prejudice against blacks was learned, irrational, and a central cause of America's racial "dilemma."

Tanner Duckrey's group, for example, tried to go beyond wartime crisis management and use the schools to prevent young children from being corrupted by adult hatreds and hostilities in the first place. To that end, the school district and the Fellowship Commission launched the Early Childhood Project in 1945. Fifteen elementary school teachers—most of them white—participated in a four-year "field experiment" aimed at finding the causes of prejudice and inoculating against it through exposure to "democratic attitudes." (When project leaders quickly learned that the children and, indeed, some of the teachers, were already prejudiced, they shifted their focus from prevention to cure.)[96] In the 1950s, the district continued to collaborate with the Fellowship Commission to build what experts praised as one of the top intergroup education programs in the country.[97] (As we will see, Marcus

Figure 1. Celebrations of interracial understanding in the mid-1950s, displayed at the H. J. Widener School as part of an "intergroup education" program run by the Philadelphia Public Schools and the Philadelphia Fellowship Commission. Intergroup education, a strand of racial liberalism prior to the 1960s, aimed to promote racial equality by teaching children not to be "prejudiced." Photo-Arts photograph, courtesy of Urban Archives, Temple University Libraries.

Foster became part of this effort when he was the principal of Dunbar Elementary School.) Teachers attended workshops where social scientists taught them how to practice as well as preach "open-mindedness." Committees of teachers and consultants scrutinized textbooks for stereotypes or prejudicial points of view and recommended books that fostered mutual understanding. Teaching guides and courses of study incorporated human relations themes.[98]

One of the most striking examples of intergroup education as a response to urban and racial problems was a program that never got off the ground. In 1953, the Fellowship Commission asked the Ford Foundation to contribute over $1 million to the proposed $6.5 million "community laboratory program in intergroup relations," a project aimed at nothing less than the democratic socialization of groups of children from eight different Philadelphia neighborhoods from the time of their arrival in kindergarten through their graduation from high school. The proposal listed more than one hundred academics and intergroup leaders who might consult on the program and included supportive letters from more than a dozen of those.[99] The Ford Foundation, reeling at the time from McCarthyite attacks on its support for school desegregation in the South, did not fund the proposal, which forcefully listed, among other problems, the "unwritten 'conspiracy'" by which blacks had been shut out of new housing within the city and in the suburbs.[100] Even so, the proposal itself tellingly distilled a growing liberal faith in the possibility of solving such problems by teaching children not to be prejudiced.

Racial liberalism and intergroup education did not change the system overnight. Critics like Floyd Logan of the Educational Equality League (EEL) and Francis Jennings of the left-wing Teachers Union (TU) believed the district failed to live up to its "impressive printed materials" on such virtues as "living together." Beginning in 1948, when the city passed a Fair Employment Practices law, both organizations repeatedly criticized the school board and its superintendent, Louis Hoyer, for their refusal to announce an official "human relations" policy. These critiques highlighted a mix of concerns among such activists—segregationist policies as well as prejudicial attitudes, with no clean line of separation between them.[101] According to an editorial in the *Teachers Union News,* for instance, the absence of written guidelines amounted to a tacit acceptance of racially biased curricula, discriminatory placements of black teachers and students, unequal facilities, and the perpetuation of harmful stereotypes. The board was not "made up of bigots," the writer continued, but, it was "so fearful of bigots that it capitulates to their demands, and sometimes even anticipates them."[102]

The critics had a point. Notwithstanding the efforts of associate superintendents like Duckrey, school district policy was still largely set behind closed doors by conservative men like Hoyer and Add Anderson, the notoriously powerful and corrupt business manager who controlled an equally conservative school board of political appointees and fiercely resisted the involvement of reformers and citizen activists.[103] In the 1950s, the district continued to restrict black teachers to a handful of all-black elementary schools like Smith and Stanton and to draw school boundaries so as to segregate the students, as well.[104] And regardless of what schools they attended, black students continued to be held to low academic standards. Leon Frisby recalls principals pressuring teachers to pass students on to the next grade even if they had failed, a practice that came to be known as "social promotion." "You were never reprimanded for passing everybody, but you could be reprimanded for failing too many," he says. "That was the attitude in the black schools."[105] Frisby and Marcus Foster had been prepared by Leslie Pinckney Hill to lead their race forward. As they began their careers, most of the teachers and administrators in the Philadelphia schools still did not share that goal.

Still, conversations about race and education were changing, and expectations of the schools as a lever of black progress were on the rise. Teachers Union President Jennings had always believed segregation to be "unwise and undemocratic," as he told the school board a few weeks after the announcement of the *Brown* decision; now, he said, it was also "unconstitutional."[106] Meanwhile, the teaching of intergroup tolerance not only anticipated some aspects of the more recent rise of "multicultural" education; it also began to reverse the low academic expectations that many teachers held for urban African American children. As one teacher said after completing an intensive, yearlong program, "I cannot understand how I was ever so blind to the possibilities of all children, irrespective of color and class."[107] The society had changed since 1935, when DuBois, frustrated over blatant institutional racism, reluctantly abandoned the goal of integrated schools. Together, activists and elites had begun to put equal education at the heart of a "Second Reconstruction."

In the summer of 1960, civil rights and school reform came together in Philadelphia in the person of a witty, twenty-five-year-old activist named Robert Blackburn. Blackburn, who would go on to become Marcus Foster's closest associate, was hired by the Citizen's Committee on Public Education (CCPE) as its first full-time executive director. He had spent his junior year in college "abroad, in the American South," as the only white student at Vir-

ginia's Hampton Institute. In the late 1950s, he landed his first civil rights job
with the Philadelphia branch of the National Conference of Christians and
Jews. When the CCPE opening came up, Blackburn wondered if school reform might be a detour from his passion for civil rights. But he was convinced
otherwise by several friends and mentors in the city's liberal human relations
establishment. School reform would not be a detour, they said; it would be a
means of pursuing civil rights.[108]

They were right. Both the CCPE and the civil rights movement were fed
up with the school district's lack of responsiveness to their concerns, and
Blackburn and his organization quickly became leaders in a challenge to
the dominance of Add Anderson (in some ways a more powerful figure
within the bureaucracy than the superintendent himself) and his hidebound school board. Anderson and Allen Wetter, the superintendent who
succeeded Louis Hoyer, "hated to get involved in a way that legitimated us,"
says Blackburn, but they could no longer ignore the Citizens Committee
and the educational ferment of which it was part.[109] The CCPE and its civil
rights allies got the Board to commission a full-scale independent survey of
the schools and a separate study of its racial policies. The dismal findings—
extreme overcrowding, the highest dropout rate in the nation's ten largest
cities, the largest number of antiquated buildings (25 percent), worsening
segregation (a majority of schools with more than 90 percent of one race),
and a continuing white middle-class exodus to the suburbs, among others—helped set a reform agenda for the new decade.[110] As the 1960s began,
liberals in Philadelphia were on their way toward securing charter reforms
that would diminish the business manager's power and force the school
board to face the electorate. The city, like the nation as a whole, had raised
its expectations of public education and was placing the schools at the heart
of the black freedom struggle.

Marcus Foster and Urban School Reform

The growing importance of schooling as a mechanism of civil rights activism
and social reform set the stage for Marcus Foster's rise as a black educational
leader in Philadelphia. Foster propelled himself upward through the school
system, from the Stanton assignment to a job as a social studies curriculum
adviser for some thirty elementary schools in District Two, to an assistant
principalship at the James Rhodes Elementary School. Then, in 1958, at the
age of thirty-five, Foster reached the highest position of school-site leader-

ship attainable by a black man at that time: principal of an all-black elementary school.

As he progressed toward that principalship, at Dunbar Elementary School in North Philadelphia, Foster increasingly drew upon several key sources of faith in education as a tool of social advancement for his people. His family and college experiences had been shaped by the African American dream of educational achievement and uplift—an optimistic assumption that African Americans could earn a better place in society by excelling in school and proving their capacity for equal citizenship. By the late 1950s, racial liberalism had begun to reinforce this dream of racial advancement through education. *An American Dilemma*, the intergroup education movement, *Brown vs. Board of Education*—all expressed the idea that blacks had been blocked by irrational white prejudice and discrimination from participating in what was otherwise an equal opportunity society. And all looked to education as an increasingly important arena in which to end the exclusion of African Americans and bring them into the mainstream of American life.

At the same time, liberal optimism was belied by worsening conditions in African American neighborhoods and schools. Much of the agenda of racial liberalism, including educational attacks on prejudice, had been directed at the legal and interpersonal obstacles that blocked an aspiring black middle class from moving into the same neighborhoods, skilled jobs, and schools as their white counterparts. For many black Philadelphians, however, the most pressing concern was neither legal barriers nor prejudicial attitudes among individual whites so much as a social and economic crisis that increasingly enveloped their daily lives. Displacement from agricultural jobs in the South, combined with industrial decline in the cities to which they relocated, helped thrust many African Americans into joblessness and poverty.[111] Ongoing discrimination in private housing and job markets (despite municipal guidelines to the contrary) trapped them in decaying, increasingly segregated neighborhoods—while the city's celebrated "urban renewal" program displaced many residents from the only housing they could afford.[112] In turn, economic decline and social isolation fueled social disintegration. Violence in segregated black neighborhoods rose at a faster rate than white-black encounters in "tension areas." In the interracial incidents that did occur, the majority of the aggressors were not hostile whites but black juvenile gang members.[113] Racial liberalism did not fully address this growing urban crisis, much less make significant progress toward resolving it. According to Paul Ylvisaker, an aide to Mayor Joe Clark and later the Ford Foundation official who helped pioneer the War on Poverty, the liberal coalition of the 1950s—including the city's "aristocratic" black leadership—failed to notice and respond to the "massive poverty . . . that was growing in North Philadelphia."[114]

As African American communities grew more isolated and impoverished in the 1950s, the schools that served them increasingly struggled to function, much less to serve as an engine of social advancement. In addition to the continuing (in some cases, worsening) problems of segregation, low expectations, and unequal resources, inner-city schools increasingly were plagued by truancy, violent behavior, and other social problems associated with urban poverty beyond school walls. Leon Frisby estimates that 60 percent of his students were from one-parent homes that were "limited in terms of resources and background. We had kids in junior high school who could hardly write their names." One of those "kids" committed a murder while under Frisby's guidance.[115]

What could educators like Frisby and Marcus Foster do to improve achievement in such schools? And just as important, what role could such efforts play in the larger struggle for racial equality? Foster himself was the product of an economically marginal family. And he was a graduate of the poolrooms, dance halls, and youth gangs of South Philadelphia—none of which had prevented him from attaining a college degree and a professional career. But Foster had been more the exception than the norm. In particular, he had benefited from a family life rich with educational and cultural resources. Could he promote achievement not just for himself, but for all students—including many whose lives were filled with great trouble?

It was a daunting challenge—and yet, an important one. Schooling mattered more than ever to economic opportunity in America. The long-term shift toward a service economy was under way, and while blacks were still plagued by racial discrimination in labor markets, the link between education and income had begun to grow tighter, for all Americans—a trend that would only accelerate in the decades ahead.[116] As Marcus Foster took over at Dunbar, the brightest futures seemed to belong more than ever to children who attained high levels of literacy and education.[117] To hold that goal for all black children was a radical departure from the days of Foster's childhood— indeed, it was a radical departure from the status quo as of 1958. Yet, it was a departure the Foster was eager to make.

CHAPTER 2

Combating Cultural Deprivation: Urban Educators and the War on Poverty

BOB Blackburn met Marcus Foster nearly a decade before becoming his right-hand man in Philadelphia and then in Oakland, California. The twenty-five-year-old Blackburn was the boyish director of Philadelphia's Citizens Committee on Public Education (CCPE). Foster, twelve years his senior, was in his third year as principal at the Dunbar Elementary School. It was the fall of 1960, and Dunbar was the first school that Blackburn and some of the women on the Citizens Committee were scheduled to visit that year. As he drove to the school one October morning, Blackburn thought of pictures he had seen of European cities after the Second World War. "A lot of buildings were empty, and some were boarded up, and some they didn't even bother to board up. There were row houses, and bad corners, and wrecked areas. And I just remember driving to this school, myself alone that morning, feeling that he's in a particularly difficult neighborhood."[1]

The day turned out to be an inspiration for Blackburn. "The general impression," he recalls, "was he's somehow made a garden in the middle of this bleakness. It was very much like going up years later to IS 201 and seeing [Harlem principal] Seymour Gang and other heroes and heroines of urban education at work."[2] I remember [Foster's] charisma, his kind of restlessness." Inside the school, he says, "there was color, there was light. There was student work everywhere. People were busy. There was an atmosphere of hubbub. It was not quiet, it was lively." Blackburn and the other visitors saw hallway displays about historical figures like Phillis Wheatley. They opened a large broom closet and saw a mother—a volunteer—tutoring a student one-on-one. They saw cafeteria

Figure 2. Foster and Sidney Glaberson *(top left)*, owner of a local clothing store, enjoy the scene as Dunbar Elementary School students show off new neckties donated by Glaberson. Reaching beyond the school to scrounge for resources needed by urban students, whether clothing or scholarship money or foundation grants and public funds, became a hallmark of Foster's career. Urban Archives, Temple University Libraries.

workers and custodians serving food or dispensing a broom as if these were mainly opportunities to interact with and influence children. Foster showed the visitors a room with clothing he had collected from local laundromats so that no child had to wear "Bureau clothes"—shabby cast-offs from the Bureau for Colored Children. Blackburn went home and told his wife he had met a "wizard of a scrounge." In all, he remembers, "You just kind of went away shaking your head in surprise, delight, and admiration. You didn't get the sense that this school was being directed from someplace else. You got the sense that this school was working together as a collaborative community, to make things work, and they were not waiting for [the school district leadership] downtown."[3]

If anything, district administrators and other concerned parties were taking cues from school leaders like Foster as they struggled to cope with the "bleakness," the devastating effects of the urban crisis, that Blackburn had seen on his way to Dunbar. More and more of Philadelphia's neighborhoods looked like that, and more and more of its schools were attended predominantly by poor, African American children whose parents, many of them southern migrants, had little educational background.[4] As a new principal in 1958, Foster took up the challenge of improving the lagging academic performance of one of those schools—and as he did so, he and his staff played a role in shaping new strategies of urban school improvement in the United States. Collaborating initially with the Philadelphia Fellowship Commission, the Dunbar School developed a program that evolved into one of the Ford Foundation's pilot projects in "compensatory education," known as the Great Cities School Improvement Program. Great Cities and other Ford-sponsored projects, in turn, helped shape the development of federal antipoverty and educational policies.

Compensatory education marked a problematic shift in liberal approaches to race and urban schooling. In the 1940s and 1950s, as we saw in the first chapter, Philadelphia and other cities struggled with the effects of economic decline and black migration from the South—including white resistance to the integration of neighborhoods, workplaces, and schools—and racial liberals tried to ease these interracial conflicts and promote integration, partly through "intergroup education" programs aimed at eradicating white "prejudice." By the late 1950s, however, as segregation and poverty only grew worse, some local officials and foundation officers were shifting their focus from white-black conflict and white prejudice to economic and cultural factors that seemed to impede black progress *within* black communities. In this context, compensatory education took shape around the idea that low achievement among urban black children was not a matter of race, per se, but a problem of poverty and social isolation in declining urban environments. In particular, inner-city children were thought to be educationally and culturally "deprived," and it was up to the schools to compensate for the alleged deficits in their attitudes and skills.[5]

Building on Ford Foundation pilot projects that were based on these ideas, the administration of Lyndon Johnson made compensatory education a core element in federal education and social policy, especially in Head Start, the Elementary and Secondary Education Act (ESEA) of 1965, and the War on Poverty. But while Head Start evolved and remained popular, even in spite of criticism, the concept of compensatory education was on its way to being discredited even as the federal government moved to embrace it.[6] The cultural deprivation thesis had originated as an alternative to biological racism, but critics, including a number of African American leaders and educators, increasingly denounced it as a new and more subtle form of racism—a liberal way for white-run school systems to blame underachievement on black students and families rather than take responsibility for it themselves.[7] Ever since, discussion of the racial achievement gap has often been marked by this conflict between those who point to the shortcomings of the schools and those who emphasize the impoverished background of the students.[8]

The Dunbar School's pilot project bridged the dichotomy between blaming schools and "blaming the victim." In particular, we see that while the compensatory education movement was indeed marred by condescending language and inegalitarian ideas, especially as it was shaped and expanded by policymakers and district administrators, it also had roots in the work of school-based educators, like Marcus Foster, who approached it as a mechanism for raising academic achievement in urban schools.[9] For most of the twentieth century, white educational leaders had consigned African Americans to separate, non-academic curricular tracks. Drawing on postwar racial liberalism as well as longstanding traditions of African American achievement—and with key financial support from the Ford Foundation— innovative schools like Dunbar began in the 1950s and 1960s to challenge this legacy of racial inequality. As practiced by educators like Foster, compensatory education confronted both home and school factors in an effort to raise academic achievement for all urban students. In doing so, this brand of compensatory education anticipated subsequent research on the importance of the cultural capital that students bring to school *and* the quality of the education they receive once they get there.[10]

Foster and others like him were not typical, so much as significant: pioneers of approaches that would become more influential over time, as indicated by recent examples such as the Knowledge Is Power Program (KIPP) and especially the Harlem Children's Zone (HCZ). The charter schools in KIPP and the HCZ have drawn lavish praise for their efforts to raise academic achievement by compensating for the social and cultural background of urban students.[11] The experiences of those schools echo a lesson that began to come into focus earlier, during Foster's time at the Dunbar School—namely, that the big problem with compensatory education was not its focus on the disadvantaged backgrounds of some students, so much as the way that policymakers promised too much for it as a solution to urban problems. As current policymakers and pundits again rush to proclaim the power of dynamic urban schools with compensatory-style approaches, this is a lesson that merits serious attention.[12]

Urban Poverty and Schooling: The Dunbar Elementary School

The history of the Paul Laurence Dunbar Elementary School is a reminder that Jim Crow-style segregation was not limited to the U.S. South. The school was built in 1931, at 12th Street and Columbia Avenue in the Temple University area of North Philadelphia. At that time the neighborhood was racially mixed, though Dunbar apparently was not, since it had a black principal, Tanner Duckrey, and blacks were not allowed to teach in or be principals of mixed schools. Indeed, Dunbar apparently was one of the handful of schools that Philadelphia created in the early twentieth century to segregate its burgeoning African American population.

Racial segregation, in itself, did not make Dunbar a troubled school. In fact, the school appears to have had a positive reputation in its early years. In 1943, the veteran African American educator Daniel Brooks extolled the "modern" facilities of Dunbar and several other black elementary schools—a big improvement, he reminded the black readership of the *Philadelphia Tribune,* over a not-so-distant past of "old, frame buildings, gas-lighted, with coal stoves in many rooms and out-door water-closets!"[13] Even more important than the attributes of its Art Deco-style brick building, however, was Dunbar's leadership. In pre-World War II Philadelphia, the school was one of only a few places where talented African American educators like Duckrey could get a job. Even as they suffered the ills of segregation, educators like Duckrey held high expectations for black children and worked to create caring and committed school communities.[14] In 1939, a journalist reported that visitors could shut their eyes in a classroom and hear only the voice of the teacher and the scraping of a foot. "Warm politeness of pupils . . . toward their teachers," he wrote, "is a Duckrey 'must,' part of a well-mapped plan to sow personal and social ethics in the juvenile minds." Quotations from Emerson adorned classroom walls and mottoes of cleanliness were written on the blackboards. Duckrey had showers installed so that all children could abide by the latter. While strict, the environment at Dunbar was caring and supportive. Duckrey insisted on a "tutor-student attitude rather than a teacher-student approach." Parents seemed to be contributing to the positive atmosphere surrounding the school; through the Parent Teacher Association, a group of them had undertaken a survey of housing conditions.[15]

Still, when Foster arrived in 1958, he reported that "the school's better days seemed to be in the past." The teachers were "digging in like beavers, working harder and harder but achieving less and less." What had changed since the 1930s and 1940s? Not race: the school continued to have an entirely black student body and staff, with the exception of two part-time secretaries. Nor had the staff changed dramatically in other ways; Dunbar continued to draw strong black educators who had few other opportunities within the system. Foster described a "highly professional faculty" and "a great esprit de corps, partly because there had been a succession of great principals." Ida Kravitz, a school-district reading specialist who worked with Dunbar during Foster's tenure, remembers the school's faculty as the "cream of the black teachers" in Philadelphia. "There were no duds," she says.[16]

Neither the racial profile of the school nor its educators had changed significantly. What had changed, though, was the socioeconomic profile of the school community. North Philadelphia underwent the same prolonged process of economic decline and demographic change, or urban crisis, that afflicted many of the nation's big cities after World War II.[17] Certainly part of the change was racial: black migration inward and white migration to the outer city and suburbs dramatically changed the makeup of the neighborhood. In just a few years in the late 1940s, the white population of the census tract next to Dunbar went from being 38 percent to 3 percent white.[18] Previously a black school in a mixed neighborhood, Dunbar now reflected its surroundings. More important than racial change, though, was the decline of the neighborhood into a more crowded and economically marginal area. Foster described a social class change that occurred as upwardly mobile black residents moved out and lower-income blacks, including migrants from the South, moved in.[19] The new residents were two or three times more likely than other Philadelphians to be unemployed, and their average income was lower by about half. Observers tended to link these economic troubles with a lack of education and skill.[20] Less often did they mention two other key factors: employment discrimination and the postwar flight of industrial jobs out of the inner city.[21]

Poverty and population growth led to the physical decline that Bob Blackburn had witnessed on his visit to Dunbar in 1960—decline that was exacerbated, rather than alleviated, by government policy. Old nineteenth-century row houses fell apart as a rising number of absentee landlords subdivided and failed to maintain them. It no longer paid to maintain or renovate such buildings because, as one observer noted, Federal Housing Authority subsidies for new construction in the suburbs and outer city (where African Americans were excluded) drove the inner city real estate market through the floor.[22] By 1950, nearly three-fourths of all units in the area were substandard (needing major repairs or lacking a private bath). More than one-third were overcrowded (more than one person per room).[23] In response to these conditions, city planners marked the greater Temple University area for "urban renewal," and indeed, they leveled and rebuilt some sections in the 1950s and 1960s.[24] Redevelopment provided some low- and moderate-income housing and enabled Temple University to undertake a vast expansion. It gave some property owners $4,000 for houses that were nearly worthless. But it hurt the neighborhood's poor residents. Most who fled the wrecking ball ended up in nearby rowhouses where the crowding was worse than before—even as the city, unable to find private developers willing to rebuild, often left vacant, rubble-strewn lots.

Social decline went hand in hand with poverty and physical dilapidation. Crime rates rose, youth gangs thrived, and students in neighborhood schools performed below grade level.[25] Ida Kravitz recalled that the school's reading scores were among the lowest in Philadelphia.[26] According to Foster, neighborhood change and the influx of lower-income blacks had created a new "teaching-learning problem" at Dunbar.

But what exactly was the problem? Like many educators who had come of age in a world reshaped by World War II and the racial liberalism of *An American Dilemma*, Foster tended to think in terms of a vicious cycle of low teacher expectations and low student aspirations. Dunbar was not a case of white teachers disparaging black students, but Foster still believed low expectations to be an issue; as he later wrote, "People have often said of these youngsters: They can't read. They can't learn. They are natural hoodlums." In turn, he continued, this view helped to fuel a self-fulfilling prophecy: "When the children, already handicapped by poverty, absorb this kind of thinking, they present a different teaching-learning problem to the school, and this was the situation at Dunbar." The teachers, however well intentioned, "did not know how to begin" teaching their increasingly poor and working-class clientele. They were saying to Foster, "What can you do?"[27]

This was the complex of problems Marcus Foster faced when he went to Dunbar—but he did not face these problems alone. At Dunbar, Foster would become part of a larger network of civil rights activists, educators, and researchers who were responding with ever-greater urgency to the problems of urban education in an age of urban crisis.

From Black-White Conflict to the Problem of Black Achievement

In the 1950s, some racial liberals who were concerned about urban education began to shift from an emphasis on the problem of interracial or "intergroup" conflict to that of academic achievement in "one-group" (i.e., all-black) schools like Dunbar. The earlier focus on interracial conflict had been a product of the social and demographic upheavals of World War II; as black migration transformed the cities and bred conflict with hostile whites, liberals increasingly looked to the schools for solutions to these social problems. Among other things, they saw schools as a place to prevent and eradicate white prejudice (including white teachers' low expectations of black students). It is important to note that the concern with white prejudice did not disappear in the 1950s and 1960s; rather, it fed into movements for school desegregation, in northern cities as well as in the South.[28] Likewise, interest in social and cultural influences on the development of poor children (including African Americans) did not come out of nowhere in the 1950s.[29] Still, the 1950s did witness a rising preoccupation with low performance among black students, in two kinds of settings: newly integrated schools, where a black-white achievement gap became increasingly apparent in the years after *Brown v. Board of Education* (1954); and a growing number of all-black schools (like Dunbar), where achievement was suffering in general. At some of these schools, urban educators—including a rising number of black administrators—played a pioneering role in confronting the problem of underachievement among black students, developing programs that resonate to this day. Those programs not only expressed a tradition of African American achievement, raising academic expectations of students who previously had been stigmatized as less capable because of their race; the programs also focused on augmenting what would now be called a lack of cultural capital, associated with the students' being *poor*.

The most famous of the 1950s pilot projects aimed at raising achievement for urban students was New York City's Demonstration Guidance Project, at Manhattanville Junior High School (JHS 43) in Harlem. It is worth discussing the Demonstration Guidance Project in some detail, given the influence it had on Marcus Foster and other urban educators across the nation. The project was launched by the New York City Board of Education (Commission on Integration), with the input of Dr. Kenneth Clark, the Harlem psychologist and civil rights advocate, whose "doll experiments" had been cited in the *Brown* decision as evidence that segregation did damage to the psyches of black children. In 1956, when the project began, the average IQ scores of black and Puerto Rican students in Harlem (and elsewhere in the nation) actually tended to drop over the course of their school careers, from around 100 in the third grade to just above 80 in the eighth grade. "If one dared to be facetious about so serious a problem," said Daniel Schreiber, the JHS 43 principal, "one could say that the longer these children remain in school, the dumber they become. Of course, this is bosh and nonsense." Indeed, nonsense it was proven to be, as the Guidance Project worked "what looked like a miracle": quantifiable improvements in its students' IQ scores, reading levels, and high school graduation and college attendance rates. Qualitative assessments by educators and community leaders also pointed to improvements in students' ambitions and attitudes about school.[30]

What had been the problem? And what did JHS 43 do to achieve such hopeful results? Clark later wrote passionately, in *Dark Ghetto* (1965), of a vicious circle of low achievement and low expectations at JHS 43 and other ghetto schools. Like Foster when he arrived at Dunbar, Clark found teachers at JHS 43 who "felt helpless to teach. Their students seemed then to be hopeless, and considered themselves failures, their teachers as enemies."[31] The Demonstration Guidance Project broke this vicious circle of failure and mutual disparagement by attacking both aspects—how the students related to school and how the school viewed the students—in mutually reinforcing ways.

The Demonstration Guidance Project was based, above all, on the belief that black children could achieve and that Harlem teachers needed to raise their expectations accordingly. Granted, JHS 43 did not apply this belief to every child; it aimed to identify the most "able" one-third of the student body. However, even this act of selectivity helped reverse a legacy of low expectations: to identify its "unpolished diamonds," the Project augmented standard IQ tests with nonverbal tests that yielded higher (that is, normal) scores, giving a "tremendous lift" to what teachers thought of their students' abilities. For the students selected by this process, the Project set no limits to achievement, urging above all that they set their sights on college. This was in sharp contrast to decades of "realistic" counseling which held that African Americans at schools like JHS 43 should limit their academic expectations to stay in tune with the discriminatory job market they would face upon graduation.

Meanwhile, JHS 43 not only raised expectations; it also helped realize those expectations with improved curriculum and instruction. Spending an extra $250 of district funds per pupil, the Guidance Project provided smaller classes, after-school programs, individualized tutoring, professional development for teachers, engaging hands-on experiences (for example, a field trip to see a play being discussed in class), and above all, an increased emphasis by all teachers on reading skills, especially in content areas.[32]

The Demonstration Guidance Project set out to alter the beliefs and practices of the JHS 43 staff. At the same time, though, it was an attempt to change the students and their families—in effect, to increase their supply of cultural capital. Schreiber provided an apt example of cultural capital in one of his presentations on the Project: in the "middle-class home," he said, "a child of nine or ten years of age knows that he will attend college." That child was familiar with the names of colleges and had visited college campuses. As early as eighth grade, that child knew to take the algebra and foreign language classes necessary for college admission. As Schreiber saw it, JHS 43 families had none of this knowledge or sense of social power, which college-bound students needed but did not learn in school; indeed, for his more economically marginal students, school typically had discouraged such ambitions. So the Project set out to fill the gap in students' knowledge and aspirations—to give them "an image of [themselves]" as college students. Schreiber and his staff put college pennants and pictures of successful "heroes and heroines" all over the school. They invited admissions officers and successful alumni to give presentations. They provided more intensive counseling. They reached out to parents, soliciting their support and educating them on the potential benefits of the program. Perhaps most important, in Schreiber's view, the Project sponsored field trips to colleges, research centers, and professional schools. These excursions—along with other field trips to plays, movies, and concerts at Carnegie Hall—were supposed to give the students a sense that "all avenues were open to them." "It is one thing to say that a door is open," Schreiber said, referring to antidiscrimination laws. "It is quite another thing to *push* that door open. We helped them push."[33]

With its mix of elevated academic expectations and cultural enrichment, the Demonstration Guidance Project had a significant influence on educators across the nation. New York City renamed the program Higher Horizons and expanded it from one school to dozens. Big-city educators looked to Higher Horizons as a model, one going so far as to say that he knew of nothing that had "more forcefully struck the imagination of educators and people who believe in equality and human rights, all over the United States."[34]

One example of a Higher Horizons type of program that achieved some national recognition was that of Dr. Samuel Shepard, Jr., in the Banneker School District of St. Louis. Shepard came naturally to a vision of African American social advancement through education; he himself had risen from poverty to earn a college degree from the University of Michigan. In the late 1950s, as civil rights activism had begun to transform the atmosphere of race relations and bring hope of imminent change, Shepard clearly saw academic achievement as being more important than ever: "We simply cannot base our possibilities on present limitations," he said. "They might be swept away tomorrow by the president of the company, and then it would be too late for preparation." Yet, as Shepard and others surveyed the results of integration in St. Louis, after *Brown v. Board of Education,* the results were not encouraging: an achievement gap between white and black students was becoming painfully apparent. A 1959 *Time* magazine story on the St. Louis situation essentially blamed black students for the achievement gap—or, to be more precise, it blamed the "mental ghettos in which thousands of dispirited Negro children live because no one—teachers or parents—can stir them to care." Shepard, in contrast, focused his attention on teachers, parents, and students alike. In 1957, he initiated Operation Motivation, which, as the name suggested, focused primarily on changing attitudes (rather than, say, curriculum). As in Higher Horizons, teachers were encouraged to "quit teaching by I.Q." and to "quit their attitudes of condescension." Students went to pep rallies and assemblies designed to motivate them to work harder. Parents were invited to meetings and deluged with letters encouraging them to push academic success as the best means of self-fulfillment and upward mobility. By 1959, after some encouraging early test scores, Shepard was receiving national press coverage for his efforts.[35]

Projects such as Higher Horizons and Banneker made an impact in Marcus Foster's hometown; in 1958, for instance—just as Foster was beginning his work at Dunbar—Philadelphia's pioneering black educator Ruth Wright Hayre launched a similar program of her own. Like Kenneth Clark and Samuel Shepard, Hayre attacked both low expectations and low cultural capital. In the 1940s, as a teacher at the racially changing Sulzberger Junior High, Hayre had been disgusted by the "insulting condescension" with which the school's white teachers treated the increasing number of black students. In the 1950s, she left Sulzberger to become the city's first black high school teacher and, eventually, principal, at William Penn High School for Girls. Unfortunately, Hayre found that William Penn's mostly white faculty reacted to an influx of black children much as Sulzberger's had: by "dumbing-down" the curriculum (the ill-defined "Common learnings" replaced English, for example) and making derogatory comments about how the school was "nothing like what it used to be." In keeping with the liberal worldview of her era, Hayre believed low teacher expectations not only degraded the curriculum for blacks, but also did damage to her students' "already fragile self-esteem and attitudes." Concerned with breaking this vicious circle, she was thrilled when, during her tenure as principal in the late 1950s, one of the school's more dynamic teachers told her about the Demonstration Guidance Project and helped raise the funds to do something similar at William Penn. The result was a program called WINGS (Work Inspired Now Gain Strength). WINGS sent students to the opera, plays, museums, and art exhibits; reached out to parents; provided extra counseling and guidance; and featured inspirational assemblies and conferences on job opportunities. By 1961, the program had boosted attendance, reduced lateness and disciplinary problems, and cut the dropout rate from 80 to 60 percent. Twenty-seven girls were headed for college, a family first for all but one, and a goal none would have reached without the program, Hayre said.[36]

A Program to "Lift Your Child above the Ordinary and Make Him Outstanding"

As the principal of Dunbar Elementary, Marcus Foster became part of the growing network of dynamic urban educators who were looking for ways to succeed with low-achieving African American students. Just as Higher Horizons was created in collaboration with Kenneth Clark, Foster's program at Dunbar developed in consultation with the Philadelphia Fellowship Commission, the consortium of civil rights organizations that mobilized during the 1940s and 1950s to end segregated housing, employment, and education. In his first year at Dunbar, Foster enrolled the school in the Fellowship Commission's Action Research Seminar (an updated version of the Early Childhood Project that was discussed in the previous chapter). In the fall of 1959, the "Dunbar team"—Foster, three teachers, and one parent—began to meet at school and at the Fellowship Commission for monthly sessions with social science consultants and teams from seven other schools. The program they created for the 1960–61 school year bore the mark of liberal social science, with its rising emphasis on addressing the alleged cultural deficiencies of the black poor. But the tone of the program, like that of Higher Horizons, was strikingly positive, with a focus on higher academic expectations among students, parents, and teachers alike.

The Fellowship Commission's education programs showed how some racial liberals were shifting their focus from white-black tensions to problems such as low achievement within African American communities. In the late 1940s, the organization's Early Childhood Project had exemplified the postwar liberal view that America's racial problems were rooted in a vicious circle of white prejudice and black cultural pathology. To break this cycle and promote social harmony, the Project proposed to educate young children and their teachers, especially whites, not to be prejudiced. In the 1950s, the Fellowship Commission joined forces with the Philadelphia Public Schools, and the project evolved into the Action Research Seminar. Granted, the program continued to focus on white prejudice and "intergroup incidents," such as skirmishes when blacks moved into previously white neighborhoods, or hostile reactions to new low-income housing projects. During Dunbar's two years in the Action Research Seminar, the eight participating schools addressed the question, "How can a school help its young people to know and work with others of the many racial, religious, and ethnic groups they meet as they move through the school system and live in the heterogeneous community of Philadelphia?"[37] In line with this theme, the Dunbar team planned films and plays with messages of tolerance. They scheduled "intervisitations" with white students and teachers from other schools, including opportunities to play music and dance for each other. Dunbar language arts teacher Alice Campbell, who was one of the fifteen original participants in the Early Childhood Project, planned to speak to parents and staff on what that experience had taught her about eliminating prejudice. At the beginning and end of the whole enterprise, teachers, students, and parents would all take tests to see if they had become more open-minded about other groups.[38]

But if the Dunbar team and other members of the Action Research Seminar still cared about ensuring social peace among diverse groups, they were even more eager to address social and educational problems in the growing number of so-called one-group (meaning Negro) schools. During the 1950s, the principals and teachers from such schools increasingly complained of "home conditions," including "anti-social children from broken homes"; and behavioral problems such as "fighting, lying, and stealing." The educators who worked with the Fellowship Commission did not use the word "poverty," but they did see their students' problems as being rooted in "economic conditions"—not only in the sense of material deprivation, but just as im-

Figure 3. Parents and faculty of the Dunbar Elementary School visit the Philadelphia Fellowship Commission, 1960. Officially they were participants in a program of intergroup, or antiprejudice, education. In practice, they focused their greatest attention on the problem of low achievement among black students, pioneering the kinds of compensatory education strategies that became a cornerstone of the federal War on Poverty. Marcus Foster is on the far left, behind a young member of his teaching staff. Bond and McGarry photograph, courtesy of Urban Archives, Temple University Libraries.

portant, in a psychological sense. In this focus on the negative psychological effects of segregation and "disadvantage," the participants were influenced by social scientists who served as consultants for the program—men such as H. Harry Giles, Professor of Education and Director of the Center for Human Relations Studies at New York University. So, for instance, participants in the program believed that isolation from the mainstream society dampened their students' aspirations for success in school and diminished their "pride in themselves and their community." The educators were also concerned that parents had little contact with the school.[39]

These were the kinds of concerns that Foster and his colleagues had in mind as they planned an intergroup education program for the 1959–60 school year. Like Daniel Schreiber in Harlem or Ruth Hayre nearby in Philadelphia, Foster and his team intended to take aim at a vicious circle of low aspirations and achievement on the part of students and low expectations on the part of their teachers. In an urban context in which teacher-student relationships were increasingly adversarial and "custodial," as Kenneth Clark had put it, Dunbar teachers received summer homework assignments aimed at helping them better understand and serve their students. The planning team gave the faculty a list of recommended books such as Clark's *Prejudice and Your Child* and Bruno Bettelheim's *Overcoming Prejudice*. The Dunbar team also planned to improve teacher-student relationships by having faculty members share their talents in a variety of clubs—orchestra, chorus, social dancing, Negro History, science, poetry, "good literature," sewing, scouting and Red Cross, and handicrafts.[40]

As the Dunbar program focused on teacher attitudes, however, it also placed a heavy emphasis on raising the academic aspirations of students and their families. Like predecessors such as Tanner Duckrey, Foster attempted to motivate his students for academic and life success by invoking a long-standing legacy of African American educational achievement. The Dunbar team planned that when the students entered the building, they would see displays about outstanding African Americans and their accomplishments on large "hero bulletin boards." They brought in "successful Negro" guest speakers as role models of achievement. They planned a curriculum with more black history and a "rich and meaningful observance of Negro History Week." They encouraged teachers and other school personnel, even custodians and cafeteria workers, to use all of these activities and materials to motivate students—to remind them that they, too, could achieve great things if they remembered the words "I CAN and I must WORK."[41] Of course, the most visible role model of this ethic of striving and black achievement was Foster himself; in many ways his program aimed to equip Dunbar students with attitudes that had helped carry him through school and life.

The Dunbar staff not only brought a wider world of black achievement to the students; they took the students beyond the school to expand their sense of belonging and agency in the larger society. Foster's interest in taking students on cultural enrichment outings was undoubtedly shaped by his own childhood memories of Boy Scout camping trips, museum visits, and trips to the zoo. Not surprisingly, field trips were a key feature of the Fellowship Commission project—not just during school time, but on Saturday mornings. And while many of the trips were designed to expand the students' horizons beyond North Philadelphia (the most ambitious outing was to the United Nations in New York), the school also made use of less obvious destinations closer to home: Temple University, the Bayuck Cigar Co., the R. W. Brown Boys Club. In the fall of 1960 Foster sent these and many other local institutions a survey and a letter saying that Dunbar students could not afford the travel costs of many firsthand educational experiences but that "we are persuaded that within walking distance of the school are 'acres of diamonds' which, when identified, will enrich the lives of our children."[42] In North Philadelphia, as in the tiny Maryland town where visits to oyster houses and other local enterprises had made his students feel "ten feet tall," Foster believed that field trips could help give students a sense of purpose and belonging within the larger society.

For Foster, as for Schreiber or Hayre, the most important form of cultural enrichment was to build academic skills—in particular, the ability to read and write in Standard English. Dunbar students spoke what scholars have come to recognize as a linguistically coherent dialect, African American Vernacular English. Foster believed his students needed to assimilate the "prestige dialect"—Standard English—in order to function successfully in the classroom and in society.[43] Black history materials and other enrichment experiences were not only meant to expand students' aspirations; they were also part of what Foster called a schoolwide "conspiracy" to "bombard" the students with Standard English—as when, for example, teachers and other staff members made a point of using the "hero of the week" display as a springboard for thoughtful exchanges with students.[44]

Cultural enrichment rested on a notion—sometimes implicit, other times openly stated—that the school needed to teach information and skills that families had not provided. In particular, Foster and his staff saw the school as needing to compensate for low motivation and inadequate academic preparation. "I was a disciple of early intervention a long time ago," Foster later said in a speech at Stanford University that touched on his years at Dunbar. "Back in those days learning for preschool children had to be a play experience. It couldn't look like real concept building. And we dared to say that we needed to consciously help fill some of the gaps in the children's background."[45] By the late 1960s, this was indeed a daring thing to say, insofar as some might have called it an example of "blaming the victim." With the rise of what came to be called compensatory education, a potentially harsh and uncomfortable spotlight began to shine on the child-rearing practices of black parents (or, to be more precise, poor and uneducated black parents).

Still, as the Dunbar team conceived it at their school, "filling gaps" did not mean blaming parents or supplanting them; it meant engaging them—indeed, in some cases *educating* them—to be more effective. As Foster went on to tell his audience at Stanford, he had never met a parent who "didn't respect education and want their children to be fully educated." The frustration was that they did not always "know how to go about it, and we were saying . . . we were going to help them help their children." One of the most striking examples of this effort to enlist parents as partners in their children's academic growth was Dunbar's preparation of a thirty-page booklet of "Hints for Helping the Preschool Child." Foster, his English teacher Alice Campbell, and others created the guide in the summer and discussed it with parents at a "Get Together and Sing Along" a few weeks before the 1960–61 school year began. The booklet told parents, "You too are a teacher," and it gave them advice on how to use nursery rhymes, stories, riddles, and other creative activities to prepare their child for success in school and especially the language arts. "Middle-class people do this all the time, automatically," Foster wrote later, and while it seemed "odd" to formalize it in a handbook, he felt his staff had an obligation as educators "to help them learn how to do it."[46]

The book of parenting tips was part of a larger strategy of parental outreach, spearheaded in large part by one especially dynamic parent. Eloise Holmes was an active member of the Home-School Association (Philadelphia's version of the Parent Teacher Association) and other civic organizations. As the parent representative on Dunbar's intergroup education team, she developed activities to get her fellow parents more involved in the school, such as "talent night," at which parents shared their often-unsung skills with the school community; and the Saturday morning field trips. She also arranged for parents to be invited to faculty meetings and sessions at the Fellowship Commission.[47]

Dunbar's outreach to parents was partly an attempt to address what some were beginning to describe as "deficits" in students' backgrounds. As it did so, however, the school conveyed a proactive sense of optimism—a feeling that, by addressing impediments to achievement both at school and outside of it, urban educators could help their students fulfill a longstanding dream of African American uplift through education. Foster captured that sense of optimism in a letter to Dunbar parents at the end of the 1959–60 school year. The letter focused on how the parents could help prepare their children for academic success. Foster urged them to take their kids on educational excursions at least once a week. "Do you believe that your child deserves the best?" he asked them. "We think that he does; and that nothing is better than a worthwhile firsthand experience." The letter contained a five-page list of such experiences—everything from museums and historical sites to a trip to the airport to see large jets land and take off. In describing the importance of these outings, Foster did use language that would stir controversy in the 1960s: without expanded life experiences, he wrote, "your child is handicapped; he is educationally crippled; he is culturally deprived." But Foster not only balanced such deficit-oriented statements with a positive focus on student potential (cultural experiences could "lift your child above the ordinary and make him outstanding"); he specifically emphasized an academic rationale for cultural enrichment, suggesting that regular excursions could stimulate a desire and a background for reading—a greater familiarity with the language and "topics of the printed page."[48]

As the 1959–60 school year approached, the Dunbar School was prepared to show that an all-black school could be a good school—a school where educators, parents, and students worked together to foster high standards and achievement, regardless of racial or socioeconomic background.

The Ford Foundation and the "Culturally Deprived" Child

Foster and his team had barely finished planning their project with the Fellowship Commission when the school was chosen to participate in the Ford Foundation's new Great Cities School Improvement Program. The Great Cities program supported pilot projects in fourteen of the nation's large urban school districts. In Philadelphia, the program centered on four predominantly black schools in North Philadelphia: a junior high school and three of its feeder schools, including Dunbar. As we will see in this analysis of Great Cities in Philadelphia, school district leaders and Ford Foundation officials did not invent compensatory education, so much as they built on the experiments of school-based educators like Marcus Foster and turned them into the centerpiece of what amounted to an "educational war on poverty."[49]

The Great Cities program grew out of a rising sense of desperation among the superintendents and board members of the nation's big-city school districts. Those officials had been gathering since 1956 to discuss common problems, including the impact of demographic change on their districts' financial and educational health. Thousands of low-income black families were still moving to the cities every year, while comparable numbers of middle-income whites continued their highway migration to the suburbs, taking tax revenue with them.[50] Philadelphia's superintendent was Allen Wetter, an earnest, soft-spoken man who had worked in the district thirty-eight years before assuming the top job in 1955. As they drew attention to urban changes, Wetter and his fellow superintendents expressed an increasingly urgent sense of alarm. Benjamin Willis of Chicago warned that the big cities would be "doomed" if something was not done for the roughly 30 percent of their school children who lived in "problem areas"—that is, the expanding black ghettos.[51]

What was the matter with such students? In a press release, the superintendents noted that "problem area" children, when compared to students from less poor and troubled parts of the cities, were six times more likely to fail in elementary school and two-and-a-half times more likely to fail in high school subjects; twice as likely to be absent and truant; and three times as likely to drop out before high school graduation. Their median achievement levels in reading and math were, respectively, four and three grades lower (though their potential seemed to exceed what test data showed). They were six times more likely to have entered—and failed—first grade without the benefit of kindergarten.[52]

The School District of Philadelphia had made a few efforts to address these problems, including the collaboration with the Fellowship Commission project that Foster and his staff had just finished planning. By the end of the 1950s, though, the big-city superintendents apparently believed that locally sponsored projects could no longer keep pace with the changes, and they went to the Ford Foundation for help. Founded in 1936 with a $25,000 gift from Henry Ford's son, Edsel, the Ford Foundation was transformed in the 1950s from a local Detroit foundation to the largest philanthropy in the world after Edsel and Henry Ford died and bequeathed to it 90 percent of the (nonvoting) stock of the Ford

Motor Company (which, by 1955, was worth some $2.5 billion).[53] In 1959, the
big-city superintendents approached Clarence Faust and Alvin "Al" Eurich, the
president and vice-president of the Ford Foundation's semi-independent spin-
off organization, the Fund for the Advancement of Education (FAE). "[The su-
perintendents] knew they were going to be clobbered, were being clobbered,
on bond issues by the new social problem," Paul Ylvisaker, the head of Ford's
Public Affairs program at the time, said later in reference to the black migration's effect on taxpayer support for the public schools. "And so they came to
Ford and asked Al, in effect, 'Give us some millions to throw at the problem.'"[54]

In going to the Ford Foundation, the superintendents began to tie their
urban school systems to broader agendas of social reform. The FAE had a
history of liberal activism on issues related to race and education. On the eve
of the *Brown* decision it had published *The Negro and the Schools,* Harry Ashmore's sympathetic study of desegregation campaigns around the country. In
the mid-1950s, it had sponsored *The Puerto Rican Study,* a collaboration with
the New York City school board on the same kinds of migration issues that
were troubling the Great Cities superintendents.[55] Granted, by the late 1950s
the momentum on these issues had slowed; boycotts of Ford dealerships in
the South, combined with McCarthyite congressional investigations, had
prompted the Ford Foundation to place an "embargo" on anything having to
do with race.[56] But some Foundation officers—notably Ylvisaker—remained
interested in getting around this embargo and addressing the kinds of urban
problems the superintendents were facing. And Ylvisaker was not inclined to
do so merely by "throwing millions" at [Chicago superintendent] "Ben Willis
and his boys."[57]

Ylvisaker had been an aide to Philadelphia mayor Joseph Clark in the
1950s, and the experience had made him wary of entrenched bureaucracies
and simplistic solutions for urban decline.[58] Having witnessed the development of the city's much-heralded urban renewal program, he decided that
"bricks and mortar" approaches were no solution for "human" problems
(In fact, he believed, urban renewal had in some ways made those problems
worse.) At Ford, Ylvisaker's goal was to push city governments, city agencies, private social welfare organizations, and yes, school districts, to make
a coordinated attack on the social problems of the black ghettos—which, in
light of the Foundation's sensitivity about racial issues, he called "gray areas."
Schools could not "go it alone," Ylvisaker thought, and he had little faith in
the school superintendents as agents of change—but still, a school reform
initiative might help pave the way for his larger vision of urban institutional

cooperation and reform.[59] With that goal in mind, Ylvisaker visited all fourteen prospective "great cities" with a team of Ford staffers and consultants, including future Secretary of Housing and Urban Development Robert Weaver, and asked the superintendents to explain, in front of city officials and other interested parties, what they planned to do with the foundation's money.[60]

Philadelphia city leaders had their trial before the Ylvisaker group on May 6, 1960, at the Bellevue-Stratford Hotel in Center City. The meeting presented school problems and programs as part of a larger urban crisis. Superintendent Wetter and other administrators presented the district's proposal, entitled "The School-Community Coordinating Team." However, in keeping with Ylvisaker's interest in a multifaceted approach to urban problems, the school leaders were joined by the city's Managing Director, its urban renewal coordinator, and the heads of the human relations and health and welfare agencies, among others. All of these city officials made presentations on the problems of the "gray areas" and participated in a general discussion of urban problems. They showed an ongoing concern, hearkening back to the 1940s and 1950s, with black-white violence in changing neighborhoods; as one participant observed, an "armed truce" existed in "those gray areas where negroes and whites are intermixed in significant proportions." At the same time, the officials seemed worried about violence and delinquency within black communities. As they told the Ford staffers, the city had seventeen "hard core" gangs, and all seventeen of those were "organized Negro groups." (This in contrast to some 150 "non-organized" groups of lesser importance and indeterminate racial composition.) In neighborhoods that were experiencing a range of "delinquency and crime incidents" ("rumbles, muggings, rapes, and occasional murders"), the hard-core black gangs were responsible for the most "overt, explicit activities of major significance."[61]

In light of such discussion, it was not surprising that Wetter and his colleagues told the Ford staffers that one of their two main goals was to identify and prevent "incipient delinquency." Meanwhile, the other major goal was the "discovery and development of talent."[62] And so, the Philadelphia proposal focused on two specific groups of students: the most troubled and the most gifted. In both instances, the proposal referred to these children not as "Negro" but as "culturally different" (no doubt, in part, because of the Ford Foundation's continuing "embargo" on race-related grants). And in both instances, district leaders portrayed school reform as a means to fulfilling larger social goals. Unfulfilled potential represented a "loss to our nation" and had "often resulted in delinquency and crime." In fact, the Philadelphia proposal to the

Ford Foundation went so far as to suggest that locating talent and controlling delinquency were crucial to winning the Cold War. In keeping with the
logic of "Cold War civil rights" that we encountered in the previous chapter,
the Philadelphians emphasized that the United States needed to fix domestic problems that put the nation in a bad light on the world stage, and that
one of those domestic issues was the "effort to have the culturally different
live in amity and peace." In this effort, the schools, with support from other
community agencies, were needed to supply "wise guidance and courageous
leadership."[63]

Expecting the schools to be the key to solving larger social problems was
likely a recipe for disillusionment. Yet district leaders and foundation officials did not exactly emphasize these grand expectations at the outset of the
Great Cities program. At the Bellevue-Stratford meeting, it was "strongly
suggested," presumably by Ford staffers, that school leaders "play down" the
antidelinquency objective and let it emerge as a "by-product" of the project.[64] Perhaps they feared that teachers and principals would not relate to
such goals—or that parents might be alienated by a program that described
their children as "incipient delinquents." Whatever the reason, superintendent Wetter and his colleagues complied with the advice, and Philadelphia
went on to become one of fourteen cities to receive roughly $100,000 in Ford
Foundation funding for its pilot project in urban school improvement.[65] In
practice, the program they laid out sounded a lot like what urban educators
like Foster and Daniel Schreiber had been devising at individual schools over
the past few years.

As the name of the project suggested, the School-Community Coordinating Team emphasized a need to address conditions beyond the schools,
especially in students' homes. In particular, school leaders expressed concern
about the impact of poverty on school performance, although they did so in
the language of culture and lifestyle. The proposal lamented the "unique and
pressing cultural and social needs" of urban families and the need to raise the
"level of family and community living." In response to these concerns, the
pilot project called for a school-community coordinator to visit the homes of
"talented or problem children" and try to motivate and enlighten their parents about educational issues. The focus of such visits was to include everything from personal hygiene to the use of local libraries to the creation of
better study conditions in the home. Echoing Paul Ylvisaker's belief in a multifaceted approach to urban social problems, the school-community coordi-

nator was also to work with the school counselor to facilitate contact between the parents and any appropriate community agencies.[66]

In the summer of 1960, Foster and his Dunbar team joined educators from the other project schools at a three-week planning workshop, where they heard a variety of presentations by school district officials and Ford Foundation consultants. In these presentations about students from "limited backgrounds," it was possible, again, to see how some liberals were shifting from a focus on segregation and white prejudice to a preoccupation with the alleged cultural deprivation of the urban poor. Granted, race and segregation were still a part of the conversation, in explicit as well as unspoken ways. In a panel entitled "The Negro in America," the Executive Director of the Philadelphia Fellowship Commission, Maurice Fagan, spoke on the need to eliminate de facto segregation. And even when race was not explicitly mentioned in discussions of "the child of limited background," it was surely a subtext, just as "Negro ghettos" were the subtext of euphemistic discussions about urban "gray areas."[67]

Still, the 1960 Great Cities workshop showed how the emphasis on cultural concerns, which had been evident in programs such as Higher Horizons and the Fellowship Commission intergroup education project, was accelerating. Social scientists were "rediscovering" poverty, and in particular an alleged "culture of poverty." Led by the anthropologist Oscar Lewis and the writer and activist Michael Harrington, proponents of the culture of poverty thesis suggested that, for some poor people, poverty had gone from being a material condition to a set of self-defeating cultural responses to that condition—a fatalistic worldview and way of life passed on from one generation to the next.[68] The presenters at the 1960 Great Cities workshop did not use the term "culture of poverty" or that closely related concept for educators, cultural deprivation (though, as we have seen in one of Foster's letters to Dunbar parents, the term was already in use). But those were the ideas that informed their discussions of the African American, Puerto Rican, and, to a lesser extent, "hillbilly" (Appalachian white) children the Great Cities program proposed to help.[69] As the professional development workshop framed them, those children's problems were rooted not in race or ethnicity, but in poverty and, in particular, in the ways in which a poor background handicapped a child's preparation for school.

The Great Cities workshop not only captured how social scientists were shifting their focus from racial segregation to the supposed cultural effects of poverty; it also revealed a rising emphasis on cognitive (in addition to attitudinal) concerns. As epitomized by *Brown v. Board of Education*, with its infamous use of Kenneth Clark's doll study, racial liberalism in the 1950s had been marked by a concern over the damage that segregation supposedly inflicted on the psyches of black children; in particular, racial isolation allegedly dampened the self-esteem and aspirations of black children, preventing them from assimilating into the mainstream of American society.[70] The social scientists who helped launch the Great Cities program added a new focus on how the economic and cultural background of many urban students supposedly affected their cognitive development. Recent research into environmental effects on cognitive development had suggested that intelligence (IQ) was not fixed and therefore that all children could learn, if properly prepared.[71] One of the leading scholars in this field, New York University psychologist Martin Deutsch, was a Ford Foundation consultant at the summer workshop in Philadelphia. Deutsch and other presenters emphasized that children from "stimulus-poor homes," including some who had not experienced "even a three-minute sequence of speech" with a parent, were at a disadvantage when it came to starting school and learning to read.[72]

If the Philadelphia Great Cities program emphasized deficits in students' homes and families, however, this was not its only focus. The program also stressed the need for changes in the schools, and in particular, the need to hold higher expectations of students. Great Cities consultants like Martin Deutsch adopted an optimistic and proactive stance with regard to the academic achievement of black children in city schools. Two points are worth emphasizing in this respect. First, the Great Cities workshop presented the educational handicaps of poverty as being reversible, rather than intractable or permanent (much as racial liberals had rejected a biological basis for racial inequalities). Second, the Great Cities presenters emphasized that schools had a responsibility to turn this potential for higher achievement into a reality. In doing so, they pointed optimistically to the leading pilot projects of the day; indeed, one of the Ford-affiliated presenters was Daniel Schreiber, who, as the founder of Higher Horizons, was able to offer a firsthand perspective on how his program had galvanized teachers, parents, and children to produce higher academic achievement. Schreiber acknowledged initial teacher resistance to Higher Horizons. However, in response to a question from Dunbar language arts teacher Alice Spotwood, he emphasized the need to break down such resistance in small groups, sometimes over a period of a year or more. Overall, Schreiber and the other presenters conveyed a sense that educators not only had the power to raise their students' performance; they had an obligation to do so. It was easy to say, "I can do nothing about this," Deutsch commented, but if teachers shared successful experiences and practices they soon would say the opposite.[73]

At the Dunbar school, Foster and his staff conveyed a sense of high expectations in their name for the Ford Foundation project: "High Roads to High Achievement." It was sometimes hard to tell High Roads apart from the Fellowship Commission project that preceded it. Reports to the Ford Foundation featured many of the same clubs, cultural enrichment trips, black history programs, assemblies, role modeling activities, and other motivational strategies that Foster and his staff had laid out during the previous year. Also similar was the underlying focus on raising achievement by reversing low expectations both in the school and at home (or, as the Dunbar team put it, more stiffly: maximizing the "total resources" of the school and its community so that "the effects of cultural deprivation can be minimized and academic achievement and latent talent can be extended beyond apparent limitations").[74]

If the Great Cities program did not invent the core elements of compensatory education at Dunbar, however, it did provide a key ingredient that the Ford Foundation was well equipped to provide: money. Ford Foundation resources provided two much-needed buses for field trips and made possible an explosion of activity in some thirty after-school programs and homework centers. (The latter were intended especially for children who lived in substandard housing.)[75] Most important, the Great Cities program enabled Foster and his staff to expand their existing efforts in two main areas: parental outreach and literacy.

Community outreach was labor intensive, and Ford Foundation resources made it possible for parent activist Eloise Holmes to do this work on a full-time basis. Holmes now received a teacher's salary as a school-community coordinator. In the fall of 1960, she went about organizing the neighborhood one block at a time, setting up a network of "commanders" who lived on each one—fifty-six in all. These served as her liaisons to the Dunbar families who resided there. Holmes then spent most of her time visiting parents at home, explaining the program to them, asking for their support and reinforcement with the children, and encouraging them to get more involved in school and community life.[76]

Similarly, the Great Cities program paid for an expansion of professional development activities in the language arts, spearheaded by the veteran reading supervisor Ida Kravitz. Kravitz was tough and dynamic; at ninety-six pounds, she had been too tiny for service in the Navy's WAVES division

Figure 4. Language arts specialist Ida Kravitz *(right)* works with first-grade teacher Nancy Fairfax during the Dunbar School's participation in the Ford Foundation's Great Cities program. While the foundation did not invent the core ideas of compensatory education, its financial support for Kravitz and other new staff and activities underscored the importance of resources in urban schools. Urban Archives, Temple University Libraries.

(Women Accepted for Volunteer Emergency Service), but once, when a junior high school student had attacked her with a knife, she won his respect by slugging him in the stomach.[77] Now, thanks to resources from the Ford Foundation, she was able to concentrate her energies on raising academic expectations and achievement in Dunbar and several other pilot schools. Rather than emphasizing deficiencies, the idea was to identify strengths and interests and build on them, gradually developing confidence and skill in teacher and student alike. For example, Kravitz suggested a school wide effort to improve the manual skill of handwriting, as a step toward more sophisticated achievements. Foster remembered that within several months students were "writing beautifully," and when they took a city test, "zoom, they made the highest scores in Dunbar's history." An aura of failure was lifting, as children began to "believe in themselves" and the teachers began to say, "look, we can do something with these kids"—the kind of transformation of expectations and relationships that, as the sociologist Charles Payne has emphasized, is often the first and most important step in the improvement of demoralized urban schools.[78]

Kravitz encouraged teachers to adjust their methods to promote success and self-esteem, but this was no reprise of the dumbed down, nonacademic curriculum Ruth Hayre had accused white educators of applying to the city's predominantly black schools. The handwriting campaign and the increased confidence it brought were a warm-up for more academic learning—especially for what Foster called "the challenge of 'the word.'" Kravitz, like Foster, believed that the most important contribution Dunbar could make to its students' educational and life opportunities was to teach them to read and write well in Standard English. Great Cities made possible a more intensive focus on this goal, not only by funding Kravitz's efforts, but by releasing fifth grade teacher Alice Campbell from the classroom and making her the head of a school "language laboratory." Kravitz and Campbell worked to foster a mutually reinforcing combination of listening, speaking, reading and writing skills. First-graders brought large boxes of leaves from the park and threw them in the air, describing how they "crackled and crunched and popped" underfoot, thus preparing themselves, Foster said, to recognize such words on the page and "to say a little more than 'the leaves fall down.'"[79] Campbell spent half of her time working with students in her lab and the rest in classrooms, demonstrating new approaches for other teachers, because, as Kravitz said, "you can't give a teacher a curriculum and say teach it."[80]

Even Dunbar's approach to tracking provided evidence of raised academic expectations for all students. Granted, the Great Cities project was infused with a heavy emphasis on differential abilities. In contrast to post-1960s movements for "detracking" and the mainstreaming of special needs students, the schools used standardized exams such as the Ginn Reading Tests and the Philadelphia Verbal Ability Test to sort the students into homogeneous "maturity groups." In keeping with the project focus on "slow" and "talented" learners, Dunbar's language lab worked with two groups in particular: younger children who "did not talk" and an older "enrichment group." The "non-verbals" were put into smaller classes. Maturity groups, like the adjustment of the curriculum in the name of self-esteem, had the potential to stigmatize and reinforce low expectations of some students. One Dunbar teacher, for example, challenged Campbell's decision "to give the 'silent ones' a chance; she felt more could be accomplished by focusing on 'children who could be helped.'"[81] However, as implemented by Campbell, Kravitz, and Foster, "maturity groups" were more like differentiated *instruction* toward common academic goals (especially literacy) than the differentiated *curriculum* that traditionally had relegated African American students to less academically rigorous programs of study. Using her resources as a Ford consultant, Kravitz recruited academics from across the country to help her create teaching materials for the Great Cities schools. The result was a flexible program involving phonics as well as methods more akin to what came to be called the "whole language" approach. "We assumed that every child could be taught to read if the method appropriate for him was used," Foster wrote. "We were not purists. We wanted results."[82]

The Great Cities program was launched at a time of burgeoning optimism about the efficacy of social programs, and it did not include, by later standards, a very extensive process for evaluating Foster's and the other educators' success. Still, quantitative as well as qualitative evidence suggested that the program did in fact help to improve student achievement. A feature in the *Philadelphia Evening Bulletin* noted that by June 1963, 137 of 140 Dunbar students could read by the end of the first grade—this at a school where whole classes of first-graders, and more than one-third of the second grade, had supposedly been unable to read in 1960.[83] The article did not say how or by whom the students' reading abilities had been measured, but the finding squared with the results of standardized testing and other district evaluations, which indicated improvement in reading and math at two of the three elementary schools, including Dunbar. (Sub-par results occurred in one school in which the program "never achieved full implementation.") Informal teacher evaluations of student reading levels were consistent with these test results, indicating that most students, instead of dropping further and further behind as they often had before, were instead making normal progress.[84]

Meanwhile, anecdotal evidence suggested that teachers, administrators, and parents felt better about the schools and the children's performance. After one year, Louis Ballen, the school district's Coordinator of Human Relations, noted that a growing number of teachers were coming to believe that "children of limited backgrounds can learn and be taught so that they want to learn," and those children, in the process, were showing "better work habits" and other positive "attitudinal" changes.[85] At Dunbar, staff members gushed over the benefits of Campbell's Language Arts demonstrations, their only complaint being that they needed even more classroom visits and special presentations. And a number of Dunbar parents reinforced the positive testimony of the staff. As one said, "I have tried very hard in many ways to get through to my daughter the importance of learning, but with little results. Since the High Roads program, the difference is remarkable." Another was glad her children had "a chance to go to many more places and see more things, also a chance to improve in their studies." Still another commented that she and her child had "learned more about themselves from the Negro History club than they had ever known before."[86]

The High Roads project did not eliminate all problems in school-parent relations. Eloise Holmes continued to perceive apathy among some parents who, she wrote, "cannot for one reason or another bring themselves out of the depressed state to cooperate in any way for the good of the school, children, and community." From a different perspective, but leading to a similar point about the limits of parental involvement at Dunbar, former teacher Lynne Yermanock Strieb remembers the school's parents as having been a valuable but untapped resource during her time as a long-term substitute in the 1962–63 school year.[87] Overall, though, the High Roads project represented a step toward greater parental involvement at Dunbar. Holmes felt that her personal visits gave many parents a "feeling of status; a sense of being needed and a desire to be counted." She also believed that those feelings translated into action, in the form of a rise of volunteerism at the school. Even after just one year as school-community coordinator, she perceived a "definite change of attitude toward school within the home."[88]

An Educational War on Poverty

With Ford Foundation support, Dunbar and other participating schools did much to demonstrate the educational potential of compensatory education. Some reformers and public officials found the Great Cities program so encouraging, in fact, that they made compensatory education a cornerstone of school and social policy during the Great Society.

To be sure, it was evident even in the pilot phase of the Philadelphia program that compensatory education was only as effective as the people carrying it out. Wesley Scott, an observer from the Ford Foundation in the early 1960s, described how Eloise Holmes, an "indigenous leader" who knew the community well, was more successful than, say, her counterpart at Ludlow Elementary, who was "overwhelmed" by the job.[89] Likewise, the skill and dedication of Ida Kravitz were key to the improvement of language arts in the project schools. Kravitz herself felt that Great Cities was "a fabulous program" but that "we saw results in direct proportion to the interest of the community and the ability of teachers."[90] Dunbar was luckier, in that regard, than other project schools that had larger numbers of inexperienced and substitute teachers.[91] This is not to mention the importance of leadership from the principal's office; as subsequent research has emphasized, having a proactive instructional leader like Marcus Foster is crucial to school improvement.[92]

Yet questions about how broadly and easily pilot programs could be replicated did not limit the rapid expansion of compensatory education. The Great Cities program was a signature example of what the historian Ellen Condliffe Lagemann has described as "strategic philanthropy," or the use of limited foundation resources to leverage action by other organizations, including the federal government.[93] As both the Ford Foundation and the district had hoped, the program became a template for the Philadelphia schools' response to the social and educational problems of the urban crisis. At the end of the initial one-year grant, the district landed a three-year, $225,000 extension from Ford and matched it, expanding the program to eight schools. Pressure from outside the system led to further expansion; in 1963, for instance, the Reverend Leon Sullivan and a group of clergy known as the "400 Ministers" launched a protest against inferior learning conditions and low academic achievement in sixty-five predominantly black schools, and they pressed the district to extend compensatory education to those schools.[94] By 1966, sixty-eight elementary schools and fourteen secondary schools would be spending $2 million of the district's regular budget in the Educational Improvement Program, a direct descendant of Great Cities.[95]

The impact of these programs reverberated beyond Philadelphia and the other localities that launched them. In June 1964, several dozen of the nation's leading psychologists, sociologists, and educators, including Erik Erikson, Benjamin Bloom, and Edmund Gordon, met in Chicago and recommended that the nation extend its efforts in compensatory education.[96] In fact, the Johnson Administration had declared the War on Poverty a few months earlier, and by the following year, it was clear that compensatory education was one of the government's main weapons. The Elementary and Secondary Education Act (ESEA), while not officially part of the poverty program, focused heavily on funding compensatory programs for poor students; indeed, Great

Cities had provided much of the basis for the testimony of Francis Keppel, Johnson's Commissioner of Education, in the 1965 congressional hearings that led to the ESEA's historic passage.[97]

Compensatory education was also at the center of one of the best-known and most controversial of the administration's antipoverty initiatives, the Community Action Program. Community Action was created as part of the Economic Opportunity Act of 1964, and it was modeled substantially on Ford Foundation projects. As he had planned to do from the start, Paul Ylvisaker tried to build on the Great Cities program by pushing urban politicians, agency heads, and educators to come up with more comprehensive approaches to solving the urban crisis.[98] The result was the Ford Foundation's Gray Areas program, and in the five cities that received funding—Philadelphia, Oakland, Boston, New Haven, and Washington, D.C.—it did lead to the creation of new agencies for receiving and re-allocating Foundation and federal resources to fight poverty. Moreover, under the eventual federal program, which called for and in some cases made possible the "maximum feasible participation" of the poor themselves, some of those Community Action Agencies (CAAs) took a far more confrontative stance toward existing institutions and social policies (including school districts) than even Ylvisaker envisioned.[99] Still, despite Ylvisaker's grander intentions, Gray Areas and eventually the federal Community Action Program relied heavily on the Great Cities approach of educational programs for the culturally deprived. Philadelphia's antipoverty agency—the Philadelphia Council for Community Advancement (PCCA), launched in January 1962 with grants from the Ford Foundation and the President's Committee on Juvenile Delinquency (PCJD)—approached the urban crisis in much the same way as did the school superintendents, emphasizing such priorities as "creating motivations toward upward mobility, e.g., job training and other education"; "removing or insulating children from negative influences in their environment"; and "acculturating newcomers."[100]

In Philadelphia and elsewhere, policymakers hoped to fight poverty by spreading, especially in the Head Start program, the kind of compensatory education approaches Marcus Foster and his colleagues had been developing at the Dunbar School. In fact, one of the PCCA's four main programs, after it received its antipoverty funds from the Johnson Administration's newly created Office of Economic Opportunity (OEO) in 1964, was to extend, at Dunbar and three other elementary schools, a pre-kindergarten experiment Foster had helped initiate.[101]

"A Curious Amalgam of Hope and Underestimation"

Foster's tenure at Dunbar thus intersected with a larger story—a story of reformers looking to early-childhood and elementary education as arenas for solving the social problems of the big cities. Unfortunately, the optimism surrounding pilot projects like Great Cities was short-lived, as compensatory education came under fire from critics who saw it as a disparagement of poor people and/or an excuse for not desegregating the schools.

Not all liberals and civil rights advocates had shifted their primary focus from integration to cultural deprivation; black civil rights leaders, in particular, continued a struggle for school desegregation that they had been waging since the 1930s. In Philadelphia, the local NAACP and the Educational Equality League (EEL) had pushed for integration not only to eliminate what they saw as a damaging aura of inferiority surrounding black schools, but to ensure that black children would enjoy the same educational resources as white children. These efforts gained some steam after the *Brown* decision, and in 1961, the leaders of the Philadelphia NAACP and the EEL—the future federal judge Leon Higginbotham and the tireless Floyd Logan, respectively— took a more confrontative stance, joining forces to sue the school district over racial discrimination in the establishment of school boundaries and the assignment of teachers. In *Chisolm v. Board of Public Education*, Higginbotham and Logan charged that the Board of Education, even if innocent of gerrymandering, had nonetheless shirked an affirmative responsibility to integrate its schools. The case ended in an out-of-court settlement and failed to make a significant dent in racial segregation. However, it did direct pressure and criticism where many civil rights leaders felt it belonged: on the school system itself, as opposed to the families it served.[102]

Civil rights activists had good reason to believe that programs like Great Cities were a diversion from, even a threat to, their goal of desegregation. In a 1963 piece in the *Atlantic Monthly*, Murray Friedman, a sociologist and a regional director of the American Jewish Committee, linked compensatory education to what he called, in dismay, a "white liberal retreat" from the goal of integration. Based largely on observations of his hometown of Philadelphia, Friedman (who himself was white) reported that white city dwellers had "pushed up enrollment at private and parochial schools, shut their eyes to the widespread practice of gerrymandering of school district lines to avoid integration, and helped to create pressures for separating slow from rapid learners in the public schools." He emphasized that these were not necessarily malicious acts; many liberal-minded people still believed in and fought for black civil rights in the abstract even as they struggled to separate themselves from the "squalor" they perceived in the expanding "slums." But the author worried that scientific racism, discredited since the 1930s, was making a comeback. Studies linking inequality to IQ had proliferated in the wake of *Brown*. Meanwhile, mainstream social scientists who still rejected racial and genetic interpretations were nonetheless backpedaling on desegregation because they felt it necessary to "upgrade Negro slum children before they are thrown into the more difficult world of the middle-class white." In other words, they felt it necessary to provide compensatory education. While Friedman was not opposed to compensatory education—he approvingly cited several examples—he was alarmed that some saw it as a substitute for, even an excuse to avoid, desegregation.[103]

Others objected to the very notion of "upgrading Negro slum children." Liberal sociologist Frank Riessman, author of *The Culturally Deprived Child* (1962), described projects like Great Cities and Higher Horizons as a "curious amalgam of hope and underestimation": reformers were right to believe they could overcome the negative effects of a child's early environment, but they mistakenly assumed that nothing in that environment was positive. Educators' and reformers' middle-class outlook, he argued, prevented them from recognizing or building on black cultural traditions, especially music, that might serve as a bridge to "high culture." Ironically, Riessman patronized and stereotyped the culturally deprived as much as other liberals did, if not more so, arguing that their "anti-intellectual" outlook called for a different curriculum based on physical modes of learning and the wisdom of the streets. This position, in contrast to the one taken by educators like Foster, did not expect or even allow for poor and minority children to build the cultural capital that would allow them to compete in the larger society. Still, as Riessman's book suggested, the liberal approach to assimilation as a one-way street—the shedding of a supposedly defective subculture in favor of the dominant one—was troublesome in its own right.[104]

Riessman's critique was echoed by the novelist Ralph Ellison, a longtime critic of liberal social scientists for their tendency to see only pathology in black culture. Ellison had taken issue with this tendency as early as 1944, in an unpublished review of Gunnar Myrdal's seminal statement of postwar liberalism, *An American Dilemma*.[105] In 1963, speaking at a seminar on "Education for Culturally Different Youth," he declared that "there is no such thing as a culturally deprived kid." In fact, he argued, the "difficult thirty percent" had shown remarkable ingenuity in adapting to their own distinctive "cultural complex," namely, life as a black American in the streets of the city. The goal for educators was not to get these children to abandon that culture, but to build a bridge to it; not simply assimilation, but a recognition of cultural pluralism, or what came to be known as multiculturalism.[106]

By 1963, when the fiery Cecil Moore replaced Leon Higginbotham as head of the Philadelphia NAACP, new black leaders were adding to Riessman's and Ellison's criticism of liberal condescension, denouncing the idea of cultural deprivation as an elitist attack on the urban poor. In his inaugural speech before the NAACP, Moore attacked white reformers in general and the city's new antipoverty agency (Philadelphia Council for Community Advancement) in particular, for promoting studies designed to expose the weakness and inferiority of blacks. Instead, he demanded an immediate program of direct action in North Philadelphia, and he threatened a boycott of Ford car dealers if the Ford Foundation continued to support the PCCA.[107]

Philadelphia's Great Cities program certainly exhibited some of the cultural biases that alienated critics like Riessman, Ellison, and Moore. The Dunbar School's reports to the Ford Foundation tended to emphasize the problem of a "defeatist environment" at home and in the community, noting, for example, that some black parents taught their children that "work and ambition were useless in a white man's world." Only occasionally did these documents mention the kinds of external forces—for example, "unfortunate . . . inter-group contacts with merchants, landlords, social workers, and police"—that might have given some parents reason to feel pessimistic. Rather, Foster and his staff tended to define their challenge as one of helping a "sub-standard" community assimilate to the school's culture of hard work and self-improvement.[108]

Despite having spent a good part of his youth wearing a zoot suit and carousing in black Philadelphia (or perhaps because of that), Foster seems to have emerged by the early 1960s with a conservative streak on issues of cultural identity. In a 1962 article on "the child of limited background," he described a process of "identity change" in starkly assimilationist language that many African Americans (including, to some extent, Foster himself) would come to reject. Foster suggested that urban educators needed to reinforce positive identity traits and root out negative ones like "unusual hair styles" and "non conformist behavior."[109] Consistent with these ideas, the High Roads project included a "good grooming campaign" that echoed Leslie Hill's regimen at Cheyney. Beyond the hygienic practice of providing showers for children who did not or could not bathe regularly at home, the school also encouraged boys and girls to wear ties and dresses (furnished by the school when necessary) and to "get rid of the many exaggerated motions in their walking posture." Even Dunbar's black history program stressed assimilation to white, mainstream society rather than distinctive cultural traditions or a legacy of struggle against oppression. The school's spectrum of role models—"Negroes whose behavior, interests, and accomplishments conform to socially accept-able standards"—included Booker T. Washington and Martin Luther King, Jr., for example, but not W. E. B. DuBois or Paul Robeson; the singers Marian Anderson and Leontyne Price, but no jazz musicians.[110]

Foster also appears to have had a somewhat conservative response to Cecil B. Moore and the rising tide of militant activism he was sparking in Philadelphia. Lynne Strieb was a young graduate student when she went to work at Dunbar in 1962 as a long-term substitute, making her the only white teacher at the school. She had heard that Dunbar had a militant principal and that the students had to play with brown-skinned dolls. Actually, the dolls had arrived at Dunbar only that very year, and the African American principal—Foster—was less involved in civil rights activities than she was (and apparently less so than other young members of his teaching staff.) Strieb had taken part in a local NAACP protest against racial discrimination in the construction industry, and she remembers that Foster did not participate—indeed, that he expressed disapproval of Moore and his confrontational tactics.[111] Her memory echoes that of Foster's boyhood friend Leon Frisby, who remembers a time in the 1940s or 1950s when Foster chose caution over confrontation in the face of racial discrimination. On a bus ride home from an overnight outing to Atlantic City, Foster and Frisby were told by the driver to move to the back of the bus. Frisby began to resist, but his friend thought otherwise. It was not the time to "make a big thing out of this," Foster told his friend. "You're either going to do it or you get off the bus."[112]

It is important to note that Foster's attitudes and actions reflected a mix of cultural bias and political savvy. Strieb says she "wanted him to be more radical," but she also notes that, as a black man aspiring to leadership in the school system, he "had to do it a certain way."[113] In a similar vein, Bob Black-burn says Foster undoubtedly "changed and grew" as the 1960s unfolded, moving toward a more expansive cultural pluralism and a more forceful cri-tique of racism—but he also believes that in the early years Foster was careful to say what he knew funders wanted to hear. "Comp Ed was a way of getting 'the Man's' money," he says. "And it was rarely discussed except socially and informally, back in those years. Marcus could put on a straight face and talk about the appropriate ingredients of an effective program, behind his back knowing, 'get me the money and I'll put this together.'" And when Foster and his colleagues "put this together," their motto was "accent the positive; play down the negative." Instead of "getting kids down on floor, and grinding them with their area of weakness," which is how Blackburn remembers Foster describing the deficit model of compensatory education, the emphasis was on "building bridges from their strengths."[114] Above all, Foster wanted his students to fit into and excel in the mainstream—not to vindicate themselves to disapproving whites, but to claim a birthright.[115]

The more serious problem with cultural and class chauvinism came as policymakers tried to implement compensatory education on a mass scale. Bob Blackburn recalls that external agencies tried to replicate what people like Marcus Foster had been "making up out of their back pocket," but that, "as soon as you had all the appropriate ingredients, one from column A, one from column B, something died in the whole Comp Ed movement." That "something" was, in part, a deeply ingrained faith in and respect for the abilities of underachieving children, qualities even well-meaning reformers and teachers often lacked. "When you see a lot of yourself in the child," Blackburn says, "it does not require an act of will to have high expectations—something that your professor in the education class told you that you should have. You intuitively have high expectations."[116]

Superintendents and other local leaders were careful to avoid generalizing about minority groups, pointing to class differences within them, yet they tended to make disparaging blanket statements about poor families' "indifference" and "apathy" toward their children's health and educational needs.[117] A telling example of well-intended but troubling condescension came from the district superintendent who supervised Great Cities in Philadelphia. Aleda Druding was a passionate believer in the program and the potential of the children it served. As she once wrote, "To be a teacher is to be bound in conscience to help each child find his own worth, his own dignity. To be a teacher is to open doors. And to be a teacher in the Great Cities School Improvement Program is to be and do all these things with renewed dedication, with loving enthusiasm."[118] And yet, in a report on the Great Cities program for the *NEA Journal*, Druding struck a different tone:

> What do these descriptions mean? Translated into daily school
> life, they mean that children come to kindergarten without
> knowing their own names. "Big Boy" or "Brother" is the only

name they have heard at home. That medical and dental checks will show hundreds of children who have never brushed their teeth or bathed regularly. Mother has never shown them how or encouraged them to brush or wash. That many children—perhaps most—have vocabularies so limited that they are unable to speak in sentences. "Huh?" "Out!" "Go On." "Shush!" plus a number of curse words may be their entire repertoire. That many children will fall asleep in class because they find it difficult to sleep at night in the noisy room they share with three or four other children and adults. That emotional problems are not unusual. One little girl, for example, will not go near the lavatory because she saw a dead man's body in the bathroom her family shares with the rest of their building.[119]

In many ways, Foster shared this administrator's concerns about the home lives of his students (though he was less inclined to generalize from the worst cases). But where he portrayed parents as an ally to be mobilized, she described them as an obstacle to be overcome. With obvious shock and dismay, Druding told of the time a mother "didn't feel like making any breakfast" for her child and Eloise Holmes did the job herself; this showed how Holmes "sometimes shames them into cooperation."[120] At a time of surging pride and self-assertion in the civil rights movement, it was no wonder such ideas and language quickly fell into disfavor.

The Limits of Compensatory Education

The Dunbar School showed that it was possible to address disadvantages associated with poverty without turning these into excuses for inaction and low expectations. Foster and his staff focused their attention beyond the school, especially by motivating parents to play a more productive role in their children's education. In the language of the time, they said they were compensating for cultural deprivation. Today we would say (at least in academic circles) they were building cultural capital. Yet Foster and his colleagues did not focus exclusively on non-school factors; they made changes at the school, as well. In the Great Cities School Improvement Program, they stood for the idea that IQ tests and prior achievement did not capture the true potential of urban students (who increasingly were black) and that educators needed to raise their expectations of such students, especially in the academic subjects of reading and mathematics. In doing so, moreover, they took inspiration not only from social scientists like Martin Deutsch, but from an African American tradition of academic achievement and from the local experiments of innovative educators and activists such as Kenneth Clark and Daniel Schreiber. In retrospect, the most serious problem with compensatory education was not the concept itself, or the fact that some advocates described or implemented it in pejorative-sounding ways. The bigger problem was the way in which policymakers made it into a centerpiece of their responses to large-scale social problems such as urban poverty and racial inequality.

For one thing, there was the matter of resources; it was expensive to reproduce pilot projects on a mass scale, in all similar schools. Of course, this was not the fault of the pilot projects, nor was it a reason not to spend the money. On the contrary, Dunbar's success with compensatory education was a compelling argument for channeling more resources to schools that served low-income students. In 1962, the journalist Charles Silberman drew precisely that conclusion in the *Fortune* magazine series "The City and the Negro." If pilot projects affected only a "minute fraction of the children needing special help," he argued, the answer was to implement them "on a mass scale" and thus exercise "positive discrimination" on behalf of urban blacks. Silberman was only repeating what Daniel Schreiber and other advocates had said before (and what current commentators such as the journalist Paul Tough have continued to say): compensatory education could raise academic achievement, but taxpayers would have to "spend for it."[121] Yet the nation did not spend for compensatory education on a large scale. As Marcus Foster said in 1969, efforts like the Educational Improvement Program in Philadelphia were conceptually sound, but "we went at the task with a teaspoon, when we needed the mighty efforts of a steam shovel."[122]

Moreover, even if Americans had made large and beneficial investments in compensatory education, schooling alone could not have solved the problems of racial inequality and urban poverty. Yet, in characteristic American fashion, echoing Horace Mann and his belief in public education as the great equalizer, this is largely what policymakers and politicians came to expect of the schools in the early 1960s. For school-based educators like Foster, compensatory education was first and foremost a means of improving academic achievement—a source of practical strategies and, not least, extra funds, for implementing remedial reading instruction, intellectually stimulating field trips, and stronger counseling and parent outreach programs, among other improvements. By contrast, as we have seen, the district leaders and Ford

Foundation officials who launched the Great Cities program saw school reform as a means to greater ends. Granted, they "played down" these goals and
described the program primarily in educational terms. But for these leaders,
compensatory education was a means to the realization of larger, and at times
contradictory, social goals: reducing juvenile delinquency, promoting social
peace and racial integration, and equalizing economic opportunities in an
increasingly knowledge-based, technological society.

Granted, it was important to link urban schools and school reform to
larger social problems—especially poverty and racial segregation. One
Philadelphia leader who did so in a thoughtful way was George Schermer,
head of the city's Commission on Human Relations (CHR). Schermer was
a passionate advocate of racial integration, and he was not one to speak in
a sensational or exaggerated way about the social problems of black Philadelphians.[123] Still, by the early 1960s, he had grown increasingly alarmed
over the apparent connections between poverty, school achievement, and
the struggle for a racially integrated society. In his experience enforcing
fair employment practices, Schermer had had difficulty finding enough
qualified black candidates for certain skilled occupations.[124] Meanwhile, as
he wrote in July of 1960, "the one persistent fear that chill[ed] the hearts
of most white people" when they contemplated racial integration of their
neighborhoods and especially their children's schools, was the "'different'
living standards and disorganized behavior" of certain black families—that
is, poor ones. Schermer quoted whites who said they were willing to integrate with "many Negro families" but not with "*that kind* of neighbor,
regardless of color."[125] He understood that some may have been making excuses for their opposition to integration of any sort. Still, Schermer and
other like-minded liberals were understandably concerned that social class
differences—including what he described, in the language of the time, as
"cultural deficits"—were as damaging to the struggle for racial integration
as racial prejudice itself.[126] As he saw it, these deficits could not be eliminated simply through school and neighborhood desegregation. Indeed, the
reverse was also true: eliminating deficits and enhancing the cultural capital
of disadvantaged students was an important aspect of achieving desegregation. With this in mind, Schermer embraced the Ford Foundation compensatory education project. However, he was careful not to overstate what
the project could accomplish. As one CHR publication emphasized, the
causes of urban school problems lay "more outside the school system than
within it," and as a consequence, Schermer continued to stress the impact

of racism on black Philadelphians and the need to keep fighting for racial equality on various fronts.[127]

George Schermer was careful not to attribute racial inequality solely to cultural deprivation, nor to seek its solution entirely in compensatory education programs. The big-city superintendents and other reformers were less careful. In a 1960 press release about Great Cities, for instance, Chicago superintendent Benjamin Willis spoke for his counterparts in the other cities when he stated that "the social and economic life of the United States—indeed, its very existence—will be in jeopardy unless the great cities take decisive steps" to boost the aspirations and achievement of those million or so children. Grandly casting schools as the centerpiece of urban social policy, Willis went on to assert that "more can be done in the classrooms of America to meet the needs of the children of limited background than can be done in any other place or in any other way."[128]

There was much to admire in a school like Dunbar, just as there is much to admire in current charter school movements that likewise aim to eliminate achievement gaps by raising academic expectations and building cultural capital. (It is worth noting that, with the exception of the Harlem Children's Zone, most of those current efforts put far less emphasis on parent and community outreach than did Foster.) But there was also a danger in holding up such schools as the key to solving bigger problems. Americans often assume that schooling was the path to opportunity for previous generations of immigrants, and in the 1960s many expected the schools to do the same for African American migrants and their children. But while educational attainment *had* come to play an increasingly important role in shaping social opportunity (a trend that has accelerated to this day), it was not as decisive a factor as Americans tended to believe. The schools had never been the main avenue of advancement, at least not in economic terms. The immigrants of the early twentieth century had survived due to a vibrant (if exploitative) industrial economy.[129] Their children were helped toward a middle-class existence by the racially discriminatory social policies of the New Deal.[130] In the postwar era, urban blacks enjoyed neither benefit; despite hopes unleashed by the war and its aftermath, they were increasingly defeated by deindustrialization and ongoing racial discrimination (in practice if not always in law). Over time, critics and scholars have been sharply critical of the War on Poverty and other social reforms of the 1960s for relying too heavily on educational solutions and failing to address the economic changes and persistent patterns of discrimination that underlay urban poverty and decline. As these scholars have suggested, overpromising for education as the great social equalizer tends to obscure those root causes and breed disillusionment with schools and/or with the families they serve.[131]

Advocates of compensatory education were not the only ones to hold inflated expectations of education; ironically, so did some of their critics within the civil rights movement. Members of both camps tended to see schools as the major mechanism of social mobility in America. But that common tendency was not obvious at the time. More clearly visible was a growing *split* within liberalism, between those who emphasized the idea of cultural deprivation and those who believed the schools themselves were to blame for low achievement.

Foster, being immersed in the daily life of his school and the idiosyncrasies of individual students, did not fit easily in either camp. But he began to change with the times, and this would be all the more evident after 1963, when the school district appointed him to be principal of the Catto Disciplinary School in West Philadelphia. Catto was one of two institutions where the superintendent sent students no one else could or would teach. Foster soon found himself in a less hopeful outpost of the school system, expressing a more critical view of its shortcomings.

CHAPTER 3

Victims, Not Hoodlums: Urban Schools
and the Crisis of Liberalism

THE summer of 1965 was a hopeful moment in the struggle for equality among African Americans. In March, just ten days after a violent attack on civil rights marchers in Selma, Alabama, President Lyndon Johnson sent Congress a bill aimed at eliminating the various strategies that southern states had used to keep blacks from exercising their Fourteenth and Fifteenth Amendment rights to vote. In addressing a joint session of Congress about the legislation, on national television, the president had stated that "we shall overcome," thus echoing the famous civil rights anthem and aligning himself with the movement. And indeed, on August 6, with Martin Luther King, Jr., Rosa Parks, and other civil rights leaders in attendance, Johnson signed the Voting Rights Act into law. Coming on the heels of the Civil Rights Act (1964), it was a heady moment. So it was surely a shock when, five days later, the Watts section of Los Angeles erupted in violence, resulting in thirty-four deaths and $40 million in property damage. For decades thereafter, historians and other analysts tended to portray Watts as the moment when the "ghettoes erupted" and the optimism of the early Sixties, especially on the issue of civil rights, suddenly gave way to a darker and more troubled time.[1]

The shift from hope to turmoil was less sudden and simple than has often been described. As we have seen, the cities—and their schools—had been wracked by racial tensions and violence for decades. Yet the national mood did shift significantly in the middle years of the decade, and the problems of urban schools and students played an important part in that shift.[2] In the early 1960s, as we have seen, racial liberals had begun to split over the idea of compensatory education for the "culturally deprived," with some civil rights leaders complaining that it stigmatized black children and lowered expectations of them. After 1964, those cracks in the liberal coalition widened into chasms. In that year—the summer before Watts—the nation's ghettos truly began to erupt in riots. Philadelphia was one of seven cities in which black residents took to the streets to express their anger at white police and white-owned businesses, resulting in three days of rioting and looting. Many of the rioters were teenagers, and some observers, including liberals eager to maintain a positive image for the civil rights movement, denounced them as maladjusted "hoodlums." Others moved toward an equally fervent denunciation of the racism that they believed African Americans had suffered in the schools and the larger society. Debate along these lines only intensified in 1965 after the even more destructive Watts riot and the release of the U.S. Department of Labor report *The Negro Family: The Case for National Action,* better known as the Moynihan Report, after its author, then-Assistant Secretary of Labor Daniel Patrick Moynihan. By the fall of that year, public debates over race and poverty had taken the form of an ideological crossfire between those who blamed the problems of African Americans (including poor school performance and high rates of juvenile delinquency) on racism and those who faulted the alleged cultural pathologies of blacks themselves.

Were disaffected urban blacks hoodlums, or were they victims? When Marcus Foster was reassigned from Dunbar Elementary to the Catto Disciplinary School in 1963, he became even more enmeshed in this deepening debate over the problems of black families and schools. Catto was one of two special schools in the city where the district concentrated its male disciplinary cases. Most, according to psychological tests conducted by school district and county court officials, were emotionally disturbed and/or had serious family problems. All were black. These were not the young children for whom the Dunbar program tried to provide early interventions: they were junior and senior high school students whose chances for a "head start" were long gone—and their teachers had little faith in the possibility of reversing the situation. As the sociologist Kathryn Neckerman has documented, some of the well-known problems of urban schools, including adversarial relationships between black students and white educators, can be traced in no small measure to the discriminatory treatment of students in the urban school systems of the early twentieth century.[3] As Foster discovered when he got there, the Catto School was a blatant example of the low expectations and educational failure that were increasingly pushing black activists to criticize the system rather than the students.

In today's terms, Catto was a school in need of a "turnaround," and the district looked to Foster to get the job done. Foster's answer was what he called the Catto Comprehensive Treatment Program (CCTP). As at Dunbar, this program was more than just a significant departure for one school; it spoke to, and offered a synthesis of, competing interpretations of the problems of urban schools. At Catto, Foster became a more assertive critic of the white-run school system and a stauncher advocate for the black families the system increasingly served. During the riot of 1964, for example, he argued that the young looters were victims of injustice, including a second-class education— a statement that presumably was informed by his work at Catto as well as his own personal history in the streets and the segregated schools of South Philadelphia. In line with this critique, his program included a revamped curriculum, including a focus on literacy and more relevant vocational education, and a push for teachers to adopt higher expectations of their students. In this sense, Foster's work at the Catto Disciplinary School was part of a growing movement among educators and activists affiliated with the civil rights movement to reverse decades of discriminatory treatment and hold urban schools more accountable for the performance of students.

At the same time, Foster continued to emphasize the importance of factors beyond the school itself, including the social and cultural backgrounds of the students and the need for additional support from the community and larger society. Yet, in contrast to the increasingly heated debate beyond the school, Foster did not pit the school against the community, or educators against students and families. As a school leader, he carefully pushed all parties—teachers, students, parents, building staff, nearby residents and merchants—to change their fundamental beliefs about the school and each other, and to contribute to reversing a cycle of low expectations and failure. And, arguably, that is just what the Catto Comprehensive Treatment Program accomplished, according to Foster and others who knew the school before.

Later in the 1960s, Foster pursued a doctorate in education at the University of Pennsylvania, and he chose to write his dissertation on the CCTP—specifically, on how it reduced truancy and delinquency.[4] His multifaceted approach to such problems offered an alternative to the increasingly polarized debates over urban youth, and since that time, it has only become clearer that school performance is shaped by a range of school and non-school factors. Also clearer than ever is the fact that education played an increasingly important role in shaping social opportunity over the latter half of the twentieth century, for Americans in general and for African Americans in particular.[5] Catto's educational successes with young black males who were at risk of dropping out and becoming incarcerated (a group that continues to be especially unlikely to benefit from civil rights progress and an expansion of public sector jobs since the 1960s) takes on special significance in this context.

Still, did Catto's program hold a key to ending poverty? Foster did not promise such grand results (though he did continue to portray school as a key path to opportunity for his students). Regardless, for the second time, his work as an urban school principal took on a larger meaning in relation to developments in national policymaking. In Philadelphia, as in the rest of the nation, the War on Poverty was fought largely with educational weapons. Programs at schools like Dunbar had helped to inspire the school district and the Ford Foundation (and eventually the federal government) with the idea of intervening in the lives of young children and preventing them from becoming delinquents and wasting talents that might prove useful against the Soviets. After 1964, Catto-style vocational education programs also played an important role in the poverty war. But while history has reinforced the importance of addressing both school and non-school factors in academic achievement—as well as the idea that such achievement is increasingly important to social mobility in America—it has been less kind to the familiar but flawed idea that schooling itself (whether in the form of compensatory education, vocational education, or otherwise) is the key to ending poverty.[6]

"The Cesspool of the School System"

The Catto School was located in West Philadelphia, at 42nd and Ludlow Streets, but it drew students from a broad territory encompassing the southern and western parts of the city, including two large, expanding areas of black settlement. A boy ended up at Catto when the principal of his neighborhood school recommended he go there, and when a district superintendent, after reviewing the case history, agreed. Most were referred from regular programs in regular schools, though about a third came from other disciplinary schools, special education classes for the "retarded educable," and other sources, such as children's shelters, social agencies, and religious institutions for wayward youth.[7]

Foster believed that some of Catto's several hundred students were unfairly assigned to the school, but he had no doubt that most presented serious educational challenges. Most of the boys were of junior and senior high school age (the former made up more than 50 percent of the student body), but they tested, on average, at third- and fourth-grade levels in math and reading, respectively—no doubt partly because they were chronic truants who tended to miss more school days than not. Half came from broken families, often because one or both parents had died. One out of five incoming students had an arrest record, and that figure shot up to more than three out of five during the time they attended Catto. Almost all, according to Foster, had a "street-corner affiliation"—a gang—and the wide geographic distribution of the student body meant that rival gang members were thrown together at Catto.[8]

Dean Cummings, a social studies teacher from the early 1960s until the mid-1980s, remembers having many kinds of students. "Some of them were hard cases, where I've had boys come right out of prison," he says. "And when they got there, [*imitates them*] 'Man, I don't want to learn, I don't be sittin' in no classroom, man I don't—everything was 'man.'" Others were "just misunderstood; something psychologically wrong with them, so they couldn't get along in a regular classroom. Maybe they were fighting with other students, or fighting with teachers because some of them didn't like their mothers, and took it out on a woman teacher . . . Everybody was a little different, and you couldn't generalize for the whole group."[9]

Catto's troublesome students represented a challenge for American ideals of universalist public education. Horace Mann and other reformers had founded public school systems to promote a "common" educational experience for all, but in reality, school attendance remained limited and uneven for decades thereafter. By the end of the nineteenth century, enrollment in high school was still the exception rather than the norm, and public schools were not expected to accommodate a broad spectrum of teenagers, much less those with significant social, emotional, and/or academic problems. During the Progressive era, however, the situation changed. The regulation of child labor and the expansion of compulsory school attendance laws (Pennsylvania passed such legislation in 1897) put greater pressure on the schools to accommodate all students. Immigration and farm-to-city migration also increased the number and variety of students that urban public schools were expected to serve. Expanded enrollments raised difficult questions, not only in terms of resources (finding enough classrooms, seats, and teachers), but in terms of mission: what would it mean for the schools to provide a common experience for a student body that varied tremendously in terms of race, ethnicity, socioeconomic status, and academic preparation? At the level of individual classrooms, how could teachers work effectively with heterogeneous groups that included a growing number of difficult-to-teach students with special social, emotional, and/or academic needs?[10]

In the end, the schools did not provide a common experience, and teachers did not end up working with such heterogeneous groups. To resolve the tension between universalist ideals and an increasingly heterogeneous student population, administrators in the Progressive era turned to various forms of curricular "differentiation," or what is now called tracking. Curriculum differentiation called for sorting a diverse student population into homogeneous groups, so that schools and teachers could educate students more "efficiently." And the emphasis was not on different routes and rates of progress toward similar goals, as in today's movement for "differentiated instruction"; it was on segregation into different classes and courses of study entirely. For the urban, working-class students who were entering the public schools in unprecedented numbers (including most African American students), curricula tended to focus on the behaviors, attitudes, and manual skills that employers thought desirable at the lower rungs of modern industrial society. For their more affluent peers (a smaller number of students), an academic education was more likely.[11]

Curriculum tracking in its various forms has generated a vast literature, both pro and con, and the issue remains controversial; indeed, the challenge to tracking since the 1960s, in the name of a more universal set of expectations, is a key story at the heart of this book.[12] Prior to the 1960s, however, with support from the growing "science" of intelligence testing, administrators promoted curriculum differentiation in idealistic terms as the most rational, efficient, and appropriate way to meet the needs of all students. Descriptions of disciplinary schools like Catto were no exception. By the 1930s, according to one account, "truant" schools were rejecting punitive approaches such as handcuffs and straightjackets for a more therapeutic emphasis on educating delinquents to grow and lead a productive life. This new style of reform school took off especially after World War II, as a new migration of black southerners coincided with an alleged epidemic of juvenile delinquency. To be sure, in the face of these trends, some educators sought to get rid of difficult students by scaling back the compulsory education laws that progressives had stiffened. However, the upshot of the black migration was an expanded reliance on disciplinary institutions.[13] In 1947, New York City established four "600" schools to which the regular schools could send "defiant, disruptive, disrespectful" students; by the mid-1960s, fifteen such day schools served about two thousand boys and girls of all ages. The goal of the "600" schools, according to a 1965 report by the New York City Board of Education, was to provide a "therapeutic educational program, non-punitive in approach, in which the anti-social, hostile, disruptive behavior would be molded and redirected through positive, constructive approaches."[14] The Catto and Daniel Boone schools were Philadelphia's version of the "600" schools. They were supposed to give troubled students the individual attention they needed and could not get in regular schools. By law, class size was limited to fifteen students.

Critics took disciplinary schools to task in the 1950s and early 1960s for their educational shortcomings; in 1957, for instance, the sociologist Robert MacIver produced a critical evaluation of the "600" schools for the Juvenile Delinquency Evaluation Project, which he headed at City College in New York.[15] However, even MacIver's critique of disciplinary schools reinforced the notion that they should be places of emotional, academic, and vocational growth. As summarized by Marcus Foster in his 1971 dissertation—because Foster saw it as relevant to his own work at Catto—the MacIver report called for better vocational programs in the "600" schools; it emphasized the importance of breaking an apparent causal link between poor reading skills and delinquency; and it claimed that, more than anything else, disciplinary schools needed a strong principal and a highly skilled teaching staff.[16] In other words, disciplinary schools, like compensatory education programs, should educate students who previously had been written off as uneducable.

From the outside, it might have seemed that Catto embodied this hopeful new mentality about disciplinary schools. Granted, the neighborhood itself was on the decline; as recently as the 1940s it had been a middle-income, Jewish area of single-family homes and small businesses, but white flight, an influx of poor black migrants, and economic decline had taken their toll. Store windows were covered with plywood. Houses had been subdivided and rented to tenants who could not afford to maintain them. But the Catto School itself was brand new, completed in 1959 as part of a district effort to modernize its facilities and keep pace with the expanded enrollment caused by the baby boom and the black migration. The atmosphere of a fresh start came through in a series of photographs taken in 1961 at the school's dedication; unidentified officials and a group of black teenagers in dark suits and ties watched intently as a metal box—presumably a time capsule—was welded shut and sealed into a wall behind the "1959" cornerstone.[17] (The photographs also conveyed that Catto was a black school built and run by whites—an image reinforced by the administration's naming of the school for Octavius V. Catto, an African American man who had emerged in the post–Civil War era as one of the city's most magnetic educators and activists, only to be ambushed and assassinated, at the age of thirty-one, for casting a vote in the election of 1871.[18])

Foster soon discovered, however, that the positive images surrounding separate classrooms and schools obscured more disturbing realities of segregation and second-class education. When he arrived at Catto in the fall of 1963, he perceived an atmosphere of abysmally low expectations in which little or no learning was taking place. The school did not come close to fulfilling the educative purpose some commentators attached to disciplinary schools. It was more like a dumping ground for difficult students.[19]

In recent decades, educational researchers have emphasized the importance of a positive school culture, defined by a sense of trust and high expectations.[20] The school culture at Catto was exactly the opposite. Starting on day one—the intake interview—administrators told incoming students and their parents that the main priority was to show up and "stay out of trouble," thus setting the stage for them to "play the adjustment game sufficiently well" to get sent back to a regular school. One rule of the game was that students could not bring anything of value to school; staff periodically searched them as they entered the building, sometimes confiscating weapons, but also taking cigarettes and anything else of value on the assumption that the boys would steal from each other. Students learned that rule well, and the searches extended to the surrounding neighborhood, where the staff sometimes found knives and other stashes of contraband. Even money was forbidden; in its place, administrators and faculty used an internal economy of tokens and free lunch both to keep the peace and to help ensure student cooperation with the staff. The boys received a free lunch and, at the end of the day, tokens for going home and returning the next morning. Rule-breakers, including those who resisted a search, lost all privileges and thus had to go hungry, walk home, or steal a subway ride. Meanwhile, boys who performed favors—errands, car polishing, repairing or making something in shop class—could earn more.[21]

If the carrot did not work, Catto staff often turned to the stick; corporal punishment, though illegal, was routine. Dean Cummings says that "everybody had to do it a little differently." In his case, the implement of choice was a fraternity paddle, the mere presence of which, he believes, made it possible to maintain

order. "I have had classes," he says, "where . . . most of the class was in there, and
one boy comes staggering in late, and they would say, 'Turn him around Mr.
Cummings, turn him around, give him a paddle!'" Cummings believed, much
to his surprise, that "some understood they needed discipline."[22]

Indeed, while they usually tried to prevent violence, Catto staff sometimes
tolerated or even encouraged fighting—if they could supervise the action.
Foster disapprovingly described classrooms where teachers sometimes handled a disagreement by pushing back the chairs and letting the boys have a
"fair one," thereby hoping to release tension and pre-empt more dangerous
battles on the way home. Staff even had been known to remove the fighters to
the auditorium and put them on stage for other students to watch.[23]

Catto's disciplinary practices brought some order to the school, but Foster
marveled at how little teaching and learning had been taking place. Teachers of the vocational courses came from industry, and Foster thought they
were "extremely competent in their fields," but he faulted the program for not
showing students how to find and keep real jobs. Even more disturbing to
the new principal was the school's atmosphere of low academic expectations.
Catto teachers received bonuses for working in a disciplinary school—a kind
of "combat pay"—but the incentives apparently did little for the academic
program. The English, social studies, and math teachers included three ex-
policemen and one part-time intake interviewer for a juvenile detention fa-
cility. Foster noted that these teachers emphasized "the custodial role rather
than instruction. A day without a major outbreak was considered successful."
Worst of all, Foster believed, the school had made next to no effort to improve poor reading skills, which Foster and many other researchers saw as a
root cause of delinquency and academic failure in the first place. Catto's two
administrators, the principal and his administrative assistant, apparently had
done little to encourage higher standards. Teachers did as they pleased, however questionable their curricula or disciplinary practices may have been.[24]

Foster above all painted the picture of a leadership vacuum at his new
school. Again, it would be difficult to imagine a starker contrast with recent
educational research, with its emphasis on principals who provide instructional leadership and set a tone of achievement and high expectations.[25] The
Catto principal and his assistant had served in the same elementary school,
as a principal and teacher, respectively, of the so-called retarded educable.
The assistant, an ex-marine captain, was respected and feared by students.
Teachers respected him, too. By contrast, the principal was neither feared nor
respected, even though he had the final say on who got to leave Catto. The

principal apparently had little to do with the boys, and when he did, his presence was hardly commanding. Students, interpreting his lack of visibility as fear, had nicknamed him "rabbit." On one occasion a group of them lured him into a restroom and stuffed him in a trashcan. Foster put it lightly when he observed that his predecessor failed to use the "hero model," or role model, style of leadership he had tried to practice at Dunbar.[26]

Perhaps the most striking aspect of the story about the principal's being dumped in the trash was the pride the staff seemed to take in recounting it for Foster. Faculty members apparently liked Foster's predecessor, and even appreciated his administrative competence, but they saw him as a failure at dealing with students. His lack of leadership, in discipline as well as curriculum, led staff members to unite for mutual support and protection from what they saw as a hostile student body and community. The staff helped each other subdue unruly students and shifted difficult ones from one class to another. On Dean Cummings's first or second day at Catto, as a substitute teacher, the gym teacher walked into the new teacher's out-of-control classroom, jumped on top of his desk, and yelled, "You all show this man the same respect you show us down in the gym, or I'll come up here and beat some ass!" The class quieted, and Cummings stayed on another twenty years. Teachers also told with pride how, in the absence of initiative from the principal, they raided an apartment where Catto students were involved in illegal activities.[27]

Oddly, such skirmishes between the students and faculty seemed to be the main source of whatever school spirit existed at Catto. Foster believed that taking disciplinary matters into their own hands and maintaining order had created an esprit de corps among the teachers. And, he wrote, students as well as teachers seemed to take pride that "you had to be 'tough' . . . to survive" at Catto. "There was the apparent desire to develop a reputation that was at least equal to that of the older disciplinary school for boys, Daniel Boone"[28]

Still, teachers had the upper hand in Catto's daily struggle for survival, and most students simply wanted to go elsewhere. Many younger boys tried to achieve this by toeing the line; Foster estimated that half of those who showed up every day seemed "willing to 'do their time' and get out." Others, usually older students, simply dropped out, and the school failed to retrieve them from the streets partly because some teachers felt the school was better off without them. Either way, the staff achieved its main objective: maintaining order.[29]

Whatever rehabilitative function it might have had in theory, the Octavius V. Catto Disciplinary School was widely viewed within the district as a "cesspool of the system."[30] The school did not handcuff its students or put them in straitjackets, like reform schools once had, but it did not do much to educate them, either. And the teachers and administrators seemed to have little interest in changing this image. Indeed, some felt that fear and punishment were what disciplinary school was all about.

Foster brought a distinctly different view: he was appalled by the practices he encountered at the Catto School and took a sympathetic view of the students, in spite of their many problems. In this, he echoed an influential new book at the time, *Delinquency and Opportunity*, by the sociologists Richard Cloward and Lloyd Ohlin. Cloward and Ohlin argued that "norm-violating" behavior, while self-destructive, was not necessarily pathological in the way social scientists and psychologists had long emphasized; rather, it was a rational response to an urban environment in which young people faced frustration and "blocked opportunities" at every turn.[31] Cloward and Ohlin portrayed delinquents as victims of oppressive institutions. For Foster, Catto was one such institution, and he intended to change it.

Who's to Blame? The Mounting Critique of Urban Schools

The Catto Disciplinary School epitomized a growing crisis within liberalism over the problems of race, poverty, and urban education. Catto was not a typical school, but its characteristics were all too typical of urban schooling in general. In the nation's big cities, academic performance was down, disciplinary caseloads were up, and segregation was only getting worse as black migration and white flight continued to change the face of the schools. The liberal response to these problems, as expressed in the Ford Foundation program that Foster had implemented at Dunbar, supposedly offered a corrective to racism and defeatism. According to this strand of liberal thought, urban blacks did not struggle in school because they were incapable; on the contrary, their true potential was stifled by a negative social and cultural environment, and the schools could compensate for such deprivation. As we have seen, critics quickly began to pounce on this idea for the way it emphasized black deficiencies and allegedly undermined the goal of desegregation. This critique intensified during Foster's time at Catto, as civil rights leaders and some black educators increasingly found fault with the schools themselves rather than with the students who attended them.

By 1963, the psychologist Kenneth Clark had emerged as a leading critic of the liberal notion of cultural deprivation. Of course, Clark himself had been a key figure within racial liberalism over the previous two decades. He had contributed research to the Myrdal report, and he and his wife, Mamie Phipps Clark, had famously influenced the outcome of *Brown v. Board of Education* (1954) with their doll experiments, which suggested that segregation produced feelings of inferiority among African American children. In keeping with this view, Clark fought to desegregate the New York City schools. However, he met stiff resistance from the school board and from white residents, and over time, his work *within* predominantly black communities in Harlem took on added significance.

Again, in many ways the efforts in Harlem shaped, and were shaped by, the racial liberalism of the postwar era. In the late 1950s, as we have seen, Clark influenced the creation of the nation's most influential compensatory education project, the Demonstration Guidance Project at Junior High School 43 in Harlem. Demonstration Guidance focused heavily on raising academic expectations among teachers, while at the same time addressing social, cultural, and economic problems beyond the school. The project was influenced by Kenneth and Mamie's work at the Northside Child Development Center, the community service organization they had founded in 1946. At Northside, the Clarks developed programs in such areas as counseling, remedial reading, nutrition, and parenting skills. In the early 1960s, they expanded these efforts by capitalizing on a groundswell of antidelinquency and antipoverty reforms at the national level. With a $230,000 grant from the President's Committee on Juvenile Delinquency (PCJD), Northside changed its name to Harlem Youth Opportunities Unlimited (HARYOU) and produced a six-hundred-page blueprint for solving the urban crisis. Entitled *Youth in the Ghetto,* it echoed, in some ways, the main themes of the Ford Foundation's Great Cities and Gray Areas programs: urban students were performing below their potential, and they needed "compensatory educational techniques" to motivate and equip them for success.[32]

At the same time, though, Kenneth Clark was moving toward a more radical and confrontative approach to the problems of underachievement and delinquency than was typical in other compensatory education programs. Like Mobilization for Youth, another PCJD-funded project that Richard Cloward had initiated on the Lower East Side of New York City, HARYOU laid most of the blame for the urban education crisis at the door of the schools themselves. According to this line of thinking, teachers and administrators were hardly the victims of a flood tide of deprived and difficult children that they claimed to be; they were guilty of "criminal educational neglect." Clark continued to speak of social "pathology" in the black ghettos; however, he emphasized that such pathology, while reinforcing a low quality of life and education, was not a root cause. The root cause of ghetto problems was racial and class oppression—and the root cause of educational failure, in particular, was the low expectations held by the teachers and the school system. Clark had been concerned about the problem of low expectations in his work with the Demonstration Guidance Project, and eighteen months of HARYOU field research deepened this concern. As he and members of his staff suggested in *Youth in the Ghetto* (which Clark later revised for a wider audience as the book *Dark Ghetto*), Harlem students were the victims of a self-fulfilling prophecy; they fell below grade level mainly because "substandard performance [was] expected of them," and they performed to this level of expectation. In this sense, America's public schools were "contaminated by the moral sickness of racism which afflicts the larger society."[33]

Clark did not limit his critique to the most malignant forms of this "sickness"; he especially found fault with "well-intentioned" liberals such as James Bryant Conant. Conant had been president of Harvard in the 1930s and 1940s, and during that time, as we saw earlier, he came to promote his vision of public education as a sorting mechanism that held the key to the future of American democracy. In particular, Conant called for the use of standardized tests (especially the SAT, which he was instrumental in promoting) to guide students fairly and rationally toward the educational and career paths that best suited them. That is to say, like most educational leaders since the Progressive era, he was a proponent of tracking, or curriculum differentiation, as the key to educating all members of a heterogeneous society. By 1960, Conant was perhaps the nation's most influential commentator on education, yet he soon found himself embroiled in the emerging controversy over race, education, and unequal achievement.

Conant's sense of urgency about public education had not previously included a focus on racial issues, but this changed when he visited a handful of big-city school systems, as part of a major study on American secondary education for the Carnegie Corporation. In *Slums and Suburbs* (1961), the second of three influential reports to come out of the Carnegie study, Conant sounded an alarm over high dropout and unemployment rates among young black men in the cities. These undereducated, unemployed teenagers were akin to "social dynamite," he said. Their mounting frustration was a weakness in a free society, exploitable by communists. But if Conant's report had the ring of news, its remedies were familiar. Essentially, Conant proposed curriculum differentiation on a metropolitan scale. Suburban schools would do the work of college preparation, especially for the gifted students who, in a Cold War context, constituted a vital national resource. Urban schools, meanwhile, should emphasize vocational education—an old idea, though with two new twists, as Conant presented it: the schools had to do a better job of coordinating with social agencies and employment offices to help graduates and dropouts actually find jobs, and racial discrimination among labor unions and employers had to be ended.[34]

Conant went out of his way to emphasize his liberal credentials. Describing himself in *Slums and Suburbs* as a "one-hundred-percent New Englander" with abolitionist forbears, he presented his call for more spending on urban education and his rejection of racial discrimination by employers and unions as part of a long, good fight against slavery and its aftereffects. White liberals tended to agree, hailing his book as a sobering call to arms.[35]

But Conant stepped on a political landmine when he declared integrationists to be "on the wrong track" and urged northern cities to forget about busing experiments and work instead to improve the schools black children already attended.[36] Civil rights leaders were outraged. At public forums in Philadelphia and elsewhere, Kenneth Clark took Conant to task not only for his opposition to desegregation but, equally important, for his desire to place urban and suburban students in separate curricular tracks, with differentiated expectations: vocational education for the former, college prep for the latter. That approach was "arrant nonsense," Clark said in a 1963 speech at a Baltimore teachers college; urban students did not do as well as suburban students mainly because their schools and teachers did not expect them to do as well, and liberals only made matters worse by labeling urban students as "culturally deprived." For Clark, that label was not an alternative to racism but a subtle form of it, a fancy way to dismiss children and shirk responsibility for educating them. Commentators like Conant laid the true social dynamite, he argued, by stigmatizing black students and applying to them a separate set of expectations. Instead, Clark urged, "let us approach these children in terms of educational requirements, standards, and demands, as if they were human beings and not lepers. Let us not teach these children as if they were different."[37]

Clark stepped up his critique of the schools in the context of a surging civil rights movement that contradicted the notion of cultural weakness and deficiency among blacks. In 1963, millions had attended the March on Washington, capping several years of sit-ins, freedom rides, and other bold, highly publicized acts of civil disobedience. Less famously, but with no less impact on urban education in the North, parents and activists staged school boycotts and other protests in New York City, Cleveland, and other big cities during the 1963–64 school year, in hopes of desegregating those school systems. (Clark remained committed to this cause.)[38]

The boycotts did not succeed in desegregating northern schools, but these and other events had done much to discredit the idea that low achievement was a result of cultural deprivation. In February 1964, for instance, President Johnson's commissioner of education, Francis Keppel, issued a highly public rejection of some of the basic assumptions that had guided liberals like him in the postwar period. Speaking to 25,000 attendees of the annual meeting of the American Association of School Administrators (AASA), Keppel stated, "For years, we have talked of the disinterest and apathy of slum parents. We have argued that we can't teach their children because they are not interested in education and because their parents have not taught them to be interested. But now, out of the civil rights movement," said Keppel, "we are learning differently. We are learning that many of these parents are interested and have finally found a way to express their interest . . . In spite of all the present difficulties, I say, thank God for the civil rights movement." In a statement that might as well have been directed at the Catto Disciplinary School, with its atmosphere of neglect and low expectations, Keppel urged the nation's educators to discard "a cluster of misunderstandings and misbegotten myths" about poor children, including the belief that "the best we can do is send them along to the 'dumping ground' that so many of our vocational training schools have been made."[39]

The nation's top education official had lent his voice to the idea that the schools, rather than the students, needed adjustment. Urban schools, said Keppel, had to do better at providing disadvantaged students with the best teachers, the least crowded classrooms, and the best educational opportunities. Still, explanations of underachievement continued to be a divisive issue at the national and local levels. Differences of opinion over whether to blame urban schools for low achievement came through in a sharp exchange between Kenneth Clark and the sociologist Nathan Glazer at a 1964 *Commentary* magazine roundtable on "Liberalism and the Negro." Clark rose from the audience to second the sentiments of panelist James Baldwin, declaring that the liberalism he had embraced as a younger man was now an "insidious type of affliction" because it blamed its failures on African American victims. As usual, urban schools were central to Clark's analysis: in Harlem they were bad and getting worse, he said, and the self-described liberals who ran the system were to blame. Glazer, like Clark, was moving away from the liberalism he formerly had embraced, but toward the right rather than the left. He agreed that the schools had declined—but was it the fault of white liberals? "Of course not," Glazer said, citing a "hundred other reasons: changes in the student body, the difficulty the Board of Education has in dealing with its own Board of Examiners, its own bureaucracy, and so on down the line."[40] Glazer doubted the ability of government policy to transform the schools and other American institutions—a stance for which critics to his left would soon dub him a "neoconservative."

In Philadelphia, perhaps the most revealing clash over low-performing urban schools came in response to a magazine article. The controversy erupted in January 1964, when *Greater Philadelphia*, a monthly magazine aimed at the business community, ran a sensational exposé, entitled "Crisis in the Classroom," on conditions in one of the city's predominantly black school districts.[41] The article and the angry rebuttals that it sparked offer a vivid picture of the context in which Marcus Foster took charge at the Catto School, and as such, it is worth recounting the exchange in some detail.

The writer of "Crisis in the Classroom," a young reporter named Gaeton Fonzi, had become interested in the problems of the Philadelphia schools through his wife, who was preparing to become a teacher. Fonzi and his editors at *Greater Philadelphia* apparently thought of themselves as liberals, though Fonzi claimed they were less motivated by ideology than by a desire to do the kind of muckraking stories they felt were missing in the local newspapers. In the fall of 1963, before riots had turned the problems of the inner cities into a national obsession, the day-to-day realities of urban schools were still an underreported story. Fonzi's wife had given him the idea to publicize and question the district's heavy use of unqualified substitutes as regular classroom teachers. To do so, he got himself hired, in spite of his utter lack of experience, as a per-diem substitute teacher. He wrote "Crisis in the Classroom" based on six days of subbing and some interviews with teachers and administrators.[42]

As planned, Fonzi cited unqualified, indifferent teachers as one of the system's main problems. However, his article mainly emphasized what was wrong with the children themselves—namely, that most of them were black and poor. According to Fonzi, Philadelphia's main problem was that it had "a Negro system" and, more important, "a ghetto system"; the schools mainly served an "economically deprived, socially suppressed class of adolescent."

In the end it did not matter who taught such students, because, he claimed, "you can't make them learn." To support this stark conclusion, Fonzi cited examples of what he and other teachers and administrators had witnessed in the schools: a classroom where every male student revealed a knife; a high school cafeteria with wire grilles on the fourth-floor windows because students had been known to throw chairs out of them; teachers who positioned themselves at regular intervals, like a "riot squad," in the hall between classes. He also offered a sensational account of his experiences tagging along with Estelle Price, an attendance officer, on her visits to the homes of truant cases. At one garbage-strewn apartment, a handful of children blasted a record player; they thought their mother was around the corner fetching coal, though the seven-year-old could not find her. At another house, an intoxicated man said he had sent his son to buy a coat instead of to school. At a third stop, Fonzi and Price left a note for a mother who was still asleep because her job as a hospital janitor had kept her out until one o'clock in the morning. Seeing these scenes filled Fonzi with a sense of futility about the Philadelphia schools. It seemed "absurd" to tell children from these kinds of homes that they had to learn algebra or proper sentence structure, when, in fact, their main concern was to scrape together enough money for lunch.[43]

Of course, educators such as Marcus Foster were trying to show that such efforts were anything but "absurd." Fonzi did not encounter Foster, but he profiled someone very much like him: James Young, a graying, African American educator in his ninth year as principal of the Roberts Vaux Junior High School in North Philadelphia. Crowded and segregated, Vaux served 2,300 students in a building meant to accommodate 1,700. Less than 1 percent of the student body—perhaps no more than ten children—was white. Like Foster, Young believed that low aspirations were a major roadblock to academic success for poor, black students and that urban educators needed to help those students raise their sights. To put this belief into practice when he arrived at Vaux in 1955, Young promoted what would come to be called "black pride" and "multiculturalism." He put replicas of African art and tribal masks on the wall so his students would learn to appreciate the beauty of their heritage. Next to the art he hung framed portraits of boys and girls who had accomplished something notable. Like Foster, he made a point of leaving his office and roaming the halls, patting students on the head and complimenting them on their "rich mahogany color." Fonzi observed that they clamored after him "as they would a movie star."[44]

James Young believed that all of these positive experiences, by transforming a child's basic attitude about himself and his school, would lead to academic improvement, too. Fonzi was not impressed, however, and his disparagement of Young's programs and others like it posed a challenge to the educational strategies that underlay Marcus Foster's career and, in a larger sense, liberalism's response to the urban crisis. Fonzi charged Young with "catering to the inherent abilities and standards of the children"—that is, dumbing-down the curriculum. He agreed that Vaux's programs made for "a happy school, a proud school," as Young had described it, but he insisted that "it [wa]sn't education" so much as an attempt to salvage some "niggling attainments" from a hopeless situation. And the same went for the rest of the district's motivational programs (which would include the Great Cities program Foster had helped create). Even if those efforts could claim success among a small number of schools and students, he wrote, they were trivial within the bigger picture, like "diamonds in a pile of manure: They don't affect the smell." For Fonzi, the smell was coming from the community itself, and no matter what the schools tried to do, they could not begin to counteract the "brutal" lessons their students were learning at home and in the streets, "nineteen hours of every day." The conclusion of the article reiterated this point with an idealistic-sounding twist: pointing fingers at the schools masked the fact that the education crisis was part of a deeper problem that cried out for more substantial social changes. "What can the schools accomplish," Fonzi asked, "when society itself condemns the bulk of this population to deprivation and second-class citizenship? The ghetto walls must come down."[45]

Committed educators and civil rights leaders were not impressed by Fonzi's final-paragraph indictment of the larger society; by the time they got that far, if they got that far, many were enraged at a piece that they felt shifted blame for the urban education crisis from the school system and the larger society to the children themselves. Marcus Foster's reaction to the article is unknown, but he probably agreed with dozens of like-minded colleagues, including some of his closest mentors, who sent angry rebuttals to *Greater Philadelphia* and the *Philadelphia Tribune,* the city's leading black newspaper. Marion Steet, president of the Philadelphia Teachers Association, the NEA local to which Foster belonged, admitted that incidents like those in the article occurred every day, and that only a "liar or a fool" would deny it. But like many educators, she charged Fonzi with making "unjust generalizations." In particular, she emphasized, it was wrong to blame the children for the problems Fonzi had witnessed. "If the finger of blame is to be pointed," she charged, "let it be pointed in many directions."[46]

For Steet, many of those directions pointed out the front door of the schools, at the larger society. In particular, she cited public apathy; private and parochial school parents who had abandoned public education; outside critics like Fonzi who vehemently attacked the schools without offering constructive solutions; and "those who gain so much from this city in profit and prestige" (presumably the business readership of *Greater Philadelphia*) while investing so little in its children and therefore its future. Educating those children was not cheap; it would take "money and vision and love and dedication and more money," she wrote, but in her most startling criticism, Steet wondered whether Fonzi had intended for his audience to "wash its hands of the Philadelphia Public Schools and to do so with a clear conscience."[47] The black administrators Robert Poindexter and Ruth Wright Hayre, both of whom were mentors to Marcus Foster within the school system, did not wonder whether the magazine had an ulterior motive; they were certain of it. Poindexter complained that "deviate behavior was played up to the hilt" in order to "embarrass all Negro citizens" during their struggle for integration and to derail public support for school bond issues. Superintendent Allen Wetter joined the chorus, complaining that the *Greater Philadelphia* article seemed "to present deliberately a false picture calculated to foment hatred and misunderstanding."[48]

In one sense, the *Greater Philadelphia* controversy united educators and black activists—everyone from longtime civil rights activist Floyd Logan to the superintendent himself—against an outside critic who made the schools and the students look bad. But the incident cut a different way, too, as the response of Ruth Hayre indicated. Hayre objected to the school system's being "relieved of all responsibility for the education of these children who are summed up as a 'waste.'"[49] She believed Fonzi gave voice to racism and low expectations that existed *within* the district and its low-performing schools. Echoing this sentiment, Marion Steet also pointed the "finger of blame" at Board of Education members who were "out of touch" and "burned-out educators who were complicit in the lowering of standards."[50]

In the end, the *Greater Philadelphia* controversy highlighted the range of problems faced by low-achieving schools, and, at the same time, the growing difficulty of discussing that mix of problems in its full complexity. Few observers denied the challenges posed by disadvantaged students; educators like Ruth Wright Hayre and Marcus Foster had long been concerned with the negative impact of racial segregation and poverty on their students' preparation for academic success. However, the *Greater Philadelphia* story highlighted the difference between acknowledging such factors and dwelling on them to the point of giving up in defeat. Fonzi later insisted that there was "no element of racism at all" in his perspective—just a journalistic commitment to reporting what he found, however unpalatable.[51] But whatever his intentions, when he wrote that "you can't make them learn," and that the schools were being "forced to deal with" an "overwhelming enormity of human waste," he understandably provoked a strong reaction from those who had dedicated their lives to African American education. For black educators such as Hayre (and, presumably, Foster), Fonzi's article illustrated Kenneth Clark's claim that cultural deprivation was becoming an excuse for inaction rather than a challenge to address. By contrast, these educators insisted that schools could help children transcend the disadvantages of racism and poverty, and, unlike Fonzi (who later admitted that his own ineptitude had shaped his pessimistic views), they applied their experience and skill to the creation of such schools. In the wake of an event like the *Greater Philadelphia* story, these educators were all the more likely to insist that the schools educate the students, with no excuses; indeed, they increasingly argued that excuses, in the form of low expectations, were a *cause* of low achievement. For a growing number of activists and educators, the backgrounds and characteristics of the students were increasingly off the table, and the failings of the schools themselves took center stage.

The Catto Comprehensive Treatment Program

Foster's work at the Catto School was in the spirit of Kenneth Clark and other leaders and activists who increasingly held the schools responsible for student failure. The new principal insisted that teachers raise their expectations of students, because, as he later wrote, "everyone knows that if teachers go into a school expecting youngsters to act like hoodlums and do sloppy work or no work at all, they will begin to produce just that behavior." Foster also intended to "help the faculty move from a punitive, vindictive attitude . . . to a more humane approach." Along those lines, one of the first things he did was distribute copies of a new school board ruling against corporal punishment, including pushing, grasping, and striking, and then collect the paddles and other instruments teachers used for this purpose. "You would have thought someone had told the teachers they would have to teach with one hand tied behind their backs," he wrote. "'What are we going to do now?' they asked." Foster's answer was, "Constructive School Discipline." It sounded fancy, but it was really a simple idea: Catto's troublemakers would behave, even learn to enjoy school, if the school would actually educate them.[52]

But what did this mean in practice? It was one thing to denounce corporal punishment and take away a teacher's paddle—but what would take its place? How to go about raising expectations of teenagers with established records of failure and delinquency? How to transform such a low-performing school? Improving the curriculum, in terms of academic as well as vocational subjects, was part of Foster's answer. But the transformation of a dysfunctional school like Catto was not simply a matter of imposing a new curriculum and new standards. If curricular change were to work, Foster would need to work on relationships, not only within the school, but between the school and its parents and surrounding community. Not only was it unhelpful to point the "finger of blame" in one direction only; in the adversarial atmosphere of the Catto School, it did not help to point fingers of blame at all. Instead, as Foster showed, it was helpful to try to understand the problem in all of its messiness and complexity—including school as well as non-school factors—and to involve all members of the school community in the development of solutions. Following this overall approach, Foster translated the critique of low expectations in urban schools into successful leadership and practice at one particular school.

Step one was to start a genuine dialogue about the big issues: Catto's philosophy, its curriculum, its approach to discipline. Foster joked that he could not change teacher attitudes and expectations "simply by printing memos and telling everybody to 'Please be loving and please have high expectations'"— so he instituted weekly staff meetings (twice the normal frequency) to talk it out. The exchanges were "sometimes abrasive," he recalled. But Catto was the place where Foster's skill at conflict resolution—a signature of his career— first came to the fore. His recounting of the early staff meetings reveals key aspects of his leadership style in the making. Foster welcomed, even demanded, input and participation from all parties: "The staff had to discover and face the problems themselves," he wrote, "with a minimum of help from me." And when that process led to dissenting opinions, he made a point of not stifling them. "These men and women had a world view and were expert with their familiar techniques," he wrote of the Catto staff. Rather than insisting that the teachers abandon those ways, which he believed would threaten them and make them even more resistant to change, he tried to create a climate "where disagreements could be aired and positions and assumptions challenged" in the process of striving for a consensus.[53] Former social studies teacher Dean

Cummings corroborates Foster's account, saying, "He wasn't always bossy. He would ask, 'What do you think?' He was always open to suggestions."[54]

Reaching a new consensus was not easy; as Foster recalled, habits were "stronger than rational arguments." But by the end of the first series of meetings, a new sense of teamwork had begun to emerge, and the staff had begun to take greater responsibility for the quality of education at the school. Together, they produced a four-page checklist for evaluating and improving their own performance. The list, which contained more than eighty items, revealed a new spirit of responsiveness; for instance, it asked whether the teacher possessed "desirable personal and social qualities" such as "fairness," "understanding of children," "tactfulness and courtesy," and "professional standards"; and whether he or she established control through "compulsion (you must or else)" or "self-control growing out of interesting purposeful activity." Together, Foster noted, the staff began "to look at some of the old techniques and ask which were pedagogically unsound."[55]

Teachers' attitudes began to shift not only because Foster sought their input; the principal was also careful not to make "low expectations" the only problem. There were other factors that contributed to low achievement, including aspects of the students' experiences at home, in their communities, and in previous schools. Foster did not ignore these factors or the difficulties they posed for his teachers. He noted that many inner-city children hit a "plateau of nonachievement" as early as the third grade (with their normal progress until that time confirming for some critics that the problem was with the educators, not the students); and that, by junior or senior high school, such students often had totally rejected the educational process. As Kenneth Clark said, "they hate teachers, they hate schools, they hate anything that seems to impose upon them this denigration."[56] Attitudes like those presented a tough challenge for any teacher, no matter how fair minded or well meaning.

Foster believed that in many cases the boys' home lives compounded the cycle of failure. Granted, this was not always the case in urban education; as Foster noted, some inner-city parents pressured teachers and schools to hold high expectations of their children, while others with less political savvy or persistence still "priz[ed] education as a way out of the ghetto." But for Catto students, and many others in the Philadelphia schools, this was not the norm. Most of Foster's students came from broken homes where the mother or even an aunt or a grandmother was the dominant figure—though the absent father sometimes was called upon to visit and dish out "harsh and excessive" corporal punishment. Raised by a single mother himself, Foster nonetheless worried about the educational impact of such homes, which, unlike the one in which he grew up, were often crowded, noisy, and "totally lacking in facilities conducive to good study habits." Worse, many of these homes tended to have an anti-intellectual atmosphere, with "little enthusiasm for learning." Foster believed that the "cross-generation poor," as he described the most down-and-out group of city residents, tended to be apathetic about schooling because they did not perceive its relevance to their daily struggle for survival.[57]

Here Foster laid out the kinds of problems that many liberals of his day had defined as cultural deprivation or a culture of poverty. Kenneth Clark had rejected that terminology, believing it had become an excuse for lowering expectations of urban children—and as we have seen, low expectations were indeed a problem. Still, as more recent debates about special education have demonstrated in an especially vivid way, educators and families face trade-offs when deciding how and whether to label the special needs that some students present at school. Labels can be stigmatizing and lead to segregation and differential expectations; yet they can also facilitate the provision of special attention and services.[58] Unlike Clark, Marcus Foster continued to speak of "cultural deprivation" among his students, but at Catto, as at Dunbar, that label did not become an excuse, in the way Clark abhorred. Instead, like currently touted initiatives such as the Knowledge is Power Program (KIPP schools) and the Harlem Children's Zone, the Catto program seems to have benefited from discussing and explicitly addressing aspects of students' backgrounds (including the negative effects of prior educational experiences) that posed a problem for school achievement.[59]

To this end, Foster put together a second round of staff meetings on "The 'Culturally-Deprived': Their Special Problems," which emphasized, among other themes, that delinquent behavior and negative attitudes toward school were defense mechanisms rooted in frustration and insecurity (and thus curable, if treated with patience and understanding). Foster believed that the seminars not only led his teachers to approach student misbehavior in a more thoughtful and productive manner, but that the experience promoted a new sense of professionalism. Faculty members gathered resources and led discussions without much intervention from their principal. Some who had felt stigmatized at district-wide meetings because of their Catto affiliation now held their heads higher because, as Foster wrote, they began to see their school as "a situation requiring the most professional of teachers, people who really knew their child psychology."[60]

Foster's comment on the importance of child psychology hinted at his own dissatisfaction with cultural deprivation arguments and other social explanations for delinquency and academic failure: they could not explain individual differences within the same urban environment. Why did some children become dropouts or disciplinary cases while others applied themselves to school? For Foster, the answer lay partly at the level of individual psychology. As he put it, drawing on his own experience and on many of the antidelinquency studies he reviewed for his dissertation, "the conditions under which a person lives are not as important as his attitude toward those conditions." Specifically, he suggested, the problem was one of "self-concept." Studies had shown that children with strong self-concepts were, in Foster's words, less likely to "succumb to deviant behavior even though they live[d] in areas with a high delinquency rate." By the same token, youths who were not "ego secure" not only found it difficult to transcend obstacles to their success; they sometimes were so plagued by segregation-induced feelings of hostility, hate, and alienation that they failed to take advantage of the educational opportunities that were available to them.[61]

To insist on personal rather than social causes of delinquency was increasingly controversial; critics who regarded the cultural deprivation label as a pernicious way to denigrate the victims of a flawed system were even less inclined to emphasize the psychological deficiencies of those individuals. Still, educators and social workers had long been among the main proponents of a clinical, psychological approach to delinquency, and Foster was no exception, even as times were changing. He saw no use to a "sterile argument" over whether Cloward's emphasis on the environmental causes of delinquency was more valid than Erik Erikson's work on personality disorder; as an educator who confronted a messy mix of social patterns and individual idiosyncrasies on a daily basis, he found both to be useful.

For boys with especially unusual or difficult problems, for example, Foster convened a Catto Case Conference Committee (CCCC) consisting of himself, the school counselors, the district's attendance supervisors, and, as necessary, outside psychiatrists, psychologists, social workers, and probation officers. The CCCC mainly dealt with severe truancy cases (one student even made the police department's missing persons list), but the teachers and counselors also referred cases like "#22," a fifteen-year-old with a history of violent outbursts; and "#23," a "very frightened" ten-year-old who had been charged with burglary. At its meetings, the counselors presented such cases and recommended courses of action both at the school and beyond: boxing lessons, new glasses, referrals to the school's reading and speech specialists, interventions with parents, medication, placement in outside organizations like the George Junior Republic boys club, and further psychiatric evaluation, among others.[62] The CCCC was a version of "child guidance," an approach that drew criticism, then and since, for allegedly reducing delinquency from a social problem to an individual, psychological one.[63] Whatever its limitations, though, child guidance was a decidedly proactive alternative to what Catto had been doing before—namely, writing off its truants and thereby increasing the likelihood that their fates would be decided by the police and the criminal justice system rather than the schools. As Foster pointed out, the school's three counselors previously had busied themselves with paperwork and placed little emphasis on the kind of "re-education and therapy"—that is, child guidance—that troubled middle-class children often received.[64]

In sum, Foster traced his students' delinquency and low achievement to many sources—educationally bankrupt schools, blighted neighborhood environments, troubled families, individual psychological problems—and he set out to address as many of these interrelated causes as possible. At Catto, as at Dunbar, the language of "self-concept" and "cultural deprivation" was less important than the tone and emphasis of the conversations that developed around these concepts—conversations that, above all, were focused on the needs of students and the creation of a more positive school culture. Foster cited studies on the importance of teachers' being role models for children with low self-esteem. He wanted his own teachers to play that role. Like the experimental programs in those studies, he wanted to show that a good school, with a "favorable emotional climate," could counteract the sense of "powerlessness" that many children picked up at home, in the streets, and—all too often—in the schools themselves.[65] And it was not just teachers and administrators who were to create that "total environment"; as at Dunbar, custodians and cafeteria workers had roles to play, too. In one instance, a young boy had watched his father kill his mother, and "nobody could reach him," Foster recalled, except the head cook, who befriended the boy and guided him back to a regular school. To encourage these kinds of interventions, Foster met regularly with non-teaching staff members to get their input on student affairs.[66]

Also as at Dunbar, extracurricular activities played an important role in changing the culture of the school. It was a radical departure for Catto to hold any kind of schoolwide event; before Foster's arrival, large gatherings of students had been considered an invitation to gang fighting. Now, a student assembly committee coordinated exhibits of student work in each department. Faculty basketball and volleyball games gave the boys "a chance to knock teachers around, legitimately." Student musical groups performed for assemblies of their peers, their parents, and other visitors. Perhaps the most unusual event was a fashion show. Parents and students came in their finest attire. Foster did not say where he found the models, but he happily noted that some of his "biggest rogues" turned out to be his most earnest helpers. Told he "must be losing [his] mind" for trying such a thing at an all-male school, Foster begged to differ: in terms of what it contributed to a new sense of pride in school and self, he said, the fashion show was "one of the most successful things we did."[67]

Foster's most immediate task at Catto was to transform the adversarial climate of the school. However, this was not a substitute for curricular change. In fact, the two priorities could not really be separated. The new principal believed that bad behavior reflected a bad educational program, and a revamped curriculum was high on his agenda. The program that he and his staff created—the Catto Comprehensive Treatment Program (CCTP)—was an academic as well as affective enterprise.

The fact that Catto was a disciplinary school put limits on the kinds of curricular changes Foster and his faculty could make; years of failure and neglect had left the students with substantial academic deficits and little time to catch up. For the older ones, especially, a year or so at Catto often marked the end of the road, educationally. The school's curriculum previously had been geared toward vocational education rather than academics partly because of these realities. Courses in shoe repair, tailoring, restaurant practice, gas station service, wood shop, and auto repair were supposed to steer students toward a constructive role in society.

Foster did not fundamentally alter Catto's vocational program—the course offerings mostly stayed the same—but he did set out to make it more relevant to the "real world of work." The key figure in this change was a new hire, the "work coordinator," who had three main tasks: to help students find part-time jobs with local merchants and manufacturers; to make sure the school's vocational courses reinforced these hands-on work experiences; and to help students keep their jobs. The coordinator's efforts were reinforced, in turn, by the Pre-Vocational Evaluation Program (PEP), a new career-planning initiative co-sponsored by the Bureau of Vocational Rehabilitation and the Philadelphia Vocational Institute. The PEP conducted physical, psychological, and vocational evaluations of Catto students and allowed them to spend part of the day at other schools according to their special aptitudes and interests.[68]

Foster maintained Catto's vocational emphasis to help ensure that no student left the school without future prospects. In this sense his program echoed James Conant's vision: more effective coordination between urban high schools and employers. Yet Foster and his staff also moved to set up a "fully respectable academic program." The principal recalled that "some people thought this was crazy at a disciplinary school"—they assumed the students were incapable of handling academic coursework—"but the fact was we had bright students who needed the challenge." Those students also needed the academic skills: Foster noted (and subsequent scholarship confirmed) that automation had eliminated many entry-level jobs and that undereducated youths consequently found themselves "unable to gain access to the portals of gainful employment that provide a path out of the slum." Ideally, as Foster saw it, Catto would be just the first step in a growth process that included returning to regular schools and someday getting "*entry* jobs that would provide *vertical* mobility."[69] In this sense, in the limited domain of a lone disciplinary school, Foster recognized and responded to the forces of deindustrialization in the postwar city and challenged the long-standing tendency—shared by Conant and most others in American education—to track disadvantaged urban students into nonacademic courses of study.

The Catto staff took steps to improve the school's social studies, math, and language arts courses, but the main thrust came in the last area. Foster was passionate about adding a remedial reading program to the school; as he noted, "every study that deals with pre-delinquent children shows that severe reading retardation is central to their failure in school." So the new principal adapted his Dunbar approach to the Catto situation. He released teachers for a crash course on the kinds of language immersion techniques he had used with the younger children. He urged the staff to build the students' confidence by starting from "where they were" (he believed it was fruitless to give ninth-grade level textbooks to students who were reading at a third-grade level)—and, at the same time, to guide them to higher levels. He promoted curricular change as part of a larger transformation of academic expectations at the school: "A lot of things were happening," he wrote, "but it all boiled down to this: the faculty began to believe in itself. They began to believe in the students. And the students began to believe."[70]

Foster furthered his focus on literacy by recruiting University of Pennsylvania students to do five-week stints as language arts tutors, and this was an example of a third key aspect of his work at Catto, in addition to his revamping of the school's culture and its curriculum: his emphasis on school-community relations. As at Dunbar, Foster reached beyond the school to solve the school's problems. He expected teachers and administrators to be as responsive to parents and neighborhood businesspeople as they were to the students. At the same time, he pushed parents and businesspeople to provide greater support for the school's programs.

Catto was an unusually difficult case in the area of school-community relations. The staff had little or no contact with neighborhood residents and business owners, whom they viewed as hostile. And with good reason: Foster noted that the neighbors and merchants despised the school, seeing its students as a menacing presence and its teachers as uncaring. Most store owners, fearing vandalism and shoplifting, closed their shops from dismissal time until the boys left the neighborhood. As for parents, what few encounters they had with the school usually resulted from suspensions and other negative incidents. Many felt guilty and embarrassed about their association with the school. "You couldn't start a Home and School Association," Foster recalled, "because if you did it was a tacit admission on the part of parents that they had a youngster in trouble."[71]

Foster began to build better relationships with parents from the day he met them in the intake interview. Instead of emphasizing rules and making threats, the first meeting was used to "learn as much as possible about the boy, the parents, the community, the home, and the perception of the family regarding the reason for the assignment. Considerable time was spent in listening." The parents then toured the building, to "dispel the notions that no learning was taking place and that the facilities were substandard," and the boy was placed in an orientation class to further assess him and settle on an appropriate program. Foster had two related goals for the new intake process: to show parents that the staff cared about their child's development, and to give them a way to participate in the school without feeling stigmatized. To accomplish the latter, he took a five-dollar contribution and signed them up for a new organization called Friends of Catto.[72]

Foster described Friends of Catto as a way to "mobilize the total resources of community"—in other words, to "scrounge," as Bob Blackburn described his former colleague's characteristic response to a shortage of resources.[73] The organization included businessmen, ministers, and other community leaders in addition to parents. Its chairman and one of its key organizers, Edward Dolbey, was the head of a medical supply company in the neighborhood. Under Dolbey, Friends of Catto used the mailing lists of social service agencies to solicit classroom materials, clothing, money, and other resources. Meanwhile, Foster went to the Kiwanis, Optimist, Rotary, and other service clubs and urged them to support the school. The scrounging paid off. Friends of Catto brought in audiovisual supplies for the art shop, funds for a library and language arts lab, and a lift and simulated gas pumps for the auto shop, among many other contributions. The service clubs sponsored school activities and donated tickets to Penn football games, plays, and other events. A local foundation helped the school extend its psychological and counseling services (the Catto Case Conference Committee was limited by a lack of available professionals) by funding the use of psychologists for group therapy sessions. Ten students received counseling while one Catto staff member watched and learned how to run his or her own group.[74]

Foster and the Friends of Catto got the community to do more for the school because they showed that the school was doing more for the community. Partly this was a matter of good public relations. Foster assigned a school-community liaison (he did not say whether she was paid) to be an "ear to the community." As the school-community coordinator reported complaints from the neighbors about student conduct, the school took immediate steps to respond. Foster also got the staff to go door-to-door in the community, soliciting input and offering to enlist the school's vocational shops in helpful tasks. Catto began to receive letters of appreciation for its new responsiveness and compliments on the students' improved behavior. The school's image was changing.[75]

Foster also got parents involved in Catto by giving them access to some of the vocational courses. In the Evening Community Extension Center, as the night school was called, parents could take many of the same classes, from the same teachers, as their children did by day, including "Shoe Service and Leathercraft"; "Gymnastics"; and "Improving Reading, Writing, and Arithmetic Skills." Foster hoped the experience would build enthusiasm and support for the school by showing that "the teachers were skilled in their fields and not primarily providing custodial care."[76]

Foster's emphasis on school community relations—indeed, his overall approach in the Catto Comprehensive Treatment Program—was echoed in subsequent scholarship on effective urban schools. According to one prominent recent study, for example, the key to success in urban schooling is to be found in a combination of five essential "supports" or ingredients: strong leadership from principals who are focused on instruction and "inclusive of others"; teachers who believe in change and participate in professional development and collaborative work; a learning climate that is safe and stimulating for all students; the forging of connections with parents and the community; and strong instructional guidance and materials.[77] While some of the language is new, these are basically the same ingredients that Marcus Foster tried to bring to the Catto School. His program attempted to change the culture of the school, including teacher expectations of students, as well as the curriculum and the community and parental supports that would be necessary if students were going to fulfill those expectations.

What kind of impact did the program have on the students? Did they perform differently than before? Evidence suggests they did, in modest but notable ways. Foster himself conducted the most detailed analysis of the program in the doctoral dissertation that he wrote in the late 1960s for the University of Pennsylvania. Foster's study tried to quantify the impact of the CCTP on behavior, as opposed to academic performance, though it did include a thorough description of all aspects of the program. In particular, he used an "index of delinquency" that was modeled on the work of one of his thesis advisers, the criminologist Marvin Wolfgang, to compare the frequency and severity of delinquent acts in an experimental group that participated in the CCTP and a control group that went through the "traditional" program before his arrival. Using this Sellin-Wolfgang index, he weighted and tracked three kinds of offenses: those that caused bodily harm; those that damaged property; and a group of "other" offenses, including "truancy, runaway, malicious mischief, trespassing, curfew violations, carrying concealed deadly weapons, intoxication, and other minor offenses such as corner lounging." Foster compared the control and experimental groups at three stages: before arrival at Catto, during enrollment, and after departure. He hypothesized that the experimental group, after leaving Catto, would commit fewer and less serious offenses in each of these three categories, and he was right four out of six times. The trend also moved in the expected direction in the two other cases. Significantly, the expected improvement came even though the CCTP inherited a more difficult group of students than the traditional program by almost every measure cited in the study. On average, Foster's students had lower IQ scores (mean of 68 versus 75); they were more likely to come from a corrective institution or some other non-regular school setting; they were older, and therefore had problems Foster believed to be more deeply ingrained; they were less likely to come from two-parent households (39 versus 50 percent); they had committed more body offenses (19 versus 11 percent), more acts of property damage (41 versus 27 percent), and a greater number of "other offenses" (51 versus 39 percent); and they were more likely to have been arrested (38 versus 20 percent).[78]

Foster hoped his write-up would help others duplicate his positive results, though it did leave some important unanswered questions. The study revealed, for example, that both the control and experimental groups had much higher arrest rates while enrolled at Catto (over 60 percent for each) than either before or after. And the same steep increase and subsequent drop occurred in all three categories of delinquent acts. Did these data show that disciplinary schools were simply a bad idea—that the mere fact of concentrating troubled students made them more likely to commit delinquent acts, no matter what kind of school program they experienced? Looked at differently, did the numbers indicate that most of these students were prone to act out at a certain age (junior high school, on average) before growing out of it? Foster himself hinted at that possibility, noting that "many changes may occur in the control group because of matura-tion and other factors unrelated to the program." Finally, Foster's study only addressed the behavioral impact of the CCTP; would standardized test scores have revealed academic benefits?[79]

Despite such unanswered questions, though, other evidence seemed to support the idea that Foster's leadership made a significant impact on stu-dents at Catto. Attendance rose from 46 to 68 percent after one year. Un-excused absences remained disturbingly high but went down significantly, from ninety-eight to seventy-five per year. Neighborhood merchants stopped closing their shops at dismissal time and even began hiring the school's stu-dents. And anecdotal evidence pointed toward academic as well as behavioral improvement. Foster recalled, for example, that some children wanted to stay at the school, and others wanted to come back after they had left, because of the academic program. Once while meeting with a writer who was doing an article on changes at Catto, a former student walked into the office and said he wanted to return to the school. Foster told the boy he had better opportu-nities—a more comprehensive curriculum—in a regular school, whereupon the writer interjected that he probably wanted to come back for the shop pro-grams. "To tell you the truth," the student replied, "I wasn't in shop. I was in the academic program."[80]

Parents saw their children making academic and social progress, too; Fos-ter recounted the time a mother called to say her son "did something today he's never done before." Ready for the worst, he relaxed when she proudly told him the boy had read a newspaper for the first time. At least some parents had such a positive view of the Catto School that they tried to enroll their non-delinquent sons. This presented a problem, Foster joked in a speech, because the student had to get in trouble first. One woman told Foster she wanted him to "handle" her eight-year-old "because you straightened my older boy out." Foster warned that "we've got big kids eighteen years old here," but she went to the superintendent and got the school to take the boy anyway, because, Foster said, "she wanted him to be part of this environment." Catto was no longer a "cesspool of the system."[81]

In all, teachers, parents, school officials, church groups, youth-serving and civic organizations, and local citizens commented on the apparent benefits of the CCTP.[82] Foster's quantitative analysis, his anecdotal evidence of student growth, and the testimony of colleagues and the community left no doubt that Marcus Foster left the O. V. Catto Disciplinary School a much better school than he found it.

An Educational War on Poverty

Foster's programs at Catto held promise as school reforms; they showed how leadership from the principal's office could help turn a demoralized school into a more positive force in the lives of troubled teenagers. Foster never claimed that these programs offered a solution for urban poverty itself. Indeed, he recognized limits to the social impact of the schools on children, noting that it was "difficult to offset the combined influence of the home, community, and the peer group during out-of-school hours. A significant level of norm-violating behavior persisted in spite of improvements" made by the CCTP.[83] And, to the extent that Foster tried to counteract those negative home and community influences, he did so as an educator rather than as a social reformer. Catto's night school may have served as a form of community organization, for example, but for Foster, this function was a means to an end. First and foremost, the night school gave him a new batch of Friends of Catto members and better mutual understanding between teachers and parents.

Still, for the second time, Foster's work as an urban school principal effectively made him part of the nation's educational war on poverty. Philadelphia's antipoverty agency—that is, the entity to which the federal Office of Economic Opportunity (OEO) distributed funding under the Economic Opportunity Act of 1964—was initially the Philadelphia Council for Community Advancement (PCCA). Launched in 1962 with grants from the Ford Foundation and the President's Committee on Juvenile Delinquency (PCJD), the PCCA had grown out of the same conversations and ideas that shaped the school district's (and Marcus Foster's) participation in the Great Cities

School Improvement Program. After receiving federal funds in 1964, the PCCA funded just a few projects before becoming embroiled in controversies that would lead to its reorganization; one of those programs, it will be recalled, was a proposal to extend a Head Start–type nursery school program that Foster had helped to start while he was at Dunbar. Two of the three other programs that received initial support from the PCCA—a Department of Labor project and the Reverend Leon Sullivan's Opportunities Industrialization Centers (OIC)—were devoted to vocational training.[84]

Sullivan launched OIC in 1964 on the heels of his successful protest campaigns against discriminatory private-sector hiring practices. By 1966, the centers had trained and placed 1,500 black workers in such fields as drafting, electronics, power sewing, and restaurant practices. By the end of the decade, the program had grown to include OEO-funded centers in more than 150 cities. President Johnson, Senator Robert F. Kennedy, and OEO chief Sargent Shriver were among those who touted Sullivan's program as a key strategy in the federal war against poverty.[85]

Marcus Foster knew Leon Sullivan, and his program at Catto was in some ways reminiscent of what Sullivan developed on a larger scale. Moreover, the parallels between Catto's programs and those of the OIC highlight the strengths as well as the limitations of educational responses to the urban crisis. Sullivan embraced an education and job training agenda out of firsthand experience with African American deficits in this area; during the "400 Ministers" boycotts of companies with discriminatory hiring practices, he had found it difficult to find qualified black applicants for the jobs in question. And though he was not an educator, his response was to train and educate those potential workers. In the "Opportunity Schools" where OIC trainees were inducted—as in Foster's public school programs at Dunbar and Catto— courses in black history and remedial reading and math not only taught skills and content; they aimed to instill pride, aspiration, and behavioral traits such as good grooming and punctuality.[86] (It will also be recalled that, in addition to the campaign against employment discrimination, Sullivan and the 400 Ministers had launched a direct attack on "inferior learning conditions and low academic achievement" in the Philadelphia schools, lobbying specifically for an expansion of the compensatory education program Foster had helped to start while at Dunbar.[87])

On the face of it, this focus on education and training—especially the part about attitudes and behavior—seems to echo the approach that has drawn such criticism from liberal-left critics of the War on Poverty, then and now.

Reviewing the Johnson administration's draft of the Economic Opportunity Act in 1964, the sociologist Christopher Jencks criticized the antipoverty legislation from the left as being "fundamentally conservative." With nine-tenths of the OEO's $962 million budget allotted to what he described as "education, training, and character building" under the Community Action Program—rather than a jobs program as the labor department had favored—Jencks complained that the administration "assumes the poor are poor not because the economy is mismanaged but because the poor themselves have something wrong with them. They live in the wrong place and won't move. They have the wrong skills and won't enroll in training programs. They have the wrong personality traits or bad health." In all, he complained, the new campaign was "not just a war on poverty but a war on the poor."[88] Historians generally have agreed, seeing social policy in the 1960s as one more chapter in a long story of Americans trying to cure the ills of urbanization, industrialization, and immigration through the limited means of schooling. And while scholars have found this approach wanting in every major era of reform, they have especially emphasized its inadequacy for the period after World War II, when large waves of unskilled black migrants arrived in the cities just as the industrial job base began to decline.[89]

The War on Poverty has been told as a "narrative of failure" for good reason, and this is not likely to change anytime soon.[90] Still, Sullivan's training programs—and, on a smaller scale, Foster's efforts at his one school—tell a slightly different story. Sullivan, like Foster, focused on the deficits of the poor themselves—yet both men did so in a spirit of pride and "self-reliance," rooted as much in long-standing traditions of black self-help as in liberal arguments about cultural pathology. Moreover, neither man focused on self-help and vocational education in isolation from the realities of the labor market. The historian Guian McKee has defined Sullivan's approach as a local version of liberalism, fueled by civil rights activism, which was in tension with the national approaches that have drawn so much criticism. Rather than approaching job training purely as a remedy for the deficiencies of the unemployed, and assuming that such newly trained workers would be lifted by a rising tide of national economic growth, Sullivan was among those who recognized deeper problems in the structure of the economy—namely, the fact that the inner cities were *not* growing like other parts of the nation. Sullivan addressed these structural problems in the labor market by coupling job training with job creation.[91]

Of course, Foster, as a school-based educator, did not take on the task of job creation. But his efforts to improve vocational education at Catto—specifically his emphasis on actually finding jobs for the students by fostering a tighter link between school and industry—was in the same spirit. Moreover, Foster's academic program was an effort to open up new avenues of vocational opportunity for young black men. Educational attainment was increasingly important for social mobility in America's emerging postindustrial economy (a trend that has only accelerated since that time).[92] Yet, even as education grew more important as a means of entry into public sector employment and other white-collar work, the quality of education received by many black males was, if anything, deteriorating. By raising expectations of these young men and improving their academic skills and literacy, Foster contributed modestly, yet notably, to their inclusion in a changing economy.

In vocational education, as in compensatory education, the problem was not the idea itself so much as the excessive expectations that reformers attached to it. Compensatory education had held promise as an educational policy aimed at raising academic achievement (and it still does, judging from recent optimism surrounding KIPP schools, the Harlem Children's Zone, and other current initiatives that echo the history of Comp Ed); it ran into trouble when reformers turned it into a centerpiece of the War on Poverty. Similarly, Foster's program at Catto, like Leon Sullivan's much larger initiatives, spoke to the importance of education, training, and jobs for young African Americans in the city; yet, education, training, and community-based job creation needed to complement, not substitute for, a more comprehensive set of urban policies that directly and decisively attacked the problems of unemployment and poverty. Once again, educational strategies were expected to pull too much weight as solutions for larger social and economic problems.

In Foster's case, the limitations of urban school reform were highlighted by a series of career conferences that the Catto School co-sponsored in May 1965 with the mayor's Manpower Utilization Commission. The conferences undoubtedly were positive experiences for some teenagers who previously had had little desire or opportunity to land any kind of job. Still, the menu of career options, including car mechanic, plumber, truck driver, barber, radio and TV repairman, and member of the armed services, did not exactly promise a future of vast and expanding opportunity.[93] It was not clear how many urban teenagers could actually find jobs to match their training in these fields, not to mention whether those occupations provided a suitable alternative to the now boarded-up factories where earlier generations of unskilled migrants and immigrants (though not African Americans) had

found work. Escaping poverty was not simply about changing one's attitude or obtaining more skills or being more resourceful, important though
these approaches were. It was also about the availability of jobs—something
Philadelphia lacked more than ever.

Victims or Hoodlums?

The North Philadelphia riot of 1964 highlighted the limitations of educational and civil rights responses to the urban crisis—as well as the increasing difficulty of even discussing the educational and social problems of black
families and youth. As in many subsequent cases across the nation—including Watts, the next summer—the immediate cause was a minor incident involving the police. Two officers (one white and one black) had tried forcibly
to remove an intoxicated African American woman from a stalled car that
was blocking an intersection. As a police wagon carted off the woman and a
bystander who had attacked the officers, bricks and bottles began to fly from
the rooftops of surrounding buildings. A weekend of violence and looting
ensued, leaving two people dead, hundreds wounded (239 residents and 100
police), and $3 million in property damage. Many of the looters were women
and teenagers.[94]

The looters' actions seemed to reveal a basic economic resentment over
being left out of the affluent society, and neither civil rights leaders nor educators nor city officials could mollify them. Raymond Pace Alexander, a prominent local judge and old-guard moderate on civil rights, climbed on top of
a car with a microphone and begged, in vain, for the rioters to go home. J.
H. Trapp, pastor of the Thankful Baptist Church, pleaded with one gang of
youths, "We have talked too much about rights and forgotten about personal responsibility"; they jeered and cursed him. The rioters dismissed these
men as "handkerchief-headed uncle Toms" whose cause—the steady pursuit
of progress through education and the enforcement of fair employment and
housing practices—was irrelevant. Even Cecil B. Moore, who prided himself
on having reached out to poor and working-class North Philadelphians during his nearly two-year tenure as head of the local branch of the NAACP, could
do little to tame the resentful crowd. Moore arrived on the scene around 3:45
A.M. on the first night of the disturbance and shouted, "I understand your
problems, but this is no way to solve them. It's late. Everybody go home to
bed." A woman with an armful of looted clothing shot back, "Listen man, this
is the only time in my life I've got a chance to get these things."[95]

The riot of 1964 may have dramatized the frustrations and anger felt by residents of North Philadelphia, but it only led other Philadelphians to take a more hostile attitude toward them. Robert N. C. Nix, the black congressman whose district included the riot zone, moved to ostracize the dissidents as "hoodlums" and "bums" who did not represent the great mass of law-abiding Negroes. Jules Cohen, the executive director of the Jewish Community Relations Council (JCRC), insisted that "we must not give aid and comfort to extremist elements who would like nothing better than to foster a 'white backlash' on which they can capitalize." Leaders like Nix and Cohen were eager to preserve the good name of the black community and its freedom struggle.[96] Yet civil rights leaders' fears of a backlash began to come true immediately. The *New York Times* reported that whites flooded the local NAACP office with calls announcing that, because of the weekend's events, they planned to vote for conservative Republican Barry Goldwater for president. Men in a tavern joked about the harsh measures they would have taken had they been mayor or chief of police. One said he would have shot the rioters with sawed-off shotguns filled with rock salt, to which the bartender replied, "The shotguns are okay, but I'd never use rock salt. It corrodes the barrels."[97]

To say the least, by 1964 the problems of the ghettos were well known among local officials and many residents in the big cities. And yet, in spite of the disturbances of 1964, many Americans remained largely unaware or unconcerned about these problems. All of that would change the next year, however, because of two events that pushed the acrimonious local debates over race and poverty into a national spotlight. One of these was the Watts riot, which was much larger in scale than the disturbances of 1964. Just as the North Philadelphia riot poisoned the atmosphere of discussion in that city, Watts transformed national discourse. Black anger became more visible—but so did white hostility toward urban blacks, who were increasingly perceived as aggressors rather than victims.

Another polarizing event of 1965 was the controversy surrounding the Moynihan Report. Just as the Watts riot was putting the problems of the ghettos on the radar of most Americans, the U.S. Department of Labor inadvertently fueled the fire by releasing Assistant Secretary Moynihan's study of "the Negro family." Among other issues, Moynihan raised alarms over the "failure of youth," including poor school performance, drug addiction, and delinquency. He believed alienated black teenagers had been key players in the riots of 1964 and, writing before Watts, he warned that more disturbances would follow if the nation failed to act.[98] Moynihan was ahead of most fed-

eral officials in recognizing these problems, and his report was an attempt to
spur those officials, including President Johnson himself, into action. Moreover, his diagnosis of the problem—that is, his view that black families were
trapped in a vicious cycle of discrimination and cultural pathology dating
back to slavery—was in many ways a summation of decades of liberal so-
cial-scientific thought on problems of race and poverty, extending from W.
E. B. DuBois's *The Philadelphia Negro* (1899) through influential works by E.
Franklin Frazier, Gunnar Myrdal, and Kenneth Clark. Like these predecessors, Moynihan did not view cultural pathology in isolation but rather as a
product of centuries of white racism. Like his boss, Secretary of Labor Willard
Wirtz—and in contrast to the administration's dominant focus on fighting
poverty through community organizing ("Community Action") and educational and social services—he emphasized the need to address the problem
of unemployment.[99]

But if Moynihan expressed timely concerns, in a way he hoped would
lead to proactive government intervention, his report had the opposite effect, shutting down serious discussions of the problems of the black ghettos. Among other problems, the Moynihan Report was sensationalist in its
tone, its language, and its emphasis. The "fundamental problem" was that of
"family structure." The Negro family was "crumbling," "deteriorating," "disin-
tegrating." It was a "tangle of pathology." In response to these depictions, one
critic, the Boston psychologist William Ryan, coined a new term: "blaming
the victim." Considering the acrimony we have seen in debates over urban
schools in this period (the *Greater Philadelphia* controversy in Philadelphia;
criticisms of James Conant at the national level), it is not hard to see why
Ryan and other critics feared that the report's unflattering generalizations
would play into the hands of conservatives eager to blame ghetto problems
on the personal and cultural characteristics of the residents themselves. Indeed, in some cases this is just what happened.[100] With tensions running high
after Watts, and with the sensationalism of *The Negro Family* lending itself
to media sound bites, it became difficult for commentators to discuss the issues in the constructive manner Moynihan had envisioned. Many ignored his
concerns about urban unemployment and his desire to spearhead a national
commitment to ending it, often because they had read journalistic coverage
rather than the report itself.[101] Debates on the problems of the black ghettos—including the situation in urban schools—had come down to a matter
of whom to blame: the inhabitants or the larger society and its institutions.

The riots and the concerns of the Moynihan Report were of direct significance to Marcus Foster. On the second day of looting in North Philadelphia, Foster issued a public statement in his capacity as chairman of the Columbia branch of the YMCA, which was located in the riot zone. His opinions, however, came out of personal experience—not only as principal of Catto, where he worked with the kinds of teenagers who were looting and vandalizing white-owned businesses, but as a man who had been no stranger to urban street life and the ills of discrimination in his own youth. Foster emphasized that the young rioters had been molded by the larger society—that is, they were victims. "We have allowed them to be undereducated," he wrote, and as a result they faced "massive unemployment and a life of frustration. We can sympathize with their unhappiness and hope that all will have compassion for this expression of their frustration." Foster did not condone the actions of these teenagers, but, in his most forceful commentary yet on the subject of racial oppression, he placed their deviance in broader perspective: "Bad as the rioting is, wrong as the looting and stealing are, they are insignificant when measured against centuries of injustice." The residents of North Philadelphia "undervalued" themselves and the larger society because they had been undervalued by others. The school principal did not take issue with other leaders' efforts to stop the rioting that continued even as he wrote, but he warned against a hard-line mentality. America, he said, echoing James Conant, was playing with "social dynamite" in places like North Philadelphia, and "repression [was] not the answer."[102]

Foster's programs at the Catto School illustrated this spirit of educating, rather than repressing, troubled black teenagers. Catto concentrated some of the most challenging students in the district, yet between 1963 and 1966 they came to school more often and got into less trouble than they had under the previous administration. They learned more from teachers who tended to see them more sympathetically and from a curriculum that offered better academic as well as vocational training. And their parents and neighbors got more involved in the life of a school that went from being a menace to a model of community participation. This was just one school, but it did exemplify the larger idea, which was growing more prominent with each new school year, that urban schools and educators needed to stop making excuses and take more responsibility for the performance of their students.

This impulse to hold the schools responsible for student success was an important and understandable aspect of civil rights activism that echoes to this day. Since *Brown v. Board of Education*, especially, civil rights leaders had lost patience with urban school officials who seemed to ignore, even reinforce, segregation and unequal educational quality.[103] As Clark had discovered in Harlem and as Foster had seen in his first encounters with the Catto School, too many school officials and educators, including some who considered themselves to be liberal, dismissed inner-city students as hopeless without really trying to teach them.

At the same time, the critique of urban education was marked by a troubling tendency to downplay the educational impact of forces beyond school walls. Civil rights activists, as much or more so than liberals who pushed compensatory education for cultural deprivation, were very much within the American tradition of looking to education as the key to social opportunity. As Clark wrote in *Dark Ghetto*'s final sentence on inner-city schools, nothing less than "the future vitality of democracy" seemed to depend on the society's ability to provide a quality education for all. But while critics were right to identify teachers' low expectations as a key obstacle to educational success, they ran the risk of overemphasizing this factor and singling out the schools for blame. Clark was aware of the pitfalls of "over-simplified either-or thinking and devil hunting," which, he said, would not solve the "fundamental problems of obtaining high quality education in our public schools." But as critics responded to one-sided arguments about cultural deprivation, they not surprisingly began to simplify their own perspectives. Clark quoted a black teacher, for example, who got "sick and tired of hearing (from white colleagues) about how our children will never amount to anything, our children are ignorant, the homes they come from are so deprived . . . even though I realize there is a problem."[104] There were problems indeed—especially those rooted in racial and socioeconomic disadvantage—and as critics such as Nathan Glazer had argued, it was not fair to single out the schools for failing to solve them.

Foster's work as a principal highlighted the challenge of expecting more from urban schools without oversimplifying the problems those schools faced. He certainly embraced the new pressure on educators: "In a crisis," he wrote, "society, rightly or wrongly, looks to its schools for solutions to its most pressing problems. This response is entirely appropriate since the school is in continuous contact with most youth over an extended period of time."[105] Still, Foster recognized that the schools faced problems beyond their making and perhaps (though he did not say so publicly) beyond their control. His own achievements had been shaped by the cultural capital he inherited from his mother and other family members—but he also knew that many urban teenagers lacked such resources and support. As a school-based urban educator who was intimately familiar with young people and the challenges they often faced beyond school walls, he was more willing than some civil rights leaders (and historians) to point to those external influences as a factor in low achievement. Foster described Catto students' problems as "multiple and complex," rooted not only in the schools but in the economy, the home, the community, and the individual psyche.[106] As he saw it from the principal's office, centuries of injustice had trapped these students and their families on the lowest rungs of the social ladder, but educators had to confront various symptoms and effects of such injustice, including low motivation for academic success, below-grade-level skills, and parents who lacked the resources, inclination, and/or know-how to promote their children's academic achievement. To call attention to these issues was not necessarily an example of blaming the victim (nor, to use current language, was it a case of making "excuses"); in fact, it was part of any comprehensive approach that did not simply blame the schools instead.

After the Moynihan controversy and the outbreak of urban riots, though, comprehensive analyses were harder to come by. Urban educators increasingly found themselves facing community criticism for the low achievement of students (and rejecting such criticism, with varying degrees of justification). In Foster's case, these pressures intensified in the spring of 1966. At that moment, parent and community protests over the abysmal quality of education at Gratz High School, in North Philadelphia, pushed the principal of that school out of his job. Ruth Hayre, who by that time was superintendent of the district in which Gratz was located, looked to Marcus Foster to turn the school around.

CHAPTER 4

Black Power, "People Power": Holding Schools Accountable for Black Achievement

F OR a few weeks in the spring of 1966, it looked as if Marcus Foster's days in the trenches as a school principal were over, at least for awhile: on March 1, he was promoted to a desk job in the school district's central offices on the Ben Franklin Parkway. There, he was charged with determining an educational use for a million-square-foot building the district planned to buy near Independence Hall.[1] But Foster was not downtown for long. By the end of the month, he had taken charge of perhaps the most troubled school in the city, Simon Gratz High School in North Philadelphia.

Foster's sudden change of plans resulted from a brouhaha stirred up by the city's black newspaper, the *Philadelphia Tribune*. On March 8, the *Tribune*—which two years earlier had rallied opposition to *Greater Philadelphia* magazine's exposé on the Philadelphia schools—launched its own muckraking series on the state of education at Gratz High School. Reporter J. Brantley Wilder, citing conversations with angry parents in the Gratz Home and School Association, as well as his own experiences as an undercover substitute teacher, reported that gangs of "hoodlums" were "terrorizing" Gratz. Students "could not walk down the halls without fearing for their safety." Faculty and administration had "given up trying to keep order." Meanwhile, Wilder quoted Principal Charles Tomlinson as saying the average Gratz student was reading at a fourth-grade level (not a third-grade level, as some teachers had told Wilder). The story provoked a torrent of responses. Hundreds of Gratz students denounced it as "slander" and threatened to picket the paper. Some parents, community members, and educators, including the black administrator Ruth Wright Hayre, praised it for taking teachers, administrators, and the school district to task. Critiques of low-performing urban schools had been building for some years, but by 1966, with new school reforms shaking up the leadership of the system in Philadelphia, the protests at Gratz led to change in a very visible way: the district forced out the embattled Tomlinson, who was white, and persuaded Foster to take over as principal.[2]

The transfer of power at Gratz was part of a new trend toward making schools more accountable to their communities, and it was a harbinger of more heated conflicts to come. Philadelphia and the country at large were entering the most intense phase of the escalating conflict over race and inequality, and the schools were, more than ever, a battleground. New York City's crisis over community control of the schools in the Ocean Hill–Brownsville section of Brooklyn is the most famous of the era's conflicts over race and education.[3] A year before Ocean Hill–Brownsville, though, Philadelphia suffered through a similarly scarring event. On November 17, 1967—a day that came to be known as Black Friday—hundreds of African American students, including many from Gratz, marched to the central administration building to issue demands for black studies curricula and other reforms, only to end up in a melee with Police Commissioner Frank Rizzo and his officers. It would prove to be the most violent and hotly disputed confrontation of the late 1960s in Philadelphia, leading eventually to the ouster of an innovative new superintendent of schools, Mark Shedd, and the election of Rizzo as mayor.

Foster had spent years wrestling with the divisive issues of school discipline and underachievement. Yet, he faced a new challenge as the head of a high school in which gang violence, fourth-grade reading levels, and student militancy had become matters of public controversy. At Gratz and other predominantly black high schools, some parents, students, and community members not only saw these issues as symptomatic of white, middle-class domination of the schools; after 1967, they began to challenge the very legitimacy of the existing school district leadership—including principals—and to advocate Black Power and community control instead.

Foster had always been more of a liberal than a radical in his basic faith in the system and his natural inclination toward diplomacy and compromise rather than confrontation. His years at Catto—the mid-1960s—had begun to test that basic orientation, pushing him toward a more forceful response to the needs of students and the failings of urban schools. In the heated atmosphere of the late 1960s, first at Gratz and then briefly in the central office as an associate superintendent, he had to work even harder to adjust to the times and maintain credibility among students and families who, in many cases, were losing faith in the system.

In the context of rising community anger at schools and educators, Foster brought a more responsive brand of leadership to Gratz. Granted, the new principal won the confidence of many parents and students partly because of his personal qualities: he was black, he had roots in South Philadelphia, he was charismatic and inspiring. As one journalist wrote during his Gratz years, he seemed "equally at home swapping 'freedom handshakes' with teenage black militants and exchanging scholarly quips with those who understand them."[4] Even more important to Foster's appeal in the Gratz community, however, were his efforts to respond to students' and parents' concerns. He pushed for higher academic expectations and achievement. He allowed parents and students to join teachers in writing a more "relevant" curriculum. Most dramatically, he responded to parents' anger about overcrowding by leading a successful confrontation with the school board and the city over expansion of the school's facilities. After a frustrating failure to achieve their goals through negotiation, Foster and some six thousand citizens descended on a school board meeting by the busload, peacefully forcing the board and the city to seize fourteen white-owned homes under eminent domain so that thousands of black students might enjoy adequate school facilities. All of these efforts blurred the dichotomy—familiar since the 1960s but increasingly subject to revision by historians—between civil rights and Black Power.[5] Foster and the Gratz community showed schools to be important sites in an ongoing freedom struggle—a struggle that encompassed northern as well as southern battles; achievement and resources as well as integration; and Black Power (or "people power," as Foster described it) as well as civil rights. In addition, their struggle for improved academic performance at Gratz shows that the urban educational activism of the 1960s was not simply a push for "equity" at the expense of "excellence" and "accountability," as President Ronald Reagan and other commentators later came to lament; rather, the activism of the 1960s was itself a call for excellent and accountable schools for *all* students.[6]

Still, at Gratz as at other schools, Foster did not simply pit the community against the schools; as liberalism continued to unravel and critics increasingly disparaged either the schools or the students they served, Foster pushed for the "total school community" to take responsibility for raising achievement. The total school community included parents who were upset by the school's failure to produce achievement and students who sought relevance and black history; but it also included teachers who were dismayed by their students' low motivation and skills. Foster was careful not to "blame the victim"; he did not portray poor and working-class parents (and their children) as helpless, passive, or indifferent. But he did recognize the fact that many Gratz parents had suffered frustration or failure in their own school careers and lacked the know-how or long-term strategic vision that more affluent parents brought to their children's academic achievement from an early age. In light of these concerns, Foster continued to pursue the compensatory education strategies which, in spite of mounting criticism, had been a staple of liberal approaches to school reform since the early 1960s. (Indeed, the continuing significance of such cultural deprivation arguments was reinforced in the year Foster went to Gratz, by publication of the massive federal study *Equality of Educational Opportunity*, better known as the Coleman Report, after lead investigator James S. Coleman.)[7]

Foster made impressive progress at Gratz—and in the process became a celebrated figure in Philadelphia—by responding to a variety of concerns and constituencies. However, as the 1960s drew to a close, he increasingly looked beyond the school and its community, focusing attention on what he saw as a fatal lack of *public* commitment to the cause of urban education. At Gratz, he reduced the dropout rate and boosted college acceptances and scholarships, but he was still a far cry from closing the academic achievement gap with the average suburban school. To do so would require what he referred to as "massive doses" of support. To insist that educators raise achievement without providing such support was, in Foster's view, a recipe for failure and disillusionment. As he moved to district leadership, first as an associate superintendent in Philadelphia from 1969 to 1970 and eventually in Oakland, Foster would be increasingly consumed by this problem of resources and public accountability.

"Why Do Gratz Students Have a Fourth-Grade Reading Level?"

The controversy at Gratz, in the spring of 1966, hinged on the answer to a basic question that continues to echo today: what was the cause of low achievement at Gratz? Students who entered the school with low skills and low motivation, products of a "culturally deprived" upbringing? Or the school itself?

Certainly there was no doubt Gratz had been affected by forces beyond school walls. Indeed, it had suffered from the same process of urban and academic decline that Foster had faced at Dunbar Elementary, located just a few miles to the south. When it was built, in 1927, Gratz served a predominantly Jewish neighborhood in North Philadelphia. Early on, it was as likely to be in the news for a debating trophy or journalism award as for negative stories. (Even the latter tended to possess a certain quaintness, as when neighbors complained in 1941 that students were lounging on their stoops and picking their flowers.[8]) In the 1930s and especially after World War II, though, white and middle-income black residents began to migrate to the suburbs and the outer city, while lower-income black residents, including many migrants from the South, moved in. Unemployment went up and incomes went down, not simply because of the new residents' lack of education and skill (the most common explanation at the time), but just as importantly because of employment discrimination and the shuttering of factories in the postwar era.[9] Poverty went hand in hand with the physical and social decline of neighborhoods. Residents crowded into properties that a rising number of absentee landlords subdivided and failed to maintain. Crime rates rose and youth gangs thrived.[10] By 1949, one law enforcement official, speaking at the trial of an ex-Gratz student and gang leader who had terrorized the school, warned of the "growing practice of hoodlumism." Indeed, in the 1950s, Gratz students made the news and got in trouble with the police for beating and robbing trolley car drivers, assaulting their classmates, and "rumbling" with youths from rival gangs, neighborhoods, and schools.[11]

It is important to note that, while Gratz was shaped by social and economic forces, it was not simply by chance or fate that it became a school with a concentrated population of low-income, African American students. Contrary to the persistent but misleading notion of unintentional, de facto segregation, school district officials apparently gerrymandered the attendance boundaries to align with black settlement patterns. Gratz drew all of its students from an area stretching far to the south—that is, from North Philadelphia. As one reporter observed, the northern boundary of the school was "practically in line with the north wall of the building," and the school got no students from "the white and more affluent Negro areas to the north." Foster later joked that a grand total of four white students "kept the place integrated."[12]

By 1966, Gratz presented one of the most difficult high school situations in the city. Granted, the *Tribune* articles, like the *Greater Philadelphia* magazine exposé two years before, exemplified a growing sensationalism in media coverage of urban education. At least some members of the Gratz community protested that the newspaper exaggerated the gang situation and other problems at

Gratz. "We are not hoodlums," said a flyer distributed by Gratz students. "We are not controlled by gangs. We have not browbeaten or intimidated any teachers." Even members of the Home and School Association, the parents' activist group which had leveled the charge of gang terror at Gratz, distanced themselves from the story, saying the reporter had told them he was "after circulation, and you cannot sell papers printing good things."[13] Still, regardless of the question of sensationalism, Gratz's performance and morale were strikingly low. Only one out of five entering freshmen went on to graduate, the worst record in the city. Of those who did graduate, less than 3 percent went on to college. The school had no band, no debate team, no swim team, no honor society, no dances. It had no football field, and therefore no home games. Its tiny, dilapidated gymnasiums were the worst in the city.[14]

If some members of the Gratz community responded to the *Tribune's* publicizing of these conditions by being angry at the paper, many others took aim at the school and school system itself. The Gratz controversy became a centerpiece of the civil rights critique of the Philadelphia schools, a symbol of the system's and the society's low expectations of black children. Parental anger focused partly on the school's inadequate facilities and resources: Gratz was built to serve twenty-four hundred students but had an enrollment of nearly four thousand. Some classes met in locker rooms.[15] But parents and activists also held the school accountable for the unruly behavior and low academic achievement of the students. National Association for the Advancement of Colored People (NAACP) branch president Cecil Moore called the Philadelphia schools a "Jim Crow plantation" that assigned incompetent teachers to black schools. He urged Gratz students to complain to school authorities who were "keeping them ignorant and making hoodlums out of them." A few days later, as if following Moore's cue, students passed out flyers that asked, "Who is responsible for the illiteracy at Gratz? Why do Gratz students have a fourth-grade reading level? Why does Gratz want its pupils to remain ignorant?"[16]

In the mounting conflict between Gratz High School and its community, perhaps no site of battle was more important than the principal's office. At Gratz, as in nearly all middle and high schools in the nation's big cities during that era, the principal's office was occupied by a white male, Charles Tomlinson. In contrast with a legacy of responsive black leadership in the segregated schools of the South or in northern elementary schools such as Dunbar, Tomlinson's leadership illustrated the low academic expectations that pervaded northern high schools where white principals served black students.[17] The African American educator Ruth Wright Hayre, in her capacity as superin-

tendent of Philadelphia's district four (in which Gratz was located), had repeatedly encouraged Tomlinson to raise standards and attendance rates at his
school. Tomlinson and members of his faculty had looked at her as if she was
"crazy" and told her, "you can't expect anything better" of students who came
from such poverty.[18]

Was it fair to hold the principal responsible for low achievement at Gratz?
Some members of the Gratz community said it was fair indeed, and they insisted that Tomlinson be replaced by a black principal who might move more
energetically to improve the school. In doing so, they were part of a larger
movement to make urban educators more accountable to the communities they served. One of the most important and influential examples of this
growing phenomenon took place—as was often the case—in New York City.
The controversy, which erupted around the same time as the Gratz crisis, had
to do with the leadership of a new school, Intermediate School 201. I.S. 201
was slated to be built at the edge of Harlem near the East River as a showcase
for "quality, integrated education," but the New York City Board of Education
was unable to recruit white students, so it built the school in the middle of
Harlem instead. When the superintendent of schools announced that I.S. 201
would open in the fall of 1966 with a white principal, Harlem parents who
previously had fought for integrated schooling shifted focus and began to insist on "community control" of the school. If white students were not going
to attend I.S. 201, they argued, the black community should at least have the
power to run the school—starting with the hiring of a black principal, who,
it was assumed, would be more effective in providing a quality education for
black students. The parents failed to achieve their immediate objective—the
white principal remained in office—but they helped launch a movement for
community control of black schools that reshaped debates over race and education across the nation.[19]

Not everyone was willing to hold principals responsible for student performance, of course. Celia Pincus, past president of the Philadelphia Federation of Teachers, was among those who argued that white educators were being scapegoated for problems beyond their control. The Gratz situation was
a "city-wide disgrace," she said, "but you can't blame the principal. He was
not provided with the help and support and curriculum those teachers and
students should have."[20] Pincus cited inadequate school resources—"help and
support and curriculum"—to prove her point that "you can't blame the principal." Others suggested that schools and their principals were hampered by
educational and cultural deprivations that plagued the children themselves.

As Foster began his tenure at Gratz, the cultural deprivation idea, controversial but persistently influential since the early 1960s, found renewed expression in the Coleman Report, a national study of educational inequality mandated by the Civil Rights Act of 1964 and spearheaded by the sociologist James Coleman. The Coleman Report suggested that factors associated with a child's family and social class background—the education level of the parents, for example, or the degree of exposure to books and other cultural materials in the home and community—had a greater impact on achievement than did resource "inputs" like the amount of school funding or the quality of the facilities.[21] Coleman's findings were controversial, especially among black activists and other critics who charged him with blaming the victims of an unequal social system.[22] Still, while analysts still debate the interplay between family background and social structure, the Coleman Report ushered in a lasting shift in social science research on education, from a focus on school factors to *non*-school factors in explaining academic achievement gaps.[23]

The impact of urban poverty on achievement at Gratz High School was vividly captured in a memoir by a twenty-four year-old white woman who spent two years teaching there. When she applied for a job at the fictitiously named "North High"—recognizable as Gratz—Sunny Decker was skeptical of conventional wisdom about the supposedly "limited" experiences of ghetto youth: "I was told to watch out for these kids who'd had babies, attacked teachers, and managed to survive in a world far bigger than mine. They were culturally deprived," she recalled with some sarcasm. But while Decker entered the classroom with some awareness and even respect for her students' range of experiences, she was nonetheless surprised by the extent to which these experiences posed a problem in the classroom. Decker's memoir, *An Empty Spoon*, movingly documents the humanity and intelligence she found in abundance at "North," as well as the low aspirations and low self-esteem. "I picture my future being nothing because I am nothing," wrote one of her students, in a sadly typical refrain.[24] Decker's students were not uninterested in learning—indeed, she found many to be quite interested—but they lacked what scholars now call cultural capital: the knowledge, skills, resources, and attitudes that affluent parents pass on to their children to help ensure their academic success.[25]

Reform for Gratz—and Philadelphia

We have already encountered this ideological crossfire between blaming schools and blaming the shortcomings of students during Foster's time at

Dunbar and especially at the Catto School. The Gratz crisis took place at a turning point in this conflict, however. The blame for low achievement was shifting more decisively than ever from the students to the schools, in ways that would change not only Gratz, but public schooling in general.

The uproar at Gratz was part of a larger context of change in Philadelphia; in 1965, the city had embarked on what many came to praise as the most ambitious and exciting school reform movement in the country. It was a dramatic turnaround for a system that previously had been regarded as one of the worst among the big cities. Years of activism by the Citizens Committee on Public Education (CCPE) and the Greater Philadelphia Movement had pressured the school board to commission several major studies of the district, and as we saw earlier, the results, which were published in 1964–65 but widely discussed before that time, were scandalous. Among other problems, these studies found that the Philadelphia schools had the highest dropout rate among the nation's ten largest cities; an alarming number of dangerously antiquated buildings (25 percent); and a teaching force in which nearly one in five members were permanent substitutes without full accreditation. Student achievement, especially in all-black schools, was thought to be far below national norms, and change did not appear likely in a system run by a notoriously conservative business manager, Add Anderson, and his all-but-hand-picked Board of Education.[26] Partly in response to this damning evidence, voters approved a new charter that introduced lasting changes in the governance of the school system—in particular, a smaller, more accountable school board, selected by a citizens' nominating panel and the mayor. With the swearing-in of the new board in the fall of 1965, the Add Anderson era came to an end. The new board president was former Democratic mayor Richardson Dilworth, a bold and colorful politician of enormous stature in Philadelphia. Dilworth helped infuse the school system with the same reformist energy he and Joseph Clark had brought to City Hall in the 1950s. Even before the new board took charge, he commissioned task forces to begin the process of remedying years of neglect with regard to funding, buildings, and programs.[27] As in the early 1960s when the district took part in the Great Cities program, the Ford Foundation was a key agent and sponsor of the new reforms, this time in the form of a $200,000 planning grant out of its Comprehensive School Improvement Program (CSIP).[28]

One immediate effect of the reform movement was the satisfaction of community demand for a black principal at Gratz. The new school charter contained a provision that exempted 5 percent of all administrative staff from the usual certification requirements, and this enabled the district, at the urging of local superintendent Ruth Hayre, to reassign Charles Tomlinson to the central office and replace him with Marcus Foster (who did not have a high school principal's credential). Hayre had known Foster since the days when he regularly fell asleep in her husband's class at Cheyney State Teachers College.[29] Despite his strong record at Dunbar and Catto, however, his appointment at Gratz was controversial. Educators at the high school and around the city grumbled that he got the job "just because he's colored." Foster later recalled the incident with thinly veiled bitterness over the absence of blacks in school administration. At several predominantly black high schools in Philadelphia, he said, "lily-white" administrative teams "deliberated on the future of thousands of black children without one black person having anything to say about it," and few complained that the situation was unfair or even newsworthy. "But my appointment was considered a 'flimflam.'"[30]

Foster's appointment was controversial, but it was also symptomatic of a larger shift in the system. The Dilworth-led school board not only appointed Foster as a new black principal; shortly thereafter, it hired a bold new superintendent, Mark Shedd, who, although he was white, earned notoriety for his sympathetic stance toward black activism and his cultivation of black educational leadership. Shedd's prior position was the superintendency of tiny Englewood, New Jersey (total student body: four thousand), but in that role he had overseen the desegregation of the schools at a time, in the early 1960s, when many northern school leaders were resisting that policy. In hiring Shedd, the Dilworth board signaled its interest in making progress on black educational issues. Indeed, Shedd moved quickly to shake up the system and make it more responsive to African Americans. In June 1967— several months before he officially took office—he told administrators and principals of his intention to decentralize the administration of the district, so that decision-making power would flow downward and outward through the system, from the central office to clusters of schools or even individual principals. As we will see, Shedd's vision of decentralization was not identical to the community control idea that was coming to the fore in many black communities. However, in calling for decentralization, he pointed to I.S. 201 as a cautionary example that would be repeated around the country "if we do not take notice. The schools must anticipate the needs of the community, the thirst of the community for control and power." Even before he had spent a day in office, Shedd had established himself as an advocate of "meaningful" community input in school affairs, toward the larger end of achieving the "quality education" that the desegregation and compensatory education movements seemed unable to produce.[31]

Related to this focus on community participation, one of the signature innovations of the Shedd years was the promotion of dynamic and responsive black educators like Foster. The controversy over Foster's appointment to a high school principalship underscored the extent to which professional opportunities for blacks had been circumscribed during his lifetime. In the late 1960s, though, grassroots activism went hand in hand with an activist administrator (Shedd) to knock down many of those barriers to black advancement in the school system. By the mid-1970s, the city would have ninety-nine African American principals. At a time when black educators were being displaced in the South (a side effect of *Brown v. Board of Education*), their counterparts in the big cities came to enjoy new opportunities—and, as it turned out, burdens.[32]

While it was not obvious in the exciting early stages of change, the opportunity to lead urban schools would prove to be a double-edged sword for black educators. Shedd's initial speech to district administrators and principals offered an especially striking hint at how his intended reforms could cut two ways. Decentralization was based on two words, wrote John Corr, the reporter who covered the speech. The first of these—"autonomy"—certainly had a welcome ring to it. Principals like Foster would enjoy greater freedom to implement ideas aimed at improving their schools, presumably in concert with concerned parents like Mary James. But with autonomy came "accountability," a concept that haunts educators to this day. For Shedd, accountability meant establishing goals and making those in charge responsible for achieving those goals. As Corr noted—showing how a focus on achievement outcomes goes back not just to the Reagan-Bush era but rather to the 1960s—"The idea is to at last introduce into the school system the kind of thing that makes business and industry click, rewards for achievement." For sure, Shedd's vision was less centrally directed, less defined by standardized testing of a few academic subjects, and less punitive than the accountability systems ushered in more recently by No Child Left Behind (2002); in particular, principals and teachers were to be "included in the setting of goals for their schools in terms of a variety of factors, such as pupil performance, retention of teachers and community relations." And yet, Shedd's language reflected the dawn of a new era, one that continues to echo in our own time, in which the blame for failure was shifting from the students to the educators.

Accountability was a matter not only of goals and planning, he said, but "outcomes," and without a focus on such "measures of performance and accountability, promotions and careers are hard to manage rationally."[33]

Then, as now, accountability seemed a promising way to improve urban schools plagued by low expectations and educators who passed the buck for failure. But to the extent that low achievement was rooted in a more complex set of problems both inside and beyond the school, it also held the potential to scapegoat educators—including the black educators whose rise to positions of authority was both a cause and effect of the new accountability—for problems that were beyond their full control. His principalship at Gratz was the first time Foster truly wrestled with this tension, which in some ways came to define and dominate the rest of his career (and the careers of many other urban school leaders).

Mobilizing the "Total School Community"

Foster faced a heightened set of expectations when he went to Gratz. Granted, some citizens and educators—including members of the Gratz faculty—continued to be daunted by the negative impact that poverty and cultural isolation supposedly had on students' abilities to achieve. And for many, the Coleman Report, which was released just a few months after Foster took over at Gratz, soon reinforced such pessimism. Yet such arguments were very much out of favor among the urban families and activists who increasingly held educators responsible for the low achievement of their children. These critics, from parents in the Gratz Home and School Association to nationally known commentators like Kenneth Clark, did not want to hear that urban children could not learn because they were poor; they expected the schools to produce academic achievement for all students, with no excuses. In this climate, not surprisingly, the most obvious characteristic of Foster's leadership was his effort to make the school more responsive and accountable to parents, students, and the larger school community. But Foster ultimately took an even broader view, emphasizing the need for the whole society—not just the principal and teachers, but families, politicians, and taxpayers as well—to be accountable for student achievement. Student achievement was a product of school *and* non-school influences, and to raise achievement, one had to mobilize what Foster called the total school community, both in and beyond the school.

Foster had confronted low achievement and low morale before, but not on the scale of a big high school like Gratz, and not with so much anger and controversy at the school itself. The most immediate challenge came from his fellow educators. At a faculty meeting, district officials tried, in vain, to put a positive spin on Tomlinson's sudden departure: he had requested a move for health reasons, they said; he was being promoted. The staff, as Foster recalled, got "so upset it seemed they were going to tear the place to pieces. People were jumping out of their seats and shouting." Foster quickly got to work applying the same charisma and communication skills he had brought to Catto and Dunbar. He acknowledged, even praised, the staff's loyalty to their ousted colleague, while at the same time asking them to transfer their loyalty to him. Someone shouted, "you're up there now, and every new principal is due for at least a year's honeymoon."[34]

Not surprisingly, given the community dissatisfaction that propelled him into office, Foster used his "honeymoon" to emphasize proactive and responsive leadership. The new principal went to great lengths to be accessible to all members of the school community. This was a new idea at Gratz; as he joked, visitors to the principal's office had to "come up the marble staircase, past the Winged Victory standing there ominously, through twelve secretaries out in the outer pool, and there I was back in the inner sanctum, cogitating." In reality, Foster did not have much time for cogitating; he was too busy roaming the halls and meeting with a steady stream of students and other visitors who took advantage his open-door policy. Moreover, for those who had difficulty getting to Gratz, Foster created off-site extensions of the main school, which operated afternoons, evenings, and weekends. The first of these, "Gratz Outpost," met four nights a week in a public housing project. Foster started it in 1966 with funding from the National Teacher Corps, a Great Society program that trained young teachers to work in urban schools. Two years later, with a $30,000 grant from the Board of Education, Foster and Gratz Teacher Corps leader Ned Van Dyke launched a more ambitious school-community partnership, the Neighborhood High School Center. Neighborhood High served young people as well as adults. Some were pregnant girls whom the Board of Education did not allow in school after the sixth month of their pregnancy. Other visitors included parents and grandparents who lived far from Gratz or had an alienating personal history with the school systeam. The "storefront school" was a place where these parents and guardians could "walk in off the streets rather than through long, marble corridors," a place where they had a "full voice in the education of their children." Indeed, the school was listening; it had a hotline that parents could use to ring Foster's desk directly.[35]

Foster's responsiveness to parents and students was also on display in his academic expectations for the school. Shortly after he took office, the new principal told a gathering of more than five hundred parents, students, and teachers that the Gratz curriculum needed "a complete overhaul." Part of the overhaul would focus on the school's vocational programs; Foster wanted to recruit experts from business and industry to share more up-to-date knowledge. But the principal also called for the school's academic program to be "second to none in the city." He declared that a Gratz graduate should be able to get accepted as a sophomore at Harvard.[36]

Like Ruth Hayre before him, Foster met resistance from some staff members when he pushed for higher academic expectations at Gratz. The new principal's tendency to advocate on behalf of students made him some enemies on the teaching staff. As Sunny Decker recalls, "Every student was an exception to the rule in his eyes," and teachers complained that "the kids got away with murder" in terms of discipline as well as academics. For example, Decker recalled visiting Foster's office with Michael, a bright student who was flunking his classes. After thirty minutes of exhortation from Foster, who spoke of "Black Power and its leaders, and their college degrees," a newly energized Michael emerged with a letter from Foster, informing the teachers that he was a college-bound student who would appreciate any extra work to make up what he had missed. "The teachers would hate that note," Decker wrote; they would see it as pressure to graduate an undeserving student.[37] Still, Foster worked to shift the focus at Gratz from alleged student shortcomings to school responsibility for achievement. He recalled one teacher for whom he had to "facilitate" a transfer to a different part of town. The man was "one of the brightest teachers I've known," Foster said, but he had "a basic, though unconscious, contempt for Gratz students." Others left the school of their own accord. Meanwhile, Foster criticized what he called the "buck-passing attitude" of fellow educators who complained they were powerless to cope with the social and economic problems that impinged on their students' lives. In what became one of his favorite analogies and arguments for school accountability, he said, "Education must be the only profession where if the patient doesn't get well, you say he's a poor patient."[38]

Foster attacked low expectations of urban children; however, at Gratz, as at Catto, he generally managed to do so without attacking the teachers themselves. To extend his medical analogy, he did not hold the teachers solely responsible for the health of their "patients"; the patients themselves—and their families—shared some of the responsibility. Speaking to Gratz attendance officers, for instance, he stressed parental responsibility: "Let's not be defensive about the school. When a parent says that 'they don't teach you anything up at Gratz,' you tell them that they might be speaking for their own child but not for the other children at Gratz. Tell them that their child hasn't learned anything because he hasn't been there. How can we teach him if he's out on the street?"[39]

Foster recognized that low achievement at Gratz was rooted not only in what he and his staff did at school, but in circumstances beyond school walls. In particular, he maintained his longstanding focus on the lack of hope and cultural capital—stemming from poverty—that Sunny Decker so poignantly captured in her portrait of Gratz students. As principal, he continued to emphasize the importance of raising poor students' "aspirations" and "respect for learning." As he said in 1969, "these children have so much more potential than test scores indicate," but the problem was not simply the biases of the test-givers and teachers; it was also that "you have to break through generations of non-achievement and sell the idea of college to these children."[40]

Foster's analysis of underachievement reflected his ongoing concern with the cultural and educational effects of poverty—still a controversial topic in the wake of the Moynihan and Coleman Reports. Yet this concern with the impact of poverty did not lead Foster to "blame the victim" or engage in what his close colleague Robert Blackburn refers to as the "socioeconomic cop-out" (i.e., declaring low socioeconomic status to be an insurmountable barrier to educational success).[41] On the contrary, he took proactive approaches to building the cultural capital of his school and his students. To be sure, the new principal began not by trying to change the current students but by attempting to recruit new ones; he and some of his staff went door-to-door to woo motivated students who lived in the Gratz attendance zone but had shunned the school due to its bad reputation. The hope was that these students would help improve the academic atmosphere of the school in general. In describing this approach, Foster explicitly cited the Coleman Report, which had confirmed his view that "you had to have a kind of cross-fertilization of upwardly aspiring children" with those who were less motivated.[42]

It was not easy to convince parents to entrust their "upwardly aspiring" students to a school like Gratz, but in their attempt to do so, Foster and his staff advertised one of the school's other main strategies for building cultural capital: the Beacon Motivation Program. The Beacon Program was a compensatory education program like the one Foster had created at Dunbar; in fact, the Gratz program had originated as part of the district's efforts to institutionalize the

Dunbar program and other pilot projects sponsored by the Ford Foundation.[43] Like its predecessors in compensatory education, the Beacon Program featured after-school tutoring, enrichment classes for gifted students, intensive counseling, and exposure to theater, concerts, and other cultural events, all to the end of helping talented underachievers develop both the skills and the aspirations to go to college.[44] All of these approaches had been central to Foster's career, and he naturally embraced and extended them at Gratz. Indeed, the continuities in Foster's career were illustrated in literal fashion by the path of one of his students. Gloria Gaymon was a pupil at Dunbar Elementary at the time when Foster established the High Roads compensatory education project there. In high school, she followed him to Gratz, despite having to travel well out of her neighborhood to get there, and entered the Beacon Program. Gaymon earned a scholarship to the University of Pennsylvania and went on to become head of the social studies department at Gratz. She credits the Beacon Program with putting her on that path; "I was not getting that (encouragement to excel academically) from some of my friends outside of school," she says.[45]

Parental outreach (Neighborhood High) and compensatory education (the Beacon Motivation Program) were two of many initiatives through which Foster attempted to raise expectations among all members of his school community and change what he called a "loser's image." Other such initiatives included his revival of the Gratz chapter of the National Honor Society, dormant for twelve years, because "no one believed the students could do outstanding work"; and his insistence that the school reorganize its band (also defunct prior to his arrival) and start to hold dances again. Of special interest to Foster were the potential benefits of a revitalized athletic program. Gratz's baseball and basketball teams had been a laughingstock, as much for their hand-me-down uniforms as for their hapless records. One of Foster's responses was to hire former Harlem Globetrotter and future NCAA coaching legend John Chaney to coach the basketball team. Chaney's four-year tenure put Gratz on a path to becoming a perennial basketball powerhouse in the state of Pennsylvania and, in the process, a prouder school.[46]

It did not take long for Foster's activities to begin showing results. In the spring of 1967, little more than a year after sparking the uproar over conditions at Gratz, the *Philadelphia Tribune* published a glowing piece on the school's "amazing transformation." The author cited statistical evidence of a "renaissance of high academic standards": fifty-three students had just been inducted into the revived National Honor Society; applications to take the PSAT had gone up 600 percent, from 38 to 238 students; and college acceptances had improved 150 percent, from 20 students to 50. "First and fore-most," however, were the intangible improvements. The students believed "in themselves, in their teachers, and their administration," the reporter wrote, and the faculty had adopted Foster's enthusiasm and expectations as their own.[47] Around this time, a professor of teacher education told Foster he could not bring his class to Gratz anymore because the school no longer encapsulated the ills of urban education. Foster, for his part, noted that many problems remained; but now, he said, "it seemed that the problems were at least reduced to human proportions. We were not going to let them steamroll us."[48]

Black Friday and Racial Polarization

Marcus Foster got off to a strong start at Gratz by mobilizing the total school community—students and parents as well as teachers—in the task of raising academic expectations and achievement. Stepping into a situation in which community was pitted against school, each blaming the other for the students' low performance, he worked to enlist both sides in a turnaround. After 1967, though, Foster faced new challenges to his ability to unify students, parents, and educators (white as well as black) around a common focus on academic achievement: a radicalized Black Power movement and a conservative backlash against it. Proponents of Black Power called for new, all-black school boards and more radical approaches to curriculum issues. As one of those advocates, the scholar Charles Hamilton, noted in 1968, some black parents, students, and teachers had gone beyond a discussion of urban schools' effectiveness to question the very legitimacy of the system's governance structure and its professed liberal goals (shared by Foster) of promoting literacy, numeracy, and opportunities for individual social mobility. According to Hamilton, the critics were focused "as much on Afro-American culture and awareness as on verbal and arithmetic skills."[49] In Philadelphia, conflict over the goals and governance of the schools came to a head in the fall of 1967, with Gratz High School as a center of controversy.

The summer of 1967 had been a pivotal turning point in the rise of a more militant brand of Black Power activism both nationally and in Philadelphia. In May, Mayor James Tate had appointed Frank Rizzo police commissioner. With his law and order reputation, Rizzo was emerging as a symbol of white working-class opposition to black activism. The summer of 1967 had been marked by escalating tensions—exacerbated by the riots in Newark and Detroit—between Rizzo's police force and Black Power activists who staged a series of rallies that drew large numbers of black youth. Meanwhile, national events such as the rise of the Black Panthers had fueled intense interest in black nationalism among young African Americans.[50] Sunny Decker noticed the change in her classes at Gratz. The previous year, when her sophomores had debated Black Power, she could not get any students to take the militant side. They were embarrassed by riots. By the fall of 1967, she noticed a new atmosphere, defined by a push for black unity—and increased hostility toward white teachers such as herself, no matter how sympathetic they might have been. "The summer had done it," she wrote. "It made Martin Luther King an Uncle Tom. It made an in-group of the black nationalists."[51]

The changing of the guard in the Philadelphia school system was also conducive to the rise of Black Power activism. The new superintendent, Mark Shedd, did not take office until September 1967, but earlier in the year he had made a point of meeting with and voicing support for parents, black militants, and gang members (the first of many controversial moves by Shedd, seeing as it came before his first formal meetings with principals, administrators, or teachers).[52] Shedd's early words and deeds encouraged Black Power activists like Walter Palmer, head of the Black People's Unity Movement (BPUM), and William Mathis, leader of the local branch of the Congress of Racial Equality (CORE). In the fall of 1967, these and other leaders moved to mobilize the city's black high school students and press more urgently for changes in curriculum and school governance.

The first significant display of this effort came at Gratz. On October 26, some 250 students exited the school through a fire door, setting off the alarm, and went across the street to hear Palmer and Mathis speak on the need for an all-black school board. For the rest of the day, until an early dismissal, chaos reigned at the school, with fires set in the hallways and much of the student body roaming the halls at will. Perhaps not coincidentally, Foster was not on campus that day; this was likely during a period when he was recovering from a heart attack. Would events have played out the same way if he had been there? Sunny Decker described how, on another occasion, the comedian and activist Dick Gregory came to give an angry speech across the street, and Foster angered some on his staff by accompanying a group of students to hear it; on that occasion, she concluded, he had minimized the disruptiveness of the situation by knowing not to fight it. In any event, due to Foster's absence, acting principal Robert Hoffman and District Four Superintendent Ruth Hayre met with Palmer and student leaders, who issued a set of demands that included black history courses taught by black teachers, the right to

Figure 5. Students walk out of Gratz High School in October 1967 to attend a Black Power rally, sparking chaos at the school. With Foster absent, apparently recuperating from a heart attack, activists and student leaders forged an agreement with the vice-principal and the district superintendent that empowered them to wear African clothing to school and to sit out the flag salute if they provided written proof that it was against their religion. Urban Archives, Temple University Libraries.

wear African-style clothing and jewelry to school, and an end to the district-mandated flag salute and to military recruiting on campus. Hoffman and Hayre reached a temporary agreement that empowered students to wear the African clothing and to sit out the flag salute if they provided written proof that it was against their religion.[53]

Despite the agreement, the situation at Gratz remained volatile, and it represented a challenge to the priorities Foster had established for the school and its students. Foster's life and career were predicated on the notion of working within the system to achieve individual mobility and group advancement. He exhorted his students to believe they could do well in school and integrate into the mainstream society. He wanted them to learn to read and speak and aspire to success like their counterparts in the suburbs. He himself lived in one of those suburbs, Rutledge, where his daughter Marsha attended a predominantly white high school.

In contrast, some of the students who embraced Black Power were more interested in their African cultural heritage than in black contributions to American society. Some were more intent upon learning Swahili than on improving their Standard English. And at Gratz and throughout the city, these students and their adult supporters were working to reshape school practices according to their views. On November 16, teenage and adult activists distributed leaflets outside the city's predominantly black high schools, urging the students to rally at the Board of Education the next day at 10:00 A.M. The immediate grievance was the suspension of sixteen students, for disciplinary reasons, at Bok Technical Vocational high school; the larger one was, as the flyer put it, the "white policy of the Board of Education."[54]

The next day would alter discussions of race and education in Philadelphia for years to come, though not in the way the students wanted. Shedd and his staff expected several hundred protesters to show up; instead, roughly thirty-five hundred African American students from ten schools (including Gratz) converged on the central administration building. For a time, the situation remained under control. Shedd met with thirty student leaders, who pressed him for the same rights and curricular changes, on a system-wide basis that activist students had been pushing for at Gratz. Eventually, though, the situation outside the building deteriorated. The *Philadelphia Inquirer* later reported that students began throwing bottles and stones at police. Other witnesses denied this. Local news footage confirmed, however, that Police Commissioner Frank Rizzo eventually called on his men to "Get their black asses."[55] David Hornbeck, a young white activist who went on to become superintendent of schools during the 1990s, watched Rizzo give the charge twice: once in person and again on the *CBS Evening News with Walter Cronkite*. Hornbeck was head of the Philadelphia Tutorial Project, a community-based organization that helped produce the leaflets urging students to protest at the board. He estimates he was one of just two white protesters that day. "The kids were just marching around the building," he says. "They were chanting, and stuff like that, but they were orderly. And then it turned into that melee."[56] That melee, according to many black as well as white witnesses, consisted of police officers beating black girls, boys, and adults, many of whom offered no resistance or were trying to leave the scene. By the end of the episode, which came to be known as Black Friday, fifty-seven protesters had been arrested and about twenty students and adults had been injured.[57]

Black Friday divided the city and further sharpened the tendency for citizens to see black teenagers either as victims or hoodlums. Initially, the actions of the police on November 17 seem to have fostered a wider show of support, if not necessarily for the student protesters' demands, then at least for their right to express themselves without being clubbed on the head. Radical activists obviously were furious, but so were civil rights leaders who, according to the *Tribune,* had "no connections whatsoever with Black Power."[58] For his part, Hornbeck began organizing a new group, People for Human Rights, consisting mainly of white citizens who were "shocked at the police action taken against the peacefully demonstrating students."[59] Such parties called for Rizzo's resignation or termination.

Still, even greater numbers seemed to agree with Rizzo's perception that the student protesters were juvenile delinquents who were guilty of terrorizing schools and teachers. Some students had reinforced this image when, on their way home from the riot, they assaulted and injured dozens of innocent white citizens, often many blocks from the scene.[60] On the day of the riot, Rizzo had a brief and hostile encounter with Shedd, in which he reportedly told the superintendent to "get those fucking black kids back to school."[61] A great many Philadelphians, especially those who were coming to be called "white ethnics," shared that sentiment. Four years later Rizzo won election as mayor, partly on the strength of his public criticisms of Shedd for coddling Black Power activists in and around the schools. Shedd, who had blamed November 17 on the police, resigned before Rizzo took office and could carry out a longstanding promise to drive him out of office, thus bringing to a bitter end what some had hoped would be among the most successful school reform efforts in the nation.[62]

Marcus Foster's activities on Black Friday are not known, but his comments about the episode reinforced the idea that it polarized Philadelphia and dealt a severe blow to school reform there, less than three months into the Shedd administration. "After November 17th," he said a year later, "the city's never been the same." Foster's belief in reforming the schools from within may have been in tension with the more radical sensibilities of the student activists; nonetheless, he was broadly sympathetic to their commitment to improving education for black students, and he saw November 17 as having a chilling effect on that effort. The students "went down there to talk about their education," he lamented, "and what everybody wound up talking about was police brutality. I think it's unfortunate that everybody got away from the issues. We've never really come back to address fully the question of the neglect of schools in the black community."[63]

Black Achievement as Black Power

After November 1968, it was a tougher climate for Foster's attempt to work with many parties and viewpoints, trying to make the system work for those who were alienated from it. Black Friday further widened the chasm between those who saw black students as victims of a racist school system and those who saw them as destructive delinquents. But even after November 17, Marcus Foster enjoyed striking success at bridging that divide. Building on the promising achievements of his first year as principal, he worked to synthesize the radical currents of the era with his ongoing effort to raise academic expectations among parents, students, and teachers. In line with the concerns of students in the Black Power movement, he grew more forceful in his critique of racism within the schools and society—even as he pushed those students to take their math classes more seriously.

The historian Matthew Countryman has argued that in local communities like North Philadelphia, Black Power was not a series of "pronouncements" from national figures such as Stokely Carmichael and Huey Newton, as some have portrayed it; rather, it was poor and working-class people organizing to challenge the decision-making structures of the city and improve the quality of their immediate lives. In the weeks and months following November 17, 1967, as Countryman notes, the African American struggle for a voice in school affairs actually intensified. Black activists continued negotiating with Shedd and convinced him to sponsor a series of retreats at which black students and community representatives met with the principals of the predominantly black high schools. Out of those retreats, which featured intense confrontations over charges of "white racism" in the schools, came the formation of Black Student Unions and the development of black studies curricula.[64]

As a principal, of course, Foster was part of the power structure the activists were challenging. Still, as someone who was basically sympathetic with the critique of racism in the school system, he helped bridge the divide and incorporate curricular changes at Gratz. In 1968, the school received a $35,000 federal grant to develop a black history curriculum for the rest of the city's high schools to follow—a striking change from less than two years before, when it would have been absurd to look to Gratz for leadership on this or any other issue. While the local papers continued to describe it in traditional fashion, as "Negro History," the Gratz project in some ways offered a striking reflection of new themes associated with Black Power. In particular, students and members of the community played a major role in shaping the curriculum. Students started the process by filling out a questionnaire on what they wanted to study. Eventually, students, parents, and other community representatives joined seventy-five members of the Gratz staff for a series of half-day curriculum writing sessions—ten in all—on Saturdays. Shedd called the project "our first big step toward recognizing the critical concerns of so many of our inner-city high school students."[65] Some observers perceived the project as a radical change and a threat; for example, the Reverend Henry Nichols, vice-president of the school board and one of its two black members, denounced it as a separate "South African Bantu system" of education. Nichols was afraid the parents and students might choose exotic courses like Swahili, which he felt would "unintentionally harm the Gratz student when it comes time for him to go to college."[66]

Of course, the last thing Marcus Foster wished to do was harm his students' chances of going to college; ultimately, he wanted to show that an African-influenced cultural identity could go hand in hand with academic excellence. In terms of content, Foster's approach to black history continued to emphasize liberal, integrationist themes (the need to put the "black threads" with white, yellow, and other colors in the human "tapestry") rather than a separate, nationalist identity. But he also embraced more radical voices, and he offered an academic rationale for doing so: "It's a good thing, a kid reading Malcolm X or Stokely Carmichael or Leroi Jones," he said. "That helps our job, which is to have him reading."[67] When students asked Foster to take a stand against teachers who refused to let them wear African dashikis to class, Foster supported them—but not without conveying a larger focus on achievement. "If wearing dashikis is going to make you come out of the lavatories and go to class," he said, "if wearing dashikis will make you get your lessons done rather than hanging on the corner, if it inspires you by symbolizing your rich heritage, then I say, by all means, wear your dashikis."[68] As he had done before—and as advocates of multicultural education and "culturally relevant pedagogy" continue to do today—Foster approached black history partly as a motivational tool, a means of inspiring African American student achievement.[69] Dashikis and pride in one's African heritage were as compatible with that approach as the "hero bulletin boards" Foster and his staff had posted at Dunbar Elementary School in the early 1960s.

In his embrace of both academic skills and African cultural identity, Foster also attempted to mediate a related controversy over the relevance of so-called middle-class values to African American ghetto youth. In the early 1960s, Frank Riessman and others had begun to charge that urban educators' middle-class outlook prevented them from validating and building upon the supposedly distinctive learning styles and cultural traits of their street-wise students. By the late 1960s, some black students and educators had come to reject so-called white middle-class values altogether, melding their cultural identities with those of the black poor instead. As the historian Jerald Podair has argued, these educators made important critiques of white racism in the school system, but they missed an opportunity to construct an identity that embraced both blackness and "the more salutary aspects of the middle-class ethos," such as respect for learning, hard work, and a desire to improve one's condition.[70]

Foster forged such an identity, which, indeed, had been central to African American educational history and continues to be so today. Like black leaders and educators from Frederick Douglass to W. E. B. DuBois to Algebra Project founder Robert Moses, Foster promoted academic achievement as a means of empowerment for African American students.[71] As Foster wrote, the "so-called middle-class way of speaking, writing, and presenting oneself is the preferred route toward getting the jobs and rewards that almost every person wants." Or, as his friend and colleague Bob Blackburn recalls Foster saying more succinctly to Gratz students, "you don't have to have middle-class values, but you do have to have middle-class *skills*."[72]

Foster's supportive stance toward Black Power and, at the same time, his embrace of what he called middle-class skills, was in some cases echoed in the thought and actions of Gratz students themselves. Undoubtedly, as one writer claimed, some students disapproved of Foster's attempt to "make Gratz . . . just as good as any school on the Main Line"—in other words, as good as any white school in the suburbs.[73] By contrast, though, Sunny Decker described her students' "outspoken concern with education—be it a prerequisite for jobs or a status symbol. 'White kids get homework every night—*that's* why I want it.'"[74] Even the Black Student Union (BSU), formed by radical students during the fight for black studies, was a diverse group whose members often supported Foster's academic approach. Gloria Gaymon went to weekly BSU meetings in the basement office Foster provided for the group. The BSU contained various factions, she says, including cultural nationalists and followers of the Nation of Islam. It also included many who, like her, were members of the Beacon Motivation Program and whose top priority was to go to college.

Gaymon says Foster "wanted people to believe in the system, that it worked," and in the case of the Black Student Union in particular, "he wanted them to believe that people would listen to them." Still, she says, he "didn't dictate" to the BSU, and he reacted supportively to its concerns, because he felt they were compatible with his overarching goal: "if there was something that he thought would steer students in a positive direction, he was for it."[75]

The mutual respect and compatible agendas that Foster shared with many of his students, including the so-called militants, were evident in the spring of 1968, when several of them joined him as speakers at a Fellowship Commission conference on racial conflict in the city. Foster took his cue from the conference title, the militant motto "Telling It Like It Is"—and no doubt from his young colleagues as well: "If you want this system to work," he told the mainly white audience, "you'd better do something soon. Put your actions where your mouth is." Meanwhile Dorothy Kennedy, a Gratz senior, spoke on Black Power in a way that echoed Foster's own academically grounded critique of the school system. "Black power has made me proud of my race," Kennedy stated, before going on to say she did not understand why white, suburban schools were superior to those of the inner city or "why we are allowed to graduate with a sixth-grade reading level."[76]

Black Power, "People Power": Gratz Versus the Larger Society

Demands for "grade level" performance and for "put[ting] your actions where your mouth is": these statements suggest that Foster and "militant" students like Dorothy Kennedy were not opponents so much as they were coming together in a challenge to the larger society, to rectify gaps in achievement levels by race and socioeconomic status. The black studies curriculum project, in addition to being an expression of cultural pride, was a demonstration of this struggle over achievement; it responded to student and community input, and it reinforced the idea that a lack of such input was partly to blame for the poor performance of black students in the system. However, perhaps the most important example of this growing critique of the system and the society arose over the inferior quality of Gratz's facilities. In the spring of 1968, Foster and a unified Gratz community—teachers as well as parents, students, and community activists—demanded more forcefully than ever before that the larger society bring its actions in line with its rhetoric about equal educational opportunity.

Community anger over Gratz's crowded and inadequate facilities had percolated throughout Foster's time at the school. In 1965, the school district and the City Planning Commission had agreed on a $2 million expansion plan, including the construction of sixteen new classrooms and a gymnasium across the street. By mid-1967, partly in response to the community anger and pressure that also brought Foster to Gratz, some $600,000 worth of improvements had gone forward. However, the most important feature of the plan, the new gym and classrooms, had not. Unfortunately for Gratz, the proposed site contained fourteen single-family houses whose forty-three residents—mostly elderly Polish Americans on fixed incomes—fought the move. The school and the residents went back and forth in their arguments. The residents spoke of the economic, emotional, and physical hardships they would suffer in leaving homes they had owned and lived in for decades. They pushed for the school to use other adjacent sites. The Gratz community responded that students would have to cross the street to get there. The residents said that a bridge could be built. Negotiations stalled for over a year. The Home and School Association, headed by parent activist Mary James, stepped up pressure on the school board, urging it to use its power of eminent domain to acquire the properties.[77]

The conflict took on enormous symbolic resonance: an overcrowded high school serving low-income African Americans—a group with a history of being displaced by "slum clearance" and urban renewal policies—was pressuring the school board to seize white-owned homes. In the fall of 1967, Mayor James Tate interceded, asking the board to wait until after the December mayoralty election. The board, in turn, advised Foster that the community should back off until after the election, at which time Gratz would get its expansion.[78]

Foster's basic faith in the give-and-take of politics led him to follow the board's request, and at first, it seemed to pay off. As he put it, "an all-black high school was trying to put fourteen white homeowners off their land." No matter that "the city and the two local universities had been relocating thousands of black people for twenty years . . . It was something else to have poor black people moving middle-class white people." Foster concluded that political leaders were afraid of losing the white vote, and he was willing to give a little in order for Gratz to get what it wanted in due time. Sure enough, about a week after the election, the school board announced its intention to take the fourteen homes—by "amicable agreement" if possible and by eminent domain, if necessary. Foster was with Mary James when the news arrived. "See this?" he asked. "We played the game and we won." The principal reveled in his sense that the system had worked: "You don't always lose if you go along with the establishment," he told James. "It isn't a black and white is-sue. They'll support blacks as well as whites if you give them half a chance." James replied that she would not celebrate until she saw "the houses torn down, the building erected, and the key for the door in our hands."[79]

But James had been right, as an avalanche of bad news soon made clear. First, Mayor Tate and members of the City Council announced their refusal to close a section of Luzerne Street that was inside the expansion site. Then the City Planning Commission reversed its longstanding call for the tract to be cleared. Finally, and most damaging of all, Tate threatened to withhold the city's portion of the school budget if the board did not drop the exten-sion plan. Not surprisingly, the board began to back down in the face of such pressure from City Hall. In February, board president Richardson Dilworth met with Tate and agreed to return the expansion plans to the City Planning Commission and the school board's planners.[80]

Foster was faced with the defining moment of his career. He had convinced the Gratz community, skeptical and impatient, to "play the game." They had lost. Indeed, he bitterly recalled, as far as the city and the board were con-cerned, "we were not even players in the game." So Foster changed his ap-proach to the expansion issue. Instead of the give-and-take of politics, he now spoke of a "struggle" between white homeowners who "represented the middle-class power structure" and a black school that "symbolized the posi-tion of the poor and powerless." The process of compromise and consensus building—one of the hallmarks of Foster's career—had become a "situation made for choosing up sides." Partly Foster chose confrontation out of intense feelings of anger and betrayal; the city's actions, he said, were a "total repudia-tion" of understandings the Gratz community had accepted "in good faith." Partly he felt he had no choice but to fight; he had convinced the community to go along with the mayor's stalling tactics, and his credibility was on the line. Whatever the mixture of motivations, Foster decided to stand with the Gratz community against the city and the school board, perhaps at the risk of his job.[81]

The strategy was to apply pressure on the school board and force it to seize the fourteen homes. Foster and the Gratz Home and School Association moved to mobilize the voices and power of those who supposedly lacked those attri-butes. They got a broad array of grassroots organizations from across the city to take part in letter-writing campaigns, demonstrations, and other efforts to sway public and board opinion in Gratz's favor. There were teachers groups, including Teachers Concerned, a black organization that formed in the wake of the November 17 debacle; parents groups such as the Home and School Associations of Wanamaker, Vaux, and Gillespie Junior High Schools; and activist groups like CORE and the councils from the Community Action and Model Cities Programs of the War on Poverty. About ten white members of David Hornbeck's new group People for Human Rights braved a bitter-cold morning to picket the nearby Catholic church that supported its congregants against Gratz. Their signs read, "Human Rights before Property Rights" and "No White Privilege in Philadelphia." The mix of supporters included "militants as well as system-oriented people," Foster said. At the school itself, Foster let the faculty know they were under no obligation to get involved, but many did so, writing letters and signing petitions in support of the cause.[82]

Students wanted to be involved, too, but with memories of Black Friday still reverberating in the city, Foster was wary. Judging from conversations he had with some of his more militant students in the days leading up to the protest, it is not hard to see why. The encounters were good natured—Foster's generally positive rapport with even the toughest students only improved when he decided to confront the board, but they revealed an extreme approach to social change that Foster felt compelled to challenge: "Some of my more active brothers [would come] into the office, saying to me, 'Mr. Foster, you've been doing a good job up here at Gratz. You just sit behind your desk, and run the school, and when we throw the first brick, they'll be glad to get out of those homes! And if we have to throw the torch, they'll run!' And I said to them, 'Fellas, that's not the way. Violence is not the way. Let's not do that yet.'" When they asked him to tell them when it *was* time, he made the same point he had made after Black Friday: the time for violence and vandalism would never come, because "violence changes the issue, and the sometimes legitimate goals that students are striving for are lost in the peripheral issues, in the tangential issues, associated with violence." In the end, Foster and other organizers asked the students to "let the adults handle this"—and the students did.[83]

The flurry of organizing around Gratz set the stage for a showdown at the next school board meeting on February 26. At mobbed evening strategy sessions at the school, parents, teachers, staff, and other citizens laid plans to bring busloads of supporters to the meeting. Students would be staying behind, but a few days before the meeting, Paul Washington, pastor at the Episcopal Church of the Advocate, told a gathering of them to "get your parents out" on the twenty-sixth; "We must be able to show thousands of people who are willing to stand with you for your education." City Council president Paul

D'Ortona, a Democrat and a Tate ally, responded to Gratz's grassroots campaign by charging, as opponents of civil rights activism often did, that the district had hired "agitators" to foment unrest at the school. (D'Ortona had also distinguished himself, some time earlier, by referring to a group from Nigeria as "our visitors from Niggeria.") However, as George Hutt, one of two black school board members, noted, the "spontaneous" outpouring of energy at Gratz reflected a deeply felt desire for quality education, and the board could not afford to back down.[84]

On the twenty-sixth, the school board actually did try to back down, at least for a few more weeks. In a private morning session, board president Dilworth convinced a majority to postpone a decision until city and school planners could complete their latest study of the issue. As Dilworth prepared to announce the decision in the public portion of the meeting, however, six busloads of Gratz supporters arrived at 21st and the Parkway and filed into the building. About two hundred filled the main meeting room on the first floor, while hundreds more jammed into a larger auditorium to watch on four closed-circuit televisions. School board officials activated a so-called war room from which they, too, viewed the meeting on television while analyzing reports from the Civil Disobedience Unit. But, as Foster recalled, "our people were pledged to nonviolence. The action was to be centered in debate."[85]

And so it was. For more than three hours, speaker after speaker demanded that the board act immediately to relieve overcrowding and improve the facilities at Gratz. Their pleas were eloquent, Foster said, "but what seemed to turn the tide was the Board's realization that the community was determined to support the Board," whatever the repercussions of defying the city. In the end, two members changed the vote they had cast in closed session, and the board decided by a 4–2 margin to acquire the homes "with dispatch."[86]

At Gratz the next day, teachers, parents, and students were "in ecstasy," Foster said. "For the first time, they had had an impact on the society that shapes their lives." Granted, some participants in the struggle were cautious about its larger significance. Walter Palmer was pleased by the board's decision, but, as he warned, "our people have to learn the difference between a skirmish and a battle, and that was just a skirmish."[87] Still, Foster felt something special and significant had occurred—once again, by working within the system. As he told a reporter, "This is important. This is terribly important, because now people might start to believe that if their cause is just and they organize in the right way and work—then they can get something done." Looking back later, he recalled how, as he looked around and listened to the reactions of diverse

Figure 6. Foster *(left)* celebrates with the Reverend Paul Washington, pastor of the Episcopal Church of the Advocate, after the Philadelphia school board voted in February 1968 to condemn fourteen white-owned homes and expand the overcrowded facilities of all-black Gratz High School. At a defining moment of his career, when the board reneged on earlier expansion plans, Foster helped mobilize hundreds of parents, teachers, and activists like Washington for a public showdown at the Board of Education, resulting in a much-heralded victory for the school. Urban Archives, Temple University Libraries.

participants—"activists and moderates . . . parents and students"—he knew it had been "an historic moment."[88]

Other black leaders and activists shared Foster's sense that the Gratz victory carried a larger historical importance as a model for making social change. A few weeks after the school board decision, the *Philadelphia Inquirer* reported that black leaders of all affiliations were calling the board action a "significant landmark for Negro leadership in Philadelphia." For once, reporter George Ingram wrote, "Negroes—with whites in supporting rather than leading roles—went after and got action by applying political pressure to a red-hot controversy . . . The Negro community flexed its muscles in the Gratz incident and found itself strong." According to Ingram, a few black activists had suggested that, as he put it, "Black Power is beginning to reach maturity." One of those activists had reacted to the board decision by saying, "Riots are out of style and Negroes know it. There is a new movement here toward political and economic pressure to solve problems." Other militants had promised to "keep things cool" that summer.[89] The *Inquirer* piece was misleading in suggesting that Black Power had thus far been synonymous with riots and that black Philadelphians had never applied organized "pressure"; the activism of the Reverend Leon Sullivan and the "400 Ministers," in particular, stands out as a prior example of successful "pressure" tactics.[90] However, the *Inquirer* was right to describe the Gratz expansion battle as an expression of Black Power, as historians have redefined it: local African American communities like North Philadelphia rejecting elite-driven reforms and taking mass action to improve the quality of their immediate lives. In the Gratz case, the new style was captured most vividly by one of the fourteen displaced homeowners, who observed the school's show of strength at the board meeting and said, "This is a tidal wave. You can't fight this thing."[91]

For his part, Foster described the Gratz victory as "people power," not "black power," no doubt because many observers had come to associate the latter term with violence and racial exclusivity. At Gratz, though, Black Power and people power were more or less the same: a community of students, staff, parents, and other activists who were, as Foster described it, "involved and pushing in the same direction." Prior to Foster's arrival, the school staff and the community had pushed against each other. Now, to a much greater extent (and despite ongoing internal divisions), they pushed together. Rather than blame each other for Gratz's problems, the various parties began to take responsibility for improving the school and, increasingly, to ask the school system and the larger society to do the same. For Foster and his community,

one lesson of the expansion controversy was that "the system had to be forced
to deliver" for urban students.[92]

In particular, the Gratz community had pressed for the system and the society to deliver more resources—not only to Gratz, but to all urban schools.
This position was in tension with the Coleman Report (1966), which had
shifted attention away from school resources and facilities and toward class
and cultural explanations for low achievement. Foster did not reject the Coleman study or suggest that resources alone were decisive; on the contrary, he
continued to emphasize that the "socio-economic mix of the students" was as
crucial to school achievement as any other factor.[93] At the same time, though,
Foster and his allies dramatized continuing disparities in resources and made
a compelling moral and educational argument for equalization.

The educational argument was presented in an especially pointed way
by Gratz's three National Teacher Corps participants, Ned Van Dyke, Janet
Greenawalt, and Edward Hecht, who issued a formal statement a few days
before the showdown at the school board. In it, the three teachers, who were
white, argued that severe overcrowding was "a basic cause of failure for the
young people at Simon Gratz High School" and that special programs and
compensatory projects were, at best, "stopgap measures to patch over a bad
situation." Great Society spending on such programs was not useless—but it
was not enough. A few days later, in front of the school board, Greenawalt
quoted one of her students to drive home the link between inadequate facilities and low achievement: "Why do you ask me not to cut?" the teenager had
asked her. "If I come to school, you know there is not enough room in the
classroom for me to sit down." For his part, Foster explained how the second-
class facilities represented a message to his students from the larger society:
It "really hurt," he said, when "our athletes often traveled to schools in the
richer areas and saw the excellent facilities. The only other schools in the city
that were in real need of new gyms were two, which, like Gratz, served mainly
poor, non-white populations."[94] This was education of a sort, too; Gratz students were learning, in a direct and visceral way, that the larger society expected little of them.

Foster, James, and the other leaders of the expansion crusade sent Gratz
students a different message that emphasized their inherent worth, their educational potential, and—not least—the larger society's moral and civic obligation to them. As Foster said a few years later at the dedication of the completed addition, amid loud cheering from students he addressed as "my young
gifted brothers and sisters," the new building was "second to none in the city,

because we are not a second-best people. We are first-class citizens and we will have first-class facilities."[95]

"Money Problems"

One writer, reflecting on a string of crises that followed in 1968, likened the Gratz expansion victory to a "champagne supper before execution."[96] By the end of the year the nation would endure, among other traumas, the assassinations of Martin Luther King, Jr. and Robert F. Kennedy, the Ocean Hill–Brownsville crisis in New York City, and the violence and chaos of the Democratic National Convention in Chicago. In Philadelphia, major confrontations between black and white students further widened the split in the Democratic coalition between liberal and radical critics of white racism and conservative proponents of a law and order agenda that was coalescing around Frank Rizzo.[97] As the rest of the city and the nation continued to grow more polarized, though, Foster made some further gains with his "total school community" approach—even as it became increasingly obvious that schools like Gratz could not solve their problems by themselves, no matter how proactive their leadership may have been.

A reduced dropout rate was one of the most dramatic results of Foster's energizing of staff, parents, students, and other members of the community. Counselor Jack Fink shaped a new program, Outreach Youth Opportunity, around his belief that each dropout suffered from some combination of low achievement, lack of interest in course content, and financial pressure. Working on a case-by-case basis, Outreach Youth Opportunity had persuaded, as of November 1967, fifty-one dropouts to return and twenty-three near-dropouts to stay. The students were lured partly by vocational opportunities provided by the Philadelphia Navy Yard, the Kennedy Center, and other employers whom the Gratz staff organized into a training and placement service called the Career Development Advisory Council.[98] But the most dramatic and direct of the anti-dropout strategies was simpler: knocking on doors. In January 1969, more than 250 teachers, administrators, students, parents, college students, and community leaders braved freezing temperatures to march through North Philadelphia in search of roughly a thousand youths who had dropped out or were on the verge of doing so. On doorsteps and in the streets they tried to convince these students to come back to school and take advantage of Gratz's improved programs. Foster borrowed the idea for the campaign from Marshall High School in Chicago. He called it "Go for Gratz."

Prior to setting out from the school, he told his interracial group of volunteers, "We're trying to rescue young people from dead-end lives." That day, the volunteers re-enrolled 150 dropouts. Within a week, 225 had returned.[99]

Returning to Gratz hardly ensured an escape from a "dead-end life." Not only did the staff lack the resources to reach their most ambitious goals (Foster, for example, complained of having just a few counselors for thirty-eight hundred students); in addition, Gratz's most vulnerable students had major personal, economic, and academic needs that could not be met by traditional school programs alone. These needs were rooted in conditions outside of the school, and Foster looked beyond Gratz for help in addressing them. He continued to reject the "socioeconomic cop-out"; if hunger and poor clothing were hindering the academic performance of students, it was up to the principal to get clothes (as he had done at Dunbar, for example, scavenging unclaimed clothing from local drycleaners.)[100] This was a demanding stance for an urban educator to take, especially considering the depth of the disparities in family resources that Coleman and subsequent researchers have documented. And yet, Foster's effort to acknowledge and fill those gaps in resources was in itself a statement that schools and principals could not transform urban schools all by themselves. In 1968–69, Gratz secured nearly $100,000 in grants from an eclectic variety of private sources, much of it for programs that the *Inquirer* described as "dealing with students' money problems." The Students' Revolving Loan Program loaned students money to buy suitable clothing and shoes for job interviews and transportation to their jobs until they got paid. The Scholarship Support Fund paid the college application fees that suburban students took for granted but that many Gratz students could not afford. Scientific and medical internships (at one point, eighty students working in sixty-five different laboratories); better counseling services for students on the verge of dropping out; a "communications skills laboratory"—all of these and more were launched in a rush of activity that highlighted the needs of urban students and schools.[101]

Gratz's efforts, both in the school community and beyond, led to some significant accomplishments. The *Philadelphia Tribune*, on its latest visit to the school, wrote that change could be "seen, felt, and heard" and that junior high schools were now sending more of their top students to the school. The *Inquirer* reported on various curricular improvements: an "academic program that bears comparison with any in the city," a computer education program, and a vocational training and placement program involving some thirty-five companies. Most important, these and other articles noted a promising rise in graduation and college admission rates. In the spring of 1968, around 20 percent of the graduating class, or 180 out of 900 students, was admitted to college—a low figure compared with the national average of 51 percent, but a major improvement for a school that two years before had sent only eighteen students to college. Another two hundred graduates had jobs lined up, also a significant gain. Of course, that left more than five hundred students, or close to two-thirds of the class, with no plans—a disappointment for Foster, who wanted to place every student in college or a job. But even the mass of graduates with no plans represented a victory; the class of 1968 was three hundred students larger than the previous year—a tribute, a reporter for the *Philadelphia Evening Bulletin* wrote, to "a school principal who has managed to get youngsters from the ghetto 'turned on' about school."[102]

Foster's accomplishments at Gratz made him into a public figure and helped to counter the disillusionment that pervaded debates over urban school reform. Most notably, he won the prestigious Philadelphia Award, given annually by the Bok Foundation for outstanding civic leadership and service. Foster was only the third African American in forty-eight years to win the $15,000 prize, after the singer Marian Anderson (1941) and the minister Leon Sullivan (1965). The award committee especially praised Foster for raising over $160,000 in scholarship aid and using it to send nearly two hundred members of the class of 1968 to college.[103]

And yet, amid the celebrations of this dynamic principal's work in transforming an urban school, troubling realities persisted. Sunny Decker marveled at Foster's accomplishments: the scholarship money, the revival of school dances and athletics, the long hours of dedicated service to students and parents. But, she said, he met his hardest challenge "when working with the kids . . . You can't expect a school with a dropout rate of more than half to suddenly graduate everyone who enters, just because you're being inspiring." Decker's account of her two years at Gratz—trying to teach students who slept in subway stations, or worked until 2:00 A.M. as the main breadwinner of the house, or made hopeful breakthroughs only to drop out and disappear—helped to illustrate why.[104]

Meanwhile, at the ceremony honoring Foster for the Philadelphia Award, the civil rights leader and U.S. District Judge A. Leon Higginbotham pointed toward a different problem, not with the students, but with a lack of commitment from the larger society. Higginbotham stated that Foster had "[made] his discoveries in one of America's most difficult laboratories—the public

Figure 7. Foster, with his wife, Albertine, in April 1969, after accepting the prestigious Philadelphia Award for outstanding civic leadership and service. He was the third African American in forty-eight years to win the award, after the singer Marian Anderson (1941) and the minister Leon Sullivan (1965). Urban Archives, Temple University Libraries.

school system"—a system he described as being "monitored by all, criticized by many, and helped by so few."[105]

Marcus Foster would continue to struggle with a combination of the problems identified by Decker and Higginbotham; that is, a public that tended to fault the schools for low performance, without adequately supporting them or acknowledging that they labored to meet greater student needs with fewer resources. Could a school like Gratz perform well not just in relation to its own dismal recent history, but in comparison with truly high-performing schools? And could its record of improvement become the rule rather than the exception among similar urban schools? After May 1969, Foster took up such questions in a new way, when the Shedd administration created a position for him as Associate Superintendent of Community Affairs. He would now promote total school community—and struggle with public commitments to urban schools—on a citywide level.

Equity and Excellence—for All Schools

Foster's new role was partly the brainchild of Robert Blackburn, the former director of the Citizens Committee on Public Education (CCPE) who, it will be recalled, had first met Foster on a CCPE visit to the Dunbar Elementary School in the fall of 1960. After his service with the CCPE and in the Peace Corps in Somalia, Blackburn had returned to Philadelphia and taken a job under Shedd, as head of the Office of Integration and Intergroup Education. The school district had created that office in 1964, as a response to pressure from civil rights organizations and Blackburn's own CCPE. By 1969, as Blackburn puts it, his staff of twelve or thirteen people had come to stand for "the black challenge to the status quo in education in Philadelphia." It had spearheaded the use of financial incentives to desegregate the teaching force and the controversial staff-community retreats to address the problem of "white racism" in the schools, among other efforts. "And I really thought," Blackburn says, "that it would probably be more appropriate to have a black leader of this black challenge." Blackburn suggested that Shedd combine the Office of Integration and Intergroup Education and a few other divisions under a new associate superintendency of "community affairs," and bring in someone like Marcus Foster to lead it. Blackburn had roomed with Foster and developed an affinity for him during one of the administrative retreats that Shedd initiated after November 17. "That was when I learned he read scripture every night," Blackburn recalls. When Shedd acted on Blackburn's suggestion and put Foster in charge of the new Office of Community Affairs (OCA), Foster became, at forty-six years old, one of the top-ranking black officials in Philadelphia. Blackburn stayed on as director of Intergroup Education and became what Foster called his "senior vice principal."[106]

Foster's job description as head of the OCA placed more emphasis on easing racial conflict and community "unrest" than it did on improving learning and achievement. But Foster, as in the early days of his involvement with intergroup education, did not separate these goals. Indeed, more than a decade before the Reagan Administration began to criticize sixties-era educators for promoting equity at the expense of excellence, Foster was pushing for both of those goals.[107] He presented integration—now one of his official responsibilities—as a function of quality educational programming. Seeking not only desegregation, but also the kind of "socioeconomic mixture" the Coleman Report had emphasized, Foster argued that Philadelphia had to have "schools of uniform *excellence* throughout the city, so that no student will feel stigmatized about attending a particular school (italics added)." And the key to "excellent" schools, he continued, was the involvement and support of parents, teachers, administrators, and other citizens—including taxpayers.[108] As an associate superintendent, Foster continued to insist that urban schools could not raise their students' achievement without all of these parties taking responsibility for the problem and working collaboratively with each other.

At the OCA, as at Gratz, Foster remained a critic of the schools, and an advocate for students and parents, even as he assumed a position of authority. As the district administrator in charge of responding to the rising tide of student activism and unrest, he continued to insist that the schools be more responsive to student concerns and take more responsibility for their achievement. He gave speeches criticizing teachers who "put kids down" as well as area residents who responded to student demands for better education by saying "throw the ringleaders out, they don't belong in school anyway." He said student activism was a positive force that could be turned to worthwhile ends. "The wrong approach," said Foster, alluding to Police Commissioner Rizzo and his followers, "is the administrator who says, 'I want you to get these pupils back in class.' It is better to say 'I want you to hear what these kids are talking about.'"[109]

Foster's insistence that schools listen to students' concerns came through most dramatically in his response to an escalating gang problem. As Foster assumed his new position at the OCA, violence among fifty-two Philadelphia gangs was resulting in roughly a murder per week, a situation that drew national media attention and prompted hearings by the State Crime Commission. Police chief Rizzo spoke for many Philadelphians—including, no doubt, a number of educators whose schools and students were negatively affected by the violence—when he proposed making gang membership illegal.[110] Foster, by contrast, strenuously rejected the notion that gangs were primarily a criminal justice problem. "How can the teacher or the principal say, 'Poverty is not my business' or 'Drugs are a medical-social problem' or 'Gangs belong to police gang-control programs?'" he asked. Foster acknowledged that gang activity in the schools was a negative behavior that had to be "controlled and eliminated," but it was "purposeful" behavior—a way to seek a sense of power and belonging. He emphasized that his own success at Gratz had been based on finding "legitimate avenues to meet those needs," and he called on other educators to do the same.[111]

Foster's most memorable plea for a deeper understanding of the gang phenomenon came on February 11, 1970, when ten black youths burst into a meeting of top district officials and began firing shots. "Hey, what are you doing?" one shouted. "Talking about gangs? We'll show you what a real gang is." As someone pushed the intruders from the room, Foster announced to the shaken officials, who had indeed been discussing the gang problem, that he had not meant to scare them too badly, but he wanted to show them "how you might feel if you were a kid and you didn't know when or where something like this would happen to you." Foster had arranged for a doctor to be present in case anyone went into shock or suffered a heart attack. However, he had not discussed his plans with Shedd, who said that "for a minute to a minute and a half it was very frightening." The event caused a minor public controversy, and Shedd admitted he did not know how he would have responded if Foster had asked for advance approval. Ever supportive of bold action in the name of change, though, he said that the episode had "brought home the terrible reality of teenage gangs to those insulated, as I was, from the everyday problems of the schools . . . Why focus on the simulation," he asked, "and overlook the fact that kids who live in ghettos face this type of thing all the time?"[112]

Foster called for educators to be more open-minded in their responses to student unrest and misconduct. However, he did not simply portray the students as victims of a failed system. In his speeches as head of the OCA, he suggested that the school system was not entirely to blame for underachievement, and the "community" had not done all it could, within existing institutions, to solve the problem. "It's no longer acceptable to say we have poor schools in our community because 'the man' won't do anything about them,"

Foster told a gathering of roughly a thousand parents at Strawberry Mansion Junior High School in North Philadelphia. Parents had to take the trouble to exercise their power: "We know how to get to 21st and the Parkway now if we want to," he said. They also had to "make education a higher value in our community and get rid of the things that hurt our children"—not simply outside sources of oppression but internal practices such as the failure to read books in the home. Many students did poorly in school because they did not feel it was "smart to be smart," Foster argued, and he called on parents to help reverse the pattern.[113]

Foster's words—his defense of troubled students as well as his call for "internal" changes within the community—were part of a continuing effort to attack urban school problems in all of their dimensions and complexity, as opposed to singling out schools or families for blame. During his time in the Office of Community Affairs, perhaps the most important example of this ever-delicate balancing act came on the issues of decentralization and community control.

In Philadelphia and many other cities, events in New York City served as a constant reminder of the volatility of the community control issue—in particular, the extent to which it had put professional educators and school systems at odds with the families they served. As we have seen, the community control movement started when parents at I.S. 201 in Harlem protested the appointment of a white principal and insisted that they be given a say in running the school. Over the next few years, this notion evolved into an experiment in community control of public schools in the predominantly black Ocean Hill–Brownsville section of Brooklyn—an experiment with aftershocks that rippled across the country. Residents of Ocean Hill–Brownsville were allowed to elect a local board to run their schools, and in the spring of 1968, this board tested the extent of its powers by firing ten white teachers who were members of the United Federation of Teachers (UFT). The union, which had a largely white and Jewish membership, had argued all along that the power to hire and fire teachers and administrators rested solely with the central Board of Education, and in the fall of 1968, after failing to reinstate the teachers by other means, it launched a series of three citywide teachers strikes over a span of nearly two months. The UFT prevailed in its effort to reinstate the teachers, but not before the city had suffered an exceedingly painful ordeal. The local board, supported by allies in the Ford Foundation, the administration of Mayor John Lindsay, and the media, charged the UFT with racism. The UFT, with backing from mainstream labor leaders and many white residents in the city's outer boroughs, charged its opponents with class bias, union-busting, and anti-Semitism. This was not simply a power struggle between unionized educators and black communities over the right to make personnel decisions; it was also fueled by the ongoing ideological clash over who was responsible for the educational failures of urban black children: culturally deprived black families who mainly needed compensatory education such as the More Effective Schools program (which UFT members had actively supported), or racist white educators who needed to be replaced by black ones?[114]

In the Philadelphia school system, Mark Shedd had begun to call for the decentralization of power in 1967, even before he took office, but not much had changed in his first year, and the issue remained potentially explosive. In 1968, for instance, the school board came into conflict with a group of citizens in Germantown, over the extent to which they would be allowed to participate in the affairs of a middle school slated to open in that neighborhood in 1970. The parents ended up with little control over appointments and reviews of personnel, which led to the establishment of a sixty-eight-member commission to study the problem.[115] Foster was a member of the decentralization commission, and after becoming the head of the OCA in 1969, he was well positioned to exercise leadership on the issue.

Foster had made his name with dynamic and responsive leadership at individual schools, so it was not surprising that he supported the idea of decentralizing power and giving schools and communities greater control over their affairs. In speeches around town, he emphasized the need for poor communities—especially poor black communities—to make their voices heard in the curriculum planning process. "White, middle-class planners don't know the suffering of the poor and alienated, haven't been in their skins to feel it, and therefore cannot do the job alone," he said to loud applause at the Strawberry Mansion gathering. "Our only power is in each other. If we get together, we can really move the world."[116]

In keeping with these views, Foster and other members of the Philadelphia decentralization commission promoted greater community participation. However, they did not support community *control*, and in making this distinction, they explicitly tried to avoid what they saw as the mistakes and excesses of Ocean Hill–Brownsville. According to a formal study conducted by the Philadelphia group, New York City had done no pre-planning for its demonstration projects, nor had the Board of Education ever officially recognized them. When Mayor John Lindsay named an advisory panel, headed by

McGeorge Bundy of the Ford Foundation, no one on the panel had notable ties to any of the major ethnic or interest groups that battled over the issue. By contrast, the Philadelphia group enlisted a broad spectrum of support and involvement from the outset. Partly under Foster's influence, the commission held thirty-eight community hearings in all eight districts, and its membership included a wide array of community people and even students. Still, in the Shedd administration, community and student involvement had its limits. Foster spoke frankly of the continued need for professional expertise and authority, stating that educators needed to "be there, participating, helping to encourage and shape this so it doesn't just veer off in all kinds of directions. When people move into an enterprise who are inexperienced, they are apt to want to do things that are inappropriate . . . We can't leave it to happenstance that the kind of community involvement that evolves will be good for children."[117] Foster did say inner-city parents deserved the same community control as suburbanites who routinely pressured school officials to fire teachers they did not like.[118] However, his idea of control—like Shedd's—did not extend to community members actually supplanting school officials in the making of such decisions, as occurred in Ocean Hill–Brownsville.[119]

During the 1969–70 school year, Foster's office mediated various crises that tested his notions of community participation, most notably a highly charged situation at West Philadelphia High School in the fall of 1969. The conflict began when black students, citing the stifling and condescending methods of their white social studies teacher, George Fishman, organized a boycott of his five classes and marched through the halls chanting, "Fishman Must Go!" Several teachers and administrators supported the students in demanding that Fishman be transferred in the name of "quality education." So did a community group that set up pickets outside the school and carried signs proclaiming, "Our Children Want Better Education" and "Quality Education for All Children." As Foster recalled, "It was quite obvious that they were going to test out the issue of community control." On the other side of the issue, the Philadelphia Federation of Teachers, well versed in the Ocean Hill–Brownsville story, certainly feared just that. When Principal Walter Scott, a white man with strong ties and support in the black community, announced he would recommend the transfer of Fishman, whom he called "a learned man but not an effective teacher," the union called for a strike vote. After several tense weeks of maneuvering and demonstrations, Shedd and the school board, eager to avoid a strike on the eve of an important bond election, sided with the union. Fishman kept his job, leaving students and community members embittered.[120]

Figure 8. During a tense situation at West Philadelphia High School in October 1969, Foster *(center)* confers with *(from left)* superintendent Mark Shedd, school board president Richardson Dilworth, school board member George Hutt, and Young Great Society president Herman Wrice. As the Associate Superintendent of Community Affairs from 1969 to 1970, Foster mediated various crises in the system; in this instance, black students were calling for an unpopular white teacher to be transferred, prompting the teachers union to threaten a strike. Urban Archives, Temple University Libraries.

The most significant development in the Fishman case, however, took place after the political conflict ended and Foster's Office of Community Affairs took up the underlying educational issues. Foster felt that legitimate student concerns over educational quality and practice had got lost in a power struggle between the teachers' union, on the one hand, and community activists and their supporters on the school staff, on the other. To refocus attention on the root causes of conflict and improve the quality of education in the school, he and the OCA formed a task force involving members of each of the main constituencies. Students, staff, parents, and community people met to discuss curricula, facilities, and student-teacher relations. They held a two-day problem-solving session involving administrators from virtually every department in the central administration. "It was exciting to watch students and teachers listening to each other and working together," Foster said. "All sides agreed that they were tired of controversy and wanted to concentrate their efforts on improving education at West Philadelphia." The West Philadelphia process led to two system-wide innovations in conflict resolution and student rights. One was a series of off-site training sessions in which students, parents, teachers, and principals received guidance from group dynamics experts on how to negotiate for change in their own schools. The other system-wide change to come out of the OCA-led process was the formation of a citywide committee charged with developing a student bill of rights. A year after the original controversy, the Board of Education formally adopted such a document.[121]

As associate superintendent, Foster tried to balance the responsibilities and power of schools and educators, on the one hand, and students and parents, on the other. Some observers emphasized the difficulty of this balancing act in crises such as the one at West Philadelphia High. Henry Resnik, author of a book on the Shedd years, quoted a Gratz teacher who said Foster was "like a man walking a tightrope. He has to be everything to everybody—white to the whites, black to the blacks, everything." The authors Les Payne and Tim Findley wrote that in his new role Foster was a "buffer Negro," a "compromiser," and a "firefighter for the school district and city." By 1970, they wrote, Foster was "caught in the middle of the controversy, feeling pressure from all sides."[122]

For his part, Foster seems to have felt comfortable, even exhilarated at times, wading into conflicts for the Office of Community Affairs. Indeed, his methods of mediating and making constructive use of the pervasive conflicts of the era were becoming a centerpiece of his contribution to urban school reform. As he argued in reflecting on the West Philadelphia story, conflict was "inevitable, and oftentimes healthy"—that is, if the energies it released could be harnessed in "charting new solutions, rather than in posturing, accusation, and suppression."[123]

A "Crisis of Expectations"

Mediating between communities and educators who often blamed each other for student failures was difficult, but it was not the biggest problem Foster faced as he tried to apply the idea of total school community to an entire system. More troubling still was what Foster perceived as a lack of support from taxpayers and public officials. As a principal, Foster had demonstrated that infusions of money were key to improving urban schools. As a top administrator in one of the nation's largest school systems, he blasted what he saw as the nation's unwillingness to provide the resources needed to make improvement on a vast scale.

Foster argued that a lack of will—not inadequate knowledge or strategies—had caused the failure of one of the major reform initiatives of the decade, the compensatory education movement. Like many others, he acknowledged the disappointing results of the remedial reading and cultural enrichment programs that formed a cornerstone of the Great Society. But unlike critics on the right, who were beginning to assert the futility of liberal spending programs in general, or those on the left, who rejected the premise of cultural deprivation on which compensatory education was based, Foster faulted a failure of will. Initiatives like the Educational Improvement Program (EIP) in Philadelphia, which he had helped to pioneer, or Higher Horizons and More Effective Schools in New York City, were conceptually sound, he argued, but they were not adequately funded. The problems were massive: escalating gang violence; a 60 percent rate of "functional illiteracy" among the city's high school graduates; college attendance rates way below national averages (even with the infusion of tens of thousands of dollars of private scholarship aid); the departure from the city of the kind of high-paying industrial jobs that might have provided a suitable alternative to college.[124] In this context, Foster argued, Americans not only needed to spend more money on education; they needed to channel a disproportionately large share toward poor minority children in the inner cities. "If we are really serious about catching up," he said, echoing those who had begun to argue for "positive discrimination," or "affirmative action" on behalf of poor minority children, "we have to recognize that slicing the pie in equal portions, when the needs are unequal, is an injustice."[125]

The "we" Foster had in mind was not simply the society in some general sense. It was "white people" who felt that to spend disproportionate amounts on black schools that were behind was to "reward ignorance and stupidity." It was the federal government and its prioritization of a "useless, meaningless" war in Vietnam, instead of education. Foster related that he and his colleagues on the national advisory board for Upward Bound, a Great Society program that helped poor students go to college, had failed to secure an additional $100 million to expand their clientele from 23,000 to 100,000 students per year—even as the Vietnam War absorbed the same sum every thirty-six hours. Likewise, he denounced the federal government's rejection of an additional $1 billion in education aid, ostensibly due to fear of inflation, in the context of its far greater expenditures for antiballistic missile systems: "When a plan doesn't work, they don't scrap it. They say, 'Let's put another billion dollars in and find out why it doesn't work.' We are spending billions to find out why systems of destruction don't work, even why they go up and the wings fall off. Let's put more into our schools," Foster urged, "and make them work."[126]

Foster cited this lack of public support and spending as the most important cause of the disillusionment and polarization that wracked urban education. As "proclaimed panaceas" like compensatory education received modest resources and accomplished only modest gains, he said, a "crisis of expectations" arose. Frustration, despair, cynicism, and rage mounted. Inner-city residents came to feel that American society was so corrupt, and so stacked against them, that it was necessary to "destroy the system and start fresh."[127]

In this instance Foster focused on families and communities—how a lack of public support left them frustrated and disillusioned by the quality of education they received. What was also becoming painfully apparent was the impact of this situation on educators such as him. Of course, Foster himself had contributed to the rising expectations of the era. He had worked his way into the principal's office, and in that role he had showed that meaningful change was possible when school communities worked together and educators stopped passing the buck for failure. And yet, Foster's experience in the late 1960s also dramatized the heavy demands of urban school leadership in a context of urban decline. Rising expectations took a toll on educators like him, especially when significant support from the rest of the society was not forthcoming.

The tough position of urban educators was perhaps most poignantly on display in one of Foster's greatest moments of triumph. The very day after the Gratz expansion victory at the school board, as he was being interviewed in his office by *Inquirer* columnist Joe McGinnis, Foster excused himself to meet with members of two opposing gangs; a Saturday-night conflict had spilled into Gratz on Monday, and a boy had been stabbed. When he rejoined McGinnis, Foster struck a rare note of weariness and pessimism about his program and at least some of his students: "I had enough experience running a disciplinary school before I came here to know that the way to solve these problems is not just throw a bunch of people out," he said. "But there comes a time when you've got to realize that some boys just don't belong; that you can never get anywhere with them. I'm afraid I'm at that point with some of these kids now. To keep them around just wouldn't be fair to the others." Meanwhile, in a sobering reminder of the physical toll of trying to educate boys like these, Foster pointed toward a cot in the corner of his office and said to McGinnis: "'Ten minutes a day,' they tell me. 'Lie on that ten minutes a day.' They don't understand I don't have 10 minutes a day." Foster was still in his early forties, but he already had suffered at least one heart attack. (A 1969 news story cited two.)[128]

The demands of being responsible for thousands of urban students also took a toll on Foster's own family. When he accepted the Philadelphia Award, he commented that he planned to spend some of the $15,000 prize on his family, in repayment for the "hours of neglect I have subjected them to." This was no exaggeration; a few months later, after yet another professional accomplishment (the promotion to associate superintendent), Foster was quoted in a Father's Day news feature as saying that he wished he could have spent more time with his daughter, Marsha, during her childhood and adolescence. (She was leaving for Tufts University that fall.) "Even though I've made a conscious effort to alter my pattern so that I could be with my family more," he said, "pressures and responsibilities have kept me long hours on the job. So I tried to make up to Marsha in the quality of our time together what it lacked in quantity."[129]

To be sure, Foster seems to have been somewhat absent from family life long before he was a principal or associate superintendent, for personal as well as professional reasons. Lifelong friend Leon Frisby remembers how he showed up the day after the Fosters' wedding, intending to go out and play pool with Marcus—"because that's what we usually did together"—and encountered stern opposition from Marcus's wife, Albertine, who said, "wait a minute, now, he doesn't go out with you; he's married!" Even so, the two men continued over the years to "go out and enjoy ourselves," despite the disapproval of their wives, who were friends with each other from Cheyney but felt their husbands were bad influences on each other (Leon's wife, Mabel, would not let him name their first son after Marcus).[130]

But while Foster had a longstanding pattern of being gone in the evening, whether because of his lifestyle with Frisby or because of work (including a stint as a cab driver in the 1950s), it seems that demands on his time—and tensions with Albertine over his absence—intensified when he became a high school principal and associate superintendent. By this time, also, Foster was involved in a dizzying array of civic activities, which included, but were not limited to, multiple board memberships (Fellowship House, Downingtown Industrial School, and the North Philadelphia YMCA, among others); committee work at the Fellowship Commission and the city's Health and Welfare Council; and religious counseling at a local prison. In this period, according to Frisby, Albertine struggled with "the idea that [Marcus] was somebody else's person. He wasn't the homebody. He was always out speaking and people calling him, and getting this award and that award, and on and on and on . . . He wasn't the family man she wanted him to be. The people *owned* him." So frustrating was this situation for Albertine, according to Frisby, that she actually relished a period when Marcus had to stay at home convalescing (presumably from his heart attack), because it was the only time she could compete with the many external demands on his time. "She got all the letters. When you inquired about him, she liked the fact that now, 'I'm in charge' of who can see him, messages, what was happening, etc. It was the one time that she was in control," he says.[131]

Among the growing swirl of people who were part of his life as an urban school leader, Foster epitomized optimism and achievement. He was charismatic and confident, a winner of awards and a role model for troubled youth. All of this was true—and yet, it did not capture more complicated realities: the man who gave so much and was so influential in his dealings with other people's children but had little time or energy left for his own family; the perennial optimist who was not sure what to do about some of his toughest students at Gratz; the school leader who was willing to accept responsibility for improving education but grew increasingly angry at what he believed to be the negligence of the larger society; the role model who struggled in private with a drinking problem (his "Achilles heel," says Frisby—though it seems his drinking never had a negative impact on his professional performance). These tensions seem to have had little or no effect on Foster's performance or public persona—in itself, a striking illustration of his basic can-do attitude. He continued to express hope that the cycle of panacea and polarization could be broken—that "this system *can* be made to work." Certainly no one had done more than he had to show that urban schools could be significantly improved. But Foster was no Pollyanna, and inspiring as he was, his work in the late 1960s also underscored the difficulties faced by even the best urban educators in a new era of rising expectations and uncertain finances.

Foster and Frisby continued to go out and "fellowship" during this time. "He loved to talk," says Frisby. "He could talk for hours. He could talk his best talk over a beer. We could talk all into the night." By the late 1960s, Frisby had been "saved" (he was later ordained as a Methodist minister), and he drank soda rather than beer. Foster had always been a spiritual man, too, reading scripture in the evening (though Frisby says he left Christian Science for Protestant churches because he violated its principles by taking medication). In the late 1960s, Frisby remembers how Foster used to turn to him at the bar and say, "It's praying time." "He'd say, 'it's praying time,' because he felt vulnerable . . . And I'd pray for him."[132]

To Oakland

In the spring of 1970, as he mediated crises and used the associate superintendency as a bully pulpit to advocate for urban schools, Foster was approached by school board members from Oakland, California. Oakland was going through its own traumas over community participation in school affairs, especially in what had become a bitter, drawn out process of hiring a new superintendent. One school board meeting had degenerated into a melee that led to the arrest and sensational trial of a group of activists who became known as the "Oakland Five." Barney Hilburn, a longtime member of the Oakland school board, had a connection to Foster and begged him to visit the city and meet with the board. Foster reluctantly agreed, as a courtesy to the desperate-sounding Hilburn, to tack the trip onto the end of a speaking engagement in the Midwest. The Oakland board quickly fell for Foster and offered him the superintendency.[133]

The Oakland offer was intriguing to Foster, not least because he wanted to be a superintendent. Many saw Foster as Mark Shedd's heir apparent in Philadelphia, but no one yet realized that Shedd's days were numbered. As far as Foster knew, he would stay an associate superintendent for some time, and the situation apparently did not sit well with him. Foster's childhood friend Leon Frisby remembers the Oakland decision as another case of Foster's ambitious and competitive nature: "He wanted to get out of situations where he couldn't be in control," he says. "He was a person who loved to be in control."[134] Related to this eagerness to be in charge, Bob Blackburn recalls that, while Foster enjoyed successes and satisfactions in the OCA, he felt less "authentic" than he had as a principal with direct responsibility for results. "He had begun to do consulting on the side, and he said at one point, 'Bob, you know, I'm forty-seven years old, I'm out here being paid to give advice to school districts and so forth, and either I'm gonna have to go do it someplace, or shut up.'"[135]

"Doing it" meant improving achievement and creating excellent schools across an entire public school system—the ultimate challenge and responsibility for an urban educator in the new era of raised expectations. As a place to take up that challenge, Foster found Oakland appealing. It was much smaller than Philadelphia—just 70,000 students, compared to 291,000. He had always emphasized the need to attack large problems in manageable steps. If he wanted to show that all schools and students could succeed, perhaps Oakland was a good place to try?

Foster went back to Philadelphia and shared his interest in the Oakland job with a few colleagues. Bob Blackburn was furious at the idea of him leaving prematurely. Before long, though, Foster had accepted Oakland's offer and convinced Blackburn to accompany him there as his deputy superintendent.

Shortly before they left, *Bulletin* columnist Harry Toland wrote that Foster would be missed in many ways, but "mostly for his optimism and hope." By way of contrast, Toland noted that another black member of the Shedd administration, Dr. Samuel Woodard, had recently quit his position and denounced the district as a "racist system" in which "whites make decisions for blacks." Strong words, said Toland, for an administration that had been accused by some whites of "giving" the system to blacks. The columnist asked Foster if Woodard was right and, characteristically, Foster offered a more positive take, emphasizing how much progress had been made in just five years, before which time there had not been even one black department chair in the system. At the same time, in a subtle way, Foster's remarks suggested that he was more optimistic about the possibility of big changes—system wide changes—in his new city than in the one he was leaving. "Oakland looks do-able," Foster said. "I know kids and teachers and communities. These basically don't change. It gives me confidence. If it works at Gratz and in sections of Philadelphia, it can work in Oakland."[136]

CHAPTER 5

Beyond Community Control: Accountability and Achievement in the Oakland Public Schools

THE Oakland Public Schools may have been a smaller and more manageable school district than its counterpart in Philadelphia, but by 1970 it,
too, was in a state of crisis. A nearly all-white city on the eve of World War
II, Oakland was transformed as dramatically as Philadelphia by the forces of
African American migration and deindustrialization. In the early twentieth
century, black residents had been confined to the segregated neighborhoods
and schools of West Oakland, but after the war they pushed into East Oakland and other parts of the "flatlands" that run alongside San Francisco Bay
and constitute roughly two-thirds of the area of the city. By 1970, African
Americans constituted 34.5 percent of the population of the city (up from
about 3 percent in 1940) and more than 50 percent of the students in the
public schools. (At this time Latinos and Asian Americans together made
up roughly 11 percent of the city's total population, a percentage that would
more than double in the following two decades.)[1] In spite of their dramatically increased presence in the schools, however, black Oaklanders continued
to have little influence on the affairs of the district. School board members
were elected at large, though by custom they resigned prior to the end of
their terms, thus enabling the remaining board members to appoint a successor to run as an incumbent; in this way the board tended to be a self-perpetu-
ating institution. And a conservative institution it was: board members were
almost entirely white, Republican, and drawn from the business and legal
communities. Only in 1958 did the board appoint its first African American,
Barney Hilburn—and he was a Republican lawyer.[2]

During the 1960s, the school board became a focal point for the anger of black Oaklanders who felt it did not include their voices or meet the needs of their children. These feelings had first erupted in a major way in 1961, over the board's decision to build a new high school in the affluent Oakland hills, with attendance boundaries that resulted in a nearly all-white student body. For several years, an interracial coalition fought to change those boundaries at Skyline High School and desegregate the city schools in general. But by the mid-1960s, as these efforts failed to change the system, black activists were shifting their focus to other priorities—in particular, a more equitable distribution of school district resources and a higher-quality education in predominantly black schools. On these issues, too, the board and the district fell into disfavor. Achievement in black schools in the flatlands lagged behind that of students in the nearly all-white schools in the hills. Meanwhile, in 1969, it was revealed that the district had misused $5.5 million in funds received under Title I of the Elementary and Secondary Education Act (ESEA) of 1965, dispersing the money throughout the district rather than channeling it to educationally disadvantaged students. By the end of the decade, anger over these and other issues turned the search for a new superintendent of schools into one of the most divisive political conflicts of the era in Oakland.[3]

From the beginning of the selection process in 1968, the school board had come into conflict with the Black Caucus, an umbrella organization representing a variety of political groups, over the extent of community input in the decision. In May 1969, the situation rapidly deteriorated when the board offered the job to Las Vegas Superintendent James Mason, a white candidate whom it had interviewed without informing the official search committee. At a packed board meeting shortly thereafter, Caucus members declared they would not leave until the board withdrew its selection of Mason. When the board attempted to adjourn anyway, Percy Moore, the executive director of Oakland's federally funded antipoverty agency, blocked the doors and scuffled with police. The police used Mace to clear the room and arrested Moore and four others, who became known as the "Oakland Five." Later that year, after Mason had rejected Oakland's offer, Black Caucus members intervened again in the selection process, this time crossing the country to "educate" the board's next choice, a black superintendent, as to "what Oakland is and what the school board is." That candidate, Ercell Watson of Trenton, New Jersey, also turned down the Oakland job, and while the Black Caucus apparently was not a factor in his decision, its actions were a dramatic rebuke to the board's authority. In the wake of the Watson rejection, the Black Caucus even set up its own superintendent-screening committee and counterparts to all of the other existing school board committees. In a testament to just how unpopular the board had become, individuals from dozens of organizations, ranging from the Black Panthers to the League of Women Voters, pledged their support for the new shadow school board.[4]

In offering the superintendency to Marcus Foster in the spring of 1970, the board tried again to hire a black educator and restore the legitimacy of the system. This time, it succeeded beyond what anyone could have imagined. In his first few years in Oakland, Foster defused the political crisis over school governance and mobilized thousands of citizens, white as well as black, in a massive campaign to improve public education. Supporters at the Ford and Rockefeller Foundations watched hopefully as Foster and his hand-picked deputy superintendent, Robert Blackburn, developed what appeared to be a viable alternative to New York City's explosive experiment in community control (which Ford, in particular, had done much to promote). The Oakland approach centered on the Master Plan Citizens Committee (MPCC)—an elaborate, three-tier structure consisting of ninety-one school site committees (one for each school), five citywide task forces, and a central council headed by the superintendent himself. Through this structure, Foster achieved, on a system-wide level, some semblance of the community participation he had promoted as a principal and associate superintendent in Philadelphia. The Foster-led school system had its critics, but their numbers and visibility dwindled precipitously as the MPCC gave all Oaklanders a vehicle not only for airing grievances, but for acting on them.[5]

Foster's superintendency in Oakland was a notable conclusion to a story of struggle in the 1960s, but it was more than that: it was also an important early chapter in a more recent history of efforts to hold schools accountable for eliminating racial and socioeconomic achievement gaps. As he had done throughout his career, Foster insisted that the Oakland schools produce results for the students and parents they served, regardless of race or social class background. Now, however, he increasingly expressed this goal in terms of accountability and "grade level achievement." This early 1970s push for accountability and achievement by an African American superintendent complicates the "equity to excellence" narrative that structures many accounts of recent U.S. educational history. In that narrative, which ranges from critical to celebratory, the publication of A Nation at Risk (1983) usually looms large as the major turning point in a shift from the desegregation efforts of the 1960s and 1970s to the business-influenced excellence and accountability schemes of recent years.[6] The equity to excellence narrative is certainly useful in a broad sense. However, as Foster's tenure in Oakland shows, the emphasis on academic achievement and accountability in our era is not simply a counter-reaction or corrective to the equity agenda of the 1960s; it is also—in part—a *legacy* of the black freedom movement.[7] When President George W. Bush and a variety of bipartisan supporters promoted education as the "new civil right" and the No Child Left Behind Act of 2002 as a corrective to the "soft bigotry of low expectations," they took their cues from the African American educators, parents, and activists of Marcus Foster's era.[8]

However, accountability has been a contested concept, shifting in response to historical and political context. In Oakland, Foster offered a vision of *shared* accountability that stands in contrast to the more recent approach of NCLB. Building on the approaches he had developed throughout the 1960s, the new superintendent insisted on accountability not only from educators but from families, taxpayers, and political and economic institutions as well. This effort to involve multiple actors was essential to a variety of accomplishments in Oakland, including the first successful bond measure in seventeen years, improvements in reading test scores, and a spectacular caravan of three thousand Oaklanders who traveled to the state capital to secure additional state funding for urban school systems. At the same time, Foster developed a forceful critique of a narrower kind of accountability, which increasingly blamed the schools—or the families they served—for persistent gaps in achievement.

The Urban Crisis and the Crisis of the Schools in Oakland

In 1966, the *Wall Street Journal* and other national publications spotlighted Oakland as a "tinderbox" that was likely to be "the next Watts."[9] As in Philadelphia, the sense of sudden crisis was understandable, but it also masked decades of social conflict. Oakland had no pre-Sixties golden age that was free of social conflict.

Granted, in the 1950s the city's political and business leaders worked hard to portray their city in such terms. In the early twentieth century, civic elites had tried to mute the rough-and-tumble conflicts of ward-based electoral politics by creating a council-manager form of government and a professionalized school bureaucracy headed by a superintendent, among other reforms characteristic of the Progressive era. In the 1940s, the Congress of Industrial Organizations (CIO) and its sympathizers had challenged that system, mounting a general strike and a class-based movement for an elected mayor, public-owned mass transit, public works, and increased funding for education and social programs.[10] But by the early 1950s, the labor-inspired challenge to Oakland's Republican business interests had gone down to defeat. For most of the decade, those interests—led by *Oakland Tribune* publisher and former Republican U.S. senator William Knowland and Kaiser Industries CEO Edgar Kaiser—spoke of Oakland, as one observer said, like members of a chamber of commerce extolling "a salutary climate, the excellence of transportation, and the friendliness and diligence of the natives." The boosterish climate reached a peak in 1956, when Oakland, under the slogan "citizens make Oakland a wonderful place," was one of eleven winners of the "All-America City" competition.[11]

But if "All-American" Oakland was run in the 1950s by a conservative political establishment with little major opposition, it also was increasingly divided by racial conflict. As of 1940, African Americans had constituted only about 3 percent of the city's population, but that would change dramatically as a result of World War II and its aftermath. Migrants from the South came in droves to work in Henry J. Kaiser's shipyards and continued to come even after the boom was over. Well before the turmoil of the 1960s, whites in Oakland and other cities violently resisted the movement of blacks out of crowded ghettos like West Oakland and into white neighborhoods and workplaces beyond.[12]

As in Philadelphia, the schools were also a site of racial conflict. Prior to the 1950s, most black students in Oakland were segregated in McClymonds High School and its feeder system in West Oakland. School board meetings were sleepy affairs with minimal public attendance. With the movement of the rapidly expanding African American community beyond West Oakland, however, came violent turf battles. The worst conflicts took place in two high schools, Oakland Technical and Castlemont, which served the racially changing areas of North and East Oakland, respectively. In 1957, gang fighting and other outbreaks of racial violence escalated to the point where the police department was dispatching fifteen squad cars to Tech every day.[13] As City Manager Wayne Thompson noted, violence in racially changing schools and neighborhoods played an important role in a larger story of urban decline: "When you have unsettled conditions and 'rumbles' and riots taking place in a school," he said, "it's amazing how many 'For Sale' signs you see in the area. The businessmen feel it very quickly. It really hurts business."[14] The "For Sale" signs were posted by whites; in the 1950s, nearly 100,000 middle-income whites left Oakland for new, racially segregated suburbs like Fremont and Hayward. Meanwhile, less affluent and educated blacks took their place; between 1940 and 1960, the black population rose 500 percent, from 14,000 to 84,000.[15]

The school disturbances of the late 1950s prodded Oakland's conservative political elite to become part of the same Ford Foundation reform effort that Marcus Foster was participating in at the Dunbar Elementary School in Philadelphia. Oakland city manager Thompson started the process in the late 1950s by spearheading the Associated Agencies, a program that got the schools, the police department, the courts, and other city agencies to coordinate their response to incidents of juvenile delinquency. Thompson and others had come to see antidelinquency efforts as the key to preventing middle-class neighborhoods from turning into poor, black ghettos. To that end, they encouraged school principals to welcome the help of police officers, rather than see this intervention as an admission of weakness. They prodded police officers to work with recreation officials rather than dismiss them as coddlers of vicious juveniles. Eventually, these antidelinquency efforts came to the attention of Paul Ylvisaker, the driving force behind the Ford Foundation's emerging involvement in urban problems, and in 1961 Oakland received a $2 million grant to continue developing its project as part of the foundation's new Gray Areas program. In their proposal for the Oakland Interagency Project (OIP), Oakland's public officials, along with corporate leaders like Kaiser and Knowland and the black leadership of the local NAACP and Urban League, said they wanted to address "broad community problems" and "get at causes"[16]

But what did it mean to "get at causes?" What was the nature of the problem, and what needed to be done? As Oakland's leaders answered these questions, the main influence on their thinking, as on that of their counterparts in the other Gray Areas cities of Philadelphia, Boston, New Haven, and Washington, D.C., was the education-based liberalism that was ascendant at the time. In other words, they had come to believe that "getting at causes" consisted of addressing a vicious cycle of racial discrimination, poverty, and cultural dysfunction among Oakland's migrant newcomers. As Oakland's Ford Foundation proposal stated, blacks had "never been permitted to participate fully" in American social and economic life—they had been excluded—and as a result, they had "lagged in acquiring the values, standards, and accepted behavior patterns of the larger society." To overcome the alleged cultural deprivation of their home and community life, including a lack of appreciation for the value of education, the newcomers were in need of "compensatory education." In keeping with these views, the Oakland Gray Areas program emphasized such elements as remedial reading instruction, after-school study programs, the addition of librarians to elementary school staffs, and in-service training for teachers, counselors, and other staff in several of Castle-mont High School's feeder schools.[17]

The educational liberalism of the early 1960s carried a mixed legacy that would echo into the 1970s and our own time. Oakland's "Comp Ed" programs, like others around the country, helped focus a new level of attention not only on the social adjustment of urban children (a longstanding focus in urban education), but on their academic performance as well. As we have seen in relation to Marcus Foster's elementary school program in Philadelphia, this focus on academic achievement and reading readiness among urban children in some ways prefigured subsequent research on the importance of high ex-pectations and cultural capital on a child's academic success. Compensatory programs showed promise as a remedy—albeit an expensive one, if pursued seriously—for low academic performance. In Oakland, for instance, elemen-tary school children who received the special reading and language programs generally did better on standardized tests than those in control groups. Such programs did not come cheap, and they were no substitute for quality per-sonnel and leadership; according to J. M. Regal, the Ford-funded evaluator of the Oakland project, schools with a dynamic principal tended to make more profitable use of the project. Despite such issues, however, the schools conducted a promising experiment—one that, according to Regal, they could improve with greater investments of research and money.[18]

If compensatory education had potential as an educational policy, however, many of its proponents promised too much for it as a social policy response to the urban crisis. Like their counterparts in Philadelphia, city leaders and school district officials pitched the Ford-funded programs as a way to im-prove schools, but unlike school-site educators, they still saw such improve-ments as a means to the larger social ends of reducing juvenile delinquency, racial violence, white flight, and poverty. In 1964, when President Lyndon Johnson declared war on poverty, Wayne Thompson and others transformed the Oakland Gray Areas project into the city's federally funded antipoverty agency, and compensatory education continued to play a big part in their plans. The Oakland Economic Development Council (OEDC), as the new agency was called, allotted nearly half of its initial $1.5 million in Office of Economic Opportunity (OEO) funds directly to the Oakland Public Schools. Oakland began to fight an educational war on poverty.[19]

Yet, Oakland's leaders erred in the extent to which they traced poverty to the cultural and educational backwardness of the poor themselves. Indeed, those leaders had themselves sowed seeds of the city's problems. As early as the 1930s, civic leaders had deemphasized the further industrial development of the central city, with its congestion and labor problems, and instead promoted a vision of Oakland as a metropolitan hub specializing in financial, transportation, and governmental services. In the 1940s and 1950s, as corporations did in fact relocate from Oakland to the newer cities and suburbs of southern Alameda County, these leaders succeeded too well; there were not enough jobs to employ the many unskilled, African American workers who had migrated to Oakland, and the jobs that did exist were controlled by exclusionary unions.[20] Compensatory education may have showed promise as an educational approach (and indeed, even this claim depended heavily on who implemented the programs), but modestly funded improvements in education and other social services could not, by themselves, solve social and economic problems that were rooted in discrimination and under- or unemployment. To place such a burden on the schools was to help set the stage for disillusionment with urban school reform.

For their part, African American migrants and other black residents were not passive victims of the changes that transformed cities in the postwar era. As the historian Robert Self argues, in Oakland they responded with a critique of urban political institutions and power arrangements—specifically, corporate, union, and political leaders' unequal distribution of jobs according to race, and the failure of liberal antipoverty policies to change such inequalities.[21] As in Philadelphia and other cities, this local movement for Black Power centered on education, too. In the flatlands, black parents and activists took an intense interest in the schools, and unlike those who lamented the alleged cultural deprivation of the city's newcomers, these parents and activists began to target the allegedly racist policies and practices of the school system itself.

For a decade prior to Marcus Foster's arrival in Oakland, the school system had been an important site of struggle over power arrangements and governance in the city. In particular, African Americans insisted they needed more control over educational policies and resources because the white-run system was harming their interests. The Skyline High School controversy of the early 1960s sowed the seeds of this conflict in an especially vivid way. Previously, the attendance boundaries for Oakland's high schools had stretched from the flatlands toward the more affluent hills, resulting in a degree of integration

(especially as black settlement expanded across Oakland). Skyline's attendance zone, by contrast, ran lengthwise across the hills: ten miles long and
a mile wide. Not only were the students in this zone nearly all white; Skyline
also catered to a kind of intra-city white flight out of the rapidly integrating
schools and low-income neighborhoods of the flatlands. District leaders apparently were trying to prevent the further exodus of white residents out of
the city and the school system. But in the wake of the *Brown* decision, at a
moment when interest in desegregation in northern cities was running high,
it was not surprising that their plans for Skyline aroused bitter and lasting
opposition.[22]

An interracial coalition of activists failed to alter the district's plans and
achieve desegregation in any substantial way, and over the course of the decade, anger at the school system evolved into the political crisis over community involvement that led to the hiring of Marcus Foster.[23] By 1967, the city's
antipoverty agency not only had stopped channeling its OEO funds to the
school board; that year, a new and more radical director of the agency, Percy
Moore, severed ties with the city altogether and launched an effort to organize low-income African Americans into a political power bloc that might
exercise greater control over the allocation of jobs and resources in Oakland
(including the main school district budget, which was more than twenty-five
times the size of the roughly $2 million budget of the poverty program). As
part of this plan, the agency piloted several attempts to create a neighbor-
hood-based school board as in Ocean Hill–Brownsville.[24] These experiments
did not go far, and by 1970, disaffection with the system had hit rock bottom.
In that year, residents of Oakland's flatlands—those whose schools were most
in need of new resources—mobilized to help defeat several school bond measures proposed by a school board they had come to see as unaccountable and,
indeed, illegitimate.

The crisis that Marcus Foster walked into in 1970 was one of school performance as well as governance; African Americans mobilized not only against
white, affluent Oaklanders' political grip on the school board and other institutions, but against what they saw as the system's responsibility for the low
academic achievement of black students. The contrast between this set of
concerns and those of Oakland's downtown leaders was evident, though not
widely appreciated, as early as 1957. In that year, as the Associated Agencies
focused on controlling violence in high schools with rising black enrollments,
a group of about twenty parents protested a record of low expectations and
achievement in the city's all-black high school, McClymonds. At a meeting

with the principal and other school staff, the parents suggested that "Mack" students were going to college in miniscule numbers because their counselors were discouraging them from applying. The staff, according to the *California Voice*, a San Francisco–based black newspaper, responded by emphasizing the students' poor preparation for high school.[25] If indeed the students were poorly prepared, the parent protesters had reason to fault the system itself. In 1952, for instance, as they constructed a new building for McClymonds, school officials angered some parents when they watered down the curriculum to fit the supposed needs of the students in the segregated school. The "modified" curriculum included biology classes that were designed to pay a "good deal of attention . . . to the care of the hair, skin, and feet." As J. M. Regal noted in his evaluation for the Ford Foundation, the schools tended to treat low achievement among poor, minority children as a given—"something which had always been."[26]

The McClymonds parents' protest over low expectations would echo and gain force up to the time of Marcus Foster's arrival. African Americans in Oakland took issue with the portrayal of poverty and school failure as problems rooted in the cultural deprivation, behavior, and aptitudes of the poor themselves. A leading promulgator of these critiques was the Ad Hoc Committee for Quality Education (AHCQE), a coalition of twenty-one groups that formed in Oakland in the spring of 1966, just as community pressure was sweeping Marcus Foster into Gratz High School on the other coast. In both cities the grievances of African American parents and community members were similar. Ad Hoc Committee members demanded that the district change its discipline and expulsion policy, which, they charged, pushed hundreds of young black males into the streets and allowed the schools to duck responsibility for educating them. The Committee drew upon the district's own publications to quantify and spotlight what would come to be called the achievement gap: students in all-black schools had less than half the average percentile rank of their counterparts at white schools; poor students actually tested worse as they advanced from grade to grade, and in the system as a whole—now more than 50 percent black—the average child tested below the national averages in math, reading, and writing. The Ad Hoc Committee report explicitly held the school system responsible for these gaps. In particular, the epigraph, by the critic John Holt, summed up the notion that liberals were blaming the victim for educational failure when in fact the schools themselves were to blame:

The conventional wisdom of our day has it that the reason that
slum children do badly in school lies in the children. It goes on
to say that the children's lack of ability and skill is not their fault,
but the fault of their environment, their neighborhoods, above
all their homes and families . . . The diagnosis is false. The most
important reasons for the failure of slum children's education lie
not in the children but in the schools.[27]

The Ad Hoc Committee and its allies offered an important critique of the liberal idea of cultural deprivation and made a compelling case that the schools
tended to use that idea to duck responsibility for improving their own performance. However, like the downtown leaders who redeveloped Oakland
and the liberals who launched the educational war on poverty, these activists
tended to oversimplify the problems facing city schools. Even the comments
of Oakland parents and activists sometimes hinted at the negative impact of
non-school factors on academic achievement; as they criticized the schools,
for instance, some expressed frustration over their friends' and neighbors'
general apathy and lack of concern about school issues. Meanwhile, the Ad
Hoc Committee admitted that "just one of these [disciplinary cases] can
mess up a class," but it offered no solution other than to suggest vaguely that
the school system "take an interest in all of its children, even the ones who
seem to give them a difficult time." As J. M. Regal wrote in his evaluation for
the Ford Foundation, community groups and other critics had attacked the
schools for failing to compensate for "the deficiencies of a society which has
deprived families of equal opportunity in employment, housing, health, and
leisure activities." Rather than single out the schools (or, for that matter, families) for blame, Regal argued, Oakland and other cities needed to examine
and address the "complex interdependence of many forces which affect the
lives of children."[28]

Oakland failed to produce such a complex response to its educational
problems in the years leading up to Marcus Foster's arrival. The failure was
dramatized in October 1966, for example, when the Ad Hoc Committee for
Quality Education, following a strategy employed by New York City parents
and activists several years before, urged students to boycott their classes for
three days and attend community-sponsored "freedom schools" instead. Not
only did few attend the freedom schools, but on the first day of the boycott,
in a continuation of gang activity and vandalism that had begun the night
before, several hundred black youths entered Castlemont High School and

assaulted five teachers, leaving one with critical head injuries. Violence and vandalism then continued through the night in East Oakland. In the days and weeks after the disturbance, which was one of the worst of the decade in Oakland, a state investigation and other efforts to make sense of the events managed only to identify opposing interpretations of who was to blame. As in Philadelphia's more severe riot of 1964, some denounced the students as hoodlums and blamed the Ad Hoc Committee for encouraging and inciting them with its boycott. Proponents of this law and order position included Superintendent Stuart Phillips, teachers who called for uniformed police protection in school buildings, and members of the Alameda County Board of Supervisors, which asked for a grand jury investigation. For their part, the Ad Hoc Committee and its sympathizers argued that the violence began before the boycott and was rooted in anger over the schools' punitive disciplinary policies and failure to provide "equal educational opportunity."[29] Lost in the controversy over who to blame was any discussion of how better to educate not only the riotous youths, but the majority of students who remained in their classrooms and in some cases helped teachers defend themselves.

Marcus Foster and Shared Accountability

Marcus Foster's arrival in 1970 marked a turning point in the crises over school governance and low achievement in the Oakland school system. In late June, just a few days before Foster began his work in Oakland, his friend U.S. Circuit Court Judge Leon Higginbotham gave a speech back at the Philadelphia Urban Coalition, which was honoring Foster in absentia. Higginbotham captured Foster's challenge, and his ambition, in Oakland: "It is time to get beyond rhetoric and polarization and name-calling," the jurist argued. "We must move from issue-raising to issue-solving." Higginbotham, no doubt thinking of Foster's accomplishments at Gratz, called for a "synthesis" of administrators, students, faculty, and community with "the capacity to accept and solve" educational problems.[30] In the next few years, Foster would make notable headway toward such a synthesis. He incorporated the concerns of black Oaklanders into the deliberations and decisions of the school district for the first time, and as he did so, he not only defused the crises of the 1960s; he also helped pioneer an ethos of urban school accountability that continues to resonate today.

At first, it seemed that Foster's selection as superintendent only exacerbated tensions in Oakland. This time, the conflict was not between black and white Oaklanders; instead, the hiring of an African American candidate highlighted competing political styles and visions within Oakland's black population. In particular, Foster's arrival divided "community leaders still on the outs with the system," as one journalist described the Black Caucus, and "those who have been brought into the system in leadership roles."[31]

Foster got off to a rough start with the Black Caucus. Its leaders were less interested in whether he was black (though that was certainly a good thing) than in whether he would be a forceful critic of the white-dominated political establishment that they saw as a root of black Oakland's problems. Foster first met with members of the Black Caucus one Sunday evening in April 1970, as part of a whirlwind tour of the city shortly after his selection. Asked about the meeting the next day, as he prepared to attend a school board ceremony in his honor and head back to Philadelphia, he told a reporter, "When brothers and sisters get together, it's always friendly." By Tuesday, however, three Black Caucus members were denouncing Foster at a press conference for "betraying" them. Dr. Norvel Smith, former head of Oakland's war on poverty program, and coincidentally a childhood classmate of Foster's in South Philadelphia, worried that Foster "wouldn't have the guts to be his own man." John George, a founder of the Ad Hoc Committee for Quality Education, called Foster a "mouthematician," full of rhetoric. Donald McCullum said the board had hired Foster as a "palliative and panacea" to provide high black visibility, and he predicted that "the anointed ones—the so-called responsible people— will be lined up soon to confirm the board's selection." Caucus members were apparently angry that Foster had not stated publicly some critical impressions of the Oakland situation he had shared with them in private.[32] Of course, this was no surprise. The Black Caucus was used to attacking the system from their position outside of it, but Foster would soon be the top man on the inside, and he no doubt had little interest in rebuffing the board that had just offered him the job.

The next day, as McCullum had predicted, a number of established black leaders called their own press conference, which they devoted as much to condemning the Black Caucus as to praising Foster's appointment. Over two hundred strong, the gathering included the two black members of the school board, numerous clergy, and representatives of the redevelopment agency, the Oakland Youth Council, and other organizations. Speakers from this group castigated the Black Caucus for being unrepresentative of Oakland's black population and unwilling to work at reforming existing institutions, including the school system. Ralph Williams of the West Oakland Planning Council, considered by many to be something of a militant advocate of the poor himself, said that "the ones who are making the most noise have no children at all in the schools. I think it is time that those of us who have children in the Oakland schools start speaking out." Black school board member Charles Goady declared that militance and activism were "commendable when promoted in dissent for the result of progress. Unfortunately," he said, referring to Percy Moore and other advocates of mobilizing the poor, "this militancy and activism has taken the cover of exploitation of some non-vocal blacks and intimidation of others, while a power base has been established for a few ambitious, power-hungry individuals."[33]

Surely the vote of confidence from other black leaders was helpful and appreciated, though it quickly became clear that Foster was more than capable of defining himself and winning the support of Oaklanders. Readers of his weekend interviews would have found it difficult to categorize him as either establishment or community, moderate or militant—and not because he failed to take a stand. In Foster, the school board had hired an educator who somehow managed to be both a defender and a critic of the school system. Certainly on some key points he echoed Goady and other critics of the Black Caucus. He said he was interested in educating children, not in using the schools to build a "power base." He rejected "non-negotiable demands" in favor of "parity involvement" and participation by "each member of the community"—including, he pointedly added, the superintendent.[34]

At the same time, Foster echoed critiques of the schools and the larger society that he and other black educators and activists had been emphasizing for years. The board and central office had to provide teachers with the resources and freedom they needed, Foster said, but "if there isn't achievement, then we should ask why." Regarding militant student activists, there was "no reason to get upset" at the sight of them chanting up and down the halls; they were sincere and deserved a hearing. The insistent, passionate tone of these and other statements could not have been more different from that of his predecessor, Stuart Phillips, and nowhere was the difference more noticeable than on questions of finance. Where Phillips lamented the district's fiscal problems and emphasized the limits they placed on the quality of education in the system, Foster complained of "too many educators holding on to the limitations of finance . . . We must all take up the cudgels of battle on this and demand that our country allocate the necessary funds to the greatest resource we have—our kids. We have to be aggressive and not apologetic about it."[35]

Foster's passionately expressed commitment to action and achievement for all students helped bridge the divisions that surrounded his appointment. He was not a "militant," in the confrontational manner of the Black Caucus, and yet, as he playfully responded to a questioner who tried to pin down his stance, he took "real pleasure" in the concept. "I myself am militant about getting children to read, persons involved," he said. "I would rather have a militant group and take my chances. It is easier than dealing with complete apathy . . . Where there's conflict, there's energy." Such forcefulness soon impressed even some of those who had been wary. Bob Blackburn relates how, after hearing Foster speak in West Oakland, one prominent activist leaned to another, and joked, "We're going to have to get guns to protect this nigger!" As Blackburn says, "I'm sure they thought he was a nine on a scale of authenticity and power, if not militancy, that night."[36]

Meanwhile, the Black Caucus's archenemy, *Oakland Tribune* editor William Knowland, was no less a fan of Foster's, saying he had "never met another communicator like that." Neither had many other Oaklanders, white as well as black. As Foster's wife Albertine wrote to Leon and Mabel Frisby back home in Philadelphia, "Everywhere we go people gather around him like he is a gift from heaven. Of course," she added, poking fun at her husband's ego, "you know he loves this."[37] Once again, personal charm and charisma played no small part in Foster's ability to bridge the racial and political divides of the era. Blackburn tells of the time at an Oakland school board meeting when a woman went to the microphone and "praised Marc to the skies," prompting applause from the audience. Foster said he was touched, almost embarrassed, at which point he turned to Blackburn and said, "Bob, please blush for me." "The room broke into gales of laughter," Blackburn says. "It was this ease, even playfulness about race—things were often tense in those days—which endeared him to everyone."[38] On another occasion, Foster returned to the office after a rare vacation and found a drawing of a scared little man standing waist-deep in a huge wing-tip shoe—Blackburn's attempt to illustrate the difficulty of filling the superintendent's shoes for a few days. Foster sent his deputy an official memo: "I got a chuckle out of the card . . . The message I got was that you were saying black folks tend to have big feet."[39]

Initially, some made the racialized assumption that while Foster had obvious flair and charisma, his white deputy (also known for his wit) must be the person of real substance behind him. But "that lasted about an hour and a half," Blackburn says, as Foster demonstrated his firm command of urban educational issues.[40] Above all, Foster's leadership in Oakland was shaped from the beginning by his longstanding insistence that the school system

Figure 9. Superintendent Foster and his deputy, Robert Blackburn *(left)*. Going back to their work together in Philadelphia, the two men had a close and comfortable bond that helped defuse the racial tensions that had permeated Oakland school politics in the 1960s. Courtesy of Robert Blackburn.

succeed with all children, regardless of their racial or socioeconomic background. In Philadelphia, when educators had complained of their inability to cope with external social and economic problems that impinged on their students' lives, Foster had criticized their "buck-passing attitude" and emphasized the need to "get youngsters learning *no matter what it takes*."[41] In Oakland, he staked out the same basic position in his first big speech, to an overflow crowd of more than 2,800 teachers and district staff who came to Oakland High School to hear him kick off the 1970–71 school year. Warming up gradually, in measured tones that contrasted with the political upheaval he described, Foster described the "dissent and turmoil" that had made school systems "both the focus and the locus of the social revolution." No other institution had promised so much, he said, "yet the chasm between our promise and our performance, particularly for the urban poor and minority groups, is there for all to see."[42] Foster's answer was not to moderate those lofty promises, but to fulfill them.

Foster's insistence that the schools fulfill the promise of public education for all children, regardless of racial or socioeconomic status, was a familiar refrain from his previous work and from the black freedom struggles of the 1960s. At the same time, his language was a harbinger of times to come in urban school reform. From the vantage point of the early twenty-first century, in the era defined by No Child Left Behind, one word stands out more than any other in Foster's inaugural speech: accountability.

Building on ideas Mark Shedd had begun to introduce in Philadelphia, Foster insisted that teachers and schools set "measurable" objectives and be accountable for meeting them. As a rudimentary example, he suggested that "if one third of your students are running out on the streets, your first objective should be to improve your attendance record—say by 50 percent within three months." A more substantial objective would be to produce grade-level reading scores on standardized tests. As the latter example suggested, Foster's argument for measurable objectives went hand in hand with testing as a means of assessment. Making a medical analogy, he described what educators today would call pre-assessment and formative assessment: "When you go to the doctor, you don't stand in front of him and say: 'Here I am. Guess what's wrong with me.' You subject yourself to a diagnostic procedure. The teacher in dealing with the student cannot simply say, 'Tell me what you need to learn.' We have to use certain diagnostic techniques to find out where he is. And that is testing, diagnostic testing." Noting that doctors conduct further testing to see if the patient is improving—"you might call this a kind of achievement test"—he went on to assert that teachers, too, must conduct such tests and use the data to adjust and improve their practices if necessary.[43]

In part, Foster's language of accountability and measurable outcomes stemmed from the world of business management, which was beginning to exert a significant influence in education. Business and political leaders were increasingly arguing that school systems should be run like businesses, with concern for cost effective, goal-oriented management.[44] But pressure from the business world was only part of the story; the more striking and important influence on Foster's notion of accountability was the ongoing African American freedom movement itself. As we have seen, the struggles of the 1960s were not simply about who would run the school system; they were also about the outcomes of urban education—specifically, a dismal record of underachievement and failure among so many African American children. That dismal record motivated John George and his colleagues to form the Ad Hoc Committee for Quality Education in 1966, and it was what motivated Marcus Foster to call for accountability in 1970. In particular, Foster promised to focus more heavily than ever on raising academic achievement in the basic skills of reading and math. "Our children are going to perform at grade level or better," he said to conclude his speech, "or we are going to know the reason why. That's what it all boils down to."[45]

Significantly, when Foster cited the driving force behind this insistence on grade-level achievement, it was not businessmen, politicians, or educators; it was parents. As Foster told the teachers, "I was somewhat shocked once when Mario Fantini, of the Ford Foundation, said to me: 'You know, Marc, the only measure of quality education that makes sense to parents, especially poor parents, is "grade level." Parents want their children to read, write, and count at the level appropriate to their age.'" At the time, Foster said, he had been "thinking about all the other things—learning to live together, learning to be a good citizen, all that stuff. But parents *first* ask about academic achievement. And that is what we are going to have to achieve first, and then build on it."[46] Foster's comments are a reminder that school reform since the 1960s is not simply a story of liberal social goals giving way to a hard-nosed emphasis on academic achievement and accountability; in significant ways, the activism of the 1960s was about achievement and accountability all along. And now, in Oakland, one of those activist-educators was running the system.

More important than who ushered in the idea of accountability, and when, was the issue of what accountability meant in practice. Here, too, Foster's experience was instructive, a reminder that accountability is a fluid concept, shifting with the historical moment and context. Foster pressed teachers to be accountable, but he also emphasized that the district would be accountable to them. In this way, Foster began to articulate a vision of shared accountability for school reform. As he said to his teachers, "It's easy to hold someone else accountable, and you sit in judgment. It's a little more difficult when you step out in the same arena and subject yourself to the same accountability." He told the teachers they should insist that he meet a number of measurable goals of his own. Furthermore, in a reflection of his roots as a teacher and principal, a number of his administrative goals addressed school-site conditions and resources that affected teachers' abilities to meet *their* objectives. For instance, he created a grant program, New Notions for Excellence, that channeled $100,000 to schools, individual teachers, and even students who came up with innovative proposals to help schools meet their objectives. In a similar vein, Foster also announced a new policy of decentralization: pending board confirmation, he said, he would split the central administration into three regional superintendencies to make it more responsive to and accountable for conditions in the field.[47]

Foster the superintendent still approached school reform much like Foster the principal: by empowering and, at the same time, insisting on accountability, from all interested parties in individual school communities. In the case of New Notions for Excellence and decentralization, the focus was on teachers and principals. In several other proposals, it was on parents and community members, whose participation and support Foster had long seen as essential to school success.

Ongoing tensions over the issue of parental and community input were evident in Foster's speech. Foster rejected a notion of community control that some Black Caucus members had endorsed during their struggle over the superintendency. "I am not talking about community control," he flatly stated in his speech to the teachers, "because there is no such thing as community control. Schools are state institutions. We are bound by state statutes; many of our powers simply cannot be given to the communities."[48] Still, Foster said he was "not talking about community involvement for window dressing," and in this spirit, he launched a new process of community participation called the Master Plan Citizens Committee (MPCC). It was in the MPCC that an ethos of shared accountability most clearly emerged in Oakland school reform.

Participation, Not Control

Foster's actions in creating the Master Plan Citizens Committee in the fall of 1970 signaled a sharp shift toward a more open and inclusive leadership style in Oakland. The new superintendent did not invent the idea of having a citizens committee draft a new master plan for quality education; the school board had taken steps in that direction before his arrival. But Foster did extend the concept of participation far beyond what the board had had in mind. Instead of a thirty-five member committee, Foster organized a series of board meetings in neighborhoods throughout the city. At those meetings, attended by over a thousand adults and students, he asked how he should go about creating the committee, how big it should be, what aspects of education it should examine, and how he might design it so as to represent all communities. After incorporating the suggestions into a proposal, he sent it to over three thousand individuals and organizations for review.[49]

The process consumed a large part of Foster's time and energy. In a letter to the Frisbys in Philadelphia, Albertine Foster wrote that Marcus was "constantly on the speaking circuit" and rarely ate dinner at home. In early November his secretary had told him he had spoken to more than a hundred groups since his arrival a few months before. "He went to the Dr. last week," Abbe wrote, "and he said he was fine, just couldn't believe it knowing all he was doing."[50]

The demands of being an urban school leader continued to leave Foster with little time for his own family, but it produced results: in January 1971, the school board established the Master Plan Citizens Committee. The MPCC ended up being larger and more ambitious than even Foster had envisioned. It was not really a committee at all, but rather many committees, operating on a pyramid structure. At the base were ninety-one local committees, one for every school. The local committees promoted grassroots participation by a variety of people in and around the schools: parents, teachers, students, even lunchroom and janitorial staff, as well as representatives of labor, business, community, and religious groups. With the agreement of the principal, the local committees could take up reforms in the curriculum, the condition of the building, and other areas.

The local committees also elected representatives to the next tier of the MPCC: five citywide task forces: on curriculum and instruction; finance; community resources; decentralization and governance; and facilities. The task forces were to examine existing programs in these areas and make policy recommendations to the school board. In addition to about 180 school representatives, both adult and student, the task forces included fifty members of various organizations and city agencies and fifty "resource group experts" like architects, engineers, and accountants.

Finally, at the top of the MPCC structure was a Coordinating Council consisting of Foster, Bob Blackburn, three representatives from each task force, and a coordinator. The council helped give the Master Plan its overall direction. The MPCC also employed six community liaisons, most of whom were older African American women, to facilitate communication between the three levels. In all, as Foster noted, the MPCC involved more than 2,400 people from every segment of Oakland's schools and broader population. A reporter joked that it was probably the world's largest committee.[51]

Much of this work cost money, and the school system would not have been able to pay for it without the support of philanthropic foundations. The Rockefeller Foundation provided the greatest share: more than $400,000 toward the salaries of the six community liaisons and various other personnel, the fees of the consultants to the task forces and local committees, and grants to the local committees. The Ford Foundation provided $127,000 for consulting and other technical services. Foster also won smaller grants of roughly $25,000 each from the San Francisco Foundation and the Danforth Foundation, which paid for program evaluation and covered child care costs that otherwise would have hampered the participation of low-income citizens.[52]

Community involvement in schooling was a hot-button topic for philanthropic foundations; the Ford Foundation, in particular, had drawn sharp criticism for supporting the Ocean Hill–Brownsville experiment in New York City. Still interested in promoting parent involvement, but smarting from the recent conflicts with teachers and principals, Ford and other foundations were impressed by how the MPCC fostered citizen participation in school affairs—without going *too* far in that direction. An internal Ford Foundation memo noted, with admiration, that none of the nation's fifty largest school districts had ever attempted such a comprehensive policy review and that nowhere had citizens representing all of the schools in a district been directly involved in planning processes. Student involvement was "significant and unique," with more than forty students (one for each five hundred students at the junior and senior high school levels) serving on the five citywide task forces.[53] At the same time, Frederick Willman, the evaluator for the Rockefeller Foundation, praised the MPCC for having the "political shrewdness and daring" to promote "participation" rather than "control." To illustrate the difference, Willman cited the contentious issue of hiring and evaluating principals. In the MPCC, school-level committees helped to select and advise principals but not to evaluate them or any other staff member. Contrasting this approach with the one taken in Ocean Hill–Brownsville, Willman noted that the MPCC had "a clear way of telling teachers and principals that the committees won't interfere with the traditional, prescribed methods of assessing a professional's performance."[54]

For sure, the MPCC's biggest selling point—its representativeness—also led to its most difficult problems. Foster was under no illusion that citizens would reach easy agreement on common interests and approaches, and indeed, tensions emerged. At a meeting of the Task Force on Desegregation, for example, a participant made a special plea for members to reduce the amount of personal animosity expressed in the meetings. Such committees were divided not only by differing agendas but also by clashing levels of expertise and leadership skill. Foster believed that lay citizens, by participating with each other and with "resource group experts," would themselves become experts and leaders in the area addressed by their task force. But different levels of skill and experience also led to frustration, especially when combined with racial, generational, and ideological tensions. A case in point was the Community Resources Task Force, which was charged with figuring out how to take advantage of museums, urban agencies, businesses, and other resources for educational purposes. The task force included a number of established white businessmen with many contacts and a great deal of leadership experience. But it accomplished little, partly because, in an expression of the egalitarianism that pervaded the program, it elected as its chairman a black college student with no such contacts or experience and little time to devote to the committee.[55]

The inclusiveness of the MPCC sparked outright resistance among principals, some of whom found the process of community involvement foreign or even threatening. This was understandable. Oakland may have stopped short of embracing community "control," but its new process for hiring principals did place unprecedented power in the hands of teachers, parents, and students. Representatives of these groups were authorized to screen and interview candidates at the school site before presenting the superintendent with a list of three choices. Not surprisingly, as the MPCC enacted this and other school-community partnerships, the principals were little involved. As Bob Blackburn wrote in a memo to Foster in the fall of 1971, many of them regarded the MPCC "like leprosy."[56]

Foster's career was a testament to the importance of the principal in school reform, and the resistance of Oakland principals highlighted the difficulty of implementing the Master Plan Citizens Committee. Over time, though, the new principal selection process epitomized the kind of joint action and citizen participation the MPCC was intended to produce. As they collaborated to advise the school board on a major policy matter, MPCC committees helped usher in a new, more responsive generation of school leadership in Oakland. During Foster's superintendency, teams of parents, teachers, and students essentially chose two-thirds of Oakland's ninety-one principals. "This is one area where he felt he was doing his most important work," Blackburn says. "He arrived in Oakland only a year removed from his principalship at Gratz. He saw the world through their [the principals'] eyes."[57] Specifically, he saw the world through the eyes of those principals who were comfortable working with and mobilizing all members of a school community, and through the Master Plan, he helped ensure that such principals would become the norm rather than the exception.

The seemingly mundane issue of rebuilding and renovating school facilities offered another striking example of how the MPCC mobilized Oaklanders to play a role in improving their schools. With help from district staff and volunteer professionals, the Buildings Task Force prepared a set of priorities for the rebuilding or strengthening of thirty-nine buildings that were not earthquake safe. Not only did the school board adopt the report; it turned the implementation of the plan over to most of the school-site committees. At Stonehurst Elementary School, for example, parents, students, and teachers visited other schools and districts, saw films, spoke to experts, interviewed architects, and selected the firm that designed the school. In this and other ways, the MPCC gave Oaklanders a new voice in the shaping of their schools and their school system.[58]

Confronting the Problem of Achievement

The Master Plan Citizens Committee was partly a response to the political crisis over community control of the schools, and in fact it defused that crisis in Oakland. After two or three years, the MPCC process, not to mention its accomplishments, were still taking shape; still, observers increasingly noted a decrease in the bitterness and polarization that had wracked Oakland school affairs prior to Foster's arrival. As a Ford Foundation observer summed it up, community input had transformed Oakland from a public school system whose board of education had been "held captive in its own chambers" (a reference to the 1969 incident involving Percy Moore) to one in which "the community rallied around the Board of Education and the superintendent." The public policy scholar David Kirp would later echo this assessment, writing that Foster had managed "what previously had seemed impossible of achievement: he served as a bridge between blacks and whites, and between school board and community groups . . . Black Caucus spokesmen moved on to other issues; the importance of the Black Panthers diminished; the reduced appeal of radical rhetoric and confrontationist strategies in the 1970s was everywhere remarked."[59]

Kirp emphasizes the political rather than educational aspects of Foster's leadership; by defusing Sixties-era political conflicts over race and power, he suggests, Foster opened the way for his successors to focus on less explicitly racial issues of academic achievement—a shift, he says, that reflected a more general change in the school policy agendas of big cities since the early 1970s.[60] Others saw the defusing of tension and confrontation as an end in itself. As the sociologist Daniel Bell had suggested in 1969, many officials, reformers, and politicians had come to see meaningful opportunities for community "participation" as a way to undercut radical critics of the system. No doubt this was part of the reason why William Knowland and the school board showed such support for Foster and his broad-based Master Plan (after years of resistance to community influence in the schools). Indeed, Foster himself partly saw the MPCC as a way to reduce the influence of radicals; in one of his first interviews in Oakland he had spoken of "bringing in other groups to neutralize" militants who, he believed, were less interested in education than in establishing a political power base.[61]

Foster's success at defusing tensions and mobilizing community support was certainly a political achievement. But it was not an end in itself, nor did it merely clear the way for his successors to focus on educational programming. For Foster, the MPCC process was inseparable from the educational vision he had developed over the course of his career. As a teacher and principal, Foster had found parental and community involvement to be crucial to his effort to raise academic achievement for all urban children. He came to describe his approach as "total school community," by which he meant not only shared power, but shared accountability, among teachers, principals, parents, students, and other concerned members of each school community. With the Master Plan Citizens Committee, Foster essentially tried to apply the notion of total school community to the raising of academic achievement across an entire urban district. The MPCC offered a way for interested parties inside and outside of the system to stop blaming each other for low achievement in the schools and start contributing to the process of improvement.

Reducing achievement gaps was a more ambitious task than reducing conflict, although Foster claimed some initial success. After a year in Oakland, in his second annual address to district staff and teachers, he proclaimed a "stunning turnabout" in the district. Elementary and senior high school absenteeism rates were down 21 and 34 percent, respectively. Twenty percent fewer students had entered juvenile institutions during the year. Most important to him, primary grade students had posted a "clear improvement" in reading scores. Deputy Superintendent Bob Blackburn echoed Foster's enthusiasm in a private communication at the end of 1971: "Our first-year statistics were pretty," he said. "Some *slight* movement of the mountain."[62]

Yet Blackburn joked about danger ahead: "Come eight months from now, our test scores will begin to be used for us or against us with a vengeance," he concluded. "Either we *do* better by the end of June, or lock Ed Larsen in a room until he can *show* we did even if we regressed!" Unfortunately, Blackburn's tongue-in-cheek comment did point to a more troubled picture than Foster had acknowledged. Oakland's "clear improvement" in primary grade reading scores was not so clear after all; it turned out the gains had occurred mainly in compensatory education programs that received extra funding per student. Referring to this example, a journalist noted that "critics say [Foster] has measured some progress that does not in fact exist."[63]

If Foster exaggerated improvements that were more "slight" than "stunning," those improvements at least suggested the effectiveness of Oakland's efforts in compensatory education. This alone might have been cause for celebration. Yet, Foster and Blackburn had little money with which to build on such progress. Foster had said in 1969 that "we *know* what to do, but we have not brought our doing in line with our knowing."[64] In Oakland, it was not the fading controversy over community control, but rather the problem of improving achievement in the face of diminishing public resources, that proved to be the consuming and defining problem of Marcus Foster's superintendency—and of every urban superintendent since.

Race, Resources, and Public Accountability

Resources had always been a key variable in Foster's efforts to improve achievement in urban schools. As a principal he had been described as a "scrounge" who drew upon everyone from the Ford Foundation to the local drycleaner to help support programs and services for his low-income, African American students. As an associate superintendent in Philadelphia (1969–70), he had sharpened his focus on the public sector, asserting not only that Americans needed to spend more money on education in general (and less on the Vietnam War), but that they needed to spend disproportionately more on the neediest inner-city children, in particular. In Oakland, Foster continued to insist that low-performing schools needed more resources and that the public had a responsibility to fulfill that need.

In his first few years in Oakland, acting on his belief that it was unfair to "slice the pie" equally when needs were unequal, Foster redistributed money from schools in the affluent Oakland hills to those in the flatlands, where the city's low-income residents lived. In doing so, he effectively satisfied the demands made by the Ad Hoc Committee for Quality Education and other critics of the school board throughout the 1960s. In particular, Foster reduced class size in the poorest schools and cut back sharply on teacher transfers requested for "racial and economic" reasons, which previously had helped concentrate the best-paid teachers in affluent hill schools. Lingering inequalities of teacher experience and training still favored the hills, but the gap was narrowing.[65]

Unfortunately, Foster's method of slicing of the pie could only accomplish so much when the pie itself was shrinking. Revenue from the district's two main sources, local property taxes and state aid, had been declining since the 1950s. The Oakland School Board, as a fiscally independent entity with a budget and taxing authority separate from those of the city, needed voter approval to raise its general monies tax rate. Since 1958, it had gone to the voters three times, and three times it had failed. Inflation took a progressively heavy toll on services, supplies, and equipment. Meanwhile, state aid had declined during the same period from 36 to 28 percent of Oakland's roughly $60 million school budget. (By comparison, the New York City Board of Education received over 50 percent of its revenues in the form of state aid.)[66]

The fiscal crisis that Marcus Foster inherited was, in its own way, as racially charged as the more overt conflicts between activists and the school board in the 1960s. Foster's arrival in Oakland capped a challenge to the white-dominated school system from the left; the fiscal crisis, in turn, was part of an emerging "taxpayer's revolt" that challenged the schools and other public institutions—increasingly identified with blacks—from the right. To be sure, economic pressures were a significant factor in the voters' decisions about school funding. A group of UC Berkeley researchers suggested that Oaklanders voted against school tax increases "not so much out of dis-like for the schools," but because it was the only portion of a sharply rising tax bill over which they had direct control. Still, these investigators added, the defeat of school tax-rate increases was "hastened" by racial divisions be-tween a predominantly white electorate without young children and a largely black school population.[67] Another scholar pointed to a nationwide backlash among taxpayers upset by the "direct interrelationship between racial strife and educational process, the disruptive behavior of the student radicals, and the observed efforts to convert the schools into centers for social reform."[68]

Taxpayer perceptions of the schools as hotbeds of racial strife and political activism played into a more general dissatisfaction with the performance of educators. As the authors of a major Urban Institute study on school finance suggested, voters were "turned off" by school officials who demanded more funds even as they stood unaccountable for pupil performance.[69] In Oakland, the Foster administration perceived such sentiment during its first major school funding crisis, in the summer of 1971. With the Oakland Federation of Teachers threatening to strike over wages and other issues, Foster and the MPCC repeatedly lobbied the City Council to levy a tax increase to help the district erase a budget deficit and open the schools on time. Fearing voter backlash, the Council refused to do so, though it did finally agree to give the district a smaller sum from an emergency fund. Reflecting on the crisis later that fall, Bob Blackburn noted that "people in this town *expect* administrators to whine and bleat about the system's poverty." The schools always opened, he continued, and to the extent that budget cuts resulted in diminished ser-vices, citizens blamed "our inefficiency, insensitivity to children's needs, or just gross immorality ('you guys are still drawing those fat paychecks, aren't you?')."[70]

Foster and Blackburn were not alone; the struggle for educational resources in the face of mounting public skepticism was increasingly a state and nation-al phenomenon. In the 1960s, civil rights activists had expressed Oakland's racial and class divide in the language of "flatlands" and "hills"; in the 1970s they and other lawyers, policymakers, and educators increasingly spoke of re-dressing inequities between cities and suburbs.[71] The result was a nationwide struggle over school finance reform that was less explicitly polarized along racial lines than battles over community control in the 1960s or busing in the 1970s, but no less racially charged. In 1971, California moved to the forefront of the school finance reform movement when the state supreme court, rul-ing in *Serrano v. Priest,* required equal per-pupil expenditures among school districts, regardless of discrepancies in the property tax base. The court relied upon the equal protection clause of the Fourteenth Amendment to call for legislative action severing the link between school resources and local wealth.

Serrano and its redistributionist goals offered some hope for financially strapped districts, but it faced obstacles in Sacramento. Governor Ronald Reagan and many of the Republican members of the legislature believed— along the lines Bob Blackburn had lamented after the showdown with the city council in 1971—that the schools needed better management, not more money. In the fall of 1970, just before Reagan's reelection to a second term as governor, top Reagan aide (and East Bay Area native) Edwin Meese had circulated a memo that exemplified a rising tide of conservative sentiment against public institutions generally and supposedly unaccountable educators in particular. Meese's memo declared an "all-out war on the tax-taker" and stated that the administration's "NUMBER ONE priority" was to place emphasis on "the student as opposed to educational frills; on basic needs as opposed to unmanageable enrichment programs; on measurable results as opposed to blind faith that an educator can do no wrong."[72]

In the midst of fiscal crisis and public skepticism, Foster and the MPCC worked harder to apply the idea of accountability to the taxpayers and politicians who held the schools' purse strings. To be sure, he still insisted that tight finances were no excuse for a record of failure in the schools; in his annual address to the staff at the start of the 1972–73 school year, Foster nearly mocked those who would "wring their hands in despair" and say, 'We don't have the resources to do anything for our children.'" As always, he praised the ingenious use of resources close at hand, including more than 2,200 parents and other registered volunteers. He marveled at how some of those parents had escorted him to the basement of the Clawson School to show him where they pressed and mended extra clothes for needy students. It was just like when he was principal at Dunbar Elementary thirteen years before, and Blackburn had marveled at how he had scrounged for dry-cleaner hand-me-downs and brought in parents as tutors. And in 1973 it was this same spirit that prompted Foster to start one of the nation's first local education funds, the Oakland Education Institute, as a vehicle for raising discretionary funds to provide student scholarships and support innovative work by teachers. (Renamed for Foster after his death, the Marcus Foster Education Fund continues to award roughly sixty yearly scholarships to Oakland high school students, among other activities.)[73]

But if Foster valued self-help strategies and scrounging in one's own backyard, he was even more adamant about achieving adequate public financing for public schools. He closed his 1972 address with a ringing call for every person associated with the Oakland schools to become an "educator-activist" in the struggle for such public support. In some of his most passionate oratory to date, he called on all district staff to help "smash through the barrier of political indifference that lets politicians sit by while schools descend to the lowest level of poverty and wallow in despair and reel from one economic crisis to the next." Foster suggested that school finance victories held a key to realizing his goal of eliminating the achievement gap. If Oaklanders pulled together as a political force, he said, they could "smash through that tie-in between poverty and scholastic achievement. You see," he concluded, "this force, pulling together, can prove that a child, because he's poor, doesn't have to be doomed to low achievement."[74]

Later that fall, Foster implemented his blend of self-help and political pressure in dramatic fashion. As the state legislature debated various school finance reform strategies in response to *Serrano v. Priest*, Foster closed the Oakland schools for a day and transported thirty busloads of administrators, teachers, parents, students, and citizens to the state capitol in Sacramento to press for additional aid to the state's big urban districts. The trip to Sacramento partly grew out of the work of the Master Plan Citizens Committee; with support from the Ford Foundation, the MPCC task force on Finance had hired a lawyer and economist to prepare a report on the implications of *Serrano* for urban school districts. The report argued that any new system of school finance in California had to account for the higher costs of educating low-income urban students. In other words, as Foster had emphasized in shifting local resources from the hills to the flatlands, mere equalization would not do in cases of unequal need.[75] The report armed Oakland with a message; the trip to Sacramento made sure that key people heard it. As the legislature debated Senate Bill 90, which would include a response to *Serrano,* the Oaklanders met with their representatives and rallied on the steps of the capitol. They declared, in a strategy suggested by Foster, that they were there to "support our legislators."[76] They joined Foster in chanting "We need relief now."

Relief soon came: shortly thereafter, Governor Reagan signed SB90 with an $82 million "urban factor" for California's five largest school districts. The governor thought the urban factor "would just be more money down a rat hole," as one official recalled, but he approved it as a concession to Willie Brown, the Democratic chair of the Ways and Means Committee from high-spending San Francisco.[77] The impact of the Oakland contingent was not clear, but, as Foster enjoyed pointing out, the legislators added $43 million (bringing the total to $82 million) the day after the buses rolled away.[78]

As with the Gratz expansion victory in the spring of 1968, Foster relished the Sacramento outing as much for the broad-based community support it engendered as for the specific material gains it brought. "Three thousand folks of all persuasions, of all hues and colors, of all socioeconomic backgrounds saying, 'We stand together for schools,'" he said later. "If we got nothing else but that, that would have been sufficient."[79]

The next year, led again by the MPCC and a citizen canvassing effort, the Foster administration achieved another major victory in its crusade to promote public accountability for the quality of education in Oakland: voters passed a bond election for the first time since 1956. Oakland had thirty-three school buildings that did not meet state earthquake safety standards. The Foster administration had failed once, in 1971, to win the two-thirds majority needed to pass a bond issue to upgrade these schools, though a strong show of support (54 percent) and a citizen-led canvassing effort had given cause for optimism. In the spring of 1973, led by the MPCC Task Force on School Buildings, the district tried again. This time, an alliance of previously adversarial interest groups, including the Black Caucus, the business community, black church leaders, parents, and staff, helped pass a $43 million measure by a vote of 66 percent—one of the largest majorities in the city's history.[80]

The "Blame Game"

Foster's work in Oakland had given him a national profile among education leaders, and by 1973, other cities and states were trying to lure him away to run their school systems. In an odd but telling twist, one of those who showed an interest in bringing Foster to his city was Frank Rizzo, the former police commissioner who was elected mayor of Philadelphia in 1971. Still drawing energy from Black Friday and other battles in the late 1960s over race and education, Rizzo had promised during the campaign that if he were elected, Mark Shedd would last just eight more minutes (he later revised it to eight seconds) in office. (Rizzo did not have the power to fire Shedd, but he did stand to appoint several new board members.) Informed shortly after the election that Rizzo wanted him to come back to Philadelphia and replace Shedd, Foster said he had no intention of leaving Oakland. "In Mark Shedd," he added pointedly, "[Philadelphia] has one of America's finest school executives." To say the least, Foster's ideas about education were closer to Shedd's than to Rizzo's. The fact that Rizzo would show an interest in someone so similar in outlook to Shedd (he reportedly admired Foster's emphasis on basic skills and his ability to motivate students, and he probably saw him as a man with whom he could do business), spoke volumes about the breadth of Foster's appeal.[81]

Not surprisingly, then, in 1973 Oakland made sure to give Foster and Blackburn new four-year contracts with pay raises. Things were going well for the two men. The bond election victory, the Senate Bill 90 urban factor, and the continuing progress of the MPCC had given them reason to believe that citizens and institutions were beginning to take shared responsibility for the achievement of all children. Compared to the moment when they had been hired three years before, the city was a portrait of unity in matters of public education. Even so, Foster grew increasingly frustrated at the persistence of an opposite tendency—the "blame game," as he called it, in which citizens, political leaders, educators, and parents pinned the shortcomings of urban schools on either educators or students.

In the spring of 1973, Foster surprised some people with an unusually caustic critique of those who would blame the problems of urban education on schools and educators. At the annual conference of the American Association of School Administrators (AASA), Foster spoke on "the politics of ethnic power," and he declared such power to be a myth. Five years before, Foster had fought for the expansion of Gratz High School and achieved what some celebrated as a victory for Black Power. Now, by contrast, he complained bitterly of how whites elevated "superblacks" to "Head Nigger in Charge" only when a situation had become hopeless. Blacks became mayors only in cities that had become "empty husks"; they became superintendents only in cities like Oakland, where the percentage of nonwhites in the schools had reached 78 percent. Alluding to the heart attack he had suffered while working fourteen-hour days at Gratz, Foster said, "We go through a coronary alley at all those tough high schools, and they tell us, 'Here it is, baby; make it fly.' Then, when you can't make it, they say, 'I told you those niggers can't do it.'"[82]

If the tone of Foster's AASA address was unexpectedly harsh, the message was but a variation on his other recent indictments of "political indifference," of misplaced national priorities, of cynically proclaimed "panaceas" that failed to address the full dimensions of the problem. Ironically, Foster himself may have helped fuel the exceedingly high expectations he was denouncing. For much of his career, he had insisted he could "make it fly," without dwelling on the frustration and the coronaries and the possibility that the situation was hopeless. Indeed, even as newspapers were recounting his "angry message" at the AASA conference, Foster was writing a letter to the editor of the *Oakland Tribune*—and sending it to all of his principals and central office staff—to emphasize a set of "more optimistic" points he had made. Oaklanders were rallying to strengthen the schools, he said, and academic achievement, test scores, and college admissions were climbing. Not only that, but the schools were proving to be "fertile ground" for a renewal of the urban community in general. "We are going to make it in Oakland," he concluded, "and history may record that our schools have led the way."[83] In fact, "history" showed that schools could *not* lead the way out of the urban crisis, and that to expect this of them was a recipe for disillusionment. J. M. Regal had made this point in his evaluation of Oakland's war on poverty, Christopher Jencks and his colleagues had done so in their recent landmark study, *Inequality* (1972), and historians and social scientists have done so since. As these scholars have argued in various ways, school reform must be part of a larger social policy program that addresses the problems of inadequate housing and health care and, most important, unemployment.[84]

Foster understood that to ignore this larger picture was to set the stage for retreat and recrimination: faced with persistent failure, some would blame schools and educators, as he had said in the AASA speech, and some would blame the deficiencies of the students themselves. And while Foster was not one to single out schools and educators, by 1973 he was even less willing to blame urban school problems on the students. In the AASA speech, he reiterated his longstanding insistence that urban students were victims of the system. He abhorred violence, he said, but he believed the riots of the 1960s had brought attention to "a whole segment of the population which was being ignored." Indeed, he said, the schools had not simply ignored urban children; they had "convinc[ed] the poor that they cannot learn. The record is clear on that point."[85] Foster had said such things before, but in the early 1970s he grew increasingly concerned and angry about the consequences of what he called the "blame the victim game." As he argued in a speech at Stanford University, "The danger of failing to educate a segment of the population consistently over time, is that some bright psychologist is going to look at the population that's uneducated . . . and say, 'It's something wrong with THEM!'" Foster no doubt had in mind, among other psychologists, Arthur Jensen of nearby UC Berkeley, who recently had injected the idea of inherited intellectual differences between blacks and whites back into the mainstream of educational debate.[86] The revival of racial conservatism prompted Foster to revisit the problem of low expectations, in a way that echoed both Myrdalian liberalism and the radical critique of racism in the schools. The "blame the victim game," he said, allowed the teacher, the principal, the superintendent—all who had to explain low achievement among students—to say, "'Hooray! I knew it all the time . . . there's something wrong with THEM! They're genetically inferior.'"[87]

Caught in Crossfire

In its own way, the 1973 school-security controversy that led to Foster's death was part of the blame game that had come to characterize debates over urban educational failure. In the fall of that year, Foster found himself in the middle of a heated controversy over discipline policy. The previous school year had been marred by forty-two incidents of assault on students and staff. A female student had been stabbed to death by a young intruder at Oakland Technical High School.

On the one side, a number of East Bay political leaders, educators, and citizens responded to the wave of school violence and vandalism by demanding a stronger showing of law and order. Two parties in particular—a group called Citizens for Law and Order, and teachers upset by a wave of violent attacks against school personnel—had helped persuade the Alameda County Grand Jury to turn its attention to the Oakland schools. The grand jury issued its scathing report in mid-July while Foster was on vacation (his first since arriving in Oakland). The report was critical of educators as well as students; for instance, it cited interviews with students in three schools to claim that many Oakland teachers were not interested in their work or their students. But the main thrust of the report was a repudiation of the violence and vandalism being committed by students, as well as a call for the schools to crack down on those acts. In addition to the forty-two violent attacks on school personnel during the previous year, the grand jury documented $700,000 in district losses due to student acts of vandalism and arson. It also called for a response—including, perhaps, the placement of armed police officers in some schools—by October 15.[88]

On the other side, the Black Panther Party and other activists portrayed students as victims of a racist school system and society. Vera Silverman, a radical, black activist with a sixteen-year-old daughter in the Oakland schools, was furious when she heard talk about new security proposals, and she made up a flier, on behalf of a group called the Coalition to Save our Schools

(CSOS), that urged people to attend the October 9 school board meeting in protest. The CSOS flier stated that the "big shots who run Oakland" blamed school violence and other problems on the students, but the real culprit was "the system." The system "jam[med] students into classes they [weren't] interested in" and taught them lies. It spent billions to bomb children in Vietnam and Africa but would not buy books for students in Oakland. And now, with the police-in-schools idea, it was making a move to "clamp down on students who fight against bad schools, racism, no jobs, frozen wages, etc." For their part, the Panthers had not been very involved in public school issues since the superintendent selection controversy of 1969–70, but they stepped in to denounce the grand jury report for what they saw as its racist emphasis on the "'deficiencies' of the students and their parents." According to *The Black Panther* newspaper, proposals for beefed-up security were an attempt to crush "admittedly high rates of truancy, vandalism and violence" with an "onslaught of police and police-types . . . Nowhere," the article concluded, taking aim at the supposed failings of the school system in general, "is there the mention that improved facilities, improved teaching methods, concerned teachers, and subject matter that relates to the students' experience and lifestyle would solve the problem."[89]

As he had done for much of his career, Foster attempted to navigate a path between the extremes. He certainly felt he had to do something in response to the grand jury. The murder at Tech and the assaults on students and staff were serious matters, and as a black superintendent, he felt especially sensitive to the potential charge that he was soft on violence and vandalism (which were most serious in predominantly black schools).[90] As a result, the Foster administration made a plan to spend nearly $1 million to involve the police department, the juvenile court system, and the county probation and parole departments in a more coordinated approach to school security. The plan had many features, including police-trained "peace officers" and "safety coordinators" in selected schools; a new truancy coordinator; and revival of a student I.D. card program that had fallen victim to budget cuts just a year before.[91] What it did *not* have, as Foster tried to explain in the press and at the October 9 board meeting, was the regular placement of police officers in the schools.[92] True, when Foster had announced the plan in his annual back-to-school speech to the district staff, he had struck a friendlier stance toward the police department than he did toward the radicals. "We're going to have to get away from the rhetoric of the sixties when police were called 'pigs,'" he pointedly remarked, before urging teachers to help students develop a more constructive understanding of the police role.[93] But in substance (if not in style), Foster was closer to the radicals on matters of campus security than he was to the advocates of law and order. This was evident not only in his full remarks to the staff, which included passionate advocacy for the rights and needs of students, but in all of his life experiences. He had maintained safe environments at Catto and at Gratz (arguably more challenging than any school in Oakland) without a permanent police presence, and he had no intention of dramatically changing his approach now.

Despite his best efforts, Foster's attempt to forge a workable compromise did not go smoothly. The Panthers not surprisingly remained distrustful of his administration's plan, not only because of his kind words for the police department, but because he had refused Panther leader Elaine Brown's request that he hire *them*—"Panthers, tough, paramilitary, who won't take any shit"— to handle school security. The October 9 board meeting was attended mainly by teachers, who were involved in contract negotiations with the district, but protesters made their mark on the proceedings anyway. Bobby Seale, who, along with Huey Newton, had co-founded the Black Panther Party less than a mile away, demanded that the board spend money on new school facilities rather than police. Elaine Brown echoed him and announced that "we did not come to play." Vera Silverman compared Oakland's proposed use of picture identification cards to Nazi Germany and South Africa, and she made a show of walking to the front of the room and cutting her daughter's new ID card to shreds (prompting Foster to point out that, due to a compromise on the issue, the card was not mandatory).[94]

In spite of all the fireworks, by late October the school security controversy showed some signs of dying down—and in any case, Foster and Blackburn were preoccupied with what they felt to be much bigger challenges. Foremost among these was the negotiation with teachers, which was made difficult by the district's extremely tight finances. Late in the month, as the security controversy simmered, the parties agreed on a new contract and narrowly averted a first-ever teachers' strike in Oakland. Around the time of that success, Foster and Blackburn joked about how lucky they were to have survived that and other big challenges, such as the bond election. "I tell you, Bob, the Lord's in this thing," Foster teased his less religious colleague as they drove through Oakland in a celebratory mood—to which Blackburn replied, "Yeah, he's saving us for some really indescribable misadventures."[95]

Blackburn had no idea how right he was. At that very moment, incredibly, a ragtag group of self-styled revolutionaries was putting the finishing touches on a plan to assassinate Foster and his deputy. Before they became famous for kidnapping Patty Hearst, the Symbionese Liberation Army (SLA) was a small group of college dropouts and escaped convicts looking for a public figure to assassinate. The choice of Foster was somewhat random—most of the other discussed targets were corporate leaders—but it possessed a certain logic for the fledgling group. The black leader, Donald DeFreeze (alias "Cinque," after the leader of the *Amistad* slave rebellion), had first met some of his white, Berkeley-based co-conspirators in Vacaville prison in 1972 when he was a prisoner, and they became politically active among the inmates. Not only did the East Bay–Vacaville activist network contain the nucleus of what became the SLA; it included Vera Silverman and at least two other members of the Coalition to Save Our Schools, who brought news of the Oakland police-in-schools controversy to the prisoners. Journalists Vin McLellan and Paul Avery later interviewed several inmates who said that by the summer of 1973, "everyone in Vacaville knew Foster as the Black Judas in Oakland."[96] One night in October, DeFreeze decided to target Foster as the group drank wine and watched local news coverage of the school security controversy. He and some of the others believed a black leader such as Foster must be a puppet of the white power structure and that by killing him, they would inspire the masses of black and other oppressed peoples. As one said, "You can't be a for-real nigger and be superintendent of the Oakland schools."[97]

On November 6, Foster made his own modest contribution to the delinquency debate that contrasted sharply with the heated ideas swirling around town. During the debate over vandalism and violence, the city had closed high school gyms for after-school recreation programs. At a City Council session on this and other budget cuts, Foster implored the city to reopen the gyms. He had prepared a speech, but as he often did, he spoke extemporaneously, imploring the councilmen to consider the "total milieu" and the needs of Oakland youth. He reminded them of the district's problems with violence, vandalism and truancy: "I shudder to think what we may see," he said, if the city eliminated the program that gave youth a place to go after school. When reminded by councilmen of the city's financial situation, Foster spoke of "false economy" versus long-term social investments.[98] It was a mundane event, one of many such appearances Foster had made in Oakland. And yet, it captured key aspects of his career as an educator: his belief in the power of schools to save urban youth, and his persistent struggle to secure the resources needed to accomplish the job.

Afterward, Foster returned to the administration building to chair a brief and uneventful school board session. Walking out to the car with him at the end of a typical eleven-hour day, Blackburn was mildly surprised when they passed two young men wearing watch caps (or were they women?) loitering for no apparent reason in the desolate alleyway behind the building. He did not give them much thought as he hurried toward the passenger side of his Chevy Vega to unlock the door for Foster. It was election day, and the two men were on their way to vote before the polls closed.

The women Blackburn had seen did not know or care about the details of the district security plan or the meetings Foster had been attending all after-noon. All they knew was that Foster and Blackburn were guilty of committing crimes "against the children and the life of the people." For this reason, they and another gunman who was hiding across from them—DeFreeze—opened fire on the two educators, catching them in a crossfire of shotgun pellets and cyanide-filled bullets.[99] Foster pitched forward and went down. Blackburn was hit, too, but he managed to stumble some sixty feet down an alleyway and up fifteen steps to unlock a back entrance to the nearly empty building. Inside, he collapsed and told a colleague, who had heard the shots and run upstairs from the basement, to go help Dr. Foster. It was too late. The super-intendent had been hit seven times in the head and back from two automatic pistols at close range. He was already dead. Blackburn heard the news about thirty minutes later, just before going into emergency surgery. He felt that "either we should both be dead or both be alive. Marc dead and myself alive seemed totally unacceptable." Blackburn survived three episodes of cardiac arrest, despite having been hit by two double aught shotgun blasts that sev-ered his spleen and damaged his central nervous system, liver, and kidneys.[100]

Three days later, SLA released a "communiqué" announcing its existence and explaining that it had "executed" Foster with cyanide-filled bullets at the behest of "the Court of the People," for his role in forming a "Special Political Police Force . . . patterned after fascist Amerikan tactics of genocide, murder and imprisonment practiced by Amerikan financed puppet governments in Vietnam, The Philippines, Chile and South Africa." As the editors of the radi-cal magazine *Ramparts* later wrote, the SLA's initial communiqué showed the group to be "far removed from the realities of the Oakland school situation (indeed, from reality itself)."[101]

Indeed, the outpouring of grief over Foster's assassination showed how be-loved he was among "the People" and how marginal and deluded his killers were. (The SLA kidnapped Hearst partly to deflect attention from their "pub-lic relations mistake," as one member coldly put it—and as Hearst-dominated

SLA stories have shown ever since, they succeeded all too well in this aim.)[102] Foster had been killed for being an alleged Uncle Tom, but tributes to him underscored his lifelong effort to change the system from within by engaging many perspectives and interests. Fellow educators mourned him as a leader in their field; James Guthrie, a UC Berkeley policy analyst who observed a number of high-level cabinet meetings within the Foster administration, called Foster the "most capable big-city school superintendent in the nation." But the praise and grief extended beyond professional circles and encompassed all points on the political spectrum. Mayor John Reading and other members of Oakland's Republican establishment were shattered by the loss of a colleague who, they felt, had done more than anyone else to bridge the city's bitter racial divide. So were left-leaning African American Oaklanders like Congressman Ron Dellums and the writer Ishmael Reed, who lamented that Foster had been cut down for being a black man who dared to compete and achieve within white, mainstream society. Even Vera Silverman said, "We liked Dr. Foster. He was all ears. We stuck our necks out and somebody took advantage." (As it turned out, of course, that "somebody" had a history of ties to Silverman's own activist circles.)[103]

Memorial services were held on both coasts. In a ceremony attended by five hundred people in the Gratz High School auditorium, the speakers included a number of friends and allies from Foster's time in Philadelphia: Mary James, Dr. Ruth Wright Hayre, the Reverend Leon Sullivan, and the Honorable Leon Higginbotham, among others. A Gratz staff member sang the spiritual "Ain't Got Time to Die," as arranged by Foster's uncle, Hall Johnson. Marvin Gambrell, a former Gratz student whom Foster had motivated to graduate and go on to earn a master's degree in medical technology, was asked by a reporter why he had returned to help with the arrangements for the service. "I loved the man," he was quoted as saying.[104] In Oakland, meanwhile, thousands assembled at multiple gatherings in the days after November 6. At the largest of these services, held in the Oakland Coliseum and attended by some 4,500 residents, Albertine Foster told of her life with Marcus and made a dramatic request. "Do something for me," she said, asking the members of the audience to take the hand of the person beside them and repeat after her, "I will do everything within my power to love my neighbor. I will pray for Dr. Foster's assassins." Meanwhile, messages and gifts poured into the Oakland Education Institute, now renamed after Foster. One was a donation from the inmates of the Santa Rita Rehabilitation Center, who proclaimed Foster "an Educational Giant."[105]

Figure 10. The Reverend Leon Sullivan delivers his remarks at a memorial service for Marcus Foster at Simon Gratz High School in Philadelphia, November 1973. Foster had left his hometown more than three years before, but he had not been forgotten, especially at the high school where he first came into public view. Among many tributes to the slain educator on both coasts, the Gratz athletic field—built as a result of the school's confrontation with the Board of Education in 1968—was renamed the Marcus Foster Memorial Stadium. Urban Archives, Temple University Libraries.

As they struggled to absorb the loss of Foster, Oaklanders reached for comparisons with the assassinations of Martin Luther King, Jr., Malcolm X, and Bobby Kennedy. The city reeled with a sense of unfulfilled potential. A few days after the killing, one Oakland official remarked, "We were beginning to heal, to get together again. And not just in the schools. What happened in the schools was affecting the whole community." Guthrie wrote that Foster had led Oakland "closer than any other major city to solving the conflict which so plagues our nation."[106]

The all-too-brief Foster era did not simply heal conflicts, though; it helped raise expectations that schools truly could be an engine of opportunity for all Americans, whatever their race or social status. That part of Horace Mann's vision—public education as the great equalizer—had long been a cruel joke for African Americans. But as Bob Blackburn memorably described it several decades after the assassination, Foster had filled a city with new hope:

> In urban schools, the unspoken worry is that things will never
> be turned around, that the crush of the effects of poverty and
> racism—in all their complexities—can for most kids never be
> overcome, that we are all doomed to sail this fundamentally
> flawed and damaged ship forever . . . Marcus' gift was to get almost
> all of Oakland to see and believe: *it doesn't have to be this way*!
> This was beyond any one or two specific moves, or the MPCC,
> or the bond election, or the in-person appearances throughout
> the community some 4 or 5 nights a week. It was all of these, plus
> some quality of his that was, for want of a better term, spiritual.
> He had come to epitomize the yearnings of parents, of teachers, of
> administrators, of community and political leaders, of the students
> themselves. At his death, few people understood why they felt so
> devastated, so stunned, so shocked, so deeply wounded. But it was
> about the loss of an imagined future, one that everyone had the
> right to want, to need, and, in fairness, to expect.[107]

As a superintendent, Marcus Foster promoted an idea that was rooted in the black freedom struggle of the 1960s: urban schools ought to be held accountable for the achievement of their students, regardless of their race or socioeconomic status. Still, Foster did not intend for schools and educators to transcend social inequality on their own; he promoted a broader public responsibility for the "imagined future" that Blackburn so eloquently describes.

And by the time he was assassinated, he was taking the larger society to task for its failure to fulfill this responsibility.

Since Foster's time, the cause of accountability has been taken up by the federal government. In their insistence that schools be held responsible for reducing or eliminating achievement gaps, proponents of No Child Left Behind and the Obama Administration's Race to the Top program take their cues not only from performance-oriented business leaders, but from Foster and others of his era. However, as we shall see in conclusion, proponents of the new accountability have only intensified the damaging tendency to single out educators and ignore the impact of external forces on the performance of schools and students.

Legacies of the 1960s in American School Reform

MARCUS Foster's life and times were marked by a monumental shift in public discourse about urban education, from racist double standards to high expectations for all students, and Foster's story counters the all-too-familiar assumption that public education has declined since the 1960s. At a time when critics routinely condemn the failures of public schools, it is instructive to recall just how blatant was the inadequate education received by ethnic-minority and working-class students in Foster's childhood prior to World War II. Even when he began his career in the 1940s, in a climate of burgeoning racial liberalism, Americans often had a simple explanation for achievement gaps: black students, as well as students from other ethnic groups and lower social classes, were less intelligent. Such thinking has never entirely disappeared from public discourse, not to mention urban classrooms, but by the time of Foster's death in the early 1970s, it was no longer the norm simply to shrug and accept as inevitable the low graduation rates and achievement levels of large numbers of poor and minority children.[1] By the time Foster died, it was schools and educators—not students and families—who increasingly found themselves having to answer for the dismal condition of urban schools. Urban educators such as Foster had helped establish the idea that, with proactive leadership and high academic expectations, urban schools could be "effective schools"—and a key to social mobility—regardless of the social and economic background of their students.

Though Foster's assassination was a devastating setback for these hopes and expectations in Oakland, the belief that urban schools should be an answer to inequality, as opposed to a reflection or even a cause of it, did not die with him.

Today's policy debates are dominated by the same basic idea that animated Foster: race and social class should not determine a student's success in school and in life, and schools should be held accountable for fulfilling that promise—specifically, by eliminating achievement gaps. A key driver of these heightened expectations has been the No Child Left Behind legislation, enacted into law by Congress and then-president George W. Bush in 2002. NCLB calls on the states to measure student achievement in math and reading, through regular standardized testing, and to use that data to hold schools accountable for reducing academic achievement gaps. The law has been unpopular for a variety of reasons, and yet NCLB's emphasis on accountability and achievement gaps has taken a firm hold in national debates on education. In those debates, the mantle of "reformer" has been claimed by those who advocate standardized testing to hold schools accountable for achievement. That group includes "get tough" school superintendents (or, as they are often called now, "CEOs"); the leaders of charter school movements such as the Knowledge Is Power Program (KIPP); advocacy groups such as the Education Trust; and officials at philanthropic foundations, especially the Bill and Melinda Gates Foundation and the Eli and Edythe Broad Foundation. It also includes President Barack Obama's secretary of education, Arne Duncan, himself the former CEO of the Chicago schools. Duncan captures the current sense of urgency, the impatience for results, when he says that children in low-performing schools "can't wait for incremental reform. They need radical change right now—new leadership, new staff, and a whole new educational approach . . . we have a moral obligation to save those kids."[2]

In Marcus Foster's story we have seen that the roots of this current focus on accountability run much deeper than is often appreciated. Prior to the Obama administration, the idea of holding schools accountable was associated especially with Republicans and conservatism, but the ethos of accountability (if not the exact form it has taken) is also a legacy of racial liberalism and civil rights activism, since World War II and especially since the late 1960s. Foster and others of his era promoted an urgent, "no excuses" mentality, as they shifted the focus of public discourse from the alleged deficiencies of urban students to those of the schools.

So what has changed in school reform between Foster's era and our own? Revisiting the 1960s and 1970s not only gives us a better sense of where the impulse toward accountability came from; it also highlights the shortcomings of our current approaches to the issue. Foster put a focus not only on schools, but on social and economic forces that shape them. His emphasis on shared accountability was validated by the Coleman Report, with its focus on family and community influences on schooling, and it was evident in his signature accomplishments. Outreach to parents from the principal's office, bus caravans to the school board and the statehouse, mobilization of a broad coalition of citizens to support a school bond measure for the first time in nearly two decades: all of these instances, and many others, showed educators, parents, students, and other citizens joining forces to confront the social and financial obstacles to urban school reform. In the last ten to fifteen years, by contrast, the nation has embraced narrow and simplistic versions of the accountability ethos that came out of Foster's era. In public debates and policies, we ignore four decades of social science research on how unequal achievement is shaped by social and economic inequalities in the larger society and how schools cannot transcend those inequalities on their own. We hear a great deal about changes in the governance and organization of school systems but less about the complexities of school and classroom life that make or break lasting reform. In these ways—and often in spite of good intentions—we run the risk of negating, rather than nurturing, a sense of hope in urban schools.

Confronting the Full Extent of the Problem: The 1970s to the Present

To be sure, the narrow vision of accountability that currently predominates did not originate with No Child Left Behind; Marcus Foster was already struggling against it in the years leading up to his death. In an essay about Foster, published just after the assassination, the education analyst John Merrow memorably described the pressures that faced urban school superintendents. Foster and others were "fighting a holding action against conditions over which [they] have no control: poverty, crime, drugs, 'white flight,' urban decay, municipal overburden, and reduced revenues." They were "accountable but not powerful."[3] Foster fought to ensure that schools received the support they needed to confront this array of problems, but he was losing that battle. As he suggested in a speech at Stanford University in the fall of 1973, the United States was "failing miserably" to educate all of its children, and the responsibility for reversing that failure lay not only with the schools, but with business, government, the family, and religion.[4] Since Foster spoke those words, educators and activists have continued his fight to end achievement gaps—including his struggle with social and economic obstacles to fulfilling that goal. For examples of that continuing struggle, we need look no further than Oakland and Philadelphia.

The Oakland schools did not always have much to celebrate in the decades after Foster's death. At the turn of the twenty-first century, achievement was abysmal: according to performance standards set by the California Department of Education, two-thirds of all elementary schools, fifteen out of sixteen middle schools, and all seven high schools were "low performing."[5] In 1996, the district gained nationwide attention—in the form of ridicule—for endorsing "bilingual" instruction in Ebonics, or African American Vernacular English, as a way to improve achievement among its struggling African American students.[6]

Still, by the late 1990s, Oaklanders had started a reform initiative that carried some of the main concerns and approaches of Foster's era into the twenty-first century. The movement was focused on creating new small schools, and it originated in grassroots activism. As they had done in the 1960s, mothers of children in overcrowded flatlands schools began to mobilize for a higher-quality education. Working through a faith-based group called the Oakland Community Organizations (OCO), these parents, in collaboration with like-minded teachers and activists, pressured the district to develop new small schools with greater control over curriculum, instruction, assessment, and budgets. By 2007, the district was operating forty-five small schools. Early on, in particular, the movement echoed Foster's Master Plan (MPCC) reforms in striking ways, especially in its focus on improving instruction through parent, community and staff collaboration at individual school sites. As the number of small schools grew, and a budget crisis led to a state takeover of the district, Oakland attracted some $26 million in funding from businesses and foundations (especially the Gates Foundation). After 2003, the thrust of the district's small schools movement shifted somewhat, as the state-appointed superintendent, Dr. Randolph Ward, pushed aggressively for accountability and a "marketplace of schooling options."[7] As in the Foster years, Oakland won praise for being a national model in school reform. Gates officials and many others had high hopes that small schools held the key to reducing dropout rates and achievement gaps. And indeed, Oakland's new schools showed some positive results. From 2003 to 2008, according to evaluators from Stanford University, the new small schools tended to outperform older schools at the elementary and high school levels. (Results in middle schools were less positive.)[8]

Still, the Oakland small schools movement was a reminder that there is no quick, inexpensive path to significant gains in urban education. The local autonomy fostered by small schools could not, by itself, raise academic achievement. Low test scores, high dropout rates, and high teacher and principal turnover continued to plague the district. By 2008, for instance, in all but three of

Oakland's new high schools, more than 80 percent of the student body scored either "below basic" or "far below basic" on state math tests.[9] Looking ahead in 2007, one analyst suggested that Oakland's fate hinged on who controlled the schools and how willing those leaders were to support charters, shut down non-performing schools, and otherwise enforce accountability and school choice.[10] But the Oakland story also highlighted deeply entrenched social and educational challenges. The Stanford evaluators, for instance, did not emphasize issues of power and governance so much as basic educational elements that can be notoriously difficult to ensure in struggling urban districts: strong leadership ("mission-driven principals"), experienced teachers, "authentic, hands-on" instruction, and commitment to parent and community engagement.[11] This was not to mention the socioeconomic issues that continued to loom large: as of 2001, nearly two-thirds of the district's students qualified for free or reduced lunch based on household income, and in most "low performing" schools, that number soared to over 90 percent.[12] Neither smallness, nor any other single reform, held the key to addressing the full range of social and educational challenges across an entire urban school district. By 2008, when its pronouncements on the transformative potential of small schools had given way to an acknowledgment of disappointing results, the Gates Foundation was shifting its focus—this time, to teacher effectiveness.[13]

Philadelphia also provided notable examples of school leaders who tried hard to end achievement gaps but could not do so—not least, they believed, because politicians and the public did not provide the necessary support. This mixed legacy of high expectations and persistent failure was apparent at the very site of Marcus Foster's most renowned accomplishments, Gratz High School. Foster set a precedent of dynamic, African American leadership at Gratz, which carried into the twenty-first century. In 1975, for example, journalists reported a "miraculous" increase in standardized test scores under principal Oliver Lancaster, who had pioneered an intensive reading program across the disciplines, including an impressive commitment to professional development for teachers.[14] Just as common in those years, however, were reports of vandalism, violence, deteriorating facilities, and academic troubles. Indeed, even the celebration of academic progress in 1975 was quickly soured by reports that a Gratz English teacher had shared vocabulary test items with her students prior to the test. The incident captured painful realities for urban school leaders like Foster and his successors. Even after the much-touted improvement in test scores from 1974 to 1975, 44 percent of Gratz students still finished below the sixteenth percentile nationally (a cutoff that was thought to indicate literacy). Many factors played a role in such low achievement; some, such as a decrepit and overcrowded physical plant, were located in the school itself, while others— gangs, poverty, lack of cultural capital—were a product of urban life beyond school walls. Yet, in spite of this difficult context, educators grew ever more accountable for results, as measured by standardized tests. As a local editorial noted in response to the 1975 controversy at Gratz, school administrators and teachers were facing "tremendous pressures . . . to see that pupils perform well on tests"—a form of "accountability," they said, which "seems to make many educators jittery."[15]

Even greater pressures faced the woman who became the city's first African American superintendent. In 1983, after forcing out "insider" superintendent Michael Marcase, the school board interviewed eighty-four candidates and hired Constance Clayton. In a district plagued by low test scores, high absentee- ism, and budget deficits, the *Philadelphia Inquirer* deemed Clayton the "closest thing to a miracle worker the board was likely to find." Like Foster, Clayton had been an original participant in Philadelphia's Great Cities program—though as a young teacher rather than a principal. Also like Foster, she largely embraced the role of miracle worker, working fourteen-hour days and promising to make Philadelphia the best urban school district in the country. Clayton's philosophy of high expectations led to some notable achievements. She instituted a new curriculum with higher academic and promotion standards, and she improved math and reading scores. She also balanced the budget, averted further teacher strikes, and generated millions of dollars of corporate contributions to the dis- trict through the Committee to Support the Philadelphia Public Schools.[16]

Still, Clayton was no more a miracle worker than Marcus Foster or any other school leader. Large achievement gaps persisted; critics noted that out of 501 school districts statewide, only one scored below Philadelphia on state read- ing and math tests. Half of the district's ninth graders were not finishing high school. Much as Foster had done late in his career, Clayton blasted the larger society (in addition to some fellow educators) for neglecting black children and then blaming them for failure. In a special issue of the *The Nation* entitled "Scapegoating the Black Family," she argued that the problem was not poverty, per se; it was the vicious cycle of low funding, low achievement, and low ex- pectations that politicians and educators—out of indifference, or racist beliefs about black inferiority, or a self-interested desire to keep poor African Ameri- cans down—fueled in *response* to poverty.[17]

The tenure of Clayton's successor, David Hornbeck, was filled with a simi- lar sense of frustration over the problem he called "citizen accountability." Like

Clayton, Hornbeck exemplified how the civil rights era helped give rise to a generation of urban school reformers as well an ethos of accountability and high expectations. In the 1960s, he directed the Philadelphia Tutorial Project, which had helped produce the leaflets urging black students to attend the ill-fated protest on November 17, 1967, and People for Human Rights, the group of white activists who had supported black students after November 17 and during the Gratz expansion controversy. During that time, the young Hornbeck, a Texan with divinity degrees from Oxford and the Union Theological Seminary and a staunch commitment to social justice, came to admire Marcus Foster, who, he believed, went beyond a general sense of the worthiness of all children and promoted high *academic* expectations—the idea that "all kids can succeed at high levels." Shaped by this past, Hornbeck earned a law degree and became a leading voice for school accountability, notably in Kentucky, where he designed one of the nation's first state-level accountability systems. In 1994, when eighty-four-year-old Ruth Wright Hayre once again played a key role in Philadelphia's educational history—a divided school board deferred to her on whether to appoint Hornbeck—she recognized Hornbeck as someone who stood for the same principles to which she and Foster and others had devoted their careers. For Hayre the decisive factor was Hornbeck's emphasis on accountability for academic achievement; as she told him and others, she "didn't know if he could do it—but at least he talked about it."[18]

Hornbeck did more than talk; in early 1995, he launched Children Achieving, in some ways the most ambitious reform program in the nation. Children Achieving was part of the standards movement that began in the 1980s and culminated in No Child Left Behind: it set the same academic standards for every child in the nation's fifth-largest school district and called for tests in the fourth and eighth grades to hold schools accountable for reaching those standards. In 1998, Hornbeck became the first superintendent in Philadelphia's history to release detailed reports on the academic performance of city schools. As it turned out, standardized reading, math, and science scores went up every year from 1996 to 2000. Less tangibly, Hornbeck and other observers believed that to make schools test thousands of students who had been written off in the past was an achievement in itself. "There's a different conversation in Philadelphia about kids and what they're capable of learning," observed Jolley Christman, principal researcher for a nonprofit research group hired to evaluate Children Achieving.[19]

Children Achieving made educators more accountable for achievement, and this led to serious friction with the Philadelphia Federation of Teachers

(PFT). However, as Hornbeck saw it, the program's biggest obstacle—and the one that led to his departure—was a failure of will among citizens and politicians. The key issue was state assistance to local school districts; by the mid-1990s, Pennsylvania ranked well below average among the states in this area, leaving districts highly dependent on local property taxes. By the time Hornbeck took office, Philadelphia was spending $1,900 less per student than the average suburban southeastern Pennsylvania district to meet educational needs that were far greater. Children Achieving asserted the moral and educational necessity of Pennsylvania spending more money on its urban poor, to the tune of $1.3 billion for such improvements as better facilities, more books, and new technology. As practiced by David Hornbeck, accountability was a two-way street, and it did not come cheap. Pennsylvania balked at spending more, however, and Hornbeck enraged state lawmakers by suggesting that their school funding decisions revealed racial biases against Philadelphia and its poorest citizens. Fittingly, the education analyst and documentarian John Merrow made Hornbeck the focus of the PBS program *The Toughest Job in America*. The program echoed Merrow's sentiments from the mid-1970s, when he had declared superintendents like Marcus Foster to be "accountable but not powerful." Airing in 2000, it noted that Hornbeck, still forging ahead after six years of constant political crises, had lasted twice as long as the average big-city superintendent. A few months later, however, Hornbeck resigned with a year remaining on his contract, citing budget cuts and the district's need for a superintendent who could establish better relations with state legislators in Harrisburg.[20]

To this day, the most promising urban school reforms struggle with a multiplicity of school and social factors. Like Foster and successors like Clayton and Hornbeck, the leaders of these reforms show an impatience for results that is in tension with their recognition of the complexity of the problems, including the challenge of meeting substantial needs on a large scale with scarce resources. Chicago is one city where the potential as well as the difficulty of school reform have become strikingly clear, not least because researchers have done such a thorough job of studying the reforms. The University of Chicago's Consortium on Chicago School Research (CCSR), for instance, has analyzed fifteen years of data on achievement in elementary schools. Like the Stanford team that evaluated small schools in Oakland, the Chicago researchers conclude that, more than the governance issues that have attracted so much attention in Chicago and elsewhere (which is better, decentralized governance or strong mayoral control?), the key to success is to be found at school sites, in a combination of five essential ingredients: instructional leadership in the principal's office, parental and community outreach, a quality teaching staff that believes in reform, a learning climate that is safe and stimulating for all students, and strong instructional guidance and materials.[21]

The Chicago study is in many ways a hopeful one. Like the activism of Foster's time, it suggests that demography is not destiny: schools with similar demographic challenges—especially a high percentage of students living in poverty—might produce dramatically different results, depending on the presence or absence of the five ingredients. The same idea is emphasized by KIPP, Teach for America (TFA), and other movements of dynamic educators who have made some hopeful gains in troubled schools, not least by focusing their efforts on the subtleties of teaching and classroom life.[22] But the difficulty of the challenge is also clear, especially if the goal is to go beyond small networks and transform all of the nation's schools. Changes in classroom teaching and learning are not easy to achieve, especially on a broad scale and in the demoralized atmosphere that pervades the lowest-performing schools.[23] And reform, according to the Chicago researchers, is like baking a cake: *all* of the ingredients must be present, or it will not work. Moreover, at the end of the Chicago study, following many chapters on the ingredients for success, comes a short but sobering comment on those "truly disadvantaged" schools whose students are most seriously affected by poverty, crime, and other damaging social forces beyond the walls of the school: they are unlikely to improve, the authors write, without bold efforts to address that broader social context.[24]

In confronting the challenges posed by such "truly disadvantaged" schools, the Chicago researchers, like many others, see hope in the social experiment known as the Harlem Children's Zone (HCZ). Founded in 1997 by social activist Geoffrey Canada, the HCZ is a non-profit organization that is attempting to transform the lives of some eight thousand children in a one-hundred block area of Harlem in New York City. As it confronts this challenge, the project highlights the depth of commitment that may be needed to raise educational achievement, not just in a few exceptional schools, but on a much broader scale. The Harlem Children's Zone is anchored by several Promise Academy charter schools. Like KIPP and other charter school movements, the Promise Academy schools have come to exemplify high expectations and an insistence on results, with no excuses. But in contrast to many other charter schools, the HCZ does not propose to change lives and raise achievement at school sites alone; it takes action in the community beyond the school. The HCZ charter schools operate in conjunction with early childhood education programs, parenting

workshops, health clinics, and other community services, in a broad attempt to
support children from birth through college graduation.[25]

As much as any school reform effort, the Harlem Children's Zone is consistent with decades of research, going back to the Coleman Report, on how low-
performing schools are shaped by, and cannot be transformed without addressing, social and economic problems beyond school walls. And the Zone's charter
schools have posted some encouraging (though by no means conclusive) gains
in achievement.[26] But even a seemingly comprehensive effort like the HCZ still
raises as many questions as it answers about the possibilities of deep and lasting
urban school reform. For one thing, the HCZ spends more money per pupil
than regular public schools in New York City, not least because it raises large
sums of private capital from Wall Street benefactors. Is it possible to replicate
such expenditures on a nationwide scale, even with support from the federal
government?[27] And even it was, would that be enough to counteract the effects
of urban poverty? Just as politicians and Ford Foundation officials had outsized
expectations for programs such as compensatory education in the 1960s, so,
too, do some backers of the HCZ seem to hold the dubious belief that educational programs can, by themselves, put the children of Harlem on an equal
footing with those in more affluent neighborhoods and towns. After all, the
social and educational services of the HCZ do not directly address the larger
economic forces that shape the lives and opportunities of Harlem residents. It is
hard enough to prepare a multitude of urban students for college; it is perhaps
even harder to supply the capital to pay for it.[28]

Urgency over Complexity: From NCLB to Obama

During the 2000 presidential election, the cover of the *New York Times
Magazine* proclaimed that "Schools Are Not the Answer" to the problem
of poverty and that they never will be. This was not an astonishing idea,
admitted James Traub, the writer of the story, but it was one that Americans still refused to accept. Revisiting the Coleman Report and more recent
research on the negative impact of poverty on school performance, Traub
argued that the nation's faith in the "omnipotence of school" was "disingenu-
ous and self-serving"; it promoted cheap and simplistic solutions to a problem with deep roots. Traub suggested an alternative view: schools were not
the answer to inequality, but it was wrong to ignore obvious success stories
and give up on reform. What was needed, Traub said, quoting a dedicated
but beleaguered urban principal whom he described as being straight out of

the "effective schools" literature, was for all Americans, from rich to poor, to "take ownership of the problem."[29]

Traub's argument was reminiscent of the balancing act that has marked the career of Marcus Foster and a number of urban educators and researchers since: an urgent, no excuses mentality combined with a recognition of the scope and complexity of the challenge, both in and outside of schools. In the past decade, however—that is, in the reform era defined by NCLB-style accountability and market-based organizational changes such as privatization and charter schools—urgency has trumped complexity. Impatient for results, the self-proclaimed reformers oversimplify the problems, and in doing so, they scapegoat educators and set the stage for cynicism and disillusionment.

To be sure, those who embrace test-driven accountability and changes in school governance have made important contributions to urban education, especially in individual schools or small networks of schools. In their emphasis on data, they have raised awareness of race- and class-based achievement gaps. In their language of equity and their impatience with excuses, they have popularized the idea that such gaps are unacceptable and have galvanized a good deal of effort and experimentation to eliminate them. Their passion for reform is captured in a statement from the Educational Equality League (EEP), a leading advocacy group in the fight against achievement gaps:

> Fifty-six years after *Brown vs. Board of Education*, forty-two years
> after the assassination of Dr. Martin Luther King, Jr. and twenty-
> seven years after the publication of A Nation at Risk, we must
> confront a shameful national reality: If you are an African American
> or Latino child in this country, the probability is high that our
> public education system will fail you, that you will not graduate
> from high school, that your ability to function successfully in the
> twenty-first century economy will be limited, and that you will have
> no real prospect of achieving the American dream.

Or, as EEP co-founder Al Sharpton has said, the achievement gap is "the civil rights issue of the 21st century."[30]

When it comes to the accountability agenda of the NCLB era, Marcus Foster's hometown of Philadelphia once again provides telling examples of national trends. Even as No Child Left Behind was just getting off the ground, the district became a laboratory for some of the more radical turnaround strategies that the law recommends for chronically underperforming schools and districts. One such strategy was state takeover. In 1998 and 2000, in response to budget battles with David Hornbeck and test scores that were still far below state averages, the Pennsylvania legislature passed laws allowing the state government to take control of the city's schools. In 2001, the state did just that, ending the era of mayor-appointed school boards that began in 1965 and creating a five-member School Reform Commission appointed primarily by the governor. State takeover went hand in hand with other NCLB-sanctioned interventions in the governance of troubled public schools. One was privatization: in the wake of the state takeover, the district "outsourced" management of forty-five of its lowest-achieving schools to a mix of for-profit businesses, nonprofit organizations, and universities. As part of this "diverse provider" model, described by some as the nation's boldest experiment in privatization of public schools, the for-profit company Edison Schools gained control of twenty schools. Public charter schools were another attempt to improve low-performing schools by changing the governance structure. The charter movement was launched prior to NCLB and the state takeover, in a 1997 state law, but it, too, was extolled by many supporters as a way to shake up school bureaucracies and make them more accountable to families who were desperate for choices and results (especially in Philadelphia, where Republican governor Tom Ridge made a point of signing the charter legislation). By 2011, Philadelphia had emerged as a national leader in the movement, with more than seventy charter schools.[31]

State takeover of the Philadelphia schools also led to the appointment of a bold new school leader, Paul Vallas, who epitomized the can-do ethos of the new accountability. Like leaders such as Alan Bersin in San Diego and Joel Klein in New York City, Vallas was part of a new wave of CEO-superintendents whose experience lay in the corporate world, the military, the law—anywhere but public schools. In Philadelphia, as in Chicago (where he earned praise for his leadership of the school system from 1995 to 2001), Vallas's aggressive leadership seemed to instill a sense of possibility in the district. In addition to managing the transition to diverse providers, he energetically developed after-school programs, new schools, and new curricula. A research study suggested that NCLB and state takeover had helped to facilitate his dynamic leadership.[32]

But if leaders like Vallas have been able to dispel defeatism with their dynamic style and their energetic commitment to action, neither they nor the radical turnaround strategies of NCLB have been able to produce major, systemic change. Nationwide, NCLB has failed to produce big improvements in student achievement or in racial and socioeconomic achievement gaps. According to the National Assessment of Educational Progress (NAEP), which most serious observers believe to be a more reliable standard than the widely varying state tests, the gap between black and white scores was narrowing at a faster rate in the three years *before* NCLB than in the years since—and it is still a substantial gap (at least 26 points on a 0-500 scale, in all subjects, at each tested grade level).[33] In Philadelphia, students did make consistent gains on state reading and math tests during the Vallas era; however, by 2006 Vallas had alienated even key supporters with his autocratic style and, not least, the revelation of an unexpected $73 million budget deficit. Having lost the support of the state board that hired him, he moved on to try to save the devastated public schools of New Orleans. Privatization (which Vallas supported, but did not initiate) ended in disappointment, too; researchers from the RAND Corporation concluded that, in general, privately managed schools matched regular schools but were outperformed by schools that were restructured by the district. By 2006, the district had cancelled its contract with Edison.[34]

Educators like Foster and Clayton and Hornbeck had met with disappointment, too—but when they did, they tended to push a broader spectrum of people (including taxpayers and politicians) to make stronger commitments to solving the problem. In the "no excuses" era, by contrast, reformers were more likely to respond to disappointing results by making inflated claims of success or cracking down harder on teachers and principals. From Houston's alleged "miracle" under future Bush education secretary Rod Paige, to Chicago's celebrated turnaround of troubled schools under Arne Duncan, to New York City's alleged progress on the racial achievement gap during the tenure of Joel Klein, the accountability era produced results that, upon closer analysis, were not as impressive as they initially seemed to be.[35] Meanwhile, to the extent that they did acknowledge disappointing results, advocates of accountability tended to single out teachers and especially their unions for blame, leading to intensified media scrutiny such as the *Los Angeles Times'* controversial decision to publish the names of six thousand teachers, ranked by how much their students' standardized test scores had improved due to a year in their classrooms.[36] In the tense atmosphere created by high-stakes accountability, it was disturbing, but perhaps not surprising, when major cheating scandals came to light in Atlanta, Philadelphia, and other cities. Using forensic reviews of erasure patterns on standardized tests, investigators uncovered systematic cheating that many observers attributed to distorted incentives and unreasonable pressures on teachers and principals in the NCLB era.[37]

Even high-performing charter schools—perhaps the most widely praised achievement of the NCLB era—were dogged by uncertainty as to whether they could equalize achievement on a broad scale. The School District of Philadel-phia used charters as a way to continue contracting with outside "providers" to run low-performing schools. Results at charters were mixed in general, though a good deal of optimism swirled around some of these efforts. In particular, the Mastery Charter Schools network earned high-profile support from the Obama administration, the Gates Foundation, and Oprah Winfrey on its way to taking charge of a growing list of schools. Compared by some to the KIPP schools, the Mastery network gained its reputation by going into dysfunctional schools and establishing order, exhorting students to set their sights on college, and posting promising test score results. The buzz surrounding Mastery was such that, in 2011, it won a bid to step into Marcus Foster's shoes and run Gratz High School, as part of Superintendent Arlene Ackerman's Renaissance Schools turnaround program.[38] In spite of some strong leadership and proud moments since the 1960s, Gratz continued to epitomize the problems of urban education. Would Mastery be able to do what neither Foster nor anyone else had been able to do and make lasting change at the school? Even more important, did charter schools like Mastery hold a key to eliminating achievement gaps and fostering social advancement on a large scale? Only time would tell, but dis-quieting reports from other supposedly high-performing charter schools cast doubt on such expectations. One example was the Bruce Randolph School in Denver. President Obama praised the previously troubled school in his 2011 State of the Union address, citing its 97 percent graduation rate as an example of "what good schools can do." And yet, in spite of some gains, achievement at Randolph was actually quite low, with middle school students showing profi-ciency on state math and science tests at rates of just 21 percent and 10 percent, respectively.[39]

The Randolph School's low pass rates were no indictment of its apparently dedicated staff, any more than Gratz's lower-than-average college admissions could have been blamed on Marcus Foster in the 1960s; both were examples of urban schools that made limited yet notable progress in challenging, high-poverty environments. The historian Diane Ravitch, who had renounced her earlier support for NCLB and emerged as the most influential critic of account-ability and market-driven reforms, pointed to the Randolph example and oth-ers like it to suggest that reformers were ignoring the negative impact of pov-erty on school performance. Of course, to them, citing poverty was an excuse. But ironically, making excuses was precisely what some reformers began to do, when faced with the limitations of their reforms. The journalist Paul Tough made a telling critique of reform advocates who argued, in response to Ravitch, that comparing high-poverty schools like Randolph with white, middle-class schools was like "comparing apples and oranges." "These are excuses," wrote Tough; "If early reformers believed in anything, it was that every student is an apple." To say otherwise now (just a decade or so into the movement) was a tacit recognition of the impact of poverty on achievement.[40]

In spite of the increasingly obvious limitations of NCLB-inspired reforms, the Obama years were defined by a continuing split between those who took a hard line on holding schools and educators accountable and those who emphasized a more complex (and therefore less easily transformed) mix of school and non-school factors. Indeed, in national policy as well as in public debates and media coverage, the accountability advocates continued to have the upper hand. Granted, Obama and Secretary of Education Duncan were critical of No Child Left Behind, and they proposed a "Blueprint" for changing the law. The Blueprint shifted the focus from punishments to incentives: annual testing in math and reading would continue, but only the bottom 10 percent of all schools would face "warnings" or sanctions (including, in many cases, the firing of all staff). The other 90 percent—many of which had been declared "failing" under the existing law—would enjoy greater flexibility and incentives to broaden their curricula. The Blueprint also recognized the impact of economic disadvantage on achievement, in the form of incentives for creating Promise Neighborhoods modeled after the Harlem Children's Zone. The administration was unable to move its Blueprint forward in Congress, and by 2011, the process of reauthorizing NCLB had stalled—but even then, Duncan took a bold stand against the most problematic aspect of the law, unilaterally overriding the requirement that 100 percent of students be proficient in math and reading by 2014.[41]

And yet, as critics argued, the administration's policies were more a continuation of NCLB-style accountability than a change. According to policy analyst Richard Rothstein, the part of Obama's Blueprint that called for Promise Neighborhoods was contradicted by the part about getting tougher on the nation's worst schools. Those lowest-performing schools have the highest concentration of disadvantaged students; according to the logic of Promise Neighborhoods, they needed extensive services in order to succeed. Yet, regardless of whether they got such services, the staff was likely to be fired if test scores did not show improvement. In this sense, the Obama Blueprint seemed to maintain the NCLB practice of holding educators solely responsible for academic achievement (the big difference being that middle-class schools would now be under less pressure). In fact, in one key respect the Obama Administration's brand of accountability went further than NCLB: it sought to tie teacher evaluation directly to standardized test scores. Under the administration's much-touted $4 billion Race to the Top (RTT) program, the chance to win competitive grants was limited to states that were willing to buck the teachers unions and embrace this new policy—in spite of warnings from leading educational testing experts that existing test-driven measures of teacher effectiveness were too inaccurate to be used in high-stakes evaluations of teachers.[42]

The Obama administration's policies reflected a larger climate of opinion: expectations of school reform ran as high as ever, as did enthusiasm for the idea that schools and educators should be held accountable for meeting those expectations. Politicians and activists across the ideological spectrum, from Newt Gingrich to Al Sharpton, passionately promoted these ideas.[43] So did media coverage of school reform, which increasingly echoed the anti-union sentiments of the accountability movement. In one especially striking (though by no means unusual) example, the cover of *Newsweek* showed the headline "The Key to Saving American Education," printed on a blackboard, surrounded by the answer, written over and over: "We must fire bad teachers." Perhaps the most influential statement in this vein was the 2010 documentary *Waiting for "Superman,"* which earned swooning reviews from Bill Gates, Oprah Winfrey, and many other commentators for its portrayal of America's urban educational problems largely as a conflict between hidebound teachers unions and high-performing charter schools (despite the film's own acknowledgment that only one in five charter schools are highly successful).[44]

Not surprisingly, educators were resistant to reforms that portrayed them as the main cause of the problem. Since 2001, teachers had been the most vocal opponents of the accountability agenda of NCLB; not only did they tend to feel that the law cheapened the educational process by forcing them to "teach to the test," but they argued that it held schools accountable for influences on achievement that were outside the school and therefore beyond their control. After 2008, educators extended this critique to the policies of the Obama administration. In response to the Blueprint for reauthorizing NCLB, Randi Weingarten, president of the American Federation of Teachers (AFT), complained, "It just doesn't make sense to have teachers—and teachers alone—bear the responsibility for school and student success." Likewise, Dennis Van Roekel, president of the National Education Association (NEA), said, "It's just not a solution to say, 'Let's get rid of half the staff.' If there's a high-crime neighborhood, you don't fire the police officers."[45]

What would Marcus Foster say about the education policies of the first African American president? About No Child Left Behind and the acrimonious debate about accountability? It is a lasting shame that the SLA deprived the nation of his contributions to these ongoing debates, and that we may only speculate. Yet, given what we know of Foster's career, and the clear connections between the challenges of his day and our own, it is not hard to imagine the broad outlines of his response. Foster would likely feel, and express, the same urgency and impatience as the current advocates of accountability; indeed, he and others of his era helped lay the groundwork for their impatience. As Foster put it in his own book on urban education, "Inner city folks . . . won't be interested in beautiful theories that explain why the task is impossible. The people believe that the job can be done. And they want it done now." This was a challenge to urban educators who held low expectations of students and refused to take responsibility for their learning—problems that continue to hold relevance for anyone hoping to raise achievement in low-performing schools. In key respects, Foster would likely fit in with the "reformers."[46]

At the same time, Foster—a former teacher and an administrator who prioritized teacher input in reform—would no doubt be concerned about the extent to which the debate has come to pit educators against everyone else. In cities that have been held up as models of reform—San Diego, Chicago, Oakland— school CEOs have pursued their agendas with little or no input from teachers or other practitioners. Randolph Ward, the administrator whom the state of California appointed in 2003 to run the Oakland schools, captured this impatience with educators when he said, in response to union and school-board criticism of his autocratic approach: "They have been sitting around singing kum-ba-ya for 30-years, while kids are dropping out and shooting each other. That's what they do in Oakland."[47] As a reformer who cut his teeth during the civil rights era, Foster would likely favor an approach that goes beyond holding teachers accountable for test scores to include a wider focus on school-community relations and societal support for the economic and health problems faced by many urban children. In this regard, he almost certainly would admire the work of a superintendent like Tony Smith, who took charge of the Oakland schools in 2009 and, like Foster four decades before, brought a strong focus on building partnerships between the schools and the larger society—not only parents, but businesses, universities, and social service organizations.[48]

It was difficult during Foster's lifetime, and it is difficult still, to combine a sense of urgency in urban school reform with a recognition of the scope and complexity of the problems—to expect much of schools, yet not too much. Similarly, it has been hard to avoid turning the unequal outcomes of public education into an either-or blame game. Who is responsible for the achievement gap—the schools? The students and their families? The larger society that produced them? For most of American history, racist or discriminatory answers held sway: working-class and minority students simply were not expected to excel. The 1960s brought challenges to the assumption that the students were the main problem, leading to a new era of pressure on the schools. Schools were now to be held accountable for the achievement of all students regardless of their race or social class status.

And yet, since the 1960s we have also gained a more accurate sense—minus the reflexive racism and defeatism of the earlier era—of just how difficult it is to ensure high achievement for all students, in every school in the land. Decades of educational and social research have showed that schools are complex organizations, shaped and constrained by internal relationships as well as the communities they serve and the resources they are provided. Inner-city students tend to lack not only experienced teachers and other educational benefits enjoyed by students in more affluent schools and districts; they suffer as well from disparities in family economic resources and cultural capital. As Marcus Foster and others of his generation envisioned it, school reform must not only address disparities in the quality of schooling that is received (no easy or inexpensive feat, if one of the goals is to provide highly qualified teachers in every classroom); it must be part of a larger set of social and economic policies aimed at addressing unequal access to higher education, health care, and stable employment.[49]

Historians are not fortune tellers, but the past does help illuminate potential pitfalls in current courses of action. And one potential pitfall is that of excessive promises. As the historian Michael Katz has emphasized, generations of reformers have looked to schools as the engine of social mobility and opportunity in America. When they have failed in this effort to overcome inequalities rooted more deeply in the fabric of social and economic life, they have retreated, and the biases of school systems—unequal resources, access, and achievement—have flourished.[50] Recent advocates of accountability largely have singled out educators and ignored the complexity of reforming urban schools, across entire districts, in ways that last. In the era of No Child Left Behind and Race to the Top, it is useful to remember a central lesson and legacy of Marcus Foster's life and times: the need for the whole society, not simply the schools, to be accountable for the educational and life success of all children.

Notes

Introduction

1. Les Payne and Tim Findley, *The Life and Death of the SLA* (New York: Ballantine Books, 1976), 16; Vin McLellan and Paul Avery, *The Voices of Guns: The SLA in History* (New York: Putnam, 1977), 68–69. See Chapter 5 for a full account of the assassination.

2. See, for example, Neil Postman, *The End of Education* (New York: Vintage Books, 1996); W. Norton Grubb and Marvin Lazerson, *The Education Gospel: The Economic Power of Schooling* (Cambridge, Mass.: Harvard University Press, 2004); and David F. Labaree, *How to Succeed in School Without Really Learning: The Credentials Race in American Education* (New Haven: Yale University Press, 1997).

3. James D. Anderson, *The Education of Blacks in the South, 1860–1935* (Chapel Hill: University of North Carolina Press, 1988); Hilary J. Moss, *Schooling Citizens: The Struggle for African American Education in Antebellum America* (Chicago: University of Chicago Press, 2009); Theresa Perry, "Up from the Parched Earth: Toward a Theory of African American Achievement," in Theresa Perry, Claude Steele, and Asa Hilliard III, *Young, Gifted, and Black: Promoting High Achievement Among African American Students* (Boston: Beacon Press, 2003); Ira Katznelson and Margaret Weir, *Schooling for All: Class, Race, and the Decline of the Democratic Ideal* (New York: Basic Books, 1985).

4. Michael B. Katz, Mark J. Stern, and Jamie J. Fader, "The New African American Inequality," *Journal of American History* 92, no. 1 (2005), http://jah.oxfordjournals.org/content/92/1/75.full (accessed January 5, 2012); Ronald F. Ferguson, *Toward Excellence with Equity: An Emerging Vision for Closing the Achievement Gap* (Cambridge, Mass.: Harvard Education Press, 2008); William Julius Wilson, *More Than Just Race: Being Black and Poor in the Inner City* (New York: W. W. Norton & Co., 2009), 6–14, 62–72. On American expectations of schools more generally, see, among many other sources, Jennifer L. Hochschild and Nathan Scovronick, *The American Dream and the Public Schools* (New York: Oxford University Press, 2003).

5. Gunnar Myrdal, *An American Dilemma: The Negro Problem and Modern Democracy* (New York: Harper and Brothers, 1944); Walter A. Jackson, *Gunnar Myrdal and America's Conscience: Social Engineering and Racial Liberalism, 1938–1987* (Chapel Hill: University of North Carolina Press, 1990), 186–245; Alice O'Connor, *Poverty Knowledge: Social Science, Social Policy, and the Poor in Twentieth-Century U.S. History* (Princeton, N.J.: Princeton University Press, 2001), 74–98.

6. In recent years historians have recast post–World War II history in general, and the history of liberalism, civil rights, and Black Power in particular, by focusing on social and political struggles that began to transform the nation's cities well before the familiar conflicts of the 1960s. See especially Thomas J. Sugrue, *The Origins of the Urban Crisis: Race and Inequality in Postwar Detroit* (Princeton, N.J.: Princeton University Press, 1996); Robert O. Self, *American Babylon: Race and the Struggle for*

Postwar Oakland (Princeton, N.J.: Princeton University Press, 2005); Matthew J. Countryman, *Up South: Civil Rights and Black Power in Philadelphia* (Philadelphia: University of Pennsylvania Press, 2006); Jeanne Theoharis and Komozi Woodard, eds., *Freedom North: Black Freedom Struggles Outside the South, 1940–1980* (New York: Palgrave Macmillan, 2003); Martha Biondi, *To Stand and Fight: The Struggle for Civil Rights in Postwar New York City* (Cambridge, Mass.: Harvard University Press, 2006); and Marilynn Johnson, *The Second Gold Rush: Oakland and the East Bay in World War II* (Berkeley: University of California Press, 1993). However, these works have tended to focus on conflicts over economic development, jobs, and housing, and less on the educational struggles that were also of vital importance to urban residents in the postwar decades. Among works that have begun to integrate education into larger narratives of racial struggle and civil rights activism in northern cities prior to the 1960s, see Sugrue, *Sweet Land of Liberty: The Forgotten Struggle for Civil Rights in the North* (New York: Random House, 2008); Jeffery Mirel, *The Rise and Fall of an Urban School System* (Ann Arbor: University of Michigan Press, 1993); Jack Dougherty, *More Than One Struggle: The Evolution of Black School Reform in Milwaukee* (Chapel Hill: University of North Carolina Press, 2004); Ansley T. Erickson, "Schooling the Metropolis: Educational Inequality Made and Remade, Nashville, Tennessee, 1945–1985" (Ph.D. diss., Columbia University, 2010); Clarence Taylor, *Knocking at Our Own Door: Milton A. Galamison and the Struggle to Integrate New York City Schools* (New York: Columbia University Press, 1997); and Adina Back, "Exposing the 'Whole Segregation Myth': The Harlem Nine and New York City's School Desegregation Battles," in *Freedom North,* ed. Theoharis and Woodard, 65–92. For discussions of the role of education (especially anti-prejudice programs) within postwar racial liberalism in particular, see Jonathan Zimmerman, "*Brown*-ing the American Textbook: History, Psychology, and the Origins of Modem Multiculturalism," *History of Education Quarterly* 44, no. 1 (2004): 46–69; Diana Selig, *Americans All: The Cultural Gifts Movement* (Cambridge, Mass.: Harvard University Press, 2008), 268–78; and Leah N. Gordon, "The Question of Prejudice: Social Science, Education, and the Struggle to Define 'the Race Problem' in Mid-Century America, 1935–1965" (Ph.D. diss., University of Pennsylvania, 2008).

7. For a discussion of this point, see Sugrue, *Sweet Land of Liberty,* 181–99.

8. On the contrast between New Deal liberalism and the education-oriented policies of the postwar era, see Harvey Kantor and Robert Lowe, "From New Deal to No Deal: NCLB and the Devolution of Responsibility for Equal Educational Opportunity," *Harvard Educational Review,* 76, no. 4 (2006): 474–502.

9. Among broad surveys of the 1960s and 1970s that emphasize the polarizing impact of northern desegregation and busing, see Thomas Byrne Edsall and Mary D. Edsall, *Chain Reaction: The Impact of Race, Rights, and Taxes on American Politics* (New York: W. W. Norton and Co., 1992); Jefferson R. Cowie, *Stayin' Alive: The 1970s and the Last Days of the Working Class* (New York: New Press, 2010); and James T. Patterson, *Grand Expectations: The United States, 1945–1974* (Oxford: Oxford University Press, 1996). More detailed treatments of busing and desegregation include Patterson, *Brown v. Board of Education: A Civil Rights Milestone and its Troubled Legacy* (New York: Oxford University Press, 2001); Ronald P. Formisano, *Boston Against Busing: Race, Class, and Ethnicity in the 1960s and 1970s* (Chapel Hill: University of North Carolina Press, 1991); J. Anthony Lukas, *Common Ground: A Turbulent Decade in the Lives of Three American Families* (New York: Alfred A. Knopf, 1985); Dougherty, *More Than One Struggle*; and Gregory S. Jacobs, *Getting Around Brown: Desegregation, Development, and the Columbus Public Schools* (Columbus: Ohio State University Press, 1998).

10. These disturbances preceded the Watts riot of the following year. For a contemporary analysis of the Philadelphia riot, see Lenora E. Berson, *Case Study of a Riot: The Philadelphia Story* (New York: Institute of Human Relations Press, 1966).

11. Jon S. Birger, "Race, Reaction, and Reform: The Three Rs of Philadelphia School Politics, 1965–1971," *Pennsylvania Magazine of History and Biography* 120, no. 3 (1996): 163–216; Countryman, *Up South,* 223–28.

12. James S. Coleman et al., *Equality of Educational Opportunity* (Washington, D.C.: Government Printing Office, 1966).

13. For the book that coined the phrase "blaming the victim," see William Ryan, *Blaming the Victim* (New York: Pantheon, 1971). For the text of the Moynihan Report and a documentary history of the controversy surrounding it, see Lee Rainwater and William L. Yancey, *The Moynihan Report and the Politics of Controversy* (Cambridge, Mass.: M.I.T. Press, 1967).

14. Michael B. Katz, *The Irony of Early School Reform: Educational Innovation in Mid-Nineteenth Century Massachusetts* (New York: Teachers College Press, 2001); Christopher Jencks et al., *Inequality: A Reassessment of the Effect of Family and Schooling in America* (New York: Basic Books, 1972); Samuel Bowles and Herbert Gintis, *Schooling in Capitalist America: Education Reform and the Contradictions of Economic Life* (New York: Basic Books, 1976); Joel H. Spring, *Education and the Rise of the Corporate State* (Boston: Beacon Press, 1972).

15. Daniel H. Perlstein, *Justice, Justice: School Politics and the Eclipse of Liberalism* (New York: Peter Lang Publishing, 2004); and Jerald E. Podair, *The Strike That Changed New York: Blacks, Whites, and the Ocean Hill–Brownsville Crisis* (New Haven: Yale University Press, 2004). As Podair emphasizes, white and black New Yorkers had come to speak "past each other" in different languages "like strangers."

16. Robert Blackburn, interviewed by the author at Blackburn's home in Oakland, California, March 5, 1998, tape recording in possession of the author.

17. Theodore Sizer, interviewed by the author at the Francis W. Parker Charter School, Harvard, Massachusetts, September 15, 1998, tape recording in possession of the author.

18. Marcus Foster, commencement address, Swarthmore High School, Swarthmore, Pennsylvania, June 9, 1969, tape recording in possession of the author.

19. For overviews of key aspects of No Child Left Behind, see Michael A. Rebell and Jessica R. Wolff, eds., *NCLB at the Crossroads: Reexamining the Federal Effort to Close the Achievement Gap* (New York: Teachers College Press, 2009).

20. For a variety of critical perspectives, see, for example, the online forum moderated by John Merrow, "Do We Need a Basic Rewrite of No Child Left Behind?" August 5–7, 2008, http://newtalk.org/2008/08/do-we-need-a-basic-rewrite-of.php (accessed September 1, 2011).

21. For a more detailed discussion of these recent developments, see the epilogue.

22. On recent divisions between self-styled "reformers" on the one hand, and teachers' unions on the other, see, for example, Dana Goldstein, "The Education Wars," *American Prospect,* March 23, 2009, http://www.prospect.org/cs/articles?article=the_education_wars (accessed September 1, 2011). On the controversy surrounding Duncan's "turnaround" initiative, see Catherine Gewertz, "Duncan's Call for School Turnarounds Sparks Debate," *Education Week,* August 11, 2009, http://www.edweek.org/ew/articles/2009/07/21/37turnaround.h28.html?tkn=PSYFxw1Jyvgk%2FgLau9 Yz5CS3EIwzCgp9kVtI (accessed September 1, 2011). Critiques of teachers and unions in the media include Evan Thomas and Pat Wingert, "Why We Must Fire Bad Teachers," *Newsweek,* March 6, 2010; Steven Brill, "The Teachers' Unions' Last Stand," *New York Times Magazine,* May 17, 2010; and, especially, a raft of coverage surrounding the documentary film, *Waiting for "Superman,"* which featured critiques of teacher unions as a prominent theme.

23. The "equity to excellence" narrative is featured in many leading textbooks of American educational history; for an especially thoughtful synthesis of changing federal policies, see Wayne Urban and Jennings L. Wagoner, Jr., *American Education: A History* (New York: McGraw-Hill, 2004), 354–58. Even those who forcefully disagree on the merits of school policymaking since the 1980s tend to emphasize the same basic framework of a Reagan-era shift toward excellence, achievement, and accountability. For a prominent critique of this shift, see the four-part PBS documentary and companion volume *School: The Story of American Public Education* (Boston: Beacon Press, 2001). Positive appraisals include Diane Ravitch, *The Troubled Crusade: American Education, 1945–1980* (New York: Basic Books, 1983), and *The Schools We Deserve* (New York: Basic Books, 1987); as well

as Koret Task Force on K–12 Education, "Are We Still at Risk," *Education Next,* Spring 2003, http://educationnext.org/are-we-still-at-risk/ (accessed September 1, 2011). The Koret report suggests, for example, that the 1983 Reagan Administration report *A Nation at Risk* "recast many people's thinking about education from a focus on resources, services, and mindless innovation that absorbed us during the 1960s and 1970s to an emphasis on achievement that remains central today." For an account that does trace recent accountability movements to the late 1960s, though with an emphasis on the influence of business interests rather than African American activism, see Larry Cuban, "Looking Through the Rearview Mirror at School Accountability," in Kenneth A. Sirotnik, *Holding Accountability Accountable: What Ought to Matter in Public Education* (New York: Teachers College Press, 2004), 18–34.

24. For a synthesis that makes a similar point about the influence of civil rights activism on accountability agendas, see William J. Reese, *America's Public Schools: From the Common School to "No Child Left Behind"* (Baltimore: Johns Hopkins University Press, 2005), 306–8.

25. The concept of cultural capital derives from the French sociologist Pierre Bourdieu. For useful reviews of the literature on cultural capital as it has been applied to scholarship on education, see Annette Lareau and Elliot B. Weininger, "Cultural Capital in Educational Research: A Critical Assessment," *Theory and Society* 32, no. 5/6 (2003): 567–606; and John L. Rury, *Education and Social Change: Themes in the History of American Schooling* (Mahwah, N.J.: Lawrence Erlbaum, 2002), 193–94. My use of the concept in this book has been influenced by Lareau's and Weininger's rejection of an "elitist" definition in favor of one that emphasizes power contestation. See further discussion in Chapters 1 and 2.

26. The sociologist Kathryn Neckerman has called for more attention to the history of classroom dynamics between teachers and students; in those classroom dynamics, she argues, we see how discriminatory school district policies (in addition to more frequently cited social and economic factors) shaped the urban school problems that plague us today. See Kathryn M. Neckerman, *Schools Betrayed: Roots of Failure in Inner-City Education* (Chicago: University of Chicago Press, 2007), 4–7.

27. For an influential contemporary statement of this idea, see Benjamin S. Bloom, Allison Davis, and Robert Hess, *Compensatory Education for Cultural Deprivation* (New York: Holt, Rinehart, and Winston, 1965).

28. See, for example, Ryan, *Blaming the Victim,* 31–62, and Kenneth B. Clark, *Dark Ghetto: Dilemmas of Social Power* (New York: Harper and Row, 1965), 111–53.

29. On social and cultural capital, see Rury, *Education and Social Change,* 193–94, and Lareau and Weininger, "Cultural Capital in Educational Research." On the impact of teachers and schools on academic achievement, see, for example, Ferguson, *Toward Excellence with Equity;* Ronald Edmonds, "Effective Schools for the Urban Poor," *Educational Leadership* 37, no. 1 (1979): 5–24; and Rhona S. Weinstein, *Reaching Higher: The Power of Expectations in Schooling* (Cambridge, Mass.: Harvard University Press, 2004).

30. Marcus A. Foster, *Making Schools Work: Strategies for Changing Education* (Philadelphia: Westminster Press, 1971), 16–17, 21.

31. Among recent works that have redefined the Black Power movement in this way, see Countryman, *Up South;* Self, *American Babylon;* Peniel E. Joseph, *The Black Power Movement: Rethinking the Civil Rights–Black Power Era* (New York: Routledge, 2006); and Jeffrey O. G. Ogbar, *Black Power: Radical Politics and African American Identity* (Baltimore: Johns Hopkins University Press, 2005).

32. Despite the overall trend of change since his childhood, Foster did live to witness—and condemn—a controversial revival of the idea of inherited intellectual differences between blacks and whites. See Arthur Jensen, "How Much Can We Boost IQ and Scholastic Achievement?," *Harvard Educational Review* 39 (1969): 1–123. For Foster's response, which he described as the "blame the victim game," see Marcus Foster, "Child of the Poor, Looking for Mitochondria," in *Readings in*

Curriculum and Supervision, ed. V. Eugene Yarbrough, William C. Bruce, and Ronald L. Hubright (New York: MSS Information Corporation, 1974), 59–60.

33. "Black Educator's Angry Message," *San Francisco Chronicle,* March 21, 1973; "School Chief Hits Black Power Myth," *Oakland Tribune,* March 21, 1973.

34. Davis Guggenheim, director, *Waiting for "Superman,"* 2010. Other films about successful urban educators include *Lean on Me,* a portrayal of Joe Clark, the black, baseball-bat-wielding principal who instilled discipline and pride in Paterson, New Jersey's troubled Eastside High, and *Stand and Deliver,* the story of Los Angeles math teacher Jaime Escalante's guidance of his poor, underachieving Chicano students to passing scores on the Advanced Placement exam in calculus. John G. Avildsen, director, *Lean on Me,* 1989; Ramón Menéndez, director, *Stand and Deliver,* 1988. Profiles of such educators in the press include, for example, Richard Louv, "Hope in Hell's Classroom," *New York Times Magazine,* November 25, 1990, on Philadelphia middle-school principal Madeline Cartwright.

35. Among many works that emphasize the limits of schooling as a mechanism of social reform, see David F. Labaree, *Someone Has to Fail: The Zero-Sum Game of Public Schooling* (Cambridge, Mass.: Harvard University Press, 2010); Kantor and Lowe, "From New Deal to No Deal"; Amy Stuart Wells, "'Our Children's Burden': A History of Federal Education Policies That Ask (Now Require) Our Public Schools to Solve Societal Inequality," in *NCLB at the Crossroads: Reexamining the Federal Effort to Close the Achievement Gap,* ed. Michael A. Rebell and Jessica R. Wolff (New York: Teachers College Press, 2009), 1–42; Harvey Kantor and Barbara Brenzel, "Urban Education and the Truly Disadvantaged: The Historical Roots of the Contemporary Crisis, 1945–1990," in *The Underclass Debate: Views from History,* ed. Michael B. Katz (Princeton, N.J.: Princeton University Press, 1993), 366–402; Jean Anyon, *Ghetto Schooling: A Political Economy of Urban Educational Reform* (New York: Teachers College Press, 1997); Richard Rothstein, *Class and Schools: Using Social, Economic, and Educational Reform to Close the Black-White Achievement Gap* (Economic Policy Institute, 2004); Michael B. Katz, "Education and Inequality: A Historical Perspective," in *Social History and Social Policy,* ed. David J. Rothman and Stanton Wheeler (New York: Academic Press, 1981); and Richard deLone, *Small Futures: Children, Inequality and the Limits of Liberal Reform* (New York: Harcourt Brace Jovanovich, 1979). The last of these is by an author who played a major role in the Philadelphia school reforms of the late 1960s but came to emphasize the limits of such reforms as antipoverty strategies.

36. For a useful discussion of increasing disparities of wealth and declining access to higher education, see Peter Sacks, *Tearing Down the Gates: Confronting the Class Divide in American Education* (Berkeley: University of California Press, 2007). Among works that critique recent federal policies for ignoring or obscuring larger structural inequalities, see Kantor and Lowe, "From New Deal to No Deal" and Alan R. Sadovnik et al., *No Child Left Behind and the Reduction of the Achievement Gap: Sociological Perspectives on Federal Educational Policy* (New York: Routledge, 2007).

37. For a seminal statement of the idea that emphasizing racial discrimination and poverty is tantamount to making excuses, see Stephan Thernstrom and Abigail Thernstrom, *No Excuses: Closing the Racial Gap in Learning* (New York: Simon and Schuster, 2003). For a rebuttal to this argument, see Aaron Pallas, "Joel Klein vs. the So-Called 'Apologists for the Failed Status Quo,'" *A Sociological Eye on Education,* June 14, 2011, http://eyeoned.org/content/joel-klein-vs-the-so-called-apologists-for-the-failed-status-quo_237/?utm_source=feedburner&utm_medium=feed&utm_ca mpaign=Feed%3A+ASociologicalEyeOnEducation+%28A+Sociological+Eye+on+Education%29 (accessed September 1, 2011).

38. Among works that emphasize the impact of teachers and schools on achievement, see, for example, Gloria Ladson-Billings, *The Dreamkeepers: Successful Teachers of African American Children* (San Francisco: Jossey-Bass, 1994); David Hornbeck with Katherine Conner, *Choosing Excellence in Public Schools: Where There's a Will, There's a Way* (Lanham, Maryland: Rowman & Littlefield Education, 2009); Ferguson, *Toward Excellence with Equity;* and, for a more conservative

analysis that emphasizes the impact of schools as well as the need for cultural and attitudinal shifts among the students themselves, Thernstrom and Thernstrom, *No Excuses*. Among those who stress social and economic constraints on school reform, important recent examples are Rothstein, *Class and Schools* and Anyon, *Ghetto Schooling*.

39. For other works that emphasize both the agency of educators and the political and social structural constraints within which they operate, see especially Pedro Noguera, *City Schools and The American Dream* (New York: Teachers College Press, 2003); Charles M. Payne, *So Much Reform, So Little Change: The Persistence of Failure in Urban Schools* (Cambridge, Mass.: Harvard Education Press, 2008); and Neckerman, *Schools Betrayed*.

40. Henry J. Perkinson, *The Imperfect Panacea: American Faith in Education* (New York: McGraw Hill, 2005).

Chapter 1

1. James D. Anderson, *The Education of Blacks in the South, 1860–1935* (Chapel Hill: University of North Carolina Press, 1988); Hilary J. Moss, *Schooling Citizens: The Struggle for African American Education in Antebellum America* (Chicago: University of Chicago Press, 2009); Theresa Perry, "Up from the Parched Earth: Toward a Theory of African American Achievement," in Theresa Perry, Claude Steele, and Asa Hilliard III, *Young, Gifted, and Black: Promoting High Achievement Among African American Students* (Boston: Beacon Press, 2003); Ira Katznelson and Margaret Weir, *Schooling For All: Class, Race, and the Decline of the Democratic Ideal* (New York: Basic Books, 1985).

2. On the Great Migration in Philadelphia, see Charles Ashley Hardy III, "Race and Opportunity: Black Philadelphia During the Era of the Great Migration, 1916–1930" (Ph.D. diss., Temple University, 1989). On educational segregation during that period, see Vincent P. Franklin, *The Education of Black Philadelphia: The Social and Educational History of a Minority Community, 1900–1950* (Philadelphia: University of Pennsylvania Press, 1979); and Judy Jolly Mohraz, *The Separate Problem: Case Studies of Black Education in the North, 1900–1930* (Westport, Conn.: Greenwood Press, 1979).

3. Leon Frisby, telephone interviews by the author, September 27, 1999 and April 25, 2000, tape recordings in possession of the author.

4. For a review of the literature on cultural capital as it has been applied to scholarship on education, see Annette Lareau and Elliot B. Weininger, "Cultural Capital in Educational Research: A Critical Assessment," *Theory and Society* 32, nos. 5–6 (2003): 567–606.

5. Thomas J. Sugrue, *Sweet Land of Liberty: The Forgotten Struggle for Civil Rights in the North* (New York: Random House, 2008); Matthew J. Countryman, *Up South: Civil Rights and Black Power in Philadelphia* (Philadelphia: University of Pennsylvania Press, 2007); Martha Biondi, *To Stand and Fight: The Struggle for Civil Rights in Postwar New York City* (Cambridge, Mass.: Harvard University Press, 2006); Walter A. Jackson, *Gunnar Myrdal and America's Conscience: Social Engineering and Racial Liberalism, 1938–1987* (Chapel Hill: University of North Carolina Press, 1990); Alice O'Connor, *Poverty Knowledge: Social Science, Social Policy, and the Poor in Twentieth-Century U.S. History* (Princeton, N.J.: Princeton University Press, 2001), 74–98.

6. I use the term "racial liberalism" to encompass not only the political and legal push for new anti-discrimination laws and agencies (what Matthew Countryman has called "civil rights liberalism") but also anti-prejudice campaigns and other educational and ideological struggles to change attitudes in support of government action. Countryman, *Up South*.

7. Jonathan Zimmerman, "*Brown*-ing the American Textbook: History, Psychology, and the Origins of Modern Multiculturalism," *History of Education Quarterly* 44, no. 1 (2004): 46–69; Leah N. Gordon, "The Question of Prejudice: Social Science, Education, and the Struggle to Define 'The Race Problem' in Mid-Century America, 1935–1965" (Ph.D. diss., University of Pennsylvania, 2008); Zoe Burkholder, *Color in the Classroom: How American Schools Taught Race, 1900–1954* (New York: Oxford University Press, 2011). On precedents for such programs during the 1920s and

1930s, see Diana Selig, *Americans All: The Cultural Gifts Movement* (Cambridge, Mass.: Harvard University Press, 2008); and Nicholas V. Montalto, *A History of the Intercultural Education Movement, 1924–1941* (New York: Garland, 1982).

8. Alfred Foster, telephone interview by the author, June 30, 2000, tape recording in possession of the author.

9. Hardy, "Race and Opportunity," 135; E. Digby Baltzell, introduction to *The Philadelphia Negro*, by W. E. B. DuBois (New York: Schocken Books, 1967), xxix; Fredric Miller, "The Black Migration to Philadelphia: A 1924 Profile," *Pennsylvania Magazine of History and Biography* 108, no. 3 (1984): 329–32. Miller cites Census data (including Enumeration Districts) as well as a 1924 survey of over 500 recently arrived black migrants.

10. Alfred Foster interview, June 30, 2000.

11. Hardy, "Race and Opportunity," 16–25, 225, 380–412; Miller, "Black Migration to Philadelphia," 320; Baltzell, introduction, xxxvii.

12. Franklin, *The Education of Black Philadelphia*, 50.

13. Franklin, *The Education of Black Philadelphia*, 37–42, 53–57; Mohraz, *The Separate Problem*; and Ruth Wright Hayre and Alexis Moore, *Tell Them We Are Rising: A Memoir of Faith in Education* (New York: J. Wiley and Sons, 1997), 27, 31–32.

14. Franklin, *The Education of Black Philadelphia*, 35–48, 169–70.

15. Hayre and Moore, *Tell Them We Are Rising*, 52–54.

16. Hayre and Moore, *Tell Them We Are Rising*, 29.

17. W. E. B. DuBois, "Does the Negro Need Separate Schools?" *Journal of Negro Education* 4, no. 3 (1935): 328–35.

18. DuBois, "Does the Negro Need Separate Schools?," 335.

19. Franklin, *The Education of Black Philadelphia*, 168–69.

20. For a seminal expression of the "oppositional culture" argument, see Signithia Fordham and John Ogbu, "Black Students' School Success: Coping with the Burden of 'Acting White,'" *Urban Review* 18, no. 3 (1986): 176–206.

21. Perry, "Up from the Parched Earth"; Anderson, *The Education of Blacks in the South*, 283–85; Kathryn M. Neckerman, *Schools Betrayed: Roots of Failure in Inner-City Education* (Chicago: University of Chicago Press, 2007), 58.

22. Alfred Foster interview, June 30, 2000.

23. Alfred Foster interview, June 30, 2000.

24. Alfred Foster interview, June 30, 2000.

25. Robert Blackburn, interviewed by the author at Blackburn's home in Oakland, Calif., March 5, 1998, tape recording in possession of the author.

26. Alfred Foster interview, June 30, 2000.

27. Alfred Foster interview, June 30, 2000.

28. Lareau and Weininger, "Cultural Capital," 583–98; John L. Rury, *Education and Social Change: Themes in the History of American Schooling* (Mahwah, N.J.: Lawrence Erlbaum, 2002), 193–94.

29. Blackburn interview, March 5, 1998.

30. Alfred Foster interview, June 30, 2000.

31. Alfred Foster interview, June 30, 2000.

32. Leon Frisby, telephone conversation with the author, April 19, 2001.

33. Alfred Foster interview, June 30, 2000.

34. Frisby interview, September 27, 1999; and conversation, April 19, 2001.

35. Frisby interview, September 27, 1999; and conversation, April 19, 2001. For an example of a fatal dance hall altercation—allegedly over possession of a glass of water—during Foster's high school years, see "'Jitterbug' Dance Hall Scene of Fatal Stabbing of Youth," *Philadelphia Tribune*, December 21, 1939, 1.

36. Robin D. G. Kelley, "The Riddle of the Zoot: Malcolm Little and Black Cultural Politics During World War II," in Kelley, *Race Rebels: Culture, Politics, and the Black Working Class* (New York: Free Press, 1994), 161–82; Stuart Cosgrove, "The Zoot-Suit and Style Warfare," *History Workshop Journal* 18 (Autumn 1984): 77–91; Steve Chibnall, "Whistle and Zoot: The Changing Meaning of a Suit of Clothes," *History Workshop Journal* 20 (Autumn 1985): 56–81. For a new interpretation that is more consistent with Frisby's testimony about Marcus Foster, see Kathy Peiss, *Zoot Suit: The Enigmatic Career of an Extreme Style* (Philadelphia: University of Pennsylvania Press, 2011). Peiss deemphasizes the notion of the zoot suit as a politicized expression of resistance.

37. Leon Frisby, telephone interview by the author, October 4, 1999, tape recording in possession of the author.

38. Alfred Foster interview, June 30, 2000.

39. Marci Shatzman, "Principal Thinks 'Gratz Is Greatest,'" *North Penn Chat*, February 8, 1968, clippings file of the *Philadelphia Evening Bulletin* (hereafter referred to as *Bulletin*), "Marcus Foster," Temple University Urban Archives (TUUA).

40. Frisby interview, October 4, 1999.

41. Alfred Foster interview, June 30, 2000.

42. On Cheyney's origins and history, see Charline H. Conyers, "A History of the Cheyney State Teachers College" (Ed.D. diss., New York University, 1960).

43. Frisby interview, October 4, 1999. On Hill's life and thought, see Sulayman Clark, "The Educational Philosophy of Leslie Pinckney Hill: A Profile in Black Educational Leadership, 1904–1951" (Ed.D. diss., Harvard University, 1984).

44. Clark, "The Educational Philosophy of Leslie Pinckney Hill," 129–30; Frisby interview, September 27, 1999.

45. Harriet Braxton Logan, telephone conversation with the author, April 17, 2001.

46. Quoted in Clark, "The Educational Philosophy of Leslie Pinckney Hill," 181. Integrationists, including Floyd Logan, did attack Cheyney when it became a Normal School in the 1920s, charging that the state's adoption of the all-black school amounted to a public policy of segregated higher education. Hill, distinguishing between voluntary and forced segregation, responded that black institutions and racial pride served, rather than conflicted with, the struggle for full inclusion in American society; see 105–13.

47. DuBois commented in 1923 that he had seen schools in two continents and ten countries and had "yet to see a finer group in character and service than the teachers of Cheyney." Quoted in Clark, "The Educational Philosophy of Leslie Pinckney Hill," 118.

48. Clark, "The Educational Philosophy of Leslie Pinckney Hill," 121, 131.

49. For a detailed account of the Cheyney experience from the perspective of one of Marcus Foster's fellow students in the 1940s, see Jo Ann Robinson's oral history with longtime Baltimore principal Gertrude Williams: *Education as My Agenda: Gertrude Williams, Race, and the Baltimore Public Schools* (New York: Palgrave, 2005), 37–48. Williams echoes the idea that Cheyney instilled a powerful sense of identity, high standards, and pride among African American students.

50. "Student Leadership Outlook Excellent," *Cheyney Record*, October, 1941, 1; "Scholars Feted Here Last Night," *Cheyney Record*, February 1942, 1; "Cheyney Thespians Triumph in Seasonal Drama," *Cheyney Record*, May 1942.

51. Ernestine Roberts, "Marcus Foster," *Cheyney Record*, December 1943, 3.

52. Hayre and Moore, *Tell Them We Are Rising*, 75.

53. Frisby interview, September 27, 1999; telephone interview by the author, December 16, 2000, tape recording in possession of the author.

54. J. David Bowick to Leon Frisby, September 1, 1982, personal collection of Leon Frisby.

55. Frisby interview, October 4, 1999.

56. Frisby interview, September 27, 1999; Alfred Foster interview, June 30, 2000.

57. Frisby interview, October 4, 1999.

58. Alfred Foster interview, June 30, 2000.

59. Leon Frisby, interviewed by the author at Frisby's home in Philadelphia, Pennsylvania, June 2, 2011, tape recording in possession of the author. Established at Howard University in 1911, the Omega Psi Phi fraternity was the first national African American fraternity to be founded at a historically black college. Penn's chapter (Mu) was established in 1920; Cheyney's (Beta Gamma) was established in 1950. In Foster's era, Omega Psi Phi already had a history of actions aimed at fostering racial equality. In the 1920s and 1930s, the fraternity made contributions to a variety of black organizations, including life memberships in the NAACP and the Association for the Study of Negro Life and History (whose founder, the historian and educator Carter G. Woodson, was a fraternity brother). In 1940, the fraternity made a point of changing jewelers in order to support one that employed African Americans. Lawrence C. Ross, Jr., *The Divine Nine: The History of African American Fraternities and Sororities* (New York: Kensington Publishing, 2001), 73–100; and Tamara L. Brown, Gregory S. Parks, and Clarenda M. Phillips, *African American Fraternities and Sororities: The Legacy and the Vision* (Lexington: University Press of Kentucky, 2010), 188–90.

60. Rufus and Estella Johnson, telephone interview by the author, July 9, 1999, tape recording in possession of the author.

61. Frisby interview, December 16, 2000.

62. Rufus and Estella Johnson interview, July 9, 1999.

63. Frisby interview, December 16, 2000; and interview, June 2, 2011.

64. Bev Mitchell and Andy Jokelson, "'Pray for the Assassins,' Foster's Widow Pleads," *Oakland Tribune*, November 13, 1973; Shatzman, "Principal Thinks 'Gratz Is Greatest.'"

65. Frisby interview, June 2, 2011; Alfred Foster interview, June 30, 2000.

66. Bev Mitchell, "Marcus Foster Believed in People Power," *Oakland Tribune*, November 7, 1973.

67. Marcus Foster, "Child of the Poor, Looking for Mitochondria," in *Readings in Curriculum and Supervision*, ed. V. Eugene Yarbrough, William C. Bruce, and Ronald L. Hubright (New York: MSS Information Corporation, 1974), 54. The article is a transcript of a speech delivered at the Center for Research and Development in Teaching, Stanford University, September 21, 1973.

68. Mitchell and Jokelson, "'Pray for the Assassins'"; Shatzman, "Principal Thinks 'Gratz Is Greatest.'" Curiously, Shatzman quoted Foster as saying that Ramseur went to Chicago after college—not Florida, as she stated.

69. Frisby interview, October 4, 1999.

70. Rayford W. Logan, ed., *What the Negro Wants* (Chapel Hill: University of North Carolina Press, 1944). See also Sterling Brown, "The American Race Problem as Reflected in American Literature," *Journal of Negro Education* 8, no. 3 (1939): 284, in which Brown placed Hill in a category of black writers who "counseled that no wrong this side of heaven was too great to be forgiven."

71. Logan, *What the Negro Wants*, vii–viii.

72. See especially Sugrue, *Sweet Land of Liberty*; Jacquelyn Dowd Hall, "The Long Civil Rights Movement and the Political Uses of the Past," *Journal of American History* 91, no. 4 (2005): 1233–63; Jeanne Theoharis and Komozi Woodard, eds., *Freedom North: Black Freedom Struggles Outside the South, 1940–1980* (New York: Palgrave Macmillan, 2003); Countryman, *Up South*; and Glenda Elizabeth Gilmore, *Defying Dixie: The Radical Roots of Civil Rights: 1919–1950* (New York: W. W. Norton & Company, 2008).

73. On the impact of the "second great migration," see Nicholas Lemann, *The Promised Land: The Great Black Migration and How It Changed America* (New York: Alfred A. Knopf, 1991); and Michael B. Katz, Mark J. Stern, and Jamie J. Fader, "The New African American Inequality," *Journal of American History* 92, no. 1 (2005), http://jah.oxfordjournals.org/content/92/1/75.full (accessed January 5, 2012). On black migration during the 1930s, see Jackson, *Gunnar Myrdal and America's Conscience*, 4. For Philadelphia population statistics, see John F. Bauman, *Public Housing, Race,*

and Renewal: Urban Planning in Philadelphia, 1920–1974 (Philadelphia: Temple University Press, 1987), 84.

74. Mary Constantine, "Philadelphia Firsts," 1949, Papers of the Philadelphia Fellowship Commission (hereafter PFC papers), Acc. 626, b. 8, f. 22, TUUA.

75. Countryman, *Up South*, 29–31.

76. Jackson, *Gunnar Myrdal and America's Conscience*; Selig, *Americans All*.

77. As Ira Katznelson and others have shown, the prominence of southern Democrats within the New Deal coalition not only led the Roosevelt Administration to neglect black concerns for the most part; in significant ways, the New Deal actually deepened the already substantial levels of inequality between the races. Social Security, labor legislation, and the G.I. Bill were all designed and administered under the strong influence of the southern wing of the party to benefit whites more than blacks. In this sense, the social legislation of the 1930s and 1940s amounted to "affirmative action for whites"—a massive transfer of public wealth that deepened the already severe economic inequality between the races. Katznelson, *When Affirmative Action Was White: An Untold History of Racial Inequality in Twentieth-Century America* (New York: W. W. Norton, 2006). See also Hall, "The Long Civil Rights Movement."

78. President's Committee on Civil Rights, *To Secure These Rights: The Report of the President's Committee on Civil Rights,* (New York: Simon and Schuster, 1947); Mary L. Dudziak, *Cold War Civil Rights: Race and the Image of American Democracy* (Princeton, N.J.: Princeton University Press, 2002).

79. Hall, "The Long Civil Rights Movement," 1248–54.

80. Founded in the early 1940s to coordinate the activities of the Society of Friends, the Council of Churches, the local NAACP, and the National Council of Christians and Jews (NCCJ), among other groups, the Fellowship Commission aimed to promote "intergroup understanding and equal treatment and opportunity for all racial, religious and nationality groups." The formation of the umbrella group was a response to ethnic and religious tensions as well as racial conflict, though by 1944 black-white relations had come to the fore. See Constantine, "Philadelphia Firsts."

81. Countryman, *Up South*, 44–47; Walter Phillips, "Interview with Paul Ylvisaker," Philadelphia, Pa., November 14, 1977, The Walter Phillips Oral History Project, b. 9, TUUA; Carolyn Teich Adams, "Philadelphia: The Private City in the Post-Industrial Era," in *Snowbelt Cities: Metropolitan Politics in the Northeast and Midwest since World War II*, ed. Richard M. Bernard (Bloomington: Indiana University Press, 1990), 212–14.

82. Gunnar Myrdal, *An American Dilemma: The Negro Problem and Modern Democracy* (New York: Harper and Brothers, 1944); Jackson, *Gunnar Myrdal and America's Conscience* ; and O'Connor, *Poverty Knowledge*, 94–98.

83. See especially Gordon, "The Question of Prejudice."

84. Jackson, *Gunnar Myrdal and America's Conscience,* 121–30. On critiques of Myrdal from the left, see also Thomas Sugrue, "Hearts and Minds," *Nation,* May 12, 2008.

85. Sugrue, *Sweet Land of Liberty*, 170; David Labaree, *Someone Has to Fail: The Zero-Sum Game of Public Schooling* (Cambridge, Mass.: Harvard University Press, 2010).

86. Ellen Condliffe Lagemann, *The Politics of Knowledge: The Carnegie Corporation, Philanthropy, and Public Policy* (Chicago: University of Chicago Press, 1989), 186–95; Nicholas Lemann, *The Big Test: The Secret History of the American Meritocracy* (New York: Farrar, Straus, and Giroux, 1999).

87. Roy Larsen, Oral History Transcript, October 25, 1972, 1–6, Ford Foundation Archives (FFA). Larsen was a first generation American with a personal devotion to the public schools as "the great equalizer"—not to mention a professional interest in the institution that cultivated literate subscribers for his company's magazines.

88. Henry S. Resnik, *Turning on the System: War in the Philadelphia Public Schools* (New York: Pantheon Books, 1970), 33–40; Walter Phillips, "Interview with Annette Temin," Philadelphia, Pa.,

April 16, 1980, The Walter Phillips Oral History Project, b. 8, TUUA; Citizen's Committee on Public Education, Reports on School Visits, 1954–55 and 1956–57, Papers of the Philadelphia NAACP (hereafter NAACP papers), Urb. 6, b. 6, f. 137–38, TUUA.

89. See especially James T. Patterson, *Brown v. Board of Education: A Civil Rights Milestone and its Troubled Legacy* (New York: Oxford University Press, 2001); and Richard Kluger, *Simple Justice: The History of Brown v. Board of Education and Black America's Struggle for Equality* (New York: Vintage, 2004).

90. For similar comments on educational history, *Brown,* and civil rights, see Jack Dougherty, *More Than One Struggle: The Evolution of Black School Reform in Milwaukee* (Chapel Hill: University of North Carolina Press, 2004), 1–8.

91. Minutes, Committee on School and Community Tensions, 1944–48, Papers of the Philadelphia Urban League (hereafter Urban League papers), Urb. 1, b. 8, f. 138, TUUA.

92. Board of Public Education, "For Every Child: The Story of Integration in the Philadelphia Public Schools" (Philadelphia, 1960), 8, Educational Resources Information Center (ERIC) document #ED020951; "Teachers Study Race Tensions," *Philadelphia Tribune,* April 8, 1944, 2.

93. Board of Public Education, "For Every Child," 1.

94. Some of the most heated battles saw white residents successfully block the construction of integrated public housing projects in their neighborhoods. Minutes, Board of Commissioners Meeting, May 21, 1956, 2–3, PFC papers, Acc. 626, b. 7, f. 27, TUUA. For other reports and discussions on interracial tensions in the mid-1950s, see b. 56, f. 2; and b. 18, f. 2. On similar interracial conflicts in other cities, during a period that earlier historians had regarded as one of "consensus," see Thomas J. Sugrue, *The Origins of the Urban Crisis: Race and Inequality in Postwar Detroit* (Princeton, N.J.: Princeton University Press, 1996); Arnold R. Hirsch, "Massive Resistance in the Urban North: Trumbull Park, Chicago, 1953–1966," *Journal of American History* 82, no. 2 (1995): 522–50; and Gary Gerstle, "Race and the Myth of the Liberal Consensus," *Journal of American History* 82, no. 2 (1995): 579–86.

95. On fears of sinking educational standards, see "Report of the Executive Director, Maurice B. Fagan," Philadelphia Fellowship Commission Annual Dinner Meeting, January 21, 1957, 3, PFC papers, Acc. 626, b. 7, f. 29, TUUA. On the flight to the suburbs of "younger white couples"— those with children of school age—see Richardson Dilworth to Time, Inc., "Telegram," February 20, 1958, Papers of the Philadelphia Housing Authority (hereafter PHA papers), b. 235, f. 3519, TUUA. On the discriminatory federal housing subsidies and loan guarantees that fueled suburbanization and helped maintain segregation on a metropolitan scale, see Kenneth T. Jackson, *Crabgrass Frontier: The Suburbanization of the United States* (New York: Oxford University Press, 1987).

96. For the book-length report on the study, see Helen G. Trager and Marian R. Yarrow, *They Learn What They Live* (New York: Harper and Brothers, 1952).

97. See the comments of Harry Giles, quoted in Mary Constantine, "The Philadelphia Childhood Relations Seminar: Six Years of Action Research in Intergroup Education" (Philadelphia: Philadelphia Fellowship Commission, 1958), PFC papers, Acc. 626, b. 47, f. 5, TUUA; and Dr. Martin P. Chworosky, Minutes, Board of Commissioners Meeting, Philadelphia Fellowship Commission, May 10, 1960, 5, PFC papers, b. 8, f. 1, TUUA. For a study of New York City's similar program, see Robert Shaffer, "Multicultural Education in New York City During World War II," *New York History* 77, no. 3 (1996): 301–32.

98. The Early Childhood Project illustrated the key role of social scientists in the liberal struggle against prejudice and racial discrimination. The Early Childhood Project, while initiated by local school officials, was designed, supervised, and evaluated by academics at MIT's Research Center for Group Dynamics and New York University's Bureau of Intercultural Education—two of the most prominent examples of "intergroup relations" centers that had sprouted at universities in the 1930s and 1940s. Some centers had been created as much in response to anxieties over the assimilation of

immigrants and their children as to white-black relations. However, the wartime riots focused their attention on the latter issue. See Selig, *Americans All;* and Gordon, "The Question of Prejudice."

99. Among those who wrote letters were Otto Klineberg, the Columbia University psychologist; Gordon Allport of Harvard's Department of Social Relations; and the national directors of the NAACP, the Urban League, and various Jewish organizations. The consultant list included such liberal academic luminaries as the sociologist E. Franklin Frazier, the educational researcher Robert Havighurst, and the psychologist Kenneth Clark. See Philadelphia Fellowship Commission, "Proposal to the Ford Foundation for the Establishment of a Community Laboratory Program in Intergroup Relations" (Philadelphia: September, 1953), PFC papers, Acc. 626, b. 57, f. 13, TUUA.

100. On the Ford Foundation's liberal activism and the right-wing backlash it sparked, see Gregory K. Raynor, "Engineering Social Reform: The Rise of the Ford Foundation and Cold War Liberalism, 1908–1959" (Ph.D. diss., New York University, 2000). Other items on Fagan's list of "intergroup problems" included, at numbers one and two, white flight and the proliferation of all-black schools. Philadelphia Fellowship Commission, "Proposal to the Ford Foundation," 5.

101. Some scholars have emphasized a distinction, within liberalism, between educational campaigns aimed at changing prejudicial attitudes, on the one hand, and activism for equal rights under the law, on the other hand; see, for example, Gordon, "The Question of Prejudice." This is certainly a valid distinction, to a point, but the critiques of Logan, Jennings, and others indicate a degree of fluidity between these concerns and causes.

102. "Human Relations in Our Schools: An Editorial," *Teachers Union News* 6, no. 5 (May 1952): 1, 4, Papers of the Teachers Union of Philadelphia (hereafter Teachers Union papers), Urb. 36, b. 1, f. 26, TUUA. For Logan's and the EEL's most forceful critique of the school system, see Educational Equality League, "Some Pertinent Facts About Philadelphia Schools," c. 1950, NAACP papers, Urb. 6, b. 19, f. 375, TUUA.

103. On Add Anderson, see Resnik, *Turning on the System,* 4, 31–32; and Jon S. Birger, "Race, Reaction, and Reform: The Three Rs of Philadelphia School Politics, 1965–1971," *Pennsylvania Magazine of History and Biography* 120, no. 3 (1996): 184–85.

104. In 1951, when asked what prevented him from appointing "colored" teachers to West Philadelphia or Germantown high schools, superintendent Hoyer said that "99.9 percent of the time the right thing is the expedient thing . . . If I were running a private school and were entirely free and I thought it best to have a mixed faculty, I would have it. But it isn't as simple as that. There are all shades of opinion," he said, alluding to whites who opposed integration. "I have to take all of them into consideration." Teachers Union, "Notes on the meeting with the Board of Education," October 26, 1951, NAACP papers, Urb. 6, b. 6, f. 137, TUUA.

105. Frisby interview, October 4, 1999. For evidence of "mass promotion" out of the lower grades and resistance to the practice among high school teachers who inherited those students, see "Mass Promotion Revolt Grows," *Bulletin,* May 31, 1947.

106. Francis P. Jennings to the Members of the Board of Public Education of the School District of Philadelphia, June 23, 1954, Teachers Union papers, Urb. 36, b. 4, f. 57, TUUA.

107. Quoted in C. Leslie Cushman, "Educators Must Be Born Again," *Intercultural Education News* 7, no. 3 (April 1946): 2, PFC papers, Acc. 626, b. 57, f. 10, TUUA.

108. Blackburn interview, March 5, 1998.

109. Blackburn interview, March 5, 1998.

110. William Odell, *Philadelphia's Public Schools: Educational Survey* (Philadelphia: Philadelphia Board of Public Education, February 1, 1965); "Report of the Special Committee on Nondiscrimination" (Philadelphia: Philadelphia Board of Public Education, July 23, 1964), ERIC document #ED20207. The two studies began to influence policy debates in Philadelphia well before the final publication of their results.

111. The southern migrants arrived in a city whose industrial plants—the shipyards, railroads, and factories to which earlier migrants flocked during wartime booms—were shutting down or

being moved by corporate leaders to the suburbs and the deep South. On the disappearance of industrial opportunities in northern cities before black men had an opportunity to take advantage of them, see Katz, Stern, and Fader, "The New African American Inequality," par. 31. On deindustrialization in Philadelphia, see Guian A. McKee, *The Problem of Jobs: Liberalism, Race, and Deindustrialization in Philadelphia* (Chicago: University of Chicago Press, 2008); and Carolyn Adams et al., *Philadelphia: Neighborhoods, Division, and Conflict in a Postindustrial City* (Philadelphia: Temple University Press, 1991).

112. Philadelphia's urban renewal program was one of the most ambitious in the nation, resulting in the demolition and rebuilding of large, dilapidated areas around Independence Hall and Society Hill; Bauman, *Public Housing, Race, and Renewal.*

113. For annual Commission on Human Relations reports on intergroup violence and tension, see PFC papers, Acc. 626, b. 56, f. 2, TUUA. In early 1955, for example, the Commission on Human Relations reported that more than 80 percent of reported incidents were instigated by black aggressors and that many of those incidents were "intra-racial." "Analysis of Tension Reports—1st Quarter 1955–1956," May 4, 1956.

114. Phillips, "Interview with Paul Ylvisaker," 14, 16; Countryman, *Up South,* 58–79. As Countryman argues, the liberal attack on discriminatory housing and labor markets in Philadelphia was largely a campaign of persuasion, waged by an elite leadership. As the Commission on Human Relations struggled to enforce fair housing and employment guidelines, some advocated that African Americans should mobilize on a mass scale to defend their rights—a vision of black politics that led to a bitter internal struggle within the local branch of the NAACP. However, racial liberals continued to be the dominant voice in the struggle against racial inequality into the 1960s, and they did not take the approach of working-class mobilization. For a somewhat different emphasis, see McKee, *The Problem of Jobs,* which argues that liberals in Philadelphia did pay attention to the problem of deindustrialization but that their efforts bifurcated along racial lines.

115. Frisby interview, October 4, 1999.

116. Katz, Stern, and Fader, "The New African American Inequality," pars. 7, 38–44, and 63–73. The authors cite civil rights legislation, the growth of public sector employment, and affirmative action as key factors that caused education to eclipse race as an influence on income from 1940 to 2000. Schooling was no panacea; as the authors emphasize, it helped some individuals and groups more than others, and the overall contours of inequality remained a major problem. Still, in the late twentieth century, education helped make possible a mass movement of blacks—especially black women—into the world of white-collar work.

117. At the turn of the century, DuBois had lamented that 88.5 percent of the women and 61.5 percent of the men in Philadelphia's Seventh Ward were domestic servants. By 1960, those numbers had dropped to 3.3 and 0.6 percent, respectively. Moreover, the steepest decline came not during the industrial boom of the war years, but in the 1950s—a decade of similarly high-percentage increases in the number of black Philadelphians employed in professional, clerical, and sales jobs. See Baltzell, introduction, xxxix.

Chapter 2

1. Robert Blackburn, interviewed by the author at Blackburn's home in Oakland, California, March 5, 1998, tape recording in possession of the author.

2. Seymour Gang gained recognition for raising academic achievement while he was principal of Public School 192 in Harlem during the 1960s. His subsequent description of this accomplishment is a reminder of how such "heroes and heroines of urban education," as Blackburn describes them, pioneered a new era of higher expectations for underachieving urban students. "Basically it's simple," Gang said. "I just told the teachers and the parents right off that their children were going to perform at grade level and that I was not going to listen to any excuses if they failed . . . We insist-

ed that every teacher should teach and every child should learn, and we held the teachers account-able." Farnsworth Fowle, "Seymour Gang, 50, Educator, Is Dead," *New York Times,* January 6, 1976.

3. Blackburn interview, March 5, 1998. Foster also made a powerful impression on Peter Binzen, then the education writer for the *Philadelphia Evening Bulletin*, who later wrote of his visit, "I will never forget the obvious signs of pupil respect and admiration accorded him that morning. I re-member thinking, 'God, what a principal!'" "2 Greats Felled in Oakland," *Philadelphia Evening Bulletin* (hereafter referred to as *Bulletin*), November 11, 1973.

4. As of 1955, Dunbar was one of thirty-nine schools in the city with more than 97 percent black enrollment. See Leonard Blumberg, "A Study of Recent Negro Migrants into Philadelphia" (Philadelphia: Temple University and Philadelphia Urban League, 1958), Papers of the Philadelphia Urban League (hereafter Urban League papers), b. 12, f. 207, Temple University Urban Archives (TUUA).

5. For an influential contemporary statement of this idea, see Benjamin S. Bloom, Allison Davis, and Robert Hess, *Compensatory Education for Cultural Deprivation* (New York: Holt, Rinehart, and Winston, 1965). The book grew out of a conference involving several dozen of the nation's leading psychologists, sociologists, and educators.

6. On debates over Head Start, see, for example, Maris A. Vinovskis, *The Birth of Head Start: Preschool Education Policies in the Kennedy and Johnson Administrations* (Chicago: University of Chicago Press, 2008); and Harold Silver and Pamela Silver, *An Educational War on Poverty: Ameri-can and British Policy-making 1960–1980* (Cambridge: Cambridge University Press, 1991).

7. See, for example, Kenneth B. Clark, *Dark Ghetto: Dilemmas of Social Power* (New York: Harp-er and Row, 1965), 111–53; and William Ryan, *Blaming the Victim* (New York: Pantheon, 1971), 31–62.

8. In recent years, critiques of the shortcomings of schools have been exemplified in the ac-countability agenda of the No Child Left Behind (2002) Act; see Michael A. Rebell and Jessica R. Wolff, eds., *NCLB at the Crossroads: Reexamining the Federal Effort to Close the Achievement Gap* (New York: Teachers College, 2009). Meanwhile, the persistence of a "culture of poverty" analysis is especially evident in the writings and popular professional development programs of educator and entrepreneur Ruby Payne; see *A Framework for Understanding Poverty* (Highlands, Tex.: aha! Process, Inc., 1996). For an overview and critique of Payne's programs, linking them to 1960s-era debates over the "culture of poverty," see Jennifer C. Ng and John L. Rury, "Poverty and Education: A Critical Analysis of the Ruby Payne Phenomenon," *Teachers College Record*, July 18, 2006, http://www.tcrecord.org/Content.asp?ContentID=12596 (accessed September 1, 2011).

9. For an emphasis on the inegalitarian aspects of compensatory education, see Adam R. Nelson, *The Elusive Ideal: Equal Educational Opportunity and the Federal Role in Boston's Public Schools, 1950–1985* (Chicago: University of Chicago Press, 2005), 31–59. Nelson traces the influence of federal funding priorities on school superintendents in Boston, arguing that district officials de-fined cultural deprivation as a form of incurable disability, in ways that reinforced the tracking and segregation of African American students. See also Jack Dougherty, *More than One Struggle: The Evolution of Black School Reform in Milwaukee* (Chapel Hill: University of North Carolina Press, 2004), 51–70; and Robert Lowe and Harvey Kantor, "Creating Educational Opportunity for African Americans Without Upsetting the Status Quo," in *Changing Populations, Changing Schools: Ninety-fourth Yearbook of the National Society for the Study of Education, Part II,* ed. Erwin Flaxman and A. Harry Passow (Chicago: University of Chicago Press, 1995), 189–92, both of which portray compensatory education as a means of acculturating and reforming black students rather than as an effort to promote their advancement and intellectual development.

10. On cultural capital, see Annette Lareau and Elliot B. Weininger, "Cultural Capital in Educa-tional Research: A Critical Assessment," *Theory and Society* 32, nos. 5–6 (2003): 567–606; and John L. Rury, *Education and Social Change: Themes in the History of American Schooling* (Mahwah, N.J.: Lawrence Erlbaum, 2002), 193–94. On the impact of teachers and schools on academic achieve-

ment, see, for example, Ronald F. Ferguson, *Toward Excellence with Equity: An Emerging Vision for Closing the Achievement Gap* (Cambridge, Mass.: Harvard Education Press, 2008); Charles M. Payne, *So Much Reform, So Little Change: The Persistence of Failure in Urban Schools* (Cambridge, Mass.: Harvard Education Press, 2008), especially 93–108 and 207–12; Ronald Edmonds, "Effective Schools for the Urban Poor," *Educational Leadership* 37, no. 1 (1979): 15–18, 20–24; and Rhona S. Weinstein, *Reaching Higher: The Power of Expectations in Schooling* (Cambridge, Mass.: Harvard University Press, 2004).

11. High-profile discussions of KIPP and the Harlem Children's Zone include Jay Mathews, *Work Hard. Be Nice.: How Two Inspired Teachers Created the Most Promising Schools in America* (New York: Algonquin Books, 2009); Malcolm Gladwell, *Outliers: The Story of Success* (New York: Little, Brown, and Co., 2008), 250–69; Karl Weber, ed., *Waiting for "Superman": How We Can Save America's Failing Public Schools* (New York: Public Affairs, 2010); and Paul Tough, *Whatever It Takes: Geoffrey Canada's Quest to Change Harlem and America* (Houghton Mifflin Harcourt, 2008). In 2006, while working on *Whatever It Takes,* Tough wrote a *New York Times Magazine* cover story that spotlighted the efforts of HCZ and KIPP schools to eradicate racial and socioeconomic achievement gaps among urban students. Echoing the language and ideas of the compensatory education movement of the 1960s (while describing these ideas as being new), he wrote that students in these schools had "missed out on many of the millions of everyday intellectual and emotional stimuli that their better-off peers have been exposed to since birth," and that, in response, the schools were making a conscious effort, using slogans, motivational posters, incentives, encouragements and punishments, to change the character of those students and "*compensate* for everything they did not receive in their first decade of life [italics mine]." Tough, "What It Takes to Make a Student," *New York Times Magazine,* November 26, 2006. See the epilogue for further discussion of these charter school programs and how they fit into a historical trajectory from the 1960s to the present.

12. For a similar critique of the claims made by current charter school advocates, see Alan R. Sadovnik, "Waiting for School Reform: Charter Schools as the Latest Imperfect Panacea," *Teachers College Record,* March 17, 2011, http://www.tcrecord.org/content.asp?contentid=16370 (accessed September 14, 2011).

13. Daniel A. Brooks, "Veteran Principal Compares Present School Conditions with those of World War I," *Philadelphia Tribune,* December 11, 1943, 20.

14. The literature on such schools focuses mainly on the South; see especially Vanessa Siddle Walker, *Their Highest Potential: An African American School Community in the Segregated South* (Chapel Hill: University of North Carolina Press, 1996); and Vanessa Siddle Walker, "Valued Segregated Schools for African American Children in the South, 1935–1969: A Review of Common Themes and Characteristics," *Review of Educational Research* 70 (Fall 2000): 253–85.

15. "Teaching is Tradition in Negro Educator's Family," *Philadelphia Evening Ledger,* September 30, 1939. As the article pointed out, Duckrey came by educational leadership naturally: his great-grandfather had helped found Wilberforce University in 1856, his uncle was a dean there, and his parents were both educators. His brothers James and William also became leading Philadelphia educators, the former eventually succeeding Leslie Pinckney Hill as president of Cheyney College.

16. Marcus A. Foster, *Making Schools Work: Strategies for Changing Education* (Philadelphia: Westminster Press, 1971), 75; Ida Kravitz, interviewed by the author at Kravitz's home in Philadelphia, Pa., April 2, 1999, tape recording in possession of the author.

17. Thomas J. Sugrue, *The Origins of the Urban Crisis: Race and Inequality in Postwar Detroit* (Princeton, N.J.: Princeton University Press, 1996).

18. The census tract was 32A. Commission on Human Relations, "Philadelphia's Negro Population: Facts on Housing" (Philadelphia: Commission on Human Relations, 1953), 18–20, Papers of the Philadelphia Housing Authority (hereafter PHA papers), b. 236, f. 3527, TUUA.

19. Foster, *Making Schools Work,* 76. The Commission on Human Relations underscored this point by contrasting its case study of the Temple area (census tract 32A) with an analysis of the

Nicetown area, where housing quality and rates of home ownership actually improved because of racial turnover; see Commission on Human Relations, "Philadelphia's Negro Population."

20. Lenora E. Berson, *Case Study of a Riot: The Philadelphia Story* (New York: Institute of Human Relations Press, 1966), 27.

21. Michael B. Katz, Mark J. Stern, and Jamie J. Fader, "The New African American Inequality," *Journal of American History* 92, no. 1 (2005), http://jah.oxfordjournals.org/content/92/1/75.full (accessed January 2012); Guian A. McKee, *The Problem of Jobs: Liberalism, Race, and Deindustrialization in Philadelphia* (Chicago: University of Chicago Press, 2008); and Carolyn Adams et al., *Philadelphia: Neighborhoods, Division, and Conflict in a Postindustrial City* (Philadelphia: Temple University Press, 1991).

22. Berson, *Case Study of a Riot*, 24–25.

23. Commission on Human Relations, "Philadelphia's Negro Population," 19.

24. Map of Temple and Poplar Redevelopment Areas, 1960, PHA papers, b. 261, f. 4318, TUUA.

25. Berson, *Case Study of a Riot*, 24–28.

26. Kravitz interview, April 2, 1999.

27. Foster, *Making Schools Work*, 75–76; Marcus A. Foster, "Motivating Children to Read via Oral Language Experiences," in *Teaching Reading: Not by Decoding Alone*, ed. Joseph P. Kender (Danville, Ill.: Interstate Printers and Publishers, 1971), 79.

28. The northern school desegregation movement of the late 1950s and early 1960s has been all but forgotten, especially in comparison with the iconic struggles of the *Brown* era in the South and the nationwide busing battles of the late 1960s and 1970s. Among works that have noted and/or begun to rectify this imbalance, see especially Gary Orfield, "Race and the Liberal Agenda: The Loss of the Integrationist Dream," in *The Politics of Social Policy in the United States*, ed. Margaret Weir, Ann Shola Orloff, and Theda Skocpol (Princeton, N.J.: Princeton University Press, 1988), 313–55; Thomas Sugrue, *Sweet Land of Liberty: The Forgotten Struggle for Civil Rights in the North* (New York: Random House, 2008); Dougherty, *More than One Struggle*; John Rury, "Race, Space, and the Politics of Chicago's Public Schools: Benjamin Willis and the Tragedy of Urban Education," *History of Education Quarterly* 39, no. 2 (1999): 117–42; and Adina Back, "Up South in New York: The 1950s School Desegregation Struggles" (Ph.D. diss., New York University, 1997).

29. Barbara Beatty, "The Debate over the Young 'Disadvantaged Child': Preschool Intervention and Developmental Psychology in the 1960s and Early 1970s," *Teachers College Record*, forthcoming fall 2011.

30. Daniel Schreiber, "What Can be Done to Reduce Academic Retardation in Minority Group Children?" (paper presented at the Invitational Conference on Northern School Desegregation: Progress and Problems, New York City, 1962), 47–56, Educational Resources Information Center (ERIC) document #ED014516. On the origins and results of the project, see also Clark, *Dark Ghetto*, 141–43; and Gerald E. Markowitz and David Rosner, *Children, Race, and Power: Kenneth and Mamie Clark's Northside Center* (Charlottesville: University of Virginia Press, 1996), 113.

31. Clark, *Dark Ghetto*, 141–42.

32. Schreiber, "What Can Be Done," 49–56; Markowitz and Rosner, *Children, Race, and Power*, 113.

33. Schreiber, "What Can Be Done," 50–53.

34. Schreiber, "What Can Be Done," 46, 56.

35. "Education: Preparation in St. Louis," *Time*, June 8, 1959, http://www.time.com/time/printout/0,8816,892587,00.html (accessed September 1, 2011). The *Time* article cited hopeful test score gains; for a later description of the program with a less positive assessment of its results, see Edmund W. Gordon and Adelaide Jablonsky, "Compensatory Education in the Equalization of Educational Opportunity I," *Journal of Negro Education* 37, no. 3 (1968): 272–73. Gordon and Jablonsky repeated Shepard's claims of improved motivation, behavior, and attendance among students, as well as better morale among teachers and excellent cooperation from parents; however, they also

cited an evaluation that showed no difference in test score results between Banneker project schools and control schools.

36. Ruth Wright Hayre and Alexis Moore, *Tell Them We Are Rising: A Memoir of Faith in Education* (New York: J. Wiley and Sons, 1997), 55–69; Doris Wiley, "Cultural Doses Spur Pupils to Fuller Lives at 2 Schools," *Bulletin,* October 29, 1961, *Bulletin* clippings file, "David Horowitz," TUUA.

37. Mary Constantine, "The Philadelphia Childhood Relations Seminar: Six Years of Action Research in Intergroup Education" (Philadelphia: Philadelphia Fellowship Commission, 1958), Papers of the Philadelphia Fellowship Commission (hereafter PFC papers), b. 47, f. 5, TUUA.

38. "Plans of the Paul Laurence Dunbar Public School, Ninth Session," May 17, 1960, Scrapbook of the Action Research Seminar (hereafter "Dunbar Scrapbook"), Paul Laurence Dunbar Elementary School.

39. Constantine, "The Philadelphia Childhood Relations Seminar." As Constantine summarized, "intergroup" educators during the 1950s had gone "far afield" of the official focus on studying and modifying prejudice—though all of these efforts were "to the good in the improvement of teaching, the understanding of children, and the solution of community problems."

40. "Plans of the Paul Laurence Dunbar Public School"; "Dunbar Scrapbook."

41. "Plans of the Paul Laurence Dunbar Public School."

42. Marcus A. Foster, September 26, 1960, "Dunbar Scrapbook." Foster's reference to "acres of diamonds" contained a rich set of historical associations in relation to issues of poverty and education. The phrase was made famous in the late nineteenth century by Russell Conwell, a Baptist minister who used it as the title for a popular inspirational lecture. Conwell suggested that, in seeking opportunity and fortune, it was possible to find "acres of diamonds" in "your own backyard"—"if you will but dig for them." The historian Howard Zinn has suggested that Conwell blamed the poor for their own condition; Howard Zinn, *A People's History of the United States* (New York: Harper and Row, 1980), 256. It is unclear what shades of meaning Foster might have attached to the phrase. If nothing else, it was a resonant one to use in a neighborhood dominated by the buildings of Temple University, which Russell Conwell had founded, partly on the strength of the wealth he had amassed from his famous speech. "Russell Conwell Explains Why Diamonds Are a Man's Best Friend," http://historymatters.gmu.edu/d/5769 (accessed September 1, 2009).

43. On controversies over the relationship between African American Vernacular English and Standard English in education, see Theresa Perry and Lisa Delpit, eds., "The Real Ebonics Debate: A Special Issue of Rethinking Schools," *Rethinking Schools* 12, no. 1 (Fall 1997).

44. Foster, *Making Schools Work,* 79, 82.

45. Marcus Foster, "Child of the Poor, Looking for Mitochondria," in *Readings in Curriculum and Supervision*, ed. V. Eugene Yarbrough, William C. Bruce, and Ronald L. Hubright (New York: MSS Information Corporation, 1974), 50. The article is a transcript of a speech delivered at the Center for Research and Development in Teaching, Stanford University, September 21, 1973.

46. Foster, *Making Schools Work,* 83; Alice P. Campbell, "Hints for Helping the Pre-School Child," 1960, Papers of the Friends Neighborhood Guild (FNG), Urb. 32, b. 3, f. 31, TUUA.

47. Foster, "Child of the Poor, Looking for Mitochondria," 50; "Plans of the Paul Laurence Dunbar School"; "Team Meeting," February 26, 1960, "Dunbar Scrapbook."

48. Marcus A. Foster, letter to parents, n.d., "Dunbar Scrapbook."

49. For this characterization of the War on Poverty, as well as a discussion of the influential role of the Ford Foundation, see Silver and Silver, *An Educational War on Poverty,* 37–47.

50. As of 1960, forty-six hundred black families were moving to Philadelphia every year. See "Notes of Discussion at the Session on 'Human Planning in the Gray Areas,'" November 3, 1960, 4, PHA papers, b. 127, f. 773, TUUA.

51. Quoted by Louis Ballen in "Minutes—Summer Workshop," June 27, 1960, 1, Grant #PA06000251, R. 0214, sec. 4, Ford Foundation Archives (hereafter FFA).

52. "The Great Cities School Improvement Program" (press release), May 17, 1960, 2, Grant #PA06000220, R. 0213, sec. 4, FFA.

53. The Fords shifted their stock to the Foundation to maintain family control over the company. See Gregory K. Raynor, "Engineering Social Reform: The Rise of the Ford Foundation and Cold War Liberalism, 1908–1959" (Ph.D. diss., New York University, 2000); and Dwight Macdonald, *The Ford Foundation: The Men and the Millions* (New York: Reynal and Company, 1956).

54. Paul Ylvisaker, Oral History Transcript, September 27, 1973, 24, FFA.

55. Harry S. Ashmore, *The Negro and the Schools*, (Chapel Hill: University of North Carolina Press, 1954); J. Cayce Morrison, ed., *The Puerto Rican Study, 1953–57: A Report on the Education and Adjustment of Puerto Rican Pupils in the Public Schools of the City of New York* (Board of Education of the City of New York, 1958).

56. Gregory K. Raynor, "The Ford Foundation's War on Poverty: Private Philanthropy and Race Relations in New York City, 1948–1968," in *Philanthropic Foundations: New Scholarship, New Possibilities*, ed. Ellen Condliffe Lagemann (Bloomington: Indiana University Press, 1999), 196–206. On the Ford "embargo" on race-related projects, see Ylvisaker, Oral History Transcript, 23.

57. Ylvisaker, Oral History Transcript, 23.

58. Regarding the impact of his time in Philadelphia, Ylvisaker said it "accounted for what I feel was a successful twelve years in the Ford Foundation. I went there when they were all thinking about God and the United Nations and the cosmos . . . and I came in and saw those leaping millions . . . and I said: look, let's work out America's urban problems." Paul Ylvisaker, interview with Walter Phillips, November 14, 1977, 25, The Walter Phillips Oral History Project, b. 9, TUUA.

59. As head of the foundation's Public Affairs division starting in 1955, Ylvisaker initially promoted research on how metropolitan units of government might stem the decline of central cities. By 1959, he had come to focus more narrowly on individual municipalities, though still with an emphasis on greater coordination among multiple agencies and entities. On this and other aspects of the development of the Great Cities and Gray Areas programs, see Alice O'Connor, "Community Action, Urban Reform, and the Fight Against Poverty: The Ford Foundation's Gray Areas Program," *Journal of Urban History* 22 (1996): 586–625; and Ylvisaker, interview with Walter Phillips, 23.

60. Ylvisaker, Oral History Transcript, 25–27; "The Schools and Urban 'Gray Areas'" (Ford Foundation internal memo from Education and Public Affairs programs, recommending action on the Great Cities grants, c. 1960), PHA papers, b. 127. f. 773, TUUA.

61. "Great Cities Project, Philadelphia Meeting," May 6, 1960, Grant #PA06000251, R.0214, sec. 4, FFA.

62. "Great Cities Project, Philadelphia Meeting."

63. School District of Philadelphia, "A Philadelphia Project Proposal: The School-Community Coordinating Team," February 2, 1960, Grant #PA06000251, R.0214, sec. 1, FFA.

64. "Great Cities Project, Philadelphia Meeting."

65. The district received $94,700 and promised to provide $60,000 in matching funds. See Philadelphia Public Schools, "Public Schools to Conduct Extensive Educational Project Under Ford Foundation Grant," Press Release, June 24, 1960, Grant #PA06000251, R. 0214, sec. 4, FFA.

66. School District, "A Philadelphia Project Proposal."

67. "Minutes—Summer Workshop," July 6, 1960. The "Negro in America" panel was to include Foster, though for unknown reasons he did not end up presenting.

68. Oscar Lewis, *The Children of Sanchez* (New York: Random House, 1961); Michael Harrington, *The Other America: Poverty in the United States* (New York: Macmillan Company, 1962).

69. Before it had an official name, the big-city superintendents referred to the emerging Great Cities program as their "culturally deprived project"; see, for example, Great Cities Program for School Improvement, Minutes of meeting at the Hilton Hotel, Chicago, Ill., May 13–14, 1960, Grant #PA06000220, R. 0213, sec. 3, FFA.

70. Daryl Michael Scott, *Contempt and Pity: Social Policy and the Image of the Damaged Black Psyche, 1880–1996* (Chapel Hill: University of North Carolina Press, 1997), 71–136.

71. Ellen Condliffe Lagemann, *The Politics of Knowledge: The Carnegie Corporation, Philanthropy, and Public Policy* (Chicago: University of Chicago Press, 1989), 211–12.

72. "Minutes—Summer Workshop," June 29 and July 7, 1960. For an analysis of Deutsch's research, see Beatty, "The Debate over the Young 'Disadvantaged Child.'"

73. "Minutes—Summer Workshop," July 7, 1960.

74. Community Coordinating Team, "High Roads Project," August 1960, 1, ERIC document #ED001020.

75. School-Community Coordinating Team, "The Dunbar High Roads Project," September 1961, 3–4; 16–18, Grant #PA06000251, R. 0214, sec. 3, FFA; Henry Saltzman to Ed Meade and Clarence Faust, December 11, 1963, Grant #PA06000251, R. 0214, sec. 3, FFA.

76. Aleda Druding, "Stirrings in the Big Cities: Philadelphia," *NEA Journal* (February 1962): 50–51.

77. Kravitz interview, April 2, 1999.

78. School-Community Coordinating Team, "The Dunbar High Roads Project," 11; Foster, *Making Schools Work*, 77; Foster, "Motivating Children to Read," 80; Payne, *So Much Reform, So Little Change*, 47–92.

79. Foster, *Making Schools Work*, 79; "Minutes—Summer Workshop," June 29; School-Community Coordinating Team, "The Dunbar High Roads Project," 37–58; Foster, "Motivating Children to Read," 82–83.

80. Kravitz interview, April 2, 1999.

81. School-Community Coordinating Team, "The Dunbar High Roads Project," 7–8, 37–45.

82. Foster, *Making Schools Work*, 83. On the issue of correcting non-standard usage of English, Alice Campbell noted that children "needed tools" if they were to learn to write well, but "caution was observed . . . there was danger in emphasizing correctness to the point where it would stifle creativity." School-Community Coordinating Team, "The Dunbar High Roads Project," 42.

83. J. William Jones, "Trips to Movies, Toys Help Pupils Learn to Read in Experiment Here," *Bulletin*, February 23,1964.

84. In the district evaluations, twelve out of twenty-one comparisons of student performances before and after the program (seven math and language arts tests at each of the three schools) showed better than expected scores for students "in schools of this type." Three test results were equal to expectations and six were below, though five of the sub-par results occurred in the one school with faulty implementation. The language arts results were especially strong, showing higher than expected gain in ten out of twelve instances. School District of Philadelphia, "Progress Report, September 1960–June 1962: The School-Community Coordinating Team," February, 1963, 14–24, Grant #PA06000251, R. 0214, sec. 3, FFA.

85. Druding, "Stirrings in the Big Cities," 50.

86. School-Community Coordinating Team, "The Dunbar High Roads Project," 3–5, 25, 48.

87. Strieb's analysis is informed by her subsequent experiences as a teacher who prioritized parental involvement and wrote a book on the subject; see Lynne Yermanock Strieb, *Inviting Families into the Classroom: Learning from a Life in Teaching* (New York: Teachers College Press, 2010).

88. School-Community Coordinating Team, "The Dunbar High Roads Project," 34–36.

89. Letter to Henry Saltzman from Wesley L. Scott, March 29, 1961, Grant #PA06000251, R. 0214, sec. 4, FFA.

90. Ida Kravitz, telephone conversation with the author, February 6, 1999.

91. School District of Philadelphia, "Progress Report, 1960–1962," 6.

92. Kathleen Cotton, *Principals and Student Achievement: What the Research Says* (Association for Supervision and Curriculum Development, 2003), 9–13, 21–29; Karen S. Crum and Whitney H.

Sherman, "Facilitating High Achievement: High School Principals' Reflections on Their Successful Leadership Practices," *Journal of Educational Administration* 46, no. 5 (2008): 562–80.

93. Lagemann, *The Politics of Knowledge,* 147–51.

94. School District of Philadelphia, "Report of the Special Committee on Nondiscrimination," (Philadelphia: Board of Education, 1964), 43; Lawrence M. O'Rourke, "Negro Ministers Start 'Direct Action' on Schools," *Bulletin,* September 9, 1963.

95. David Horowitz to Paul Ylvisaker, January 11, 1966, Grant #PA06000251, R. 0214, sec. 3, FFA.

96. See Bloom, Davis, and Hess, *Compensatory Education for Cultural Deprivation,* for a write-up of the conference proceedings by three of its leading participants. Among the thirty-six named participants and observers, three—Ford staffer Henry Saltzman, Martin Deutsch, and Ida Kravitz (one of only a few K–12 educators in attendance)—had played a role in Philadelphia's Great Cities program.

97. Joel Spring, *Revisiting the Sorting Machine: National Educational Policy Since 1945* (New York: Longman, 1989), 218.

98. For minutes of two of Philadelphia's three sessions on "Human Planning in the Gray Areas," see PHA papers, b. 127, f. 773; and b. 128, f. 782, TUUA.

99. For an example of radicalization in the Community Action Program, in which poor residents gained representation in a city's OEO-funded antipoverty agency and used their power to divert federal funds from the public school system and other existing bureaucracies to groups that openly challenged the status quo of urban politics and policy, see Chapter 5, on Oakland. On the origins of the Community Action Program in the antidelinquency efforts of the President's Committee on Juvenile Delinquency (PCJD) and the Ford Foundation, see Peter Marris and Martin Rein, *Dilemmas of Social Reform: Poverty and Community Action in the United States* (New York: Atherton Press, 1967); Allen J. Matusow, *The Unraveling of America: A History of Liberalism in the 1960s* (New York: Harper and Row, 1984), 107–27; and Nicholas Lemann, *The Promised Land: The Great Black Migration and How it Changed America* (New York: Alfred A. Knopf, 1991), 119–29, among many other studies. On the development of the War on Poverty as an amalgam of approaches and assumptions, including but not limited to Community Action, and cobbled together through compromise and contestation within the Johnson administration, see Michael B. Katz, *The Undeserving Poor: From the War on Poverty to the War on Welfare* (New York: Pantheon Books, 1989), 79–123.

100. "Notes on third session on 'Human Planning,'" 1. Marris's and Rein's classic account of the Gray Areas program described the PCCA as wanting to make the schools and other urban institutions more effective at "raising (the poor citizen's) dejected posture of resigned incompetence," *Dilemmas of Social Reform,* 96. On the similar educational emphasis of the New Haven Gray Areas project, see Daniel C. Humphrey, "Teach Them Not to Be Poor: Philanthropy and New Haven School Reform in the 1960s" (Ed.D. diss., Teachers College, 1992). Nicholas Lemann notes that even Mobilization for Youth (MFY), Richard Cloward's politically confrontational project in the Lower East Side of New York City, had much in common with education-based programs such as that in New Haven; *The Promised Land,* 122–23.

101. "Progress Report of the Experimental Nursery School Program, 1964–65" (Philadelphia: Philadelphia Council for Community Advancement, 1965), ERIC document #ED021880; Marris and Rein, *Dilemmas of Social Reform,* 111.

102. The prospect of *Chisolm* going to trial helped pressure the district into forming a special committee to study many of the integration strategies other cities were considering, including Princeton Plans, busing, and educational parks. School District of Philadelphia, "Report of the Special Committee on Nondiscrimination."

103. Murray Friedman, "The White Liberal's Retreat," *Atlantic* 211 (January 1963): 42–46. For a

similar discussion of tracking and liberal resistance to integration, see Bruno Bettelheim, "Sputnik and Segregation," *Commentary*, October 1958, 332–39.

104. Frank Riessman, *The Culturally Deprived Child* (New York: Harper and Row, 1962), 108, 111.

105. Ralph Ellison, "*An American Dilemma*: A Review," in *Shadow and Act* (New York: Random House, 1964), 303–17. On the Myrdal study, see Chapter 1.

106. Ralph Ellison, "What These Children Are Like," in *Going to the Territory* (New York: Random House, 1986), 64–75.

107. Marris and Rein, *Dilemmas of Social Reform*, 105.

108. School-Community Coordinating Team, "The Dunbar High Roads Project," 1, 10.

109. Marcus A. Foster, "The Child of Limited Background and the Self Concept," *News Letter: Official Publication of the Philadelphia Teachers Association* 61, no. 2 (1962): 6, 14. The Philadelphia Teachers Association (P.T.A.) was a local of the National Education Association.

110. School-Community Coordinating Team, "The Dunbar High Roads Project," 15; "Biographic Briefs," January 1964, Grant #PA06000251, R. 0214, sec. 4, FFA.

111. Strieb, *Inviting Families Into the Classroom,* 13–14; 39; and conversation with the author, April 11, 2011.

112. Leon Frisby, interviewed by the author at Frisby's home in Philadelphia Pennsylvania, June 2, 2011, tape recording in possession of the author.

113. Strieb conversation, April 11, 2011.

114. Robert Blackburn, interviewed by the author at Blackburn's home in Oakland, California, March 11, 1998, tape recording in possession of the author; Frederick Willman, "Developing a Sense of Community: A Report on the Master Plan of the Oakland Unified School District" (New York: The Rockefeller Foundation, 1975), 20–21. Lynne Strieb recalls that Foster "didn't like the term 'culturally deprived'" and said so at a faculty meeting during the 1962–63 school year; Strieb conversation, April 11, 2011.

115. On the distinction between blacks "vindicating" their community to whites, on the one hand, and engaging in self-help as a source of race pride, on the other, see Ronald E. Butchart, "'Outthinking and Outflanking the Owners of the World': A Historiography of the African-American Struggle for Education," *History of Education Quarterly* 28, no. 3 (1988): 337.

116. Blackburn interview, March 11, 1998.

117. "The Great Cities Program" May 17, 1960; "Minutes—Summer Workshop."

118. "Ford Projections: The Ford Foundation Project Schools Newsletter," December 1960, ERIC document #ED001011.

119. Druding, "Stirrings in the Big Cities," 48.

120. Druding, "Stirrings in the Big Cities," 51–52.

121. Charles Silberman, "The City and the Negro," *Fortune*, March 1962, 151; Schreiber, "What Can be Done," 54; and Tough, "What It Takes to Make a Student." For a 1960s-era review of compensatory education programs that emphasizes their high cost, see also Gordon and Jablonsky, "Compensatory Education."

122. Marcus Foster, commencement address, Swarthmore High School, Pennsylvania, June 9, 1969, tape recording in possession of the author. See also Lowe and Kantor, "Creating Educational Opportunity," 192. As the authors emphasize, program success has been strongly influenced by the amount and duration of funding, and well-funded, sustained commitments have been "atypical."

123. In 1959, to counter national periodicals that he believed were "having a field day" publicizing problems associated with the black migration (including "extreme but untypical" problems with discipline and declining achievement in some schools), Schermer emphasized a variety of more hopeful data in such areas as black home ownership. See "Tension in the North—Race Riots Break Out Again," *U.S. News and World Report*, June 13, 1958, 85–86; and George Schermer, "The

Real Story About the Big City" (unpublished article), February 6, 1959, PFC papers, b. 56, f. 4, TUUA.

124. "Notes on third session of group considering Human Planning in Gray Areas," March 28, 1961, 3, PHA papers, b. 128, f. 782, TUUA.

125. George Schermer, "Desegregation: A Community Design" (Revision of an article that previously appeared in ADA News, July 1960) (Commission on Human Relations, 1961), ERIC document #ED001939.

126. Schermer's findings in Philadelphia were echoed, for example, in a study of "white flight" conducted in the 1950s by New York University's Center for Human Relations and Community Studies. The study concluded that rising black and Puerto Rican enrollment was the biggest factor in the exit of white families from the public schools. The key factor, however, was not simply racial prejudice, but a more complicated mix of ideas at the intersection of race, class, and culture. Parents objected to their children being "plunged into an atmosphere of slum children who through no fault of their own started out from a completely different and lower level of manners and conduct." Liberal, middle-class whites were especially eager to steer their children away from urban public schools when racial integration—which many of them supported—seemed to mean social class integration. Meanwhile, middle-income black families, shut out of the suburbs by discrimination, looked for educational alternatives in parochial schools and even in the South. One father who chose the latter option said the New York City schools had "just too much juvenile delinquency and racial tension." See Back, "Up South in New York."

127. Commission on Human Relations, "A Statement of Concern for Public Education in Philadelphia, with Particular Reference to the Special Needs of Children in Underprivileged, Segregated Areas," May 17, 1960, 1, 17, ERIC document #ED020950.

128. "Great Cities School Improvement Program," May 17, 1960. On Willis's own ouster as a result of controversies over racial inequality and segregation in the Chicago Public Schools, see Rury, "Race, Space, and the Politics of Chicago's Public Schools."

129. William J. Reese, *America's Public Schools: From the Common School to "No Child Left Behind"* (Johns Hopkins University Press, 2005), 233; Diane Ravitch *The Troubled Crusade: American Education, 1945–1980* (New York: Basic Books, 1983), 150.

130. Ira Katznelson, *When Affirmative Action Was White: An Untold History of Racial Inequality in Twentieth-Century America* (New York: W. W. Norton, 2006).

131. For early critiques in this vein, see Christopher Jencks, "Johnson vs. Poverty," *The New Republic*, March 24, 1964, 18; and Jencks et al., *Inequality: A Reassessment of the Effect of Family and Schooling in America* (New York: Basic Books, 1972). Among subsequent scholarly critiques, see Harvey Kantor and Robert Lowe, "From New Deal to No Deal: NCLB and the Devolution of Responsibility for Equal Educational Opportunity, *Harvard Educational Review*, 76, no. 4 (2006) 474–502; Amy Stuart Wells, "'Our Children's Burden': A History of Federal Education Policies That Ask (Now Require) Our Public Schools to Solve Societal Inequality," in *NCLB at the Crossroads: Reexamining the Federal Effort to Close the Achievement Gap*, ed. Michael A. Rebell and Jessica R. Wolff (New York: Teachers College Press, 2009), 1–42; Jean Anyon, *Ghetto Schooling: A Political Economy of Urban Educational Reform* (New York: Teachers College Press, 1997), and *Radical Possibilities: Public Policy, Urban Education, and a New Social Movement* (New York: Routledge, 2005). On cycles of "overpromising" and "disillusionment" in the history of American school reform, see especially David Tyack and Larry Cuban, *Tinkering Toward Utopia: A Century of Public School Reform* (Cambridge, Mass.: Harvard University Press, 1995), 3; and Michael B. Katz, "Education and Inequality: A Historical Perspective," in *Social History and Social Policy*, ed. David J. Rothman and Stanton Wheeler (New York: Academic Press, 1981), 62, 92–100.

Chapter 3

1. For characterizations of this long-familiar narrative, see Jeanne Theoharis, "Introduction," and Robin D. G. Kelley, "Afterword," in *Freedom North: Black Freedom Struggles Outside the South, 1940–1980*, ed. Jeanne Theoharis and Komozi Woodard (New York: Palgrave Macmillan, 2003), 1–5, 313–14.

2. Among works that have helped to integrate conflicts over schooling into the urban and civil rights history of the North during the 1960s, see Thomas J. Sugrue, *Sweet Land of Liberty: The Forgotten Struggle for Civil Rights in the North* (New York: Random House, 2008); Jeffery Mirel, *The Rise and Fall of an Urban School System* (Ann Arbor: University of Michigan Press, 1993); Daniel H. Perlstein, *Justice, Justice: School Politics and the Eclipse of Liberalism* (New York: Peter Lang Publishing, 2004); Jerald E. Podair, *The Strike That Changed New York: Blacks, Whites, and the Ocean Hill–Brownsville Crisis* (New Haven: Yale University Press, 2004); Clarence Taylor, *Knocking at Our Own Door: Milton A. Galamison and the Struggle to Integrate New York City Schools* (New York: Columbia University Press, 1997); Jack Dougherty, *More than One Struggle: The Evolution of Black School Reform in Milwaukee* (Chapel Hill: University of North Carolina Press, 2004); and Matthew J. Countryman, *Up South: Civil Rights and Black Power in Philadelphia* (Philadelphia: University of Pennsylvania Press, 2007).

3. Kathryn M. Neckerman, *Schools Betrayed: Roots of Failure in Inner-City Education* (Chicago: University of Chicago Press, 2007).

4. Marcus A. Foster, "Utilizing the Sellin-Wolfgang Index of Delinquency to Determine the Efficacy of a Treatment Program for Delinquent and Predelinquent Boys" (Ed.D. diss., University of Pennsylvania, 1971).

5. Michael B. Katz, Mark J. Stern, and Jamie J. Fader, "The New African American Inequality," *Journal of American History* 92, no. 1 (2005), http://jah.oxfordjournals.org/content/92/1/75.full (accessed January 5, 2012), especially pars. 7, 38–44, 55, 63–73; Ronald F. Ferguson, *Toward Excellence with Equity: An Emerging Vision for Closing the Achievement Gap* (Cambridge, Mass.: Harvard Education Press, 2008); and William Julius Wilson, *More than Just Race: Being Black and Poor in the Inner City* (New York: W. W. Norton, 2009), 6–14, 62–72.

6. Among sources cited in the previous chapter on this point about schooling and poverty, see, for example, Harvey Kantor and Robert Lowe, "From New Deal to No Deal: NCLB and the Devolution of Responsibility for Equal Educational Opportunity," *Harvard Educational Review* 76, no. 4 (2006): 474–502; Michael B. Katz, "Education and Inequality: A Historical Perspective," in *Social History and Social Policy*, ed. David J. Rothman and Stanton Wheeler (New York: Academic Press, 1981); and Jean Anyon, *Ghetto Schooling: A Political Economy of Urban Educational Reform* (New York: Teachers College Press, 1997).

7. Foster, "Sellin-Wolfgang Index," 106–8.

8. Foster, "Sellin-Wolfgang Index," 31, 56, 104–31; Marcus A. Foster, "Meeting the Needs of Disadvantaged Youth in a Disciplinary School," in *Preparing to Teach the Disadvantaged*, ed. Bruce W. Tuckman and John L. O'Brian (New York: Free Press, 1969), 113–15.

9. Dean Cummings, telephone interview by the author, April 28, 2000, tape recording in possession of the author.

10. Joseph Tropea, "Bureaucratic Order and Special Children: Urban Schools, 1890s–1940s," *History of Education Quarterly* 27, no. 1 (1987): 29–53; William J. Reese, *America's Public Schools: From the Common School to "No Child Left Behind"* (Baltimore: Johns Hopkins University Press, 2005), 149–58.

11. Edward R. Krug, *The Shaping of the American High School, 1890–1920* (New York: Harper and Row, 1964); Wayne Urban and Jennings L. Wagoner, Jr., *American Education: A History* (New York: McGraw-Hill, 2004), 206–13; Barry M. Franklin, "Progressivism and Curriculum Differentiation: Special Classes in the Atlanta Public Schools, 1898–1923," *History of Education Quarterly*

29, no. 4 (1989): 571–93; Judy Jolley Mohraz, *The Separate Problem: Case Studies of Black Education in the North, 1900–1930* (Westport, Conn.: Greenwood Press, 1979).

12. Jeannie Oakes, *Keeping Track: How Schools Structure Inequality*, 2nd ed. (New Haven: Yale University Press, 2005) is the landmark study that has influenced a trend toward "detracking" in recent years. For an overview of the debate with a more critical assessment of detracking, see Tom Loveless, "The Tracking and Ability Grouping Debate" (Thomas B. Fordham Institute, 1998), http://www.edexcellence.net/publications-issues/publications/tracking.html (accessed September 1, 2011).

13. Harry Manuel Shulman, *Juvenile Delinquency in American Society* (New York: Harper and Row, 1961), 691–722. Shulman placed disciplinary schools and compensatory programs in the same broad context of "progressive" approaches to educating the "problem" child. Seeing academic retardation as the root of most behavioral "maladjustment," he emphasized the importance of a progressive emphasis on individualized (including remedial) instruction.

14. Committee on the "600" Schools, "'600' Schools, Yesterday, Today, and Tomorrow" (New York: Board of Education, 1965), 1–2.

15. "The '600' Day Schools," Interim Report III, Juvenile Delinquency Evaluation Project of the City of New York, April 1957.

16. Foster also noted MacIver's recommendation of "school-community coordinators" and after-school clubs, both of which had been key elements of his compensatory education program at Dunbar. Foster, "Sellin-Wolfgang Index," 50.

17. Photographs #7796 and #7797, "Catto" file, Pedagogical Library, School District of Philadelphia.

18. Daniel R. Biddle and Murray Dubin, *Tasting Freedom: Octavius Catto and the Battle for Equality in Civil War America* (Philadelphia: Temple University Press, 2010). Black Philadelphians voted in 1871 for only the second time since 1838 and for the first time without federal protection against the kind of violence that killed O. V. Catto. Dorothy Gondos Beers, "The Centennial City," in *Philadelphia: A 300-Year History*, ed. Russell F. Weigley (New York: W. W. Norton, 1982), 438. Another all-black school, defunct by the 1950s, had previously been named for Catto.

19. In all likelihood, this was by design. As Stephen Lockard, an English teacher at Catto in the 1980s, noted, "the idea has always been that you can teach to a class if you take the troublemakers out." Lockard, telephone conversation with the author, April 28, 2000. See also Tropea, "Bureaucratic Order and Special Children: Urban Schools, 1890s–1940s"; and "Bureaucratic Order and Special Children: Urban Schools, 1950s–1960s," *History of Education Quarterly* 27, no. 3 (1987): 339–61. Tropea argues that, from the turn of the century into the 1960s, progressive rhetoric regarding the individual "interests of the child" helped administrators justify separate classes and other practices aimed primarily at removing difficult students from regular classrooms.

20. Among many examples, see, for example, Anthony S. Bryk et al., *Organizing Schools for Improvement: Lessons from Chicago* (Chicago: University of Chicago Press, 2010); Gerald Grant, *The World We Created at Hamilton High* (Cambridge, Mass.: Harvard University Press, 1989); and Sara Lawrence-Lightfoot, *The Good School: Portraits of Character and Culture* (New York: Basic Books, 1983).

21. Cummings interview, April 28, 2000; Foster, "Sellin-Wolfgang Index," 54–57.

22. Cummings interview, April 28, 2000.

23. Foster, "Sellin-Wolfgang Index," 54.

24. Foster, "Sellin-Wolfgang Index," 58–63; Marcus Foster, "Foster's Travels: A Twenty Year Adventure in the Philadelphia Schools," *About Education*, Fall 1968, 24.

25. Kathleen Cotton, *Principals and Student Achievement: What the Research Says* (Alexandria, Va.: Association for Supervision and Curriculum Development, 2003), 9–13, 21–29; Karen S. Crum and Whitney H. Sherman, "Facilitating High Achievement: High School Principals' Reflections on Their Successful Leadership Practices," *Journal of Educational Administration* 46, no. 5 (2008): 562–80.

26. Foster, "Sellin-Wolfgang Index," 57–61.

27. Cummings interview, April 28, 2000; Foster, "Sellin-Wolfgang Index," 59–63.

28. Foster, "Sellin-Wolfgang Index," 55.

29. Foster, "Sellin-Wolfgang Index," 57–63.

30. Marcus A. Foster, Philadelphia Award Acceptance Speech, Philadelphia, Pennsylvania, April 1969, tape recording in possession of the author.

31. Richard A. Cloward and Lloyd E. Ohlin, *Delinquency and Opportunity: A Theory of Delinquent Gangs* (Glencoe, Ill.: Free Press, 1960).

31. Harlem Youth Opportunities Unlimited Inc., *Youth in the Ghetto: A Study of the Consequences of Powerlessness and a Blueprint for Change* (New York: HARYOU, 1964), 31–35. On the Northside Child Development Center, see Gerald E. Markowitz and David Rosner, *Children, Race, and Power: Kenneth and Mamie Clark's Northside Center* (Charlottesville: University of Virginia Press, 1996).

33. Harlem Youth Opportunities Unlimited Inc., *Youth in the Ghetto,* 236, 426–30; Kenneth B. Clark, *Dark Ghetto: Dilemmas of Social Power* (New York: Harper and Row, 1965).

34. James B. Conant, *Slums and Suburbs* (New York: McGraw-Hill, 1961).

35. Conant, *Slums and Suburbs,* 8–9. For an example of a sympathetic review of *Slums and Suburbs,* see Agnes E. Meyer, "Slums and Schools: Dr. Conant's New Report," *Atlantic Monthly* 209, no. 2 (February 1962): 76–79.

36. Conant, *Slums and Suburbs,* 27–31.

37. Kenneth B. Clark, "Clash of Cultures in the Classroom," in *Learning Together: A Book on Integrated Education,* ed. Meyer Weinberg (Chicago: Integrated Education Associates, 1964), 18–25. See also Robert H. Terte, "Conant Scored by School Groups," *New York Times,* October 17, 1961, 35. In Philadelphia, *Slums and Suburbs* appeared just weeks before *Chisolm v. Board of Public Education* was slated for trial in U.S. District Court (see Chapter 2). Floyd Logan, head of the Educational Equality League in Philadelphia, worried that Conant's book would aid the opposition, so he organized a public forum to counteract its "harmful influence." Kenneth Clark was among those who spoke at the event. "'The Educational Equality League Presents Dr. Kenneth B. Clark and Dr. Joshua A. Fishman in 'An Educational Forum: Northern and Southern Style Public School Segregation,'" December 1, 1961; A. Leon Higginbotham to Floyd L. Logan, November 20, 1961, Floyd Logan papers (hereafter Logan papers), b. 8, f. 18, Temple University Urban Archives (TUUA).

38. Sugrue, *Sweet Land of Liberty,* 297–99; Taylor, *Knocking at Our Own Door;* Leonard Nathaniel Moore, "The School Desegregation Crisis of Cleveland, Ohio, 1963–1964: The Catalyst for Black Political Power in a Northern City," *Journal of Urban History* 28, no. 2 (2002): 135–57.

39. Peter A. Janssen, "Keppel Explodes Slum School 'Myths,'" *Philadelphia Inquirer,* February 16, 1964.

40. James Baldwin et al., "Liberalism and the Negro: A Roundtable Discussion," *Commentary* (March 1964): 39. The panel participants included the sociologists Gunnar Myrdal and Nathan Glazer, the philosopher Sidney Hook, and the writer James Baldwin.

41. Gaeton Fonzi, "Crisis in the Classroom," *Greater Philadelphia,* January 1964, 28–31, 60–68, 73–77.

42. Fonzi, "Crisis in the Classroom," 30; Gaeton Fonzi, telephone conversation with the author, October 12, 1999.

43. Fonzi, "Crisis in the Classroom," 30, 60, 65–68, 73, 77.

44. Fonzi, "Crisis in the Classroom," 74–75.

45. Fonzi, "Crisis in the Classroom," 76–77.

46. Letter to the editor of *Greater Philadelphia* magazine from Marion L. Steet, January 20, 1964, Logan papers, b. 9, f. 16, TUUA.

47. Letter to the editor, Marion L. Steet.

48. Robert L. Poindexter to E. Washington Rhodes, Publisher, *Philadelphia Tribune,* January 21,

1964, Logan papers, b. 9, f. 16, TUUA; Chris J. Perry, "School Superintendent Dr. Wetter Admits Magazine Duped Him in Quest for Sensational Story on Negroes," *Philadelphia Tribune,* January 21, 1964, 1.

49. Ruth Wright Hayre, "William Penn High Principal Sees Article as 'Plant' to Kill White Community Support of Education," *Philadelphia Tribune*, January 18, 1964, 1, 4. On Hayre's response to the *Greater Philadelphia* article, see also Matthew Delmont, "The Plight of the 'Able Student': Ruth Wright Hayre and the Struggle for Equality in Philadelphia's Black High Schools, 1955–1965," *History of Education Quarterly* 50, no. 2 (2010): 222–27.

50. Letter to the editor, Marion L. Steet.

51. Fonzi conversation, October 12, 1999.

52. Marcus A. Foster, *Making Schools Work: Strategies for Changing Education* (Philadelphia: Westminster Press, 1971), 91–92; Foster, "Sellin-Wolfgang Index," 69.

53. Foster, "Foster's Travels," 24; Foster, *Making Schools Work*, 95; and Foster, "Sellin-Wolfgang Index," 70.

54. Cummings interview, April 28, 2000.

55. Foster, *Making Schools Work,* 90, 95; Foster, "Sellin-Wolfgang Index," 163–67.

56. Clark, "Clash of Cultures," 24; Foster, "Sellin-Wolfgang Index," 5–6.

57. Foster, "Sellin-Wolfgang Index," 2, 5; Foster, "Meeting the Needs of Disadvantaged Youth," 114.

58. For a discussion of the trade-offs of labeling in special education, see James M. Kauffman and Daniel P. Hallahan, *Special Education: What It Is and Why We Need It* (Boston: Allyn and Bacon, 2004).

59. Paul Tough, *Whatever It Takes: Geoffrey Canada's Quest to Change Harlem and America* (Boston: Houghton Mifflin, 2008); Jay Mathews, *Work Hard. Be Nice.: How Two Inspired Teachers Created the Most Promising Schools in America* (Chapel Hill, N.C.: Algonquin Books, 2009). See the epilogue for further discussion of these programs.

60. Foster, "Sellin-Wolfgang Index," 70–72; Foster, *Making Schools Work,* 90.

61. Foster, "Sellin-Wolfgang Index," 35, 48. Delinquency studies that influenced Foster's view on the importance of "self-concept" included Bernard Lander, *Toward an Understanding of Juvenile Delinquency* (New York: Columbia University Press, 1954), a Baltimore study that found no significant correlation between delinquency, on the one hand, and poverty, ethnic group concentration, or industrialization, on the other; Gerald J. Pine, *Social Class, Social Mobility, and Delinquent Behavior* (Washington, D.C.: Personnel Guidance Association, n.d.), which suggested, according to Foster, that "the status one is aspiring to reach is more significant in delinquent behavior than one's present status"; and Charles V. Willie, "Anti-Social Behavior among Disadvantaged Youth: Some Observations on Prevention for Teachers," *Journal of Negro Education* 33 (Spring 1964): 176–81.

62. Foster, "Sellin-Wolfgang Index," 81, 153–59.

63. Frank Riessman and S. M. Miller, "Social Change Versus the 'Psychiatric World View,'" *American Journal of Orthopsychiatry* (January 1964): 30–31; Daniel Knapp and Kenneth Polk, *Scouting the War on Poverty: Social Reform Politics in the Kennedy Administration* (Lexington, Mass.: Heath Lexington Books, 1971), 57–60. For Foster's review of the literature on Child Guidance, including the pioneering works of William Healy, see Foster, "Sellin-Wolfgang Index," 27–29.

64. Foster, "Sellin-Wolfgang Index," 60.

65. Foster cited the New York State Youth Commission report *Reducing Juvenile Delinquency: What New York State Schools Can Do* (Albany, 1952) to suggest that a "favorable emotional school climate" could reduce delinquency rates, especially when "home conditions are poor." On the power of "hero models," see his discussion of Manson E. Hall, Jr., "Saving the Trouble Prone," *N.E.A. Journal* 54 (April, 1965): 26–28. Foster, "Sellin-Wolfgang Index," 49, 51–52.

66. Foster, "Foster's Travels," 24.

67. Foster, "Foster's Travels," 25.

68. Foster, "Sellin-Wolfgang Index," 75, 79–80.

69. Foster, *Making Schools Work*, 92; Foster, "Meeting the Needs of Disadvantaged Youth," 119; and Foster, "Sellin-Wolfgang Index," 2, 65. On economic trends that have favored skilled or educated workers since the 1960s, see Wilson, *More than Just Race*, 6–14.

70. Foster, "Sellin-Wolfgang Index," 83; Foster, *Making Schools Work*, 92, 99; and Foster, "Meeting the Needs of Disadvantaged Youth," 116.

71. Foster, "Sellin-Wolfgang Index," 59–61; and "Philadelphia Award Acceptance Speech."

72 Foster, "Sellin-Wolfgang Index," 66–67, 85.

73. Robert Blackburn, interviewed by the author at Blackburn's home in Oakland, Calif., March 5, 1998, tape recording in possession of the author. See also Chapter 2.

74. Foster, "Sellin-Wolfgang Index," 89–90. The group therapy program, called the Catto Child Guidance Clinic, was a collaboration with a nearby social service agency, the Child Study Center. The Study Center already provided the handful of psychologists who sat on the CCCC; the Child Guidance Clinic was an attempt to spread the impact of those same professionals.

75. Cummings interview, April 28, 2000; Foster, "Sellin-Wolfgang Index," 9, 73, 84, 89–93.

76. Foster, "Sellin-Wolfgang Index," 88.

77. Bryk et al., *Organizing Schools for Improvement*. For an overlapping set of characteristics, growing out of the earlier "Effective Schools" movement, see Ronald Edmonds, "Effective Schools for the Urban Poor," *Educational Leadership* 37, no. 1 (1979): 5–24.

78. Foster, "Sellin-Wolfgang Index," 97–131.

79. Foster used standardized reading and math test scores to compare the control and experimental groups before their enrollment at Catto, but not after. Both groups entered at roughly a fourth-grade level in math and a third-grade level in reading. Foster, "Sellin-Wolfgang Index," 9, 104.

80. Foster, "Foster's Travels," 25; Foster, "Sellin-Wolfgang Index," 72, 81–82, 87, 104.

81. Foster, "Philadelphia Award Acceptance Speech"; Foster, "Foster's Travels," 24.

82. Foster, "Sellin-Wolfgang Index," 59.

83. Foster, "Sellin-Wolfgang Index," 118.

84. On PCCA funding for early childhood education, see Chapter 2. On the early demise of the PCCA, in November 1964, because of tensions between social scientists, social workers, city officials, and civil rights leaders who vied to shape the program, see Peter Marris and Martin Rein, *Dilemmas of Social Reform: Poverty and Community Action in the United States* (New York: Atherton Press, 1967). On the reorganization of the PCCA into the Philadelphia Anti-Poverty Action Committee (PAAC), and the subsequent history of that organization, see Guian A. McKee, *The Problem of Jobs: Liberalism, Race, and Deindustrialization in Philadelphia* (Chicago: University of Chicago Press, 2008), 96–106.

85. Countryman, *Up South*, 112–16; McKee, *The Problem of Jobs*.

86. Leon H. Sullivan, *Build, Brother, Build* (Philadelphia: Macrae Smith Company, 1969), 99–102.

87. School District of Philadelphia, "Report of the Special Committee on Nondiscrimination" (Philadelphia: Board of Education, 1964), 43; Lawrence M. O'Rourke, "Negro Ministers Start 'Direct Action' on Schools," *Philadelphia Evening Bulletin* (hereafter referred to as *Bulletin*), September 9, 1963.

88. Christopher Jencks, "Johnson vs. Poverty," *New Republic*, March 24, 1964, 18.

89. On the post-1945 period, see Amy Stuart Wells, "'Our Children's Burden': A History of Federal Education Policies That Ask (Now Require) Our Public Schools to Solve Societal Inequality," in *NCLB at the Crossroads: Reexamining the Federal Effort to Close the Achievement Gap*, ed. Michael A. Rebell and Jessica R. Wolff (New York: Teachers College Press, 2009), 1–42; Anyon, *Ghetto Schooling*; Kantor and Lowe, "From New Deal to No Deal"; and Harvey Kantor and Barbara Brenzel, "Urban Education and the 'Truly Disadvantaged': The Historical Roots of the Contemporary

Crisis, 1945–1990," in *The Underclass Debate: Views from History*, ed. Michael B. Katz (Princeton, N.J.: Princeton University Press, 1993), 366–402. On earlier periods, see Katz, "Education and Inequality."

90. On the "narrative of failure" surrounding the War on Poverty, see Michael B. Katz, "Narratives of Failure? Historical Interpretations of Federal Urban Policy," *City and Community* 9 (March 2010): 13–22, http://onlinelibrary.wiley.com/doi/10.1111/j.1540-6040.2009.01312.x/full (accessed September 1, 2011). As Katz notes, federal antipoverty policies have been criticized from across the political spectrum: while liberals have pointed to inadequate government funding and a lack of attention to job creation (among other problems), conservatives have tended to see government programs as wasteful, inherently ineffective, and/or damaging to the development of market-based solutions.

91. McKee, *The Problem of Jobs*. McKee also emphasizes Sullivan's "reappropriation" of "self help" and "uplift" strategies, including his pursuit of those strategies in combination with a demand for greater government support.

92. Katz, Stern, and Fader, "The New African American Inequality"; Wilson, *More than Just Race*, 6–14; 62–72. For a contemporary discussion of the rising importance of education in a postindustrial economy, see Charles Silberman, *Crisis in Black and White* (New York: Random House, 1964), 252–54.

93. Foster, "Sellin-Wolfgang Index," 85.

94. Lenora E. Berson, *Case Study of a Riot: The Philadelphia Story* (New York: Institute of Human Relations Press, 1966), 15–22, 154–60.

95. Berson, *Case Study of a Riot*, 17–18; Joseph Lelyveld, "1,500 Policemen Bar New Rioting in Philadelphia," *New York Times*, August 30, 1964.

96. Lelyveld, "1,500 Policemen Bar New Rioting"; "Memorandum," Jules Cohen to JCRC Officers, Board of Directors, Member Agencies and Neighborhood Divisions, August 31, 1964, Papers of the Philadelphia Fellowship Commission (PFC papers), Acc. 626, b. 22, f. 16, TUUA. Black leaders of all stripes, fearful that the riot would set back their cause, called for "law and order" even more emphatically than did politicians or the police; five thousand of them volunteered to be deputized in order to help curb the mayhem. (The offer was not acted upon.) Berson, *Case Study of a Riot*, 19.

97. "Philadelphia Police Find Arms in Raid," *New York Times*, August 30, 1964.

98. For the text of the Moynihan Report and a documentary history of the controversy surrounding it, see Lee Rainwater and William L. Yancey, *The Moynihan Report and the Politics of Controversy* (Cambridge, Mass.: M.I.T. Press, 1967). The Watts riot occurred less than a month after *The Negro Family* began circulating within the Johnson administration.

99. James T. Patterson, *Freedom Is Not Enough: The Moynihan Report and America's Struggle over Black Family Life—from LBJ to Obama* (New York: Basic Books, 2010), 26–36.

100. William Ryan, *Blaming the Victim* (New York: Pantheon, 1971); Daryl Michael Scott, "The Politics of Pathology: The Ideological Origins of the Moynihan Controversy," in *Integrating the Sixties*, ed. Brian Balough (University Park: Pennsylvania State University Press, 1996), 98–101; Michael B. Katz, *The Undeserving Poor: From the War on Poverty to the War on Welfare* (New York: Pantheon Books, 1989), 29–35.

101. Rainwater and Yancey noted that many critics read only incomplete newspaper summaries that focused on problems like out-of-wedlock childrearing while ignoring Moynihan's comments on unemployment and discrimination.

102. "YMCA Asks 'Compassion' for Young N. Phila. Rioters," *Bulletin*, August 30, 1964, *Bulletin* clippings file, "Marcus Foster," TUUA.

103. A report for the U.S. Commission on Civil Rights suggested that Philadelphia school authorities had committed acts that "verged on gerrymandering," and that the board was contradicting official policy by purposefully assigning black teachers to black schools and white teachers to

white schools. Still, the report was inconclusive. Albert P. Blaustein, "Philadelphia, Pennsylvania," in *Civil Rights U.S.A.: Public Schools, Cities in the North and West, 1962* (New York: Greenwood Press, 1968), 105–73.

104. Clark, *Dark Ghetto,* 117–18, 137, 153.

105. Foster, "Sellin-Wolfgang Index," 4.

106. Noting that liberal usage of "damage imagery" (such as Moynihan's call for government assistance to transform the supposed cultural pathology of the ghettos) has been adopted by conservatives to justify retrenchment, the historian Daryl Michael Scott, for instance, understandably urges that "inner lives" be "off limits" to experts who study social groups and engage in policy debates. By contrast, Foster, as an educator who worked with individual students, found it necessary almost by definition to address aspects of his students' inner lives and cultural backgrounds that affected their performance in school. Daryl Michael Scott, *Contempt and Pity: Social Policy and the Image of the Damaged Black Psyche, 1880–1996* (Chapel Hill: University of North Carolina Press, 1997), xviii–xix.

Chapter 4

1. Marcus A. Foster, *Making Schools Work: Strategies for Changing Education* (Philadelphia: Westminster Press, 1971), 101–2.

2. J. Brantley Wilder, "Parents Claim Gangs Rule Gratz High School," *Philadelphia Tribune,* March 8, 1966; Jacob Sherman, "Gratz High Students Threaten Protest March on Tribune," *Philadelphia Tribune,* March 12, 1966; J. Brantley Wilder and J. Donald Porter, "Dr. Hayre, Cecil Moore Hail Gratz Series," *Philadelphia Tribune,* March 15, 1966; Wilder and Porter, "Gratz Gets Negro Principal," *Philadelphia Tribune,* March 22, 1966.

3. Jerald E. Podair, *The Strike That Changed New York: Blacks, Whites, and the Ocean Hill–Brownsville Crisis* (New Haven: Yale University Press, 2002); Daniel H. Perlstein, *Justice, Justice: School Politics and the Eclipse of Liberalism* (New York: Peter Lang, 2004).

4. Rich Aregood, "He's Selling Education—and N. Philadelphia Is Buying," *Philadelphia Daily News,* February 6, 1968, 4.

5. Among recent works that have redefined the Black Power movement not as a moment of decline for the civil rights movement but as a continuation and extension of the movement's tradition of grassroots activism, see Matthew J. Countryman, *Up South: Civil Rights and Black Power in Philadelphia* (Philadelphia: University of Pennsylvania Press, 2007); Peniel E. Joseph, *The Black Power Movement: Rethinking the Civil Rights-Black Power Era* (New York: Routledge, 2006); and Jeffrey O. G. Ogbar, *Black Power: Radical Politics and African American Identity* (Baltimore: Johns Hopkins University Press, 2005).

6. The notion that the 1980s marked a return to "excellence" and "achievement," after several decades in the pursuit of desegregation and other "equity" agendas, is closely associated with the Reagan administration report *A Nation at Risk* (1983). Among historians, Diane Ravitch has been a leading proponent of this version of the equity vs. excellence dichotomy; see *The Troubled Crusade: American Education, 1945–1980* (New York: Basic Books, 1983).

7. James S. Coleman et al., *Equality of Educational Opportunity* (Washington, D.C.: Government Printing Office, 1966).

8. See, for example, "Simon Gratz High Teams Capture Debating Trophy," *Philadelphia Evening Bulletin* (hereafter referred to as *Bulletin*), April 16, 1931; "Simon Gratz Paper Wins," *Bulletin,* May 9, 1936; "Gratz High Debaters Are City Champions," *Bulletin,* June 15, 1949; "Gratz Greats: Alumni Star in Many Fields, High School Finds as It Marks 20th Anniversary," *Bulletin,* December 3, 1947; "Seven Pupils Arrested," *Bulletin,* May 7, 1941. Unless otherwise noted, all *Bulletin* articles cited in this chapter can be found in the "Simon Gratz High School" or "Marcus Foster" envelopes of the *Bulletin* clippings file, Temple University Urban Archives (hereafter TUUA). In some cases, as

indicated, articles from the *Philadelphia Inquirer* and other newspapers may also be found in the *Bulletin* file.

9. On Philadelphia's industrial decline, see Carolyn Adams et al., *Philadelphia: Neighborhoods, Division, and Conflict in a Postindustrial City* (Philadelphia: Temple University Press, 1991).

10. Lenora E. Berson, *Case Study of a Riot: The Philadelphia Story* (New York: Institute of Human Relations Press, 1966), 25–28.

11. "Gratz 'Dragon' Sent to Prison," *Bulletin,* December 20, 1949; "Patrolmen Guard Route 21 Trolleys," *Bulletin,* March 7, 1955; "Boy Shot, 2 Cut After Game," *Bulletin,* October 28, 1955; "200 Pupils Riot at 17th, Erie, Police Seize 20, Find Zip Gun," *Bulletin,* April 18, 1956; "3 Boys Seized in School Row," *Bulletin,* November 4, 1958; "Arrest of 4 Nips School 'Rumble,'" *Bulletin,* May 24, 1960; "Pupils Battle in N. Broad St. Subway Stop," *Bulletin,* October 29, 1963.

12. John P. Corr, "Crummy? Marcus Foster Proves 'Gratz Is Great,'" *Philadelphia Inquirer,* March 10, 1968; Foster, *Making Schools Work,* 110; Richard H. deLone, "McIntosh Accuses Schools of Setting Boundaries to Skirt Integration," *Bulletin,* April 13, 1966. For a useful commentary on the idea of de facto segregation in the North, emphasizing that it was not simply a product of individual decisions in the private housing market but also a result of government policies, see Jeanne Theoharis, "'I'd Rather Go to School in the South': How Boston's School Desegregation Complicates the Civil Rights Paradigm," in *Freedom North: Black Freedom Struggles Outside the South, 1940–1980,* ed. Jeanne Theoharis and Komozi Woodard (New York: Palgrave Macmillan, 2003), 125–27.

13. "Gym, Auto Shop, Better Teachers Sought for Gratz," *Philadelphia Inquirer,* March 18, 1966, *Bulletin* file, "Gratz High School," TUUA; Sherman, "Gratz High Students Threaten Protest." For his part, the *Tribune* reporter J. Brantley Wilder said he had told the Home and School Association that "a 'Sunday School' story would only cover up the real facts in the situation and wouldn't help to cause any changes." J. Donald Porter, "Board Calls Story Factual; Exaggerated," *Philadelphia Tribune,* March 12, 1966.

14. Foster, *Making Schools Work,* 109–11.

15. Foster, *Making Schools Work*; Marci Shatzman, "Principal Thinks 'Gratz Is Greatest,'" *North Penn Chat,* February 8, 1968, *Bulletin* file, "Marcus Foster," TUUA.

16. Wilder and Porter, "Dr. Hayre, Cecil Moore"; "Gym, Auto Shop, Better Teachers Sought."

17. In the South, prior to *Brown v. Board of Education* (1954), black educators and students were confined to separate schools with inadequate resources; yet, even as they suffered the ills of segregation, they struggled to create schools that were noted for their responsiveness and commitment to students and their families. See, for example, Vanessa Siddle Walker, *Their Highest Potential: An African American School Community in the Segregated South* (Chapel Hill: University of North Carolina Press, 1996). In northern cities like Philadelphia, blacks shaped strong and supportive school communities at the elementary school level—Foster's leadership at Dunbar, as recounted in Chapter 2, is a notable example—but before the 1960s, they rarely occupied the principal's office, or even the classroom, at the middle and secondary level.

18. Ruth Wright Hayre and Alexis Moore, *Tell Them We Are Rising: A Memoir of Faith in Education* (New York: J. Wiley and Sons, 1997), 71–74.

19. Podair, *The Strike That Changed New York,* 34–47; Nat Hentoff, "Making Public Schools Accountable: A Case Study of P.S. 201 in Harlem," *Phi Delta Kappan* 48, no. 7, March 1967, 332–35.

20. Peter A. Janssen, "Ghetto High School Gets New Principal," *Philadelphia Inquirer,* March 27, 1966, *Bulletin* file, "Gratz High School," TUUA.

21. Coleman et al., *Equality of Educational Opportunity.*

22. See, for example, Ronald Edmonds et al., "A Black Response to Christopher Jencks's *Inequality* and Certain Other Issues," *Harvard Educational Review* 43, no. 1 (1973): 77–78, 83–89.

23. For analyses in the immediate aftermath of the report, see Frederick Mosteller and Daniel P. Moynihan, eds., *On Equality of Educational Opportunity* (New York: Random House, 1972);

and Christopher Jencks et al., *Inequality: A Reassessment of the Effect of Family and Schooling in America* (New York: Basic Books, 1972). Among more recent studies that emphasize the impact of non-school influences on academic performance, see Richard Rothstein, *Class and Schools: Using Social, Economic, and Educational Reform to Close the Black-White Achievement Gap* (Washington, D.C.: Economic Policy Institute, 2004); Jean Anyon, *Ghetto Schooling: A Political Economy of Urban Educational Reform* (New York: Teachers College Press, 1997); and Alan R. Sadovnik et al., *No Child Left Behind and the Reduction of the Achievement Gap: Sociological Perspectives on Federal Educational Policy* (New York: Routledge, 2007).

24. Sunny Decker, *An Empty Spoon* (New York: Harper and Row, 1969), 19, 45.

25. For more extensive definition and discussion of the concept of cultural capital as it is used in this book, see Chapter 1. See also Annette Lareau and Elliot Weininger, "Cultural Capital in Educational Research: A Critical Assessment," *Theory and Society* 32, nos. 5–6 (2003): 567–606; and John L. Rury, *Education and Social Change: Themes in the History of American Schooling* (Mahwah, N.J.: Lawrence Erlbaum, 2002), 193–94.

26. William Odell, *Philadelphia's Public Schools: Educational Survey* (Philadelphia: Philadelphia Board of Public Education, February 1, 1965); "Report of the Special Committee on Nondiscrimination" (Philadelphia: Philadelphia Board of Public Education, July 23, 1964), Educational Resources Information Center (ERIC) document #ED20207.

27. John N. Patterson, William L. Rafsky, and Donald Rappaport, "Reports of the Task Forces to the Incoming Board of Education," November 8, 1965, Grant #G06600189, R. 0399, sec. 4, Ford Foundation Archives (hereafter FFA). For contemporary accounts that emphasize the "revolutionary" aspects of Philadelphia school reform in the late 1960s, see Henry S. Resnik, *Turning on the System: War in the Philadelphia Public Schools* (New York: Pantheon Books, 1970), 3–25; and Marilyn Gittell and T. Edward Hollander, "The Process of Change: Case Study of Philadelphia," in *The Politics of Urban Education*, ed. Marilyn Gittell and Alan G. Hevesi (New York: Praeger, 1969), 217–35. Gittell and Hollander refer to the Dilworth era as "the most dramatic revolution in a city school system in the postwar period."

28. The Dilworth board used the Ford Foundation grant to establish an office of planning, aimed at fostering longer-range strategic thinking in response to the considerable challenges facing the district, especially with regard to "white flight," low achievement, and "lack of aspiration and motivation among students leading to early dropouts." The head of the planning office was Associate Superintendent David Horowitz, who also had played a key leadership role in the Great Cities program. Among various internal memoranda that discuss the grant and the situation in the Philadelphia schools, see Memorandum to McGeorge Bundy from Clarence Faust, "Grant Request: Education Program," March 31, 1966, Grant #G06600189, R0399, sec. 1, FFA.

29. Hayre and Moore, *Tell Them We Are Rising*, 74.

30. Foster, *Making Schools Work*, 106–7.

31. John P. Corr, "Shedd's Bombshell: Reorganization Plan," *Philadelphia Inquirer*, June 11, 1967. For an excellent overview of the Shedd years, see Jon S. Birger, "Race, Reaction, and Reform: The Three Rs of Philadelphia School Politics, 1965–1971," *Pennsylvania Magazine of History and Biography* 120, no. 3 (1996): 163–216.

32. Acel Moore, "Gratz Principal Resigns for Post in N.Y.," *Philadelphia Inquirer*, 1976. On the displacement of African American educators in the South after *Brown*, see Michael Fultz, "The Displacement of Black Educators Post-Brown: An Overview and Analysis," *History of Education Quarterly* 44, no. 1 (2004): 11–45.

33. Corr, "Shedd's Bombshell."

34. Foster, *Making Schools Work*, 108–9.

35. Vincent J. Nazzaro, "School That Looks like a Store," *Sunday Bulletin Magazine*, February 9, 1969; "Storefront School Is to Be 'Neighborhood High,'" *Bulletin*, January 28,1968; Marcus Foster, "Child of the Poor, Looking for Mitochondria," in *Readings in Curriculum and Supervision*, ed. V.

Eugene Yarbrough, William C. Bruce, and Ronald L. Hubright (New York: MSS Information Corporation, 1974); Foster, *Making Schools Work*, 123.

36. J. Brantley Wilder, "New Gratz Principal Launches Crash School Upgrading Program," *Philadelphia Tribune*, April 23,1966, 1; Aregood, "He's Selling Education."

37. Decker, *An Empty Spoon*, 43, 94–95.

38. Foster, *Making Schools Work*, 16–17, 21; Aregood, "He's Selling Education."

39. Foster, *Making Schools Work*, 112.

40. Aregood, "He's Selling Education"; Nazzaro, "School That Looks like a Store."

41. Robert Blackburn, interviewed by the author at Blackburn's home in Oakland, California, March 11, 1998, tape recording in possession of the author.

42. Marcus Foster, "Foster's Travels: A Twenty Year Adventure in the Philadelphia Schools," *About Education*, Fall 1968, 28–29; Foster, "Child of the Poor, Looking for Mitochondria," 53.

43. See Chapter 2 on the evolution of Philadelphia's Ford Foundation pilot projects into the Educational Improvement Program, which by 1966 included sixty-eight elementary and fourteen secondary schools.

44. Gratz Seeks Better Image Through 'Project Beacon,'" *Bulletin,* September 28, 1965; Decker, *An Empty Spoon,* 98–100; "Mr. Green Guides 'Beacon Project,'" *Spotlight* (Simon Gratz High School newspaper), October 18, 1965, 1, Simon Gratz High School library, Philadelphia, Pa.; "Gratz Launches Beacon Program," *Spotlight,* March 6, 1967, 1, Simon Gratz High School library, Philadelphia, Pa.

45. Gloria Gaymon, interviewed by the author at Gratz High School, November 26, 2001.

46. Foster, *Making Schools Work*, 117–19; Herm Rogul, "Mr. Chaney Becomes Mr. Cheyney," *Bulletin,* August 29, 1972, *Bulletin* file, "John Chaney," TUUA.

47. "A New Look at Simon Gratz High," *Philadelphia Tribune,* May 2, 1967.

48. Foster, *Making Schools Work*, 127, 131.

49. Charles V. Hamilton, "Race and Education: A Search for Legitimacy," *Harvard Educational Review* 38, no. 4 (1968): 669–84.

50. Countryman, *Up South,* 228–36.

51. Decker, *An Empty Spoon,* 58–63.

52. Wallace Roberts, "Can Urban Schools Be Reformed?" *Saturday Review, Education Supplement,* May 17, 1969, 88.

53. "250 at Gratz Quit School to Hear Protests," *Bulletin,* October 27, 1967; Len Lear and John Brantley Wilder, "Negro History Courses Demanded by Students," *Philadelphia Tribune,* November 4, 1967, 1; Decker, *An Empty Spoon,* 63–66. In his book on the Shedd years in Philadelphia, Henry Resnik writes of an occasion when "several left-oriented community leaders failed in their attempt to stage a minor coup at a time when Foster was seriously ill only because he made a miraculous eleventh-hour appearance after rising from his sickbed to stop them." This may be a description of the events of October 26, but if so, it is not clear why the newspapers did not mention Foster's "eleventh-hour" effort. Resnik, *Turning on the System,* 134.

54. "'Unite Against White Policy,' Leaflets Urge Negro Pupils," *Bulletin,* November 16, 1967.

55. For detailed accounts of these events, see Birger, "Race, Reaction, and Reform," 163–69; and Countryman, *Up South,* 223–28.

56. David Hornbeck, interviewed by the author in the Office of the Superintendent, Philadelphia Public Schools, April 25, 2000, tape recording in possession of the author.

57. "Cop Brutality Protests Flood Tribune Office," *Philadelphia Tribune,* November 21, 1967, 1.

58. Joe Hunter, "Negroes, Whites Join Hands in Blasting Police Tactics," *Philadelphia Tribune,* November 21, 1967, 2.

59. Hornbeck interview, April 25, 2000; "Demonstration Set Wednesday," *Philadelphia Tribune,* November 21, 1967.

60. Birger, "Race, Reaction, and Reform," 168, 172–76.

61. Joseph Daughen and Peter Binzen, *The Cop Who Would Be King: Mayor Frank Rizzo* (Boston: Little, Brown, and Co., 1977), quoted in Birger, "Race, Reaction, and Reform," 168.

62. "Ousting a Reformer," *Time,* December 20, 1971, 58.

63. Foster, "Foster's Travels," 30.

64. Countryman, *Up South,* 7–9, 241–44, 255–57. On the intensity of the retreats, see also Resnik, *Turning on the System,* 13.

65. "Gratz High Overhauls Curriculum to Emphasize the Negro's Gains," *Philadelphia Tribune,* n.d.; "Gratz Given Grant to Plan Negro History Curriculum," *Bulletin,* January 24, 1968.

66. John T. Gillespie, "Nichols Says Gratz Plan Is like South African," *Bulletin,* December 12, 1967.

67. "Gratz High Overhauls Curriculum; Aregood, "He's Selling Education."

68. Foster, *Making Schools Work,* 49–50.

69. See, for example, Sonia Nieto and Patricia Bode, *Affirming Diversity: The Sociopolitical Context of Multicultural Education,* 5th ed. (Boston: Allyn & Bacon, 2007); and Gloria Ladson-Billings, *The Dreamkeepers: Successful Teachers of African American Children,* 2nd ed. (San Francisco: Jossey-Bass, 2009).

70. Jerald Podair, "'White' Values, 'Black' Values: The Ocean Hill–Brownsville Controversy and New York City Culture, 1965–1975," *Radical History Review* 59 (1994): 54.

71. Robert P. Moses and Charles E. Cobb, *Radical Equations: Civil Rights from Mississippi to the Algebra Project* (Boston: Beacon Press, 2002). On longstanding traditions of African American achievement encompassing such figures as Douglass and DuBois, see Theresa Perry, "Up from the Parched Earth: Toward a Theory of African American Achievement," in Theresa Perry, Claude Steele, and Asa Hilliard III, *Young, Gifted, and Black: Promoting High Achievement Among African American Students* (Boston: Beacon Press, 2003); and James D. Anderson, *The Education of Blacks in the South, 1860–1935* (Chapel Hill: University of North Carolina Press, 1988).

72. Robert Blackburn, interviewed by the author at Blackburn's home in Oakland, California, March 5, 1998, tape recording in possession of the author. See also Foster, *Making Schools Work,* 127.

73. Resnik, *Turning on the System,* 134.

74. Decker, *An Empty Spoon,* 30.

75. Gaymon interview, November 26, 2001.

76. Betty Medsger, "Principal and Gratz High Seniors 'Tell It Like It Is' to 185 Here," *Evening Bulletin,* March 10, 1968.

77. Albert J. Haas, "Protests of Residents Stall Expansion of Nicetown's Gratz High," *Philadelphia Inquirer,* May 4, 1967; John T. Gillespie, "Hunting Park Ave. Residents Protest Plan for Gratz School Extension," *Bulletin,* December 13, 1967; Rowland T. Moriarty, "Families Up from Poverty Face School Bulldozers," *Bulletin,* February 18, 1968; "200 at Board Meeting Urge Gratz Expansion," *Bulletin,* February 26, 1968. See also Foster, *Making Schools Work,* 135.

78. Foster, *Making Schools Work,* 135; "200 at Board Meeting Urge Gratz Expansion."

79. Gillespie, "Hunting Park Ave. Residents Protest"; Foster, *Making Schools Work,* 135–36.

80. John T. Gillespie, "Tate Opposes Closing Street for Gratz Extension," *Bulletin,* December 21, 1967; "Nicetown Residents Win Fight to Save 14 Houses," *Bulletin,* January 24, 1968; John T. Gillespie, "Tate Warns Schools to Drop Gratz Annex Plans," *Bulletin,* February 6, 1968; "School Board to Go Ahead on Gratz Plan," *Bulletin,* February 26, 1968.

81. Foster, *Making Schools Work,* 133, 138–39. Foster was especially incensed when a politician suggested that he put the gym on another parcel and wait ten or fifteen years ("Ten years! Fifteen years!" he recalled in disbelief) for the homeowners to die and their homes to be turned into an athletic field.

82. Foster, *Making Schools Work,* 139; John P. Corr, "Negro Parents Pledge to 'Fight to the Wire' for Gratz Expansion," *Philadelphia Inquirer,* February 23, 1968.

83. Marcus Foster, commencement address, Swarthmore High School, Swarthmore, Pennsylvania, June 9, 1969, tape recording in possession of the author.

84. Foster, *Making Schools Work*, 141; "Mr. D'Ortona and the Schools," *Bulletin*, March 8, 1968; Joe McGinnis, "A Victory for Gratz High," *Philadelphia Inquirer*, February 28, 1968; Corr, "Negro Parents." Corr, in an apparent reference to D'Ortona, later wrote, "These are the people who, when a riot or other disturbance occurs, blame the 'lawless element,' or 'Communists' or 'outside agitators.' One thing Philadelphia does not need," Corr concluded, referring to the depth of anger at Gratz over the resources issue, "is 'outside' agitators." See Corr, "Crummy? Marcus Foster Proves 'Gratz Is Great'"; D'Ortona's "Niggeria" comment is cited in Decker, *An Empty Spoon*, 83.

85. Foster, *Making Schools Work*, 143.

86. John P. Corr and George Ingram, "Razing of 14 Homes Voted for Gratz High Expansion," *Philadelphia Inquirer*, February 27, 1968; "School Board to Go Ahead on Gratz Plan"; Foster, *Making Schools Work*, 143.

87. Alfred Klimcke, "Negro Leaders Hail Gratz High 'Victory,'" *Philadelphia Inquirer*, February 27, 1968; Foster, *Making Schools Work*, 144.

88. McGinnis, "A Victory for Gratz High"; Foster, *Making Schools Work*, 144–45.

89. George Ingram, "Gratz Called Negro Milestone," *Philadelphia Inquirer*, March 10, 1968, *Bulletin* file, "Simon Gratz High School," TUUA.

90. See Chapter 3.

91. Klimcke, "Negro Leaders."

92. Foster, *Making Schools Work*, 132, 138.

93. Medsger, "'Tell It Like It Is'; "Survival at Stake in Cities, Foster Says in Swarthmore," *Bulletin*, March 14, 1968.

94. "3 in Teacher Corps Urge Approval of Gratz Addition," *Bulletin*, February 22, 1968. Foster, *Making Schools Work*, 134.

95. Foster, *Making Schools Work*, 134; Laura Murray, "3,000 Pupils Cheer Foster at Dedication of Gratz Unit," *Bulletin*, February 16, 1972. Foster attended the Gratz ceremony as a visitor, having by that time moved to Oakland.

96. Resnik, *Turning on the System*, 139.

97. Countryman, *Up South*, 247–55.

98. J. Brantley Wilder, "New Program Lowers Rate of Dropouts at Gratz High School," *Philadelphia Tribune*, November 18, 1967, 3.

99. "'Go for Gratz' March Planned Saturday to Convince Pupils to Stay in School," *Philadelphia Inquirer*, January 9, 1969; Betty Medsger, "Gratz Fields 79 Teams to Bring Back Dropouts," *Bulletin*, January 12, 1969; Martin Weston, "Gratz Principal Given $15,000 Phila. Award," *Bulletin*, April 8, 1969.

100. Foster, *Making Schools Work*, 20–22.

101. The funders included white business leaders, the professional fraternity Sigma Pi Phi, and the Black Coalition, an umbrella community organization headed by Black Power activist Stanley Branche. "$21,000 Grant to Aid Programs at Gratz," *Philadelphia Inquirer*, June 18, 1968; and David J. Umansky, "Gratz Project, Funded by Black Coalition, Gets Started," *Philadelphia Inquirer*, April 24, 1969. Foster also conceived a campaign to bring Gratz graduates of the 1930s and 1940s together with those of 1968 in order to "end the growing polarization of the races"—and to generate scholarship money and job opportunities. Most of the earlier grads were Jews who had had little to do with their alma mater since it had become a predominantly black school. With Foster's encouragement, they now began supporting it with time and money. Martin Weston, "Gratz Alumni Are Urged to Give Talents to School," *Bulletin*, March 20, 1969.

102. William C. Green, "Simon Gratz Hi School Changes Are Now Being Seen, Felt, Heard," *Philadelphia Tribune*, February 24, 1968; Corr, "Crummy? Marcus Foster Proves 'Gratz Is Great'";

Carol Innerst, "Gratz Sets Records, Sends 100 on to College," *Bulletin,* May 5, 1968; Weston, "Gratz Principal Given $15,000."

103. Weston, "Gratz Principal Given $15,000."

104. Decker, *An Empty Spoon,* 5, 27, 44–45, 111–15.

105. Weston, "Gratz Principal Given $15,000."

106. Blackburn interview, March 5, 1998.

107. For a useful discussion of the rise of the "excellence" agenda in the 1980s, including the critique of 1960s-era priorities, see Wayne Urban and Jennings L. Wagoner, Jr., *American Education: A History* (New York: McGraw-Hill, 2004), 354–58.

108. Daniel J. McKenna, "Foster Sees Public Interest as 'Critical' Problem for Philadelphia Schools," *Bulletin,* May 27, 1969.

109. Jack Smyth, "Foster Calls for Innovation to Stem Unrest," *Bulletin,* March 11, 1970.

110. William K. Mandel, "Gang Victim's Mother Asks Solution to Street Violence," *Bulletin,* December 17, 1969; Albert V. Gaudiosi, "Gang Fighting Here 'Unique,' Expert Says," *Evening Bulletin,* July 8, 1969; "Return of the Rumble," *Newsweek,* September 8, 1969, 51–52.

111. Smyth, "Foster Calls for Innovation"; Foster, *Making Schools Work,* 16–17.

111. "Blank Shots Frighten Schoolmen," *Bulletin,* February 23, 1970.

113. Robert Rafsky, "'Good Schools Up to You,' Official Tells 1,000 Parents," *Bulletin,* October 29, 1969.

114. Podair, *The Strike That Changed New York;* Perlstein, *Justice, Justice.*

115. Resnik, *Turning on the System,* 15.

116. Harry G. Toland, "Schools Plan Carefully on Decentralization," *Bulletin,* August 25 1969; Rafsky, "'Good Schools Up to You.'"

117. Toland, "Schools Plan Carefully"; Robert Rafsky, "'Poor People Are Not Dumb. It's Just That Their Energies Are Drained in Making It,'" *Bulletin,* March 1, 1970.

118. Marcus Foster, commencement address, Downington High School, Pennsylvania, June 15, 1969, tape recording in possession of the author.

119. Foster's remarks in these various speeches echoed the ideas Shedd had held about decentralization all along. In 1967, for instance, when Shedd announced his plans for decentralization, he emphasized participation and partnership, as opposed to control by the community. "[Decentralization] is a way to use and channel the interest and the talent of the community," he said, "to form an alliance, a compact with those the schools serve . . . We must reach out and create the kind of relationship with the community . . . which will make a harmonious partnership possible." Corr, "Shedd's Bombshell."

120. Foster, *Making Schools Work,* 52–57; "Lord Refuses to Supersede State Court," *Bulletin,* November 4, 1969; John T. Gillespie, "Fishman to Remain at School," *Bulletin,* November 11, 1969.

121. Foster, *Making Schools Work,* 57–60.

122. Resnik, *Turning on the System,* 134; Les Payne and Tim Findley, *The Life and Death of the SLA* (New York: Ballantine Books, 1976), 153–54.

123. Foster, *Making Schools Work,* 60.

124. "Phila. Award Winner Hits 'Staid Concepts' in Educational Field," *Philadelphia Inquirer,* April 8, 1969, *Bulletin File,* "Marcus Foster"; Margaret Halsey, "60% of Grads Are Illiterate, Foster Says," *Bulletin,* April 13, 1970.

125. Foster, Swarthmore High School; Foster, Downington High School. For an example of the emerging legal argument for "positive discrimination," see David Kirp, "The Poor, the Schools, and Equal Protection," in *Equal Educational Opportunity* (Cambridge, Mass.: Harvard University Press, 1969.).

126. Foster, Swarthmore High School; Foster, Downington High School; Halsey, "60% of Grads Are Illiterate."

127. Foster, Swarthmore High School; Halsey, "60% of Grads Are Illiterate."

128. McGinnis, "A Victory for Gratz High"; John Gillespie, "Marcus Foster of Gratz Gets New School Post," *Bulletin*, May 26, 1969.

129. Untitled clipping, June 15, 1969, *Bulletin* file, "Marcus Foster"; "Phila. Award Winner Hits 'Staid Concepts.'"

130. Leon Frisby, telephone interview by the author, September 27, 1999, tape recording in possession of the author.

131. Leon Frisby, telephone interviews by the author, April 25, 2000 and December 16, 2000, tape recordings in possession of the author. Albertine Ramseur Foster and Marsha Foster Boyd did not wish to be interviewed.

132. Frisby interviews, April 25, 2000 and December 16, 2000.

133. Robert Blackburn, telephone interview by the author, January 21, 2002, tape recording in possession of the author.

134. Leon Frisby, telephone interview by the author, October 4, 1999, tape recording in possession of the author.

135. Blackburn interview, March 5, 1998; Frederick Willman, "Developing a Sense of Community: A Report on the Master Plan of the Oakland Unified School District" (New York: Rockefeller Foundation, 1975), 19.

136. Harry G. Toland, "A Philadelphia Optimist Finds Honor 'in the Field,'" *Bulletin*, June 14, 1970.

Chapter 5

1. "Here's Breakdown of Census Figures," *Oakland Tribune*, March 4, 1971; Larry Spears, "How Oakland Handles Education of Minorities," *Oakland Tribune*, August 11, 1968.

2. David Kirp, *Just Schools: The Idea of Racial Inequality in American Education* (Berkeley: University of California Press, 1982), 220.

3. Kirp, *Just Schools*, 220–41.

4. "OEDC Blasts School Tax," *Oakland Tribune*, May 29, 1969; "Uproar Follows Offer to Black Superintendent," *Montclarion*, October 20, 1969; "Meeting on Mason Selection," *Oakland Tribune*, May 17, 1969; "Community Groups Pledge Help to School Plan," *Montclarion*, November 15, 1969.

5. For a detailed account of Foster's tenure in Oakland, see Jesse J. McCorry, *Marcus Foster and the Oakland Public Schools: Leadership in an Urban Bureaucracy* (Berkeley: University of California Press, 1978). McCorry's book originated as a political science dissertation that drew upon direct observation of Foster in numerous meetings of his cabinet, and as such is the most substantial work on Foster's superintendency. However, in approaching Foster's superintendency as a case study of theories of organizational change, McCorry generally does not emphasize his educational ideas, nor does he analyze the significance of those approaches in relation to the era's polarized debates over race and urban education.

6. For a prominent critique of "equity to excellence," see the four-part PBS documentary and companion volume *School: The Story of American Public Education* (Boston: Beacon Press, 2001). For a more celebratory version of this narrative, see Koret Task Force on K–12 Education, "Are We Still At Risk," *Education Next*, Spring 2003, http://educationnext.org/are-we-still-at-risk/ (accessed September 1, 2011). See also note 23, Introduction to the present volume.

7. For an account that does trace recent accountability movements to the late 1960s, see Larry Cuban, "Looking Through the Rearview Mirror at School Accountability," in Kenneth A. Sirotnik, *Holding Accountability Accountable: What Ought to Matter in Public Education* (New York: Teachers College Press, 2004), 18–34. Cuban perceptively examines the rising influence of business managerial trends on education as well as increased governmental attention to policy evaluation in the wake of the new Elementary and Secondary Education Act (ESEA) of 1965; he does not, however, explore the influence of urban African American educators and activists on the emerging

interest in educational "outcomes." For a contemporary critique of the 1970s-era developments that Cuban analyzes, see also Don T. Martin, George E. Overholt, and Wayne Urban, *Accountability in American Education: A Critique* (Princeton, N.J.: Princeton Book Company, 1975).

8. See, for example, "Text: President Bush's Acceptance Speech to the Republican National Convention," *Washington Post*, September 2, 2004, http://www.washingtonpost.com/wp-dyn/articles/A57466-2004Sep2.html (accessed September 1, 2011). In 2011, President Obama stated that educational inequality and achievement gaps are the "civil rights issue of our time." Helene Cooper, "Obama Takes Aim at Inequality in Education," *New York Times*, April 6, 2011, http://www.ny-times.com/2011/04/07/us/politics/07obama.html?_r=1&emc=tnt&tntemail1=y (accessed September 1, 2011).

9. Amory Bradford, *Oakland's Not for Burning* (New York: David McKay Company, 1968), 36.

10. Marilynn Johnson, *The Second Gold Rush: Oakland and the East Bay in World War II* (Berkeley: University of California Press, 1993), 18; Edward C. Hayes, *Power Structure and Urban Policy: Who Rules in Oakland?* (New York: McGraw-Hill, 1972).

11. J. M. Regal, "Oakland's Partnership for Change" (Oakland, California: Department of Human Resources, 1967), 3; "Civic Action Brings Tops in U.S. Citation," *Oakland Tribune*, December 28, 1956; "Citizens Make Oakland a Wonderful Place," Application for All-America City Award, Subject Files, "City Planning," Professional Library, Oakland Unified School District (OUSD).

12. Johnson, *The Second Gold Rush*; Robert O. Self, *American Babylon: Race and the Struggle for Postwar Oakland* (Princeton, N.J.: Princeton University Press, 2003). On other cities, see also Thomas J. Sugrue, *The Origins of the Urban Crisis: Race and Inequality in Postwar Detroit* (Princeton, N.J.: Princeton University Press, 1996) and Arnold R. Hirsch, "Massive Resistance in the Urban North: Trumbull Park, Chicago, 1953–1966," *Journal of American History* 82, no. 2 (1995): 522–50.

13. Mayor's Committee on the White House Conference, "White House Conference on Children and Youth: Resource Book" (Oakland, Calif.: Council of Community Services, 1960), 10–11; Oakland History Room (OHR), Oakland Public Library; Wayne E. Thompson, "Law Enforcement Is Everyone's Business" (paper presented at the Seventh Annual Institute on Police and Community Relations, University of Southern California, February 6, 1964), 9, Grant #07200042, R. 2944, Ford Foundation Archives (FFA).

14. Quoted in Judith May, "Struggle for Authority: A Comparison of Four Social Change Programs in Oakland" (Ph.D. diss., University of California, Berkeley, 1973), 92.

15. The Mayor and City Council of Oakland et al., "Proposal to the Ford Foundation for a Program of Community Development" (Oakland, Calif., 1961), 3, Oakland Public Library.

16. Wayne E. Thompson, "City's War on 'People Problems' Unites Agencies," *Public Management* (September 1965): 212; Peter Marris and Martin Rein, *Dilemmas of Social Reform: Poverty and Community Action in the United States* (New York: Atherton Press, 1967), 18–19; The Mayor and City Council, "Proposal to the Ford Foundation," 3.

17. The Mayor and City Council, "Proposal to the Ford Foundation," 3, 9, 13, 19–20; Marris and Rein, *Dilemmas of Social Reform*, 56.

18. The Mayor and City Council, "Proposal to the Ford Foundation," 21; Regal, "Oakland's Partnership for Change," 42–49. Regal's Ford-funded study was a history and evaluation of Oakland's Gray Areas Project. His evaluations of the school programs synthesized what he considered a rigorous, though not definitive, body of in-house evaluations conducted by the Oakland Public Schools.

19. Regal, "Oakland's Partnership for Change," 99.

20. Self, *American Babylon*; Gretchen Lemke-Santangelo, "Capital Flight and Urban Resistance in Oakland, California, 1945–1996" (paper presented at the annual meeting of the Organization of American Historians, April 1997).

21. Self, *American Babylon*.

22. Robert Crain, *The Politics of School Desegregation* (Chicago: Aldine Publishing Co., 1968); Ira M. Heyman, "Oakland," in *Civil Rights U.S.A.: Public Schools: Cities in the North and West:*

1963 (Washington, D.C.: United States Commission on Civil Rights, 1983); and Kirp, *Just Schools,* 220–26.

23. An excellent account of the rise and fall of the Oakland desegregation movement can be found in Kirp, *Just Schools,* 220–41.

24. "New York School Plan Urged in Oakland," *Oakland Tribune,* November 5, 1968.

25. Tom Nash, "Parents Probe Local High School Staff," *California Voice,* May 24, 1957; "Attempt to 'Whitewash' Mack Failing," *California Voice,* June 7, 1957; Raymond Lawrence, "At Home and Abroad," *Oakland Tribune,* September 14, 1957. For its part, the executive board of the McClymonds Parent Teacher Association defended the school and stressed that parents were responsible for the success of their children. See "Mack P-TA Executive Board Answers 'Negligence Charge,'" *California Voice,* May 31, 1957.

26. Rex H. Turner and George T. McKee, "High School Planned to Serve Youths and Adults in a Low-Rent Community," *Nation's Schools* 49, no. 6 (June 1952): 62–64, Subject Files, "McClymonds," OUSD; Regal, "Oakland's Partnership for Change," 50–51.

27. Ad Hoc Committee for Quality Education in Oakland, "A Report on the Oakland Schools: Part I," December 1966, Subject Files, "Integration," OHR.

28. "Bussing No Answer for Unequal Schools—*Flatlands* Interviews Flatlands Parents," *Flatlands,* September 24–October 8, 1966; "Oakland Schools' Forgotten Kids," *Flatlands,* September 24–October 8, 1966; Regal, "Oakland's Partnership for Change," 49–50.

29. "Widespread Tries to Block Violence," *Oakland Tribune,* October 26, 1966; Commission on Equal Opportunities in Education, "Report Concerning Disturbances in East Oakland on October 19, 1966," n.d., Subject Files, "Citizens Council on Human Relations, 1965," OUSD.

30. Clemson N. Page, Jr., "'We've No Shortage of Issue-Raisers,' Judge Higginbotham Tells Educators," *Philadelphia Evening Bulletin* (hereafter referred to as *Bulletin*), June 30, 1970.

31. "Controversy in Black," *Montclarion,* April 15, 1970, Subject File, "Blacks: Black Caucus," OHR.

32. "Controversy in Black"; Peggy Stinnett, "Educator Expresses Views on Education: An Interview with Marcus Foster," *Montclarion,* April 6, 1970.

33. "Solid Support for New School Chief," *Oakland Tribune,* April 9, 1970; "Oakland's Black Leaders Support Marcus A. Foster," *Post,* April 16, 1970.

34. Stinnett, "Educator Expresses Views"; Bev Mitchell, "New School Chief Urges Integration," *Oakland Tribune,* April 5, 1970.

35. Stinnett, "Educator Expresses Views"; Mitchell, "New School Chief Urges Integration."

36. Robert Blackburn, interviewed by the author at Blackburn's home in Oakland, Calif., March 5, 1998 and November 20, 1997, tape recordings in possession of the author.

37. Stinnett, "Educator Expresses Views"; Albertine Foster to Leon and Mabel Frisby, November 2, 1970, personal collection of Leon Frisby.

38. Blackburn, private e-mail message to the author, August 5, 2011.

39. "Memo to Robert Blackburn from Marc Foster," personal collection of Robert Blackburn.

40. Blackburn interview, March 5, 1998.

41. Marcus A. Foster, *Making Schools Work: Strategies for Changing Education* (Philadelphia: Westminster Press, 1971), 16–17, 21.

42. Marcus A. Foster, "Oakland's Time Is Now," speech to certificated staff, Oakland, California, September 10, 1970, tape recording in possession of the author. For a modified version of the speech, see Foster, *Making Schools Work,* ch. 12.

43. Foster, "Oakland's Time Is Now."

44. Cuban, "Looking Through the Rearview Mirror"; Martin, Overholt, and Urban, *Accountability in American Education.*

45. Foster, "Oakland's Time Is Now."

46. Foster, "Oakland's Time Is Now."

47. Foster, "Oakland's Time Is Now." New Notions for Excellence was Foster's attempt to replicate Philadelphia's "creative teacher" grants and, in particular, the ways in which that grant program had stimulated innovation at his own Gratz High School.

48. Foster, "Oakland's Time Is Now."

49. "Board Agrees to Master Planning," *Montclarion,* March 18, 1970; Foster, *Making Schools Work,* 150; Letter to Joshua L. Smith from Marcus Foster, May 18, 1971, Grant #07200042, R. 1303, sec. 1, FFA; "Background," n.d., Grant #07200042, R. 1303, sec. 1, FFA.

50. Albertine Foster to Leon and Mabel Frisby.

51. Frederick Willman, "Developing a Sense of Community: A Report on the Master Plan of the Oakland Unified School District" (New York: Rockefeller Foundation, 1975), 3, 7, 26; Memorandum to the Files from Joshua L. Smith, "Close-out Memorandum, Oakland Unified School District," January 24, 1975, Grant #07200042, R. 1303, sec. 3, FFA; "Background," 5; David Holmstrom, "Oakland Rolls Up Educational Sleeves," *Christian Science Monitor,* December 11, 1971.

52. Willman, "Developing a Sense of Community," 4.

53. "Background," 3–4.

54. Willman, "Developing a Sense of Community," 6–7.

55. Report to Joshua L. Smith from Marcus Foster, February 13, 1973, 3, Grant #07200042, R. 1303, sec. 1, FFA; Richard A. Lacey to the Files, "Master Plan Citizens Committee (MPCC)," December 27, 1972, Grant #07200042, R. 1303, sec. 4, FFA.

56. McCorry, *Marcus Foster and the Oakland Public Schools,* 52–54; Willman, "Developing a Sense of Community," 6; Robert Blackburn to Marcus Foster, December 12, 1971, personal collection of Robert Blackburn.

57. Larry Wood, "A School System That Beat Apathy," *Christian Science Monitor,* August 26, 1974; Robert Blackburn, telephone conversation with the author, March 23, 2002.

58. Report to Smith from Foster, 3.

59. Smith, "Close-out Memorandum"; Kirp, *Just Schools,* 244–45.

60. Kirp, *Just Schools,* 244–45. Kirp's interpretation is in some ways echoed in Gary Yee, "Miracle Workers Wanted: Executive Succession and Organizational Change in an Urban School District" (Ed.D. diss., Stanford University, 1996), 91. Yee suggests, based on oral history interviews with teachers and administrators who worked with Foster, that "his curriculum and instructional reforms were much less clearly defined" than his efforts in the area of community involvement.

61. Daniel Bell and Virginia Held, "The Community Revolution," *Public Interest* 16 (Summer 1969): 158; Mitchell, "New School Chief Urges Integration."

62. Oakland Unified School District, "Supt. Foster Praises Staff for Helping Write Educational History," *Superintendent's Bulletin* 52, no. 1 (September 20, 1971): 6; Blackburn to Foster, December 12, 1971.

63. Blackburn to Foster, December 12, 1971; Thomas Hine, "Foster Finds Pressure Works in Oakland, Too," *Philadelphia Inquirer,* April 1972.

64. Marcus Foster, commencement address, Swarthmore High School, Pennsylvania, June 9, 1969, tape recording in possession of the author.

65. Frank Levy, Arnold J. Meltsner, and Aaron Wildavsky, *Urban Outcomes: Schools, Streets, and Libraries* (Berkeley: University of California Press, 1974), 67–90; Ray Giles, "Educational Methods Examined by Foster," *Sun-Star,* April 27, 1972.

66. "Oakland School Problems Aired," *Oakland Tribune,* May 12, 1968.

67. Levy, Meltsner, and Wildavsky, *Urban Outcomes,* 30.

68. James Buchanan, "Taxpayer Constraints on Financing Education," in *Economic Factors Affecting the Financing of Education,* ed. Roe Johns et al. (Gainesville, Fla.: National Education Finance Project, 1970), 265, 287, cited in Betsy Levin et al., *Public School Finance: Present Disparities and Fiscal Alternatives* (Washington, D.C.: Urban Institute, 1972), 2.

69. Levin et al., *Public School Finance,* 2.

70. "Oakland, Calif. 'At the Crossroads,'" *Newsweek,* September 13, 1971; McCorry, *Marcus Foster and the Oakland Public Schools,* 67–68; Blackburn to Foster, December 12, 1971.

71. The focus on metropolitan inequities was not entirely new; in studying the Chicago school system for the U.S. Civil Rights Commission in the mid-1960s, for instance, lawyer John Coons decided he was "asking the wrong question; the really large differences in expenditures were not between black and white schools in Chicago, but between Chicago schools and suburban schools." Quoted in Milbrey McLaughlin and Richard Elmore, *Reform and Retrenchment: The Politics of California School Finance Reform* (Cambridge, Mass.: Ballinger Publishing Co., 1982), 28.

72. Quoted in Lou Cannon, *Reagan* (New York: G. P. Putnam's Sons, 1982), 166.

73. Oakland Unified School District, "Supt. Foster Notes Progress; Calls 1972–73 'Year of Achievement,'" *Superintendent's Bulletin* 53, no. 1 (September–October 1972): 12–13. On the Marcus Foster Education Fund, see "About > History," http://www.marcusfoster.org/ (accessed August 10, 2011).

74. Oakland Unified School District, "Supt. Foster Notes Progress," 12–13.

75. Joshua L. Smith, "Close-out Memorandum"; Lacey, "Master Plan Citizens Committee"; Report to Smith from Foster, February 13, 1973. On the Ford Foundation's work in school finance reform, see Elmore and McLaughlin, *Reform and Retrenchment,* 61; and Richard Magat, *The Ford Foundation at Work: Philanthropic Choices, Methods, and Styles* (New York: Plenum Press, 1979), 144–46.

76. Blackburn interview, November 20, 1997.

77. Kenneth Hall, quoted in Elmore and McLaughlin, *Reform and Retrenchment,* 97–98.

78. Marcus Foster, "Child of the Poor, Looking for Mitochondria," in *Readings in Curriculum and Supervision,* ed. V. Eugene Yarbrough, William C. Bruce, and Ronald L. Hubright (New York: MSS Information Corporation, 1974), 57.

79. Foster, "Child of the Poor," 57.

80. Holmstrom, "Oakland Rolls Up Educational Sleeves"; Willman, "Developing a Sense of Community," 29; Yee, "Miracle Workers Wanted," 84.

81. John Gillespie, "An Odd Choice by Mr. Rizzo," *Bulletin,* November 11, 1971; and Daniel J. McKenna, "Rizzo Wants Foster to Head Phila. Schools," *Bulletin,* November 7, 1971, *Bulletin* clippings file, "Marcus Foster," Temple University Urban Archives (TUUA); "'I'll Stay in Oakland,' Foster Says," *Oakland Tribune,* November 7, 1971.

82. "Black Educator's Angry Message," *San Francisco Chronicle,* March 21, 1973; "School Chief Hits Black Power Myth," *Oakland Tribune,* March 21, 1973.

83. Marcus A. Foster, "Schools Are Improving," *Oakland Tribune,* April 3, 1973.

84. Regal, "Oakland's Partnership for Change"; Christopher Jencks et al., *Inequality: A Reassessment of the Effect of Family and Schooling in America* (New York: Basic Books, 1972). Among many subsequent works that have emphasized the limits of schooling as a means of social reform, see David F. Labaree, *Someone Has to Fail: The Zero-Sum Game of Public Schooling* (Cambridge, Mass.: Harvard University Press, 2010); Jean Anyon, *Ghetto Schooling: A Political Economy of Urban Educational Reform* (New York: Teachers College Press, 1997); Richard Rothstein, *Class and Schools: Using Social, Economic, and Educational Reform to Close the Black-White Achievement Gap* (Washington, D.C.: Economic Policy Institute, 2004); Harvey Kantor and Barbara Brenzel, "Urban Education and the Truly Disadvantaged: The Historical Roots of the Contemporary Crisis, 1945–1990," in *The Underclass Debate: Views from History,* ed. Michael B. Katz (Princeton, N.J.: Princeton University Press, 1993), 366–402; and Michael B. Katz, "Education and Inequality: A Historical Perspective," in *Social History and Social Policy,* ed. David J. Rothman and Stanton Wheeler (New York: Academic Press, 1981), 57–101.

85. "Black Educator's Angry Message"; "School Chief Hits Black Power Myth."

86. Arthur Jensen, "How Much Can We Boost IQ and Scholastic Achievement? *Harvard Educational Review* 39 (1969): 1–123. On at least one other occasion Foster had chided the conclusions of an unnamed "U.C. Berkeley professor"; see Giles, "Educational Methods Examined by Foster."

87. Foster, "Child of the Poor," 59–60.

88. Bev Mitchell and Richard Paoli, "Letter of Foster's Killers Cites Little-Known Facts," *Oakland Tribune,* November 11, 1973; James S. Tunnell, "Foster Had Tough Streak; It Was Hurting Black Radicals," *Bulletin,* November 11, 1973, *Bulletin* file, "Marcus Foster," TUUA.

89. *The Black Panther,* October 13, 1973.

90. Blackburn interview, November 20, 1997.

91. Tunnell, "Foster Had Tough Streak"; "How Schools Will Deal with Problem of Juvenile Crime," *Montclarion,* September 12, 1973.

92. A watered-down version of the police-in-schools idea had been advocated by the California Council on Criminal Justice (CCCJ), a group that was allied with the Alameda County Grand Jury. The school district was slated to receive $275,000 of the funds for its new security proposal from the CCCJ. Just before he was scheduled to present the proposal at the October 9 board meeting, Foster discovered, to his chagrin, that the CCCJ had modified what supposedly had been a final draft, adding a requirement that the new civilian security aides have a background in law enforcement. Foster caught the change just in time to remove the security proposal from the board meeting agenda, though the draft in question already had been released to the public, thus adding to the controversy and misunderstanding that surrounded the plan. See Vin McLellan and Paul Avery, *The Voices of Guns: The SLA in History* (New York: Putnam, 1977), 141–43.

93. "Foster Calls for Change: New Attitude on Cops," *Montclarion,* September 12, 1973.

94. "Foster Calls for Change," 143; "Community Unites Around Teacher's [*sic*] Demands," *The Black Panther,* October 20, 1973.

95. Blackburn interview, November 20, 1997.

96. McLellan and Avery, *Voices of Guns,* 68–69. DeFreeze was transferred out of Vacaville before the Oakland schools controversy exploded among the inmates, but he remained in contact with another prisoner, Thero Wheeler, who was greatly affected by the issue and who escaped and joined the SLA in the fall of 1973 (as its only other black member), only to break with DeFreeze over the decision to murder Foster. See also Les Payne and Tim Findley, *The Life and Death of the SLA* (New York: Ballantine Books, 1976), 16, on how Silverman "allegedly voiced her outrage on a visit to Vacaville" and SLA members discussed the schools controversy "in group session with their convict buddies."

97. Payne and Findley, *Life and Death of the SLA,* 166.

98. Fran Dauth, "An Eloquent Plea Before His Death," *Oakland Tribune,* November 7, 1973; "November 6, 1973: It Began as Typical Day," *Montclarion,* November 14, 1973.

99. In 1974, two men—Russell Little and Joseph Remiro—were convicted of killing Foster. Little was later acquitted in a retrial. Little has since stated that DeFreeze's accomplices in the attack on Foster and Blackburn were Patricia "Mizmoon" Soltysik and Nancy Ling Perry; see Robert Stone, director, *Guerrilla: The Taking of Patty Hearst,* 2004, transcript available at http://www.pbs.org/ wgbh/amex/guerrilla/filmmore/pt.html (accessed September 1, 2011). Russell's statement was corroborated by Patty Hearst's testimony in court, based on what she said SLA members Bill and Emily Harris had told her. McClellan and Avery, *Voices of Guns,* 131–32.

100. McLellan and Avery, *Voices of Guns,* 129.

101. McLellan and Avery, *Voices of Guns,* 132–36; The Editors, "The Symbionese Liberation Army: Terrorism and the Left," *Ramparts,* May 1974, 21–27.

102. Bob Blackburn laments that as former SLA members have come out of hiding or been retried in recent years, media accounts of the group continue to focus only on the Hearst kidnapping and all but ignore "the two primary victims": Foster and Myrna Opsahl, a bystander killed during a 1975 SLA bank robbery. See Guy Ashley, "SLA's Forgotten Victims," *Contra Costa Times/West County Times,* January 28, 2002; and Peggy Stinnett, "Justice for SLA Overdue," *Oakland Tribune,* January 18, 2002.

103. James W. Guthrie, "Marcus A. Foster: Tribute and Reflection," *Phi Delta Kappan,* February

1974, 414; Ishmael Reed, "The Writer as Seer: Ishmael Reed on Ishmael Reed," in *Conversations with Ishmael Reed,* ed. Bruce Dick and Amritjit Singh (Jackson: University Press of Mississippi, 1995), 65; "Leaders Pay Tribute to Marcus A. Foster," *Oakland Tribune,* November 8, 1973. For Silverman's remark, see Earl Caldwell, "Killings in Oakland Turn Air of Optimism into One of Rising Fear," *New York Times,* November 20, 1973.

104. Mark Manoff, "Foster Hailed by 5,000 at Gratz," *Bulletin,* November 17, 1973; "Memorial Services for Marcus A. Foster," November 16, 1973, personal collection of Leon Frisby.

105. Bev Mitchell and Andy Jokelson, "'Pray for the Assassins,' Foster's Widow Pleads," *Oakland Tribune,* November 13, 1973; "Foster Fund Grows, Messages Pour In," *Montclarion,* December 12, 1973.

106. Tunnell, "Foster Had Tough Streak"; Guthrie, "Marcus A. Foster."

107. Robert Blackburn, private e-mail message to the author, November 24, 2004.

Epilogue

1. Arthur Jensen had revived the idea of inherited intellectual differences between blacks and whites in his notorious 1968 article in the *Harvard Educational Review,* and his hereditarian ideas were later echoed in Richard Herrnstein and Charles Murray's best-selling book, *The Bell Curve: Intelligence and Class Structure in American Life* (New York: Free Press, 1994). In the 1990s, Herrnstein received standing ovations from white audiences at presentations of *The Bell Curve;* see Lisa D. Delpit, commentary in "Saving Public Education," *Nation* 264, no. 6 (February 17, 1997): 20.

2. Arne Duncan, "States Will Lead the Way Toward Reform," Remarks at the 2009 Governors Education Symposium, June 14, 2009, http://www.ed.gov/news/speeches/states-will-lead-way-toward-reform (accessed August 16, 2011).

3. John Merrow, Richard Foster, and Nolan Estes, *The Urban School Superintendent of the Future* (Durant, Okla.: Southeastern Foundation, 1974), 3–4.

4. Marcus Foster, "Child of the Poor, Looking for Mitochondria," in *Readings in Curriculum and Supervision,* ed. V. Eugene Yarbrough, William C. Bruce, and Ronald L. Hubright (New York: MSS Information Corporation, 1974), 59.

5. Pedro A. Noguera, "Racial Isolation, Poverty, and the Limits of Local Control in Oakland," *Teachers College Record* 106, no. 11 (2004): 2151.

6. For different views on the Ebonics controversy, see Theresa Perry and Lisa Delpit, eds., "The Real Ebonics Debate: A Special Issue of Rethinking Schools," *Rethinking Schools* 12, no. 1 (Fall 1997); John H. McWhorter, *Losing the Race: Self-Sabotage in Black America* (New York: Free Press, 2000), 184–211; and Peter Applebome, "Dispute over Ebonics Reflects a Volatile Mix That Roils Urban Education," *New York Times,* March 1, 1997.

7. Joe Williams, "National Model or Temporary Opportunity: The Oakland Education Reform Story" (Washington, D.C.: Center for Education Reform, 2007), http://www.edreform.com/Archive/?National_Model_or_Temporary_Opportunity_The_Oakland_Education_Reform_Story (accessed August 16, 2011); Roberta Furger, "Oakland's Big Plans: Small-School Reform," *Edutopia,* April 29, 2003, http://www.edutopia.org/oaklands-big-plans-small-schools (accessed August 16, 2011); Seema Shah, Kavitha Mediratta, and Sara McAlister, "Building a Districtwide Small Schools Movement" (Providence, R.I.: Annenberg Institute for School Reform, 2009), http://www.piconetwork.org/ocosmallschools (accessed August 16, 2011).

8. Ash Vasudeva, Linda Darling-Hammond, Stephen Newton, and Kenneth Montgomery, *Oakland Unified School District: New Small Schools Initiative Evaluation* (Stanford: School Redesign Network at Stanford University, 2009), http://www.srnleads.org/resources/publications/ousd/ousd.html (accessed August 16, 2011). The Stanford team's analysis was based on a measure of "productivity"—that is, a school's "capacity to *add value* to students' learning in ways that disrupt the traditional relationship between school outcomes and numerous variables and prior achievement." Taking into

account factors such as prior achievement, socioeconomic status, ethnicity, and English language learner status, the evaluators compared achievement for each student with the achievement of similar students in the Oakland Unified School District (OUSD) from 2002–3 through 2007–8. "Productive" schools produced achievement that was significantly higher than that of schools serving similar students.

9. "Oakland's Small Schools Movement, Ten Years Later," *Oakland Tribune*, May 6, 2009, http://www.oaklandcommunity.org/media-coverage?id=0001 (accessed August 16, 2011).

10. Williams, "National Model or Temporary Opportunity." See especially the section "Ten Lessons Learned from Oakland's Reforms," which is focused almost exclusively on matters of governance and accountability—saying little, by contrast, about curriculum and instruction.

11. Vasudeva et al., "Oakland Unified School District," ii–vi.

12. Noguera, "Racial Isolation," 2152, 2161–62. Noguera, a scholar with a deep immersion in Oakland schools and a documented dedication to ending achievement gaps, argues that "the simple fact is that the schools cannot serve the needs of Oakland's poorest children without greater support. Oakland residents need decent paying jobs, affordable housing, health care, and a variety of social services for the quality of life in the city to improve."

13. Jay Greene and William C. Symonds, "Bill Gates Gets Schooled," *Bloomberg Businessweek*, June 26, 2006, http://www.businessweek.com/magazine/content/06_26/b3990001.htm (accessed August 16, 2011).

14. William Raspberry, "An Academic Miracle at Gratz," *Washington Post*, October 22, 1975; Steve Twomey, "Lowly Simon Gratz High Takes a Giant Step Up," *Philadelphia Inquirer*, September 29, 1975, both articles from clippings file of the *Philadelphia Evening Bulletin* (hereafter referred to as *Bulletin*), "Oliver Lancaster," Temple University Urban Archives (hereafter TUUA). For other examples of leadership at Gratz since Foster's departure, see Fletcher J. Clarke, "New-Breed Principal Is Trying to Close Student-Teacher Gap," *Bulletin*, April 30, 1971, *Bulletin* file, "Fred Holliday," TUUA; Acel Moore, "'Doc' Big Brother to Gratz Students," *Philadelphia Inquirer*, September 16, 1970; Lezlie B. McCoy, "Gratz Welcomes Prince Andrew," *Philadelphia Tribune*, September 24, 2002; and Greg Johnson, "Simon Gratz High School Is a Hub of Learning," *Philadelphia Tribune*, February 21, 2006.

15. On the testing controversy and subsequent low achievement at Gratz, see Steve Twomey, "Gratz Teacher Gave Test Words to Pupils," *Bulletin*, October 30, 1975; Carole Rich, "Test Scores at Gratz High Fall in Year," *Bulletin*, July 24, 1976; Editorial, "Grading the Teacher," *Bulletin*, December 1, 1975. For other negative incidents, see "Phila. School Problem: Apathy, Not Violence," *Bulletin*, January 24, 1971; "Gratz HS Fire Seen as Arson," *Bulletin*, June 16, 1976; Laura Murray, "Gang War Again at Gratz," *Bulletin*, December 15, 1977; and Mary Bishop, Thomas Ferrick, Jr., and Donald Kimelman, "At Gratz, They Try to Overcome Rust, Rot, and Rain," *Philadelphia Inquirer*, September 3, 1981. All articles in *Bulletin* file, "Simon Gratz High School" and "Gratz High School, Editorials," TUUA.

16. Martha Woodall, "The Power and Passion of Constance Clayton," *Philadelphia Inquirer* magazine, September 13, 1987.

17. Woodall, "The Power and Passion"; William Celis, 3d, "Education Consultant Faces Career Challenge as Philadelphia School Chief," *New York Times*, March 22, 1995; Constance Clayton, "We Can Educate All Our Children," *Nation* 249, no. 4 (July 24–31, 1989): 132–35.

18. David Hornbeck, interviewed by the author in the Office of the Superintendent, Philadelphia Public Schools, April 25, 2000, tape recording in possession of the author; Mary B. W. Tabor, "Head of Philadelphia Schools Faces Battles on All Fronts," *New York Times*, July 24, 1996.

19. Robert C. Johnston, "Taking the High Road," *Education Week*, November 3, 1999; Susan Snyder, "Hornbeck: Too Little Money," *Philadelphia Inquirer*, June 6, 2000. For an overview of "Children Achieving" and the Hornbeck era, see William Lowe Boyd and Jolley Bruce Christman, "A Tall Order for Philadelphia's New Approach to School Governance: Heal the Political Rifts,

Close the Budget Gap, *and* Improve the Schools," in *Powerful Reforms with Shallow Roots: Improving America's Urban Schools,* ed. Larry Cuban and Michael Usdan (New York: Teacher's College Press, 2003), 96–124.

20. Eva Travers, "Philadelphia School Reform: Historical Roots and Reflections on the 2002–2003 School Year Under State Takeover," *Penn GSE Perspectives on Urban Education* 2, no. 2 (Fall 2003), http://urbanedjournal.org/archive/Issue4/commentaries/comment0007.html (accessed August 16, 2011); Ann Bradley, "Philadelphia Story," *Education Week,* February 19, 1997; John M. Baer, "Funding Still the Hot Issue," *Philadelphia Daily News,* June 6, 2000; Bob Warner, "'Toughest Job' to Air on Ch. 12," *Philadelphia Daily News,* June 6, 2000. For Hornbeck's extended reflections on "Children Achieving," and especially his emphasis on the importance of public will and "citizen accountability," see his book, *Choosing Excellence in Public Schools: Where There's a Will, There's a Way* (Lanham, Md.: Rowman & Littlefield Education, 2009).

21. Anthony S. Bryk et al., *Organizing Schools for Improvement: Lessons from Chicago* (Chicago: University of Chicago Press, 2010).

22. Jay Mathews, *Work Hard. Be Nice.: How Two Inspired Teachers Created the Most Promising Schools in America* (New York: Algonquin Books, 2009); Teach For America and Steven Farr, *Teaching as Leadership: The Highly Effective Teacher's Guide to Closing the Achievement Gap* (San Francisco: Jossey-Bass, 2010); Doug Lemov, *Teach Like a Champion: 49 Techniques That Put Students on the Path to College* (San Francisco: Jossey-Bass, 2010).

23. On the paramount importance, and difficulty, of improving teaching and learning in classrooms, see, for example, David Tyack and Larry Cuban, *Tinkering Toward Utopia: A Century of Public School Reform* (Cambridge, Mass.: Harvard University Press, 1995), 134–40; Larry Cuban, *As Good as It Gets: What School Reform Brought to Austin* (Cambridge, Mass.: Harvard University Press, 2010); and James W. Stigler and James Hiebert, *The Teaching Gap: Best Ideas from the World's Teachers for Improving Education in the Classroom* (New York: Free Press, 2009). On the special challenges of implementing reform in demoralized school environments, see Charles M. Payne, *So Much Reform, So Little Change: The Persistence of Failure in Urban Schools* (Cambridge, Mass.: Harvard Education Press, 2008).

24. Bryk et al., *Organizing Schools for Improvement,* 209–11. For another story of notable progress in urban school reform, marked nonetheless by limited results among the most underachieving students, see Cuban, *As Good as It Gets.*

25. Paul Tough, *Whatever It Takes: Geoffrey Canada's Quest to Change Harlem and America* (Boston: Houghton Mifflin, 2008).

26. For a generally positive evaluation of the impact of the Harlem Children's Zone, see Will Dobbie and Roland G. Fryer, Jr., "Are High-Quality Schools Enough to Close the Achievement Gap? Evidence from a Bold Social Experiment in Harlem" (April 2009), http://www.economics.harvard.edu/faculty/fryer/files/hcz%204.15.2009.pdf (accessed August 16, 2011). For a more critical assessment of the impact of the community services part of the HCZ, see Grover J. Whitehurst and Michelle Croft, "The Harlem Children's Zone, Promise Neighborhoods, and the Broader, Bolder Approach to Education" (Brown Center on Education Policy, Brookings Institute, July 20, 2010), http://www.brookings.edu/reports/2010/0720_hcz_whitehurst.aspx (accessed August 16, 2011). Whitehurst and Croft note that, while the HCZ "Promise Academy I" performed well in comparison with regular New York City schools, it was outperformed by other charter schools in New York City, including several KIPP schools. From this finding they conclude that "school-only" approaches are just as effective as, if not more than, the school-plus-community-services model practiced by HCZ. Their critique raises valid questions about the efficacy of the HCZ approach, relative to its cost. However, because their report goes to the heart of the debate over what schools can and cannot be expected to accomplish as agents of social advancement, it is important to note several potential flaws in their argument. Whitehurst and Croft present their conclusions as being "consistent with" available data, but they admit that they cannot make causal claims about the

effects of the different schools. That is, while they factor in the socioeconomic and racial/ethnic background of the students, there is no way to control for the key variable of parental motivation. Students in the HCZ and other charter schools may have similar demographic backgrounds, but within particular demographic categories, households may vary significantly in terms of motivation and cultural capital. As some analysts have suggested, parents who go to the trouble to seek out charters such as KIPP may be self-selected for educational success (especially in comparison with a program such as the HCZ, which aims to take in all students in a defined geographic area). In addition, as HCZ founder Geoffrey Canada points out, Whitehurst and Croft apply a narrow focus in their comparison, ignoring both Promise Academy II (which posted even more impressive test scores than Promise Academy I) and the fact that HCZ services are enjoyed not only by Promise Academy charter students, but by all students in the Zone, including those who attend traditional schools. See Geoffrey Canada, "The Harlem Children's Zone Response to the Brookings Institute's Report" (July 2010), http://www.hcz.org/images/stories/pdfs/Brookings%20Institute%20study%20response.pdf (accessed August 16, 2011).

27. Sharon Otterman, "Lauded Harlem Schools Have Their Own Problems," *New York Times*, October 12, 2010.

28. For an analysis that puts the Harlem Children's Zone and other education-based social programs in a broader context of liberal social policy approaches—including employment and welfare policies that were more widely accepted in the 1960s but are "off the table" now—see James T. Patterson, *Freedom Is Not Enough: The Moynihan Report and America's Struggle over Black Family Life—From LBJ to Obama* (New York: Basic Books, 2010), 209–12.

29. James Traub, "What No School Can Do," *New York Times Magazine*, January 16, 2000.

30. Education Equality Project, "Statement of Principles," http://www.educationequalityproject.org/pages/principles (accessed August 16, 2011). The Education Equality Project (EEP) was founded during the 2008 presidential campaign by a group of superintendents, political figures, and activists.

31. On the state takeover, see Travers, "Philadelphia School Reform"; and Boyd and Christman, "A Tall Order." On the origins of the experiment in privatization and "diverse providers," see Brian Gill, "Takeover Overtaken: Public Management of Philadelphia Schools Leaves Private Management Behind in Math," *Rand Review* 31, no. 1 (2007), http://www.rand.org/publications/randreview/issues/spring2007/takeover.html (accessed August 17, 2011); Susan Snyder and Martha Woodall, "42 Schools to Be Privatized," *Philadelphia Inquirer*, April 18, 2002; and William C. Kashatus, "Public Education in Private Hands," *New York Times*, February 2, 2002. On the rapid expansion of the charter school movement in Philadelphia, see Dale Mezzacappa, "Charter Boom: No End in Sight," *Notebook* 17, no. 6 (Summer 2010), http://www.thenotebook.org/summer-2010/102543/charter-boom-%E2%80%93-no-end-sight (accessed August 17, 2011).

32. Elizabeth Useem, Jolley Bruce Christman, and William Lowe Boyd, *The Role of District Leadership in Radical Reform: Philadelphia's Experience under the State Takeover, 2001–2006* (Philadelphia: Research for Action, July 2006), http://www.researchforaction.org/publication-listing/?id=258 (accessed August 17, 2011). See also Dale Mezzacappa, "The Vallas Effect: The Supersized Superintendent Moves to the Superdome City," *Education Next* (Spring 2008), http://educationnext.org/the-vallas-effect/ (accessed August 17, 2011).

33. Alan Vanneman et al., "Achievement Gaps: How Black and White Students in Public Schools Perform in Mathematics and Reading on the National Assessment of Educational Progress" (Washington, D.C.: U.S. Department of Education, 2009), http://nces.ed.gov/PUBSEARCH/pubsinfo.asp?pubid=2009455 (accessed August 17, 2011); Diane Ravitch, *The Death and Life of the Great American School System: How Testing and Choice Are Undermining Education* (New York: Basic Books, 2010), 102–3.

34. Mezzacappa, "The Vallas Effect"; Brian P. Gill, Ron Zimmer, Jolley Bruce Christman, and Suzanne Blanc, *Student Achievement in Privately Managed and District-Managed Schools in*

Philadelphia Since the State Takeover (Pittsburgh: RAND Corporation, 2007), http://www.rand.org/pubs/monographs/MG533.html (accessed August 17, 2011).

35. Michael Winerip, "The 'Zero Dropout' Miracle: Alas! Alack! A Texas Tall Tale," *New York Times,* August 13, 2003; Marisa de la Torre and Julia Gwynne, *When Schools Close: Effects on Displaced Students in Chicago Public Schools* (Chicago: Consortium on Chicago School Research, 2009), http://ccsr.uchicago.edu/content/publications.php?pub_id=136 (accessed August 17, 2011); Sam Dillon, "Report Questions Duncan's Policy of Closing Troubled Schools," *New York Times,* October 28, 2009; Sharon Otterman and Robert Gebeloff, "Triumph Fades on Racial Gap in City Schools," *New York Times,* August 15, 2010.

36. "Los Angeles Teacher Ratings," *Los Angeles Times,* http://projects.latimes.com/value-added/ (accessed August 17, 2011).

37. Kim Severson, "Systematic Cheating Is Found in Atlanta's School System," *New York Times,* July 5, 2011; Michael Winerip, "Pennsylvania Joins the List of States Facing a School Cheating Scandal," *New York Times,* August 1, 2011. Georgia investigators found the Atlanta cheating to be caused "primarily by the pressure to meet targets in the data-driven environment . . . A culture of fear, intimidation and retaliation existed in APS, which created a conspiracy of silence and deniability with respect to standardized test misconduct." "Deal Releases Findings of Atlanta School Probe," July 5, 2011, http://gov.georgia.gov/00/press/detail/0,2668,165937316_165937374_173112104,00.html (accessed August 17, 2011). In response to a *New York Times* editorial that stated, "It's the cheats who need to go, not the tests," the director of the organization FairTest cited the social scientific adage known as "Campbell's Law": "The more any quantitative social indicator is used for social decision making, the more subject it will be to corruption pressures, and the more apt it will be to distort and corrupt the social processes it is intended to monitor." Monty Neill, "Letter to the Editor," *New York Times,* July 18, 2011.

38. Benjamin Herold, "Mastery Ascends to National Stage," *Notebook,* February 23, 2011, http://www.thenotebook.org/blog/113377/mastery-ascends-national-stage (accessed August 16, 2011); Benjamin Herold, "Mastery's Big Gamble Set to Pay Off," *Notebook,* March 14, 2011, http://www.thenotebook.org/blog/113444/masterys-big-gamble-pays (accessed August 16, 2011). On the widely variable performance of charters nationwide, including a sixteen-state study showing that just 17 percent of charters outperformed traditional public schools, see various reports from Stanford University's Center for Research on Education Outcomes, available at http://credo.stanford.edu/ (accessed August 17, 2011).

39. Diane Ravitch, "Waiting for a School Miracle," *New York Times,* May 31, 2011. Ravitch discussed Randolph as one of several examples of highly touted schools at which achievement data proved to be ambiguous. For a source of her data, see Noel Hammatt, "Shifting Standards in the World of School Reform," *Nieman Watchdog,* May 25, 2011, http://www.niemanwatchdog.org/index.cfm?fuseaction=ask_this.view&askthisid=00511&fontsize=down (accessed August 17, 2011). On skepticism surrounding the highly touted charter schools in the Harlem Children's Zone, see Otterman, "Lauded Harlem Schools."

40. Paul Tough, "No, Seriously: No Excuses," *New York Times,* July 10, 2011; Ravitch, "Waiting for a School Miracle." For her comments on the Randolph School, Ravitch was criticized by Secretary of Education Duncan for "insulting" America's teachers, principals, and students; see Jonathan Alter, "Don't Believe Critics, Education Reform Works," *Bloomberg View,* June 3, 2011, http://www.bloomberg.com/news/2011-06-03/don-t-believe-critics-education-reform-works-jonathan-alter.html (accessed August 17, 2011). On Ravitch's critique of the reform movement and her own earlier positions, see Ravitch, *The Death and Life of the Great American School System.*

41. U.S. Department of Education, "A Blueprint for Reform: Reauthorization of the Elementary and Secondary Education Act" (March 2010), http://www2.ed.gov/policy/elsec/leg/blueprint/index.html (accessed August 17, 2011). Duncan's override of NCLB consisted of allowing states to apply for waivers and come up with their own alternatives to 100 percent proficiency; Sam Dillon, "Overriding a Key Education Law," *New York Times,* August 8, 2011.

42. Richard Rothstein, "A Blueprint That Needs More Work" (Washington, D.C.: Economic Policy Institute, 2010), http://www.epi.org/publications/entry/a_blueprint_that_needs_more_work/ (accessed August 17, 2011); Economic Policy Institute, "News from EPI: Leading Experts Caution Against Reliance on Test Scores in Teacher Evaluations" (August 30, 2010), http://www.epi.org/publications/entry/news_from_epi_leading_experts_caution_against_reliance_on_test_scores_in_te/ (accessed August 17, 2011).

43. See, for example, Education Equality Project, "Statement of Principles." Gingrich, Sharpton, and 140 other EEP signatories were clear in assigning responsibility for ending the achievement gap: nearly all of the organization's proposed steps focused on factors within schools and school systems—for instance, an effective teacher in every classroom (and fewer union restrictions on firing ineffective ones); expansion of charter school options for parents; and the need to hold teachers, principals, and administrators "accountable for student progress."

44. Evan Thomas and Pat Wingert, "Why We Must Fire Bad Teachers," *Newsweek*, March 6, 2010; Davis Guggenheim, director, *Waiting for "Superman,"* 2010. Among many laudatory articles on *Waiting for "Superman,"* see the following cover story: Amanda Ripley, "A Call to Action for Public Schools," *Time*, September 20, 2010. The *New York Times* emerged as another prominent voice in the critique of teacher unions; for a contrast with its previous Sunday magazine story by Traub, which emphasized how schools are shaped by larger social and economic forces, see the more recent cover story, Steven Brill, "The Teachers' Unions' Last Stand," *New York Times Magazine*, May 17, 2010; and the editorial "The Fight over Education in Washington," July 30, 2010, which charged "teachers unions and other forces of the status quo" with "trying to subvert" the Obama administration's competitive grant program, Race to the Top.

45. Randi Weingarten, "Press Release on the Obama Administration's Plan for Federal Education Law," March 13, 2010, http://www.aft.org/newspubs/press/2010/031310.cfm (accessed August 17, 2011); Sam Dillon, "Array of Hurdles Awaits New Education Agenda," *New York Times,* March 15, 2010. For teacher critiques of NCLB, see, for example, a variety of position papers on the web site of the American Federation of Teachers (AFT), http://www.aft.org/issues/schoolreform/nclb/index.cfm (accessed August 17, 2011).

46. Marcus A. Foster, *Making Schools Work: Strategies for Changing Education* (Philadelphia: Westminster Press, 1971), 21–22. On the persistence of low expectations in urban schools, see, for example, Payne, *So Much Reform,* esp. 72–80.

47. Williams, "National Model or Temporary Opportunity," 5. Williams himself is part of the self-proclaimed reform wing of the Democratic party, and his account of the Oakland story reflects an obvious impatience with unions and "tenured teachers"; see p. 9. On San Diego and the treatment of teachers as obstacles to reform, see Ravitch, *The Death and Life of the Great American School System,* 47–67. On reformers' "contempt" for teachers in Chicago and other cities, see Payne, *So Much Reform,* 179–85.

48. Gerry Shih, "Oakland Schools Struggle, but Emeryville May Point a Way Up," *New York Times,* July 22, 2010. Smith's plans, in addition to echoing Foster's superintendency, reflected his admiration for the Harlem Children's Zone and his prior record of success in the nearby Emeryville school district.

49. For important recent statements of these arguments by an advocacy group that seeks to shift the direction of reform, see the website, "Broader, Bolder Approach to Education," http://www.boldapproach.org/index.php?id=01 (accessed August 16, 2011).

50. Michael B. Katz, "Education and Inequality: A Historical Perspective," in *Social History and Social Policy,* ed. David J. Rothman and Stanton Wheeler (New York: Academic Press, 1981), 62, 92–100. See also Tyack and Cuban, *Tinkering Toward Utopia,* 134, on "cycles of gloomy assessments of education and overconfident solutions." "Hyperbole," they write, "has often produced public cynicism and skepticism among teachers."

Index

Acknowledgments

HOW difficult yet rewarding to try to give adequate thanks to the many individuals who have made this book possible. Some of those people paved the way long before I began my work. My parents, Molly and George Spencer, supported me in everything, including the education that was in many ways the foundation for this project. Mom, Dad: the book is finally done—and your love and support are one of the biggest reasons why. My maternal grandparents, Omar C. "Slug" Palmer and Connie Palmer, gave much to me—not least, a powerful sense of connection to the past. It gives me great pleasure to think of how proud they would be today. In my own schooling I was fortunate to have teachers like Shirley Malcolm, Doug Morten, and Dave Bailey, who showed me there can be excitement in learning and great dignity in teaching.

I am especially eager to thank three individuals who shaped my work from the beginning and gave me the inspiration and the skills I needed to complete it. Daniel Walkowitz read the roughest drafts, and his sharp intellect and editing skills have left a mark on me and on every chapter of this book. Ellen Condliffe Lagemann's wisdom and encouragement have meant the world to me at a number of key moments over many years. The late Ted Sizer was my touchstone in education and a trusted guide as I worked to understand the events in this book. I feel blessed to have had such wise and generous mentors.

Many librarians and archivists have been helpful over the years. At the top of the list is Brenda Galloway-Wright and the rest of the staff at the Temple University Urban Archives, a remarkable resource for the study of urban history. I also wish to thank helpful staff members in the Myrin Library at Ursinus College; the Ford Foundation Archives; the Pedagogical Library of the School District of Philadelphia; the Professional Library of the Oakland Unified School District; the Cheyney University Archives; the Oakland Public Library; and the Simon Gratz High School library. Other individuals loaned me items from their personal collections. I thank Leon Frisby, Robert Blackburn, Albertine Foster, and Marsha Foster Boyd for entrusting me with precious documents and tapes; and Murray Suid for giving me copies of *Making Schools Work* and *About Education.*

My research for this book came to life in the interviews I was lucky enough to conduct with key participants; I am grateful to Robert Blackburn, Alexis Moore Bruton, Peter Buttenwieser, Dean Cummings, Gaeton Fonzi, Alfred Foster, Leon Frisby, Gloria Gaymon, David Hornbeck, Al Jackson, Rufus and Estella Johnson, Ida Kravitz, Harriet Braxton Logan, Electra Kimble Price, Seymour Rose, Ted Sizer, James Slaughter, and Lynne Yermanock Strieb. I have done my best, and no doubt failed in some instances, to tell a story that is true to the experiences they related to me. Two interviewees deserve special mention. Leon Frisby told parts of the story that no one else could tell; I thank him for opening his heart to a stranger. Bob Blackburn's contribution is in a category apart. His eloquence and insight have improved the book immeasurably, in ways that surely will be evident to readers.

I have benefited from the guidance of a number of historians and educators at Brown University, at New York University, and beyond. Michael S. Harper, Paul Mattingly, William McLoughlin, Carl Prince, and Marilyn Young provided early encouragement and assistance. Barbara Beatty and Kate Rousmaniere made it possible for me to adapt parts of the book for publication in journals, and their skills and insights as editors have been enormously helpful. Barbara, in particular, has been so supportive, in so many instances, that I am running out of ways to say thank you. Nancy Beadie, Kim Tolley, Wayne Urban, and Jonathan Zimmerman read parts of the book and provided encouragement and smart advice. Marybeth Gasman, Ellen Condliffe Lagemann, and Maris Vinovskis gave valuable feedback in conference sessions. William Cutler, James Fraser, Robert Hampel, and John Rury have been kind in sharing their considerable wisdom. Many of these individuals have helped to make the History of Education Society a vibrant intellectual home for me, and on that note, I also wish to thank Christina Collins, Charles Dorn, Jack Dougherty, David Gamson, Judith Kafka, Heather Lewis, Hilary Moss, Bethany Rogers, and Tracy Steffes for their camaraderie at annual meetings and the example of their own excellent work.

I am especially indebted to two individuals who made major contributions to the final manuscript. Michael Katz read a full draft as an outside reviewer for the University of Pennsylvania Press, and his comments were exceptionally helpful. Michael's own books have had a huge influence on this project, and I deeply appreciate his insights and encouragement. The same goes for my editor at the University of Pennsylvania Press, Robert Lockhart. Bob's sharp editing skills, his engagement with matters of content as well as structure and style, and, above all, his faith and good judgment, have made this book possible. I am so glad the project ended up in his expert hands. I am also pleased that the book is part of the Penn Press series "Politics and Culture in Modern America"; thanks to the series editors, and especially to Thomas Sugrue and Michael Kazin, who have been important influences on my work. And finally, I am grateful to a second anonymous reader for the press, to Erica Ginsburg and others at Penn Press for their careful handling of the production of the book, and to many other scholars whose books have shaped my work, as is evident in my endnotes. Of course, all remaining flaws and errors are mine alone.

I am fortunate to have worked toward completion of the book while teaching at Ursinus College. Ursinus supported my writing with several summer grants and a semester leave. Even more important, it has provided a vibrant community of scholars, educators, and students. Among the many individuals who make Ursinus a place I am happy to call my academic home, I especially wish to acknowledge Kneia DaCosta, Sheryl Goodman, Dave Greason, Dallett Hemphill, Elizabeth Kessler, Stephanie Mackler, Susan Masciantonio, Charles Rice, Carol Royce, Patti Schroeder, Kelly Sorensen, the late John Strassburger, and especially Ross Doughty, Del Engstrom, and Judith Levy for all they have done to support my growth and progress thus far.

Other institutions and individuals have been important to me along the way. These include former colleagues at Rowan University, especially Donna Jorgensen, Jill Perry, and Anne Phillips in the College of Education and James Heinzen and other members of the history department who discussed my book prospectus; Josh Brown, Ellen Noonan, Jerry Markowitz, Andrea Ades Vasquez, Pennee Bender, Frank Poje, and the late Roy Rosenzweig, among others in the extended family of historians and educators at the American Social History Project/Center for Media and Learning at the Graduate Center, CUNY; and Gaea Leinhardt, Anita Ravi, and Kate Stainton at the Institute for Learning at the University of Pittsburgh. The *Journal of Educational Administration and History* published an abbreviated version of Chapter 4, and *Teachers College Record* published a modified version Chapter 2. Many teachers have helped keep me grounded in the daily experience of schools; in particular I take inspiration from Julie Craven, Penny Glackman, George Heidemark, Debbie Miller, Laurie Miller, Mike Segal, Jan Swenson, and Alexandra Wagner. The students who have inspired my scholarship are too numerous to list individually, but they, too, have played a vital role in my work.

Family and friends have sustained me while I worked to complete the book. Ellen Weiss, Leon Weiss, Lori Woolfrey, Greg Spencer, Arthur Spencer, and my many brothers- and sisters-in-law have all been unfailingly supportive. My fellow historians Karl Hagstrom-Miller and Ellen Noonan have shared many highs and lows from the beginning; they are great colleagues and even better friends. Steven Lewis and Seth Tager were there for me especially when I struggled to get the project off the ground, and Andreas Bollmann, Melissa Bollmann-Jenkins, Charles Gallagher, and Alex Schuh have helped me in various ways to get over the finish line. Peter D'Agostino was a brilliant historian and a unique combination of friend and mentor; I miss him dearly. Greg Raynor played an especially important role in the development of this book. His death left a hole that will never be filled, but he lives in these pages, and in me, always.

One of the most challenging tributes to put into words is the one I feel compelled to make to the man at the center of this book, Marcus Foster. I have tried to maintain a critical analytical stance that is true to my discipline of history. At the same time, my analysis led me to a deep admiration for my subject. Whatever usefulness this book might have is due in large part to the work that he did, on behalf of so many children. I hope I have made a worthy contribution to his legacy.

Finally, my debt is greatest, and my words least satisfying, when it comes to the most important contributor to this project and to my life: my wife, Eve Weiss. I could not have done this without her, and there is no way I can adequately express my thanks for her support and sacrifice. She has shared me with this book for many years, as have our children, Ella and Owen. It is with the deepest love and gratitude that I dedicate it to her, and them.